Lecture Notes in Computer Science 9278

Commenced Publication in 1973
Founding and Former Series Editors:
Gerhard Goos, Juris Hartmanis, and Jan van Leeuwen

Editorial Board

More information about this series at http://www.springer.com/series/7408

Danny Weyns · Raffaela Mirandola
Ivica Crnkovic (Eds.)

Software
Architecture

9th European Conference, ECSA 2015
Dubrovnik/Cavtat, Croatia, September 7–11, 2015
Proceedings

 Springer

Editors
Danny Weyns
Department of Computer Science
Linnaeus University
Växjö
Sweden

Ivica Crnkovic
Chalmers University of Technology
Gothenburg
Sweden

Raffaela Mirandola
Dipartimento di Elettronica,
    Informazione e Biongegneria
Politecnico di Milano
Milano
Italy

ISSN 0302-9743   ISSN 1611-3349   (electronic)
Lecture Notes in Computer Science
ISBN 978-3-319-23726-8   ISBN 978-3-319-23727-5 (eBook)
DOI 10.1007/978-3-319-23727-5

Library of Congress Control Number: 2015947954

LNCS Sublibrary: SL2 – Programming and Software Engineering

Springer Cham Heidelberg New York Dordrecht London
© Springer International Publishing Switzerland 2015

Printed on acid-free paper

Springer International Publishing AG Switzerland is part of Springer Science+Business Media
(www.springer.com)

Preface

The European Conference on Software Architecture (ECSA) is the premier European software architecture conference, providing researchers, practitioners, and educators with a platform to present and discuss the most recent, innovative, and significant findings and experiences in the field of software architecture research and practice. The 9th edition of ECSA featured a research track, an educational track, an industrial track, keynotes, workshops, and tool demonstrations. The conference was held in Cavtat, Croatia, in September 2015.

Software architecture has become a very prominent topic in software engineering as testified by the record number of 104 submissions the conference received for the research track and educational track. In addition, eight workshops were organized in conjunction with the conference.

The 12 full papers, three education and training papers, and 15 short papers presented in this volume were carefully reviewed. The research papers span a variety of topics. Classic topics include design approaches, decisions, and analysis and automation. The conference also attracted a substantial number of papers on popular and new emerging topics, such as adaptation, services, cloud, ecosystems, agility and architecture, and smart systems. Finally, the volume contains three educational papers that address different challenges and best practices in teaching and training of software architecture.

We are grateful to all those who contributed to the successful organization of ECSA 2015, in particular, the ECSA Steering Committee, the Program Committee, and the Local Organizing Committee. We hope that the papers of this volume will stimulate further research in software architecture and contribute to enhancing engineering practice.

July 2015

Danny Weyns
Raffaela Mirandola
Ivica Crnkovic

Organization

The 9th European Conference on Software Architecture was organized during September 7–11, 2015 in Cavtat, Croatia.

Organizing Committee

General Chair

Ivica Crnkovic   Chalmers University of Technology, Sweden

Program Chairs

Raffaela Mirandola   Politecnico di Milano, Italy
Danny Weyns   Linnaeus University, Sweden

Conference Chair

Goran Martinović   J.J. Strossmayer University of Osijek, Croatia

Workshop Chair

Matthias Galster   University of Canterbury, New Zealand

Tool Demo Chair

Bedir Tekinerdogan   Wageningen University, The Netherlands

Industry Chair

Roland Weiss   ABB, Germany

Publicity Chair

Patrizia Scandurra   University of Bergamo, Italy

Local Chair

Malin Roqvist   Mälardalen University, Sweden

Web Chairs

Zdravko Krpić   J.J. Strossmayer University of Osijek, Croatia
Josip Maras   University of Split, Croatia

Mobile App Chair

Reid Holmes   University of Waterloo, Canada

Program Committee

Anna Liu	NICTA/UNSW, Australia
Anton Jansen	Mälardalen University/ABB Corporate Research, Sweden
Antonia Bertolino	ISTI-CNR, Italy
Carlos E. Cuesta	Rey Juan Carlos University, Spain
Claudia Raibulet	University of Milano-Bicocca, Italy
Claus Pahl	Dublin City University, Ireland
David Garlan	Carnegie Mellon University, USA
Dewayne E. Perry	ESEL, The University of Texas at Austin, USA
Eduardo Almeida	Recife Center for Advanced Studies and Systems, Brazil
Elena Navarro	University of Castilla-La Mancha, Spain
Elisa Yumi Nakagawa	University of Sao Paulo, Brazil
Eoin Woods	Endava
Flavio Oquendo	IRISA (UMR CNRS) - Univ. Bretagne-Sud, France
Gerald Kotonya	Lancaster University, UK
Henry Muccini	University of L'Aquila, Italy
Ian Gorton	SEI, Carnegie Mellon University, USA
Ipek Ozkaya	SEI, Carnegie Mellon University, USA
Jan Bosch	Chalmers University of Technology, Sweden
Janet Burge	Wesleyan University, USA
Jennifer Perez	Technical University of Madrid, Spain
Jesper Andersson	Linnaeus University, Sweden
John Grundy	Swinburne University of Technology, Australia
José Carlos Maldonado	ICMC-USP, Brazil
Judith Stafford	University of Colorado, USA
Khalil Drira	LAAS-CNRS, France
Laurence Duchien	University of Lille, France
Len Bass	NICTA, Australia
Liming Zhu	NICTA, Australia
Luciano Baresi	DEIB - Politecnico di Milano, Italy
Mourad Oussalah	University of Nantes, France
Muhammad Ali Babar	IT University of Copenhagen, Denmark
Olaf Zimmermann	HSR FHO, Switzerland
Paola Inverardi	Università dell'Aquila, Italy
Paris Avgeriou	University of Groningen, Netherlands
Patricia Lago	VU University Amsterdam, Netherlands
Rafael Capilla	Universidad Rey Juan Carlos, Madrid, Spain
Rainer Weinreich	Johannes Kepler University Linz, Austria
Rami Bahsoon	University of Birmingham, UK
Riccardo Scandariato	Chalmers University of Technology, Sweden
Rich Hilliard	Independent Software Systems Architect
Rick Kazman	SEI, Carnegie Mellon University, USA
Robert Nord	SEI, Carnegie Mellon University, USA

Rogerio De Lemos	University of Kent, UK
Sam Malek	George Mason University, USA
Stefan Biffl	Technical University Wien, Austria
Steffen Becker	University of Technology Chemnitz, Germany
Thais Batista	Federal University of Rio Grande do Norte, Brazil
Tomi Mnnist	University of Helsinki, Finland
Uwe Van Heesch	Fontys University of Applied Sciences, Netherlands
Uwe Zdun	University of Vienna, Austria
Volker Gruhn	Universität Duisburg-Essen, Germany
Wilhelm Hasselbring	Kiel University, Germany
Wouter Joosen	KU Leuven, Belgium

Website

http://ecsa-conference.org/2015/

Keynotes Research Track

What Architecture Can Teach Us About When, Where, and Why Software Systems Decay

Nenad Medvidovic

Computer Science Department
University of Southern California
Los Angeles, CA, USA
neno@usc.edu

Abstract. Engineers frequently neglect to carefully consider the impact of their changes to a software system. As a result, the software system's architecture eventually deviates from the original designers' intent and degrades through unplanned introduction of new and/or invalidation of existing design decisions. Architectural decay increases the cost of making subsequent modifications and decreases a system's dependability, until engineers are no longer able to effectively evolve the system. At that point, the system's actual architecture may have to be recovered from the implementation artifacts, but this is a time-consuming and error-prone process, and leaves critical issues unresolved: the problems caused by architectural decay will likely be obfuscated by the system's many elements and their interrelationships, thus risking further decay. In this talk I will focus on pinpointing the locations in a software system's architecture that reflect architectural decay, the points in time when that decay tends to occur, and the reasons why that decay occurs. Specifically, I will present an emerging catalogue of commonly occurring symptoms of decay — architectural "smells". I will illustrate the occurrence of smells identified in the process of recovering the architectures of a large number of real-world systems. I will also discuss the relationship between architectural smells and the much better understood code smells. Finally, I will discuss several undesirable but common occurrences during the evolution of existing systems that directly contribute to decay. I will conclude by identifying a number of simple steps that engineers can undertake to stem software system decay.

Keywords: Software architecture · Architecture recovery · Architectural decay · Architectural smell · Code smell.

Adaptive Collective Systems
Are We Ready to Let Go of Control?

Maarten van Steen

Centre for Telematics and Information Technology
University of Twente
Enschede, The Netherlands
m.r.vansteen@utwente.nl

Abstract. The field of computer science is rapidly changing, and we often barely seem to notice it. For years we have been working on the same topics, and many of us expect to continue do so for still a long time to come. Moore's law is no longer determining the speedups of our programs: new algorithms and insights are pushing us further to an extent that some believe we need to start worrying about Artificial Intelligence. Computer science is eating the world, and we are the ones responsible for that. Yet, we want to stay in control. I argue that we need get into a different mindset: let go of control.

A while back, I joined a team of experts on computational intelligence in an attempt to write a booklet on adaptive collective systems. It taught me a lot about how colleagues in the same field were looking at what is important in computer science. Coming from computer systems research, it now seems to me that my view is conservative. Many colleagues concentrating on developing software constructs are often being conservative as well. We need to let a few things go.

I will talk about adaptive collective systems as being a special type of distributed computer system in which control, or rather, the lack of control, plays a crucial role. Control is no longer fixed; it evolves through learning mechanisms. The take-away message is that our future distributed systems need to be architected with learning facilities. However, considering that there are so many different types of computer systems, it is not obvious how learning should be incorporated.

Keywords: Adaptive collective systems · Distributed computer systems · Control systems

Contents

Education and Training

Cloud and Green

Agile and Smart Systems

Analysis and Automation

Services and Ecosystems

Adaptation

High-Level Language Support
for Reconfiguration Control
in Component-Based Architectures

Frederico Alvares[1]([⊠]), Eric Rutten[1], and Lionel Seinturier[2,3]

[1] INRIA Grenoble, Montbonnot-saint-martin, France
{frederico.alvares,eric.rutten}@inria.fr
[2] University of Lille 1, Villeneuve D'ascq, France
[3] INRIA Lille, Lille, France
lionel.seinturier

Abstract. Architecting in the context of variability has become a real need in todays software development. Modern software systems and their architecture must adapt dynamically to events coming from the environment (e.g., workload requested by users, changes in functionality) and the execution platform (e.g., resource availability). Component-based architectures have shown to be very suited for self-adaptation especially with their dynamical reconfiguration capabilities. However, existing solutions for reconfiguration often rely on low level, imperative, and non formal languages. This paper presents Ctrl-F, a domain-specific language whose objective is to provide high-level support for describing adaptation behaviours and policies in component-based architectures. It relies on reactive programming for formal verification and control of reconfigurations. We integrate Ctrl-F with the FraSCAti Service Component Architecture middleware platform, and apply it to the Znn.com self-adaptive case study.

1 Introduction

From tiny applications embedded in house appliances or automobiles to huge Cloud services, nowadays software-intensive systems have to fulfill a number of requirements in terms safety and Quality of Service (QoS) while facing highly dynamic environments (e.g., varying workloads and changing user requirements) and platforms (e.g., resource availability). This leads to the necessity to engineer such software systems with principles of self-adaptiveness, i.e., to equip these software systems with capabilities to cope with dynamically changes.

Component-Based Architecture. Software architecture and more specifically software components have played a very important role in self-adaptiveness. Besides the usual benefits of modularity and reuse, adaptability and reconfigurability are key properties which are sought with this approach: one wants to be able to adapt the component assemblies in order to cope with new requirements and new execution conditions occurring at run-time. Component-based Architecture defines

© Springer International Publishing Switzerland 2015
D. Weyns et al. (Eds.): ECSA 2015, LNCS 9278, pp. 3–19, 2015.
DOI: 10.1007/978-3-319-23727-5_1

the high-level structure of software systems by describing how they are organized by the means of a composition of components [15], which are usually captured by an Architecture Description Languages (ADL). In spite of the diversity of ADLs, the architectural elements proposed in almost all of them follow the same conceptual basis [13]. A *component* is defined as the most elementary unit of processing or data and it is usually decomposed into two parts: the implementation and the *interface*. The implementation describes the internal behaviour of the component, whereas the interfaces define how the component should interact with the environment. A component can be defined as *atomic* or *composite*, i.e., composed of other components. A *connector* mediates diverse forms of interactions of inter-component communications, and *configuration* corresponds to a directed graph of components and connectors describing the application's structure. Other elements like attributes, constraints or architectural styles also appear in ADLs [13], but for brevity we omit further details on these elements.

Initial assemblies (or configurations) are usually defined with the help of ADLs, whereas adaptive behaviours are achieved by programming fine-grained actions (e.g., to add, remove, connect elements), in either general-purpose languages within reflective component-based middleware plaforms [20], or with the support of reconfiguration domain-specific languages (DSLs) [8]. This low level of abstraction may turn the definition of transitions among configurations into a very costly task, which consequently may lead to error-prone adaptive behaviours. In fact, it may be non-trivial, especially for large and complex architectures, to obtain assurances and guarantees about the result of these reconfiguration behaviours. We claim that there is a need for a language, not only for the definition of configurations in the form of component assemblies, but also for the explicit specification of the transitions among them and the policies driving when and under which conditions reconfigurations should be triggered.

This paper presents Ctrl-F, a language that extends classic ADLs with high-level constructs to express the dynamicity of component-based architectures. In addition to the usual description of assemblies (configurations), Ctrl-F also comprises a set of constructs that are dedicated for the description of: (i) behavioural aspects, that is, the order and/or conditions under which reconfigurations take place; and (ii) policies that have to be enforced all along the execution.

Heptagon/BZR. We formally define the semantics of Ctrl-F with Heptagon/BZR [10], a Reactive Language based on Finite State Automata (FSA). It allows for the definition of generalized Moore machines, with mixed data-flow equations and automata. A distinguished characteristics is that its compilation involves formal tools for Discrete Controller Synthesis (DCS): a controller is automatically generated so as to enforce that a system behaves at runtime in concordance with the specification. The Heptagon/BZR definition of Ctrl-F programs allows to benefit from: (i) guarantees on the correctness of adaptive behaviours by either verification or control (i.e., by DCS); (ii) the compilation of adaptive behaviours towards executable code in general purpose languages (e.g., Java or C). Due to space limitation, the detailed definition is reported on elsewhere [1].

In the remainder of this paper, Section 2 presents the self-adaptation case study Znn.com [7], used all along the paper. Section 3 presents the Ctrl-F language. Section 4 provides some details on its integration with a real component platform as well as the evaluation of its applicability through *Znn.com*. Related work is discussed in Section 5 and Section 6 concludes this paper.

2 The Znn.com Example Application

Znn.com [7] is an experimental platform for self-adaptive applications, which mimics a news website. Znn.com follows a typical client-server n-tiers architecture where a load balancer redirects requests from clients to a pool of replicated servers. The number of active servers can be regulated in order to maintain a good trade-off between response time and resource utilization. Hence, the objective of Znn.com is to provide news content to its clients/visitors within a reasonable response time, while keeping costs as low as possible and/or under control (i.e., constrained by a certain budget).

At times, the pool of servers is not large enough to provide the desired QoS. For instance, in order to face workload spikes, Znn.com could be forced to degrade the content fidelity so as to require fewer resource to provide the same level of QoS. For this, Znn.com servers are able to deliver news contents with three different content fidelity: (i) high quality images, (ii) low quality images, and (iii) only text. The objectives are: (1) Keep the performance (response time) as high as possible; (2) Keep content fidelity as high as possible or above a certain threshold; (3) Keep the number of active servers as low as possible or under a certain threshold. In order to achieve them, we may tune: (1) The number of active servers; (2) The content fidelity of each server.

As a running example for our proposal, in the next section, we extend Znn.com by enabling its replication in presence of different content providers: one specialized in soccer and another one specialized in politics. These two instances of Znn.com will be sharing the same physical infrastructure. Depending on the contract signed between the service provider and his/her clients that establishes the terms of use of the service, Znn.com Service Provider can give more or less priority to a certain client. For instance, during the World Cup the content provider specialized in soccer will always have priority over the other one. Conversely, during the elections, the politics-specialized content provider is the one that has the priority.

3 Ctrl-F Language

3.1 Overview and Common Concepts

Ctrl-F is our proposal for a domain-specific language that extends classic ADLs with high-level constructs for describing reconfigurations' behaviour and policies to be enforced all along the execution of the target system.

The abstract syntax of Ctrl-F can be divided into two parts: a static one, which is related to the common architectural concepts (components, connections, configurations, etc.); and a dynamic one, which refers to reconfiguration behaviours and policies that must be enforced regardless of the configuration.

The static part of Ctrl-F shares the same concepts of many existing ADLs (e.g., Fractal [6], Acme [13]). A *component* consists of a set of *interfaces*, a set of *event ports*, a set of *attributes* and a set of *configurations*. *Interfaces* define how a component can interact with other components. So they are used to express a required functionality (*client interface*) that may be provided by another *component* and/or to express a provided functionally (*server interface*) that might be used by other *components*. *Event Ports* describe the events, of the given *Event Type*, a *component* is able to emit (*port out*) and/or listen to (*port in*). A *configuration* is defined as a set of *instances* of *components*, a set of *bindings* connecting *server* and *client interfaces* of those *instances* (i.e., an assembly), and/or a set of *attribute* assignments to *values*.

The dynamic part consists of a *behaviour* and a set of *policies* that can be defined for each component. A *behaviour* takes the form of orders and conditions (w.r.t. *events* and attribute *values*) under which transitions between configurations (reconfigurations) take place. The *policies* are high-level objectives/constraints, which may imply in the inhibition of some of those transitions.

The Znn.com example application of Section 2 can be modeled as a hierarchical composition of four components: *Main, Znn, LoadBalancer*, and *AppServer*. These components are instantiated according to execution conditions, the system current state (architectural composition), adaptation behaviours and policies defined within each component. Listing 1.1 shows the definition of such components with the static part of Ctrl-F.

The *Main* component (lines 1-14) encompasses two instances of *Znn*, namely *soccer* and *politics* within a single configuration (lines 7 and 8). The server interfaces of both instances (lines 9 and 10), which provides access to news services, are bound to the server interfaces of the *Main* component (lines 3 and 4) in order for them to be accessed from outside. A policy to be enforced is defined (line 13) and discussed in Section 3.3.

Component *Znn* (lines 16-33) consists of one provided interface (line 18) through which news can be requested. The component listens to events of types *oload* (overload) and *uload* (underload) (lines 20 and 21), which are emitted by other components. In addition, the component also defines two attributes: *consumption* (line 23), which is used to express the level of consumption (in terms of percentage of CPU) incurred by the component execution; and *fidelity* (line 24), which expresses the content fidelity level of the component.

Three configurations are defined for *Znn* component: *conf1, conf2* and *conf3*. *conf1* (lines 26-33) consists of one instance of each *LoadBalancer* and *AppServer* (lines 27 and 28); one binding to connect them (line 29), another binding to expose the server interface of the *LoadBalancer* component as a server interface of the *Znn* component (line 30), and the attribute assignments (lines 31 and 32). The attribute *fidelity* corresponds to the counterpart of instance *as1*, whereas for the *consumption* it corresponds to the sum of the consumptions of instances *as1* and *lb*. *conf2* (lines 34-39) *extends conf1* by adding one more instance of *AppServer*, binding it to the *LoadBalancer* and redefining the attribute values with respect to the just-added component instance (*as2*).

In that case, the attribute fidelity values the average of the counterparts of instances *as1* and *as2* (line 37), whereas for the consumption the same logics is applied so the consumption of the just-added instance is incorporated to the sum expression (line 38). Due to lack of space we omit the definition of configuration *conf3*. Nevertheless, it follows the same idea, that is, it extends *conf2* by adding a new instance of *AppServer*, binding it and redefining the attribute values.

Listing 1.1. Architectural Description of Components *Main*, *Znn*, *Load Balancer* and *AppServer* in Ctrl-F.

```
1  component Main {
2
3    server interface sis
4    server interface sip
5
6    configuration main {
7      soccer:Znn
8      politics:Znn
9      bind sis to soccer.si
10     bind sip to politics.si
11   }
12
13   policy {...}
14 }
15
16 component Znn {
17
18   server interface si
19
20   port in oload
21   port in uload
22
23   attribute consumption
24   attribute fidelity
25
26   configuration conf1 {
27     lb:LoadBalancer
28     as1:AppServer
29     bind lb.ci1 to as1.si
30     bind lb.si to si
31     set fidelity to as1.fidelity
32     set consumption to sum(as1.
              consumption,lb.consumption
              )
33   }
34   configuration conf2 extends conf1
              {
35     as2:AppServer
36     bind lb.ci2 to as2.si
37     set fidelity to avg(as1.
              fidelity,as2.fidelity)
38     set consumption to sum(as1.
              consumption,as2.
              consumption,lb.consumption
              )
39   }
40
41   configuration conf3 extends conf2
              {...}
42
43   behaviour {...}
44   policy {...}
45 }
46
47 component LoadBalancer {
48   server interface si
49   client interface ci1,ci2,c3
50
51   port out oload
52   port out uload
53
54   attribute consumption=0.2
55 }
56
57 component AppServer {
58   server interface si
59
60   port in oload
61   port in uload
62
63   attribute fidelity
64   attribute consumption
65
66   configuration text {
67     set fidelity to 0.25
68     set consumption to 0.2
69   }
70   configuration img-ld {
71     set fidelity to 0.5
72     set consumption to 0.6
73   }
74   configuration img-hd {...}
75
76   behaviour {...}
77   policy {...}
78 }
```

Component *LoadBalancer* (lines 47-55) consists of four interfaces: one provided (line 48), through which the news are provided; and the others required (line 49), through which the load balancer delegates each request for balancing purposes. We assume that this component is able to detect overload and underload situations (in terms of number of requests per second) and in order for this information to be useful for other components we define two event *ports* that are used to emit events of type *oload* and *uload* (lines 51 and 52). Like for component *Znn*, attribute *consumption* (line 54) specifies the level of consumption of the component (e.g., 0.2 to express 20% of CPU consumption). As there is no explicit definition of configurations, *LoadBalancer* is implicitly treated as a single-configuration component.

Lastly, the atomic component *AppServer* (lines 57-78) has only one interface (line 58) and listens to events of type *oload* and *uload* (lines 60 and 61). It has also two attributes: fidelity and consumption (lines 63 and 64), just like component *Znn*. Three configurations corresponding to each level of fidelity (lines 66-69, 70-73 and 74) are defined, and the attributes are valuated according to the configuration in question, i.e., the higher the fidelity the higher the consumption.

3.2 Behaviours

A particular characteristic of Ctrl-F is the capability to comprehensively describe behaviours in component-based applications. We mean by behaviour the process in which architectural elements are changed. More precisely, it refers to the order and conditions under which configurations within a component take place.

Behaviours in Ctrl-F are defined with the aid of a high-level imperative language. It consists of a set of behavioural statements (*sub-behaviours*) that can be composed together so as to provide more complex behaviours in terms of sequences of configurations. In this context, a *configuration* is considered as an atomic behaviour, i.e., a behaviour that cannot be decomposed into other *sub-behaviours*. A reconfiguration occurs when the current configuration is terminated and the next one is started. We assume that configurations do not have the capability to directly terminate or start themselves, meaning that they are explicitly requested or ended by behaviour *statements* according to the defined events and policies. Nevertheless, as components are capable to emit events, it would not be unreasonable to define components whose objective is to emit events in order to force a desired behaviour.

Statements. Table 1 summarizes the behaviour statements of the Ctrl-F behavioural language. During the execution of a given behaviour B, the *when-do* statement states that when a given event of event type e_i occurs the configuration(s) that compose(s) B should be terminated and that (those) of the corresponding behaviour B_i are started.

The *case-then* statement is quite similar to *when-do*. The difference resides mainly in the fact that a given behaviour B_i is executed if the corresponding condition c_i holds (e.g., conditions on attribute values), which means that it does not wait for a given event to occur. In addition, if none of the conditions holds ($c_1 \wedge ... \wedge c_n = 0$), a default behaviour ($B_e$) is executed, which forces the compiler to choose at least one behaviour. The *parallel* statement states that two behaviours are executed at the same time, i.e., at a certain point, there must be two independent branches of behaviour executing in parallel. This construct is

Table 1. Summary of Behaviour Statements.

Statement	Description
B **when** e_1 **do** B_1, ... , e_n **do** B_n **end**	While executing B when e_i execute B_i
case c_1 **then** B_1, ... , c_n **then** B_n **else** B_e **end**	Execute B_i if c_i holds, otherwise execute B_e
$B_1 \mid B_2$	Execute either B_1 or B_2
$B_1 \parallel B_2$	Execute B_1 and B_2 in parallel
do B **every** e	Execute B and re-execute it at every occurrence of e

also useful in the context of atomic components like *AppServer*, where we could, for instance, define configurations composed of orthogonal attributes like fidelity and font size/color (e.g., `text || font-huge`).

The *alternative* statement allows to describe choice points among configurations or among more elaborated sequential behaviour statements. They are left free in local specifications and will be resolved in upper level assemblies, in such a way as to satisfy the stated policies, by controlling these choice points appropriately. Finally, the *do-every* statement allows for execution of a behaviour B and re-execution of it at every occurrence of an event of type e. It is noteworthy that behaviour B is preempted every time an event of type e occurs. In other words, the configuration(s) currently activated in B is (are) terminated, and the very first one(s) in B is (are) started.

Example in Znn.com. We now illustrate the use of the statements we have introduced to express adaptation behaviours for components *AppServer* and *Znn* the of *Znn.com* case study. The expected behaviour for component *AppServer* is to pick one of its three configurations (*text*, *img-ld* or *img-hd*) at every occurrence of events of type *oload* or *uload*. To that end, as it can be seen in Listing 1.2, the behaviour can be decomposed in a *do-every* statement, which is, in turn, composed of an *alternative* one. It is important to mention that the decision on one or other configuration must be taken at runtime according to input variables (e.g., income events) and the stated policies, that is, there must be a control mechanism for reconfigurations that enforces those policies. We come back to this subject in Section 4.1.

Regarding component *Znn*, the expected behaviour is to start with the minimum number of *AppServer* instances (configuration *conf1*) and add one more instance, i.e., leading to configuration *conf2*, upon an event of type (*oload*). From *conf2*, one more instance must be added, upon an event of type *oload* leading to configuration *conf3*. Alternatively, upon an event of type *uload*, one instance of *AppServer* must be removed, which will lead the application back to configuration *conf1*. Similarly, from configuration *conf3*, upon a *uload* event, another instance must be removed, which leads the application to *conf2*. It is notorious that this behaviour can be easily expressed by an automaton, with three states (one per configuration) and four transitions (triggered upon the occurrence of *oload* and *uload*). However, Ctrl-F is designed to tackle the adaptation control problem in a higher level, i.e., with process-like statements over configurations.

For these reasons, we describe the behaviour with two embedded *do-every* statements, which in turn comprise each a *when-do* statement, as shown in Listing 1.3 (lines 6-14 and 8-12). We also define two auxiliary configurations: *emitter1* (line 2) and *emitter2* (line 3), which extend respectively configurations *conf2* and *conf3*, with an instance of a pre-defined component *Emitter*. This component does nothing but emit a given event (e.g., *e1* and *e2*) so as to force a loop step and thus go back to the beginning of the *when-do* statements. The main *do-every* statement (lines 6-14) performs a *when-do* statement (lines 7-13) at every occurrence of an event of type *e1*. In practice, the firing of this event allows going back to *conf1* regardless of the current configuration being executed. *conf1* is executed until the occurrence of an event of type *oload* (line 7), then the innermost *do-every* statement is executed (lines 8-12), which in turn, just like the other one, executes another *when-do* statement (lines 9-11) and repeats it at every occurrence of an event of type *e2*. Again, that structure allows the application to go back to configuration *conf2*. Configuration *conf2* is executed until an event of type either *oload* or *uload* occurs. For the former case (line 9), another *when-do* statement takes place, whereas for the latter (line 10) configuration *emitter1* is the one that takes place. Essentially, at this point, an instance of component *Emitter* is deployed along with *conf2*, since *emitter1* extends *conf2*. As a consequence, this instance fires an event of type *e1*, which forces the application to go back to *conf1*. The innermost *when-do* statement (line 9) consists in executing *conf3* until an event of type *uload* occurs, then configuration *emitter2* takes place, which makes an event of type *e2* be fired in order to force going back to *conf2*.

It is important to notice that this kind of construction allows to achieve the desired behaviour while sticking to the language design principles, that is, high-level process-like constructs and configurations. It also should be remarked that while in Listing 1.3 we present an imperative approach to forcibly increase the number of *AppServer* instances upon *uload* and *oload* events, in Listing 1.3 we leave the choice to the compiler to choose the most suitable fidelity level according to the runtime events and conditions. Although there is no straightforward guideline, an imperative approach is clearly more suitable when the solution is more sequential and delimited, whereas as the architecture gets bigger, in terms of configurations, and less sequential, then a declarative definition becomes more interesting.

3.3 Policies

Policies are expressed with high-level constructs for constraints on configurations, either temporal or on attribute values. In general, they define a subset of all possible global configurations, where the system should remain invariant: this will be achieved by using the choice points in order to control the reconfigurations. An intuitive example is that two component instances in parallel branches might have each several possible configurations, and some of them to be kept exclusive. This exclusion can be enforced by choosing the appropriate configurations when starting the components.

Constraints/Optimization on Attributes. This kind of constraints are predicates and/or primitives of optimization objectives (i.e., maximize or minimize) on component attributes. Listing 1.4 illustrates some constraints and optimization on component attributes. The first two policies state that the overall fidelity for component instance *soccer* should be greater or equal to 0.75, whereas that of instance *politics* should be maximized. Putting it differently, instance *soccer* must never have its content fidelity degraded, which means that it will have always priority over *politics*. The third policy states that the overall consumption should not exceed 5, which could be interpreted as a constraint on the physical resource capacity, e.g., the number of available machines or processing units.

Listing 1.2. AppServer's Behaviour.

```
1 component
2      AppServer {
3  ...
4  behaviour {
5   do
6     text |
7     img-1d |
8     img-hd
9   every
10    (oload
11       or uload)
12  }
13 }
```

Listing 1.3. Znn's Behaviour.

```
1 component Znn {...
2   configuration emitter1 extends conf2 { e:Emitter }
3   configuration emitter2 extends conf3 { e:Emitter }
4
5   behaviour {
6    do
7     conf1 when oload do
8      do
9       conf2 when oload do (conf3 when uload do
             emitter2 end),
10               uload do emitter1
11      end
12     every e2
13    end
14    every e1
15   }
16 }
```

Temporal Constraints. Temporal constraints are high-level constructs that take the form of predicates on the order of configurations. These constructs might be very helpful when there are many possible reconfiguration paths (by either *parallel* or *alternative* composition, for instance), in which case the manual specification of such constrained behaviour may become a very difficult task.

To specify these constraints, Ctrl-F provides four constructs, as follows:

- $conf_1$ **precedes** $conf_2$: $conf_1$ must take place right before $conf_2$. It does not mean that it is the only one, but it should be among the configurations taking place right before $conf_2$.

- $conf_1$ succeeds $conf_2$: $conf_1$ must take place right after $conf_2$. Like in the precedes constraint, it does not mean that it is the only one to take place right after $conf_2$.
- $conf_1$ during $conf_2$: $conf_1$ must take place along with $conf_2$.
- $conf_1$ between $(conf_2, conf_3)$: once $conf_2$ is started, $conf_1$ cannot be started and $conf_3$, in turn, cannot be started before $conf_2$ terminates.

Listing 1.5 shows an example of how to apply temporal constraints, in which it is stated that configuration *img-ld* comes right after the termination of either configuration *text* or configuration *img-ld*. In this example, this policy avoids abrupt changes on the content fidelity, such as going directly from text to image high definition or the other way around. Again, it does not mean that no other configuration could take place along with *img-ld*, but the *alternative* statement in the behaviour described in Listing 1.2 leads us to conclude that only *img-ld* must take place right after either *text* or *img-hd* has been terminated.

Listing 1.4. Example of Constraint and Optimization on Attributes.

Listing 1.5. Example of Temporal Constraint.

```
1  component Main { ...
2  policy { soccer.fidelity >= 0.75 }
3  policy { maximize politics.fidelity }
4  policy { (soccer.consumption +
5            politics.consumption) <= 5 }
6  }
```

```
1  component AppServer { ...
2  policy { img-ld succeeds text }
3  policy { img-ld succeeds img-hd }
4  }
```

4   Heptagon/BZR Model and Implementation

4.1   Modeling Ctrl-F in Heptagon/BZR

As architectures get larger and more complex, conceiving behaviours that respect the stated policies becomes a hard and error-prone task. This is the main reason why we model Ctrl-F behaviours and policies with Heptagon/BZR. Indeed, the FSA-based model of Heptagon/BZR allows programs to be formally exploited and verified by model checking tools [10]. The general model of Ctrl-F behaviours is as surveyed in Figure 1. Basically, each component accommodates an automaton corresponding to its adaptive behaviour, in which states correspond to configurations and transitions to reconfigurations. So, based on a vector of input events (e.g., *oload* and *uload*, in the Znn.com example) and runtime conditions (e.g., on the attribute values), transitions may be triggered while emitting signals for stopping the current configuration and starting the new one. In the case the behaviour contains choice points, that is, *alternative* statements, we model the transition conditions to each one of the choice branches as free-variables. The resulting controller from the DCS, which takes the form of a deterministic automata, is in charge of the control on those variables such that, regardless of the input events, the stated policies are enforced. It is noteworthy that although the DCS algorithms has exponential complexity as any other model checking approach, the controller is synthesized in an off-line manner and thus with no impact on the running controlled system. The same structural translation is performed hierarchically for every sub-component, i.e., in every component instantiated within another component. Due to space limitation, we have to omit the details on the translation schemes, but the full translation of Ctrl-F behaviour statements and policies to Heptagon/BZR is available in [1].

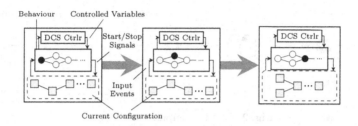

Fig. 1. Role of the Behaviour Automaton over the Transitions.

4.2 Compilation Tool-Chain

As can be seen in Figure 2, the compilation process can be split into two parts: (i) the reconfiguration logics and (ii) the behaviour/policy control and verification. The reconfiguration logics is implemented by the *ctrlf2fscript* compiler, which takes as input a Ctrl-F definition and generates as output a script containing a set procedures allowing going from one configuration to another. To this end, we rely on existing differencing/match algorithms for object-oriented models [23].

The behaviour control and verification is performed by the *ctrlf2ept* compiler, which takes as input a Ctrl-F definition and provides as output a synchronous reactive program in Heptagon/BZR. The result of the compilation of an Heptagon/BZR code is a sequential code in a general-purpose programming language (in our case Java) comprising two methods: **reset** and **step**. The former initializes the internal state of the program, whereas the latter is executed at each logical step to compute the output values based on a given vector of input values and the current state.

These methods are typically used by first executing **reset** and then by enclosing **step** in an infinite loop, in which each iteration corresponds to a reaction to an event (e.g., *oload* or *uload*), as sketched in Listing 1.6. The step method returns a set of signals corresponding to the start or stop of configurations (line 4). From these signals, we can find the appropriate script that embodies the reconfiguration actions to be executed (lines 5 and 6).

We wrap the control loop logics into three components, which are enclosed by a composite named *Manager*. Component *EventHandler* exposes a service allowing itself to be sent events (e.g., *oload* and *uload*). The method implementing this service is defined as non-blocking so the incoming events are stored in a First-In-First-Out queue. Upon the arrival of an event coming from the *Managed System* (e.g., Znn.com), component *EventHandler* invokes the step method, implemented by component *Architecture Analyzer*. The step method output is sent to component *Reconfigurator*, that encompasses a method to find the proper reconfiguration script to be executed.

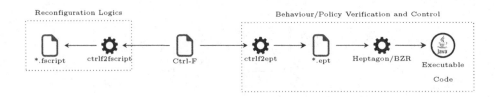

Fig. 2. Ctrl-F Compilation Chain.

Listing 1.6. Control Loop Sketch.

```
1 reset();
2 ...
3 on event oload or uload
4 <...,stop_conf1,start_conf2,...>=step(oload,uload);
5 reconfig_script=find_script(...,stop_conf1,start_conf2,...);
6 execute(reconfig_script);
```

In this work, we rely on the Java-based Service Component Architecture (SCA) middleware FraSCAti [20], since it provides mechanisms for runtime reconfiguration. The FraSCAti Runtime is itself conceived relying on the SCA model, that is, it consists of a set of SCA components that can be deployed *a la carte*, according to the user's needs. For instance, in our case, the *Manager* instantiates the *frascati-fscript* component, which provides services allowing for the execution of an SCA-variant of FPath/FScript [8], a domain-specific language for introspection and dynamic reconfiguration of Fractal components. The *frascati-fscript* component relies on other components integrating the middleware, inside the FraSCAti Composite, to perform introspection and runtime reconfiguration on the managed system's components.

4.3   Adaptation Scenario

We simulated the execution of the two instances of *Znn.com* application, namely *soccer* and *politics*, under the administration of the *Manager* presented in last section, to observe the control of reconfigurations taking into account a sequence of input events. The behaviours of components *AppServer* and *Znn* are stated in Listings 1.2 and 1.3, respectively, while policies are defined in Listing 1.4 and 1.5.

As it can be observed in the first chart of Figure 3, we scheduled a set of overload (*oload*) and underload (*uload*) events (vertical dashed lines), which simulate an increase followed by a decrease of the income workload for both soccer and politics instances. The other charts correspond to the overall resource

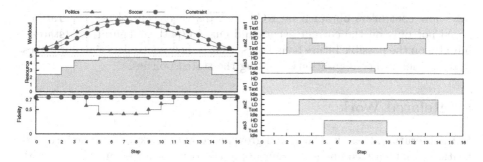

Fig. 3. Execution of the Adaptation Scenario.

consumption, the overall fidelity, and the fidelity level (i.e., configurations *text*, *img-ld* or *img-hd*) of the three instances of component *AppServer* contained in both instances of component *Znn*.

As the workload of *politics* increases, an event of type *oload* occurs at step 2. That triggers the reconfiguration of that instance from *conf1* to *conf2*, that is, one more instance of *AppServer* is added within the *Znn* instance *politics*. We can observe also the progression in terms of resource consumption, as a consequence of this configuration. The same happens with *soccer* at step 3, and is repeated with *politics* and *soccer* again at steps 4 and 5. The difference, in this case, is that at step 4, the *politics* instance must reconfigure (to *conf3*) so as to cope with the current workload while keeping the overall consumption under control. In other words, it forces the *AppServer* instances *as2* and *as3* to degrade their fidelity level from *img-hd* to *img-ld*. It should be highlighted that although at least one of the *AppServer* instances (*as2* or *as3*) could be at that time at maximum fidelity level, the knowledge on the possible future configurations guarantees the maximum overall fidelity for instance *soccer* to the detriment of a degraded fidelity for instance *politics*, while respecting the temporal constraints expressed in Listing 1.5. Hence, at step 5, when the last *oload* event arrives, the fidelity level of *soccer* instance is preserved by gradually decreasing that of *politics*, that is, both instances *as2* and *as3* belonging to the *politics* instance are put in configuration *text*, but without jumping directly from from *img-hd*. At step 9, the first *uload* occurs as a consequence of the workload decrease. It triggers a reconfiguration in the *politics* instance as it goes from *conf3* to *conf2*, that is, it releases one instance of *AppServer* (*as3*). The same happens with *soccer* at step 10, which makes room on the resources and therefore allows *politics* to bring back the fidelity level of its *as2* to *img-ld*, and to the maximum level again at step 11. This is repeated at steps 13 and 14 for instances *politics* and *soccer* respectively, bringing their *consumptions* at the same levels as in the beginning.

The adaptation scenario is very useful to understand the dynamics behind an *Manager* that is derived from a synchronous reactive programming, which is in turn, obtained from Ctrl-F. Moreover, the scenario illustrates, in a pedagogical way, how controllers obtained by DCS are capable to control reconfigurations based not only on the current events and current/past configurations (states), but also on the possible future behaviours, that is, how controllers avoid branches that may lead to configurations violating the stated policies.

5   Related Work

In the literature, there is a large and growing body of work on runtime reconfiguration of software components. Our approach focuses on the language support for enabling self-adaptation in component-based architectures while relying on reactive systems and the underlying formal control tools for ensuring adaptation policies. This section summarizes the related work, more detailed elsewhere [1].

Classically, runtime adaption in software architectures is achieved by first relying on ADLs such as Acme [13] or Fractal [6] for an initial description of the software structure and architecture, then by specifying fine-grained reconfiguration actions with dedicated languages like Plastik [3] or FPath/FScript [8], or simply by defining Event-Condition-Actions (ECA) rules to lead the system to the desired state. A harmful consequence is that the space of reachable configuration states is only known as side effect of those reconfiguration actions, which makes it difficult to ensure correct adaptive behaviours. Moreover, a drawback of ECA rules is that, contrary to Ctrl-F, they cannot describe sequences of configurations. Even though, ECA rules can be expressed in Ctrl-F with a set of *when-do* (for the E part) and *case* (for the C and A parts) statements in parallel.

Rainbow [12] is an autonomic framework that comes with Stitch, a domain-specific language allowing for the description of self-adaptation of Acme-described applications. It features system-level actions grouped into *tactics*, which in turn, are aggregated within a tree-like strategy path. We can draw an analogy between tactics and the set of actions triggered upon a reconfiguration; as well as strategies and behaviours in the Ctrl-F language. Nonetheless, alternative and parallel, as well as event-based constructs make Ctrl-F more expressive. Furthermore, Ctrl-F's formal model enables to ensure correct adaptation behaviours.

A body of work [2][4][5][17][21][22][22] focus on how to plan a set of actions that safely lead component-based systems to a target configuration. These approaches are complementary to ours in the sense that our focus is on the choice of a new configuration and its control. Once a new configuration chosen, we rely on existing mechanisms to determine the plan of action actually leading the system from the current to the next configuration.

In [18], feature models are used to express variability in software systems. At runtime, a resolution mechanism is used for determining which features should be present so as to constitute configuration. In the same direction, Pascual et al. [19] propose an approach for optimal resolution of architectural variability specified in the Common Variability Language (CVL) [14]. A drawback of those approaches is that in the adaptation logics specified with feature models or CVL, there is no way to define stateful adaptation behaviours, i.e., sequences of reconfigurations. The resolution is performed based on the current state and/or constraints on the feature model. While in our approach, in the reactive model based on FSA, decisions are taken also based on the history of configurations which allows us to define more interesting adaptation behaviours and policies.

W.r.t. formal methods, Kouchnarenko and Weber [16] propose the use of temporal logics to integrate temporal requirements to adaptation policies. While in this approach, enforcement and reflection are performed at runtime in order to ensure correct behaviour, we rely on discrete controller synthesis.

As in our approach, in [11], authors also rely on Heptagon/BZR to model adaptive behaviours of Fractal components. However, there is no high-level description (e.g., ADL) like Ctrl-F, and reconfigurations are controlled at the level of fine-grained reconfiguration actions, which can be considered time-consuming and difficult to scale. Delaval et al. [9] propose to have modular controllers that can be coordinated so as to work together in a coherent manner. The approach is complementary to ours in the sense that it does not provide high-level language support for describing those managers, although the authors provide interesting intuitions on a methodology to do so.

6 Conclusion

This paper presented Ctrl-F, a high-level domain-specific language that allows for the description of adaptation behaviours and policies of component-based architectures. A distinguished feature of Ctrl-F is its formalization with the synchronous reactive language Heptagon/BZR, which allows to benefit, among other things, from formal tools for verification, control, and automatic generation of executable code. In order to show the language expressiveness, we applied it to Znn.com, a self-adaptive case study, and we integrated it with FraSCAti, a Service Component Architecture middleware.

For future work, we intent to address issues of modularity and coordination of controllers, as well as their distribution. The reactive language and models we rely on have recent results that can be exploited, and can lead to deploy controllers taking into account the physical location of components.

References

1. Alvares, F., Rutten, E., Seinturier, L.: Behavioural model-based control for auto-nomic software components. In: Proc. 12th Int. Conf. Autonomic Computing (ICAC 2015), Grenoble, France. (extended version available as a Research Report: https://hal.inria.fr/hal-01103548), July 2015
2. Arshad, N., Heimbigner, D.: A Comparison of Planning Based Models for Com-ponent Reconfiguration. Research Report CU-CS-995-05, U. Colorado, September 2005
3. Batista, T.V., Joolia, A., Coulson, G.: Managing dynamic reconfiguration in component-based systems. In: Morrison, R., Oquendo, F. (eds.) EWSA 2005. LNCS, vol. 3527, pp. 1–17. Springer, Heidelberg (2005)

4. Becker, S., Dziwok, S., Gerking, C., Heinzemann, C., Schäfer, W., Meyer, M., Pohlmann, U.: The mechatronicuml method: model-driven software engineering of self-adaptive mechatronic systems. In: Companion Proceedings of the 36th International Conference on Software Engineering, ICSE Companion 2014, pp. 614–615. ACM, New York (2014). http://doi.acm.org/10.1145/2591062.2591142

5. Boyer, F., Gruber, O., Pous, D.: Robust reconfigurations of component assemblies. In: Proc. 2013 Int. Conf. on Software Engineering, ICSE 2013, pp. 13–22 (2013)

6. Bruneton, E., Coupaye, T., Leclercq, M., Quema, V., Stefani, J.-B.: An open component model and its support in Java. In: Crnković, I., Stafford, J.A., Schmidt, H.W., Wallnau, K. (eds.) CBSE 2004. LNCS, vol. 3054, pp. 7–22. Springer, Heidelberg (2004)

7. Cheng, S.W., Garlan, D., Schmerl, B.: Evaluating the effectiveness of the rainbow self-adaptive system. In: ICSE Workshop on Software Engineering for Adaptive and Self-Managing Systems, SEAMS 2009, pp. 132–141, May 2009

8. David, P.C., Ledoux, T., Léger, M., Coupaye, T.: FPath & FScript: Language support for navigation and reliable reconfiguration of Fractal architectures. Annals of Telecommunications: Special Issue on Software Components (2008)

9. Delaval, G., Gueye, S.M.K., Rutten, E., De Palma, N.: Modular coordination of multiple autonomic managers. In: Proc. 17th Int. ACM Symp. on Component-based Software Engineering, CBSE 2014, pp. 3–12 (2014)

10. Delaval, G., Marchand, H., Rutten, E.: Contracts for modular discrete controller synthesis. In: ACM International Conference on Languages, Compilers, and Tools for Embedded Systems (LCTES 2010), Stockholm, Sweden, April 2010

11. Delaval, G., Rutten, E.: Reactive model-based control of reconfiguration in the fractal component-based model. In: Grunske, L., Reussner, R., Plasil, F. (eds.) CBSE 2010. LNCS, vol. 6092, pp. 93–112. Springer, Heidelberg (2010)

12. Garlan, D., Cheng, S.W., Huang, A.C., Schmerl, B., Steenkiste, P.: Rainbow: Architecture-based self-adaptation with reusable infrastructure. Computer **37**(10), 46–54 (2004)

13. Garlan, D., Monroe, R.T., Wile, D.: Acme: architectural description of component-based systems. In: Leavens, G.T., Sitaraman, M. (eds.) Foundations of Component-Based Systems, pp. 47–68. Cambridge University Press (2000)

14. Haugen, O., Wasowski, A., Czarnecki, K.: Cvl: common variability language. In: Proceedings of the 17th International Software Product Line Conference, SPLC 2013, pp. 277–277. ACM, New York (2013)

15. Jacobson, I., Griss, M., Jonsson, P.: Software reuse: architecture process and organization for business success. ACM Press books, ACM Press (1997)

16. Kouchnarenko, O., Weber, J.-F.: Adapting component-based systems at runtime via policies with temporal patterns. In: Fiadeiro, J.L., Liu, Z., Xue, J. (eds.) FACS 2013. LNCS, vol. 8348, pp. 234–253. Springer, Heidelberg (2014)

17. Luckey, M., Nagel, B., Gerth, C., Engels, G.: Adapt cases: extending use cases for adaptive systems. In: Proceedings of the 6th International Symposium on Software Engineering for Adaptive and Self-Managing Systems, SEAMS 2011, pp. 30–39. ACM, New York (2011). http://doi.acm.org/10.1145/1988008.1988014

18. Morin, B., Barais, O., Nain, G., Jezequel, J.M.: Taming dynamically adaptive systems using models and aspects. In: Proc. 31st Int. Conf. on Software Engineering, ICSE 2009, pp. 122–132. IEEE (2009)

19. Pascual, G.G., Pinto, M., Fuentes, L.: Run-time support to manage architectural variability specified with CVL. In: Drira, K. (ed.) ECSA 2013. LNCS, vol. 7957, pp. 282–298. Springer, Heidelberg (2013)

20. Seinturier, L., Merle, P., Rouvoy, R., Romero, D., Schiavoni, V., Stefani, J.B.: A component-based middleware platform for reconfigurable service-oriented architectures. Software: Practice and Experience **42**(5), 559–583 (2012)
21. da Silva, C.E., de Lemos, R.: Dynamic plans for integration testing of self-adaptive software systems. In: Proc. 6th Int. Symp. on Software Engineering for Adaptive and Self-Managing Systems, SEAMS 2011, pp. 148–157 (2011)
22. Tichy, M., Klöpper, B.: Planning self-adaption with graph transformations. In: Schürr, A., Varró, D., Varró, G. (eds.) AGTIVE 2011. LNCS, vol. 7233, pp. 137–152. Springer, Heidelberg (2012)
23. Xing, Z., Stroulia, E.: Umldiff: an algorithm for object-oriented design differencing. In: Proc. 20th IEEE/ACM Int. Conf. on Automated Software Engineering, ASE 2005, pp. 54–65 (2005)

Architectural Reasoning Support for Product-Lines of Self-adaptive Software Systems - A Case Study

Nadeem Abbas[(⊠)] and Jesper Andersson

AdaptWise Department of Computer Science, Linnaeus University, Växjö, Sweden
{nadeem.abbas,jesper.andersson}@lnu.se

Abstract. Software architecture serves as a foundation for the design and development of software systems. Designing an architecture requires extensive analysis and reasoning. The study presented herein focuses on the architectural analysis and reasoning in support of engineering self-adaptive software systems with systematic reuse. Designing self-adaptive software systems with systematic reuse introduces variability along three dimensions; adding more complexity to the architectural analysis and reasoning process. To this end, the study presents an extended Architectural Reasoning Framework with dedicated reasoning support for self-adaptive systems and reuse. To evaluate the proposed framework, we conducted an initial feasibility case study, which concludes that the proposed framework assists the domain architects to increase reusability, reduce fault density, and eliminate differences in skills and experiences among architects, which were our research goals and are decisive factors for a system's overall quality.

1 Introduction

Software architecture provides the cornerstones for software system design and development. A high-quality architecture is a necessary condition if a software system should satisfy its requirements [6]. This condition becomes more vital when developing large and complex software systems.

While designing an architecture, software architects have to analyze and reason about design choices. The design choices are analyzed with respect to combinations of design parameters and their consequences. The design parameters affect the architecture decision process and include among others development time and cost, user goals, application requirements, and the operating environment. The architects select choices with outcomes that best matches the design parameters. The difficulty of architectural analysis and reasoning parallels the complexity growth in projects. To support architecture analysis and reasoning for complex systems, architects may use architectural reasoning frameworks [8,11].

We encountered several architectural analysis and reasoning challenges in our research on support for strategic reuse with Software Product Line Engineering (SPLE) [21] for Self-Adaptive Software Systems (SASS) [1]. Our goal

© Springer International Publishing Switzerland 2015
D. Weyns et al. (Eds.): ECSA 2015, LNCS 9278, pp. 20–36, 2015.
DOI: 10.1007/978-3-319-23727-5_2

is to develop assets that can be reused both vertically and horizontally [22] to support realization of self-management properties across products and product domains. The term "self-management" here refers to those characteristics which enable a software system to adapt itself in response to changes in its requirements, goals, environment and the system itself [10]. Self-configuration, self-healing, self-optimization, and self-protection are the four widely known self-management properties [18]. Realizing self-management properties is known to be a hard problem for a single self-adaptive system and becomes even more challenging when combined with reuse across products and products domains.

Self-adaptation combined with the product-line approach introduces variability along three dimensions. Domain variability, the first dimension, originates from the SPLE domain. It refers to differences among products in a product line. Run-time variability, the second dimension, comes from the self-adaptive software systems. It refers to run-time changes in a system's requirements, goals, environment, and the system itself [10]. The third dimension, cross-domains variability, stems from horizontal reuse, that is reuse across product domains. It refers to differences among products in two or more domains. The combination of three dimensions expands the design space architects have to consider, and consequently architectural reasoning and analysis become more complex.

In our work, we discovered that this increased complexity affected our primary goal, reusability, negatively. With increase in complexity, the importance of architects' skills and experience was elevated. We hypothesized that the lack of dedicated support for architecture reasoning with self-adaptation and strategic reuse was a primary reason. To that end, we adopted existing methods and techniques to develop an extended Architectural Reasoning Framework (eARF) [2].

The framework provides models and techniques that assist architects in analysis and reasoning in context of the variability described above. In this paper, we introduce the eARF elements and outline a workflow. The workflow provides step by step instructions to identify domain requirements along with their variability, extract design choices to realize requirements, analyze and reason about design choices, and finally map decisions to a reference architecture.

We have conducted an initial evaluation of the framework in a case study with final year master students [17]. The goal was to investigate its feasibility. The results indicate that use of the eARF framework provides better architectural analysis and reasoning support compared to the reference approach. It helps architects to design assets with increased reusability and reduced fault density. By providing architects with required knowledge encapsulated in the form of tactics and patterns, it also reduces the effect of differences in architects' skills and experience. The combined results indicate that our working hypothesis is correct. However, further evaluation is required to support the findings.

The remainder of this paper is organized as follows. Section 2 introduces the eARF and some of its artifacts and activities. Section 3 describes the case study. In Section 4, we analyze data and discuss results, which is followed by Section 4.4 that discusses threats to validity. Section 5 positions our work with respect to related work. We conclude and discuss future work in Section 6.

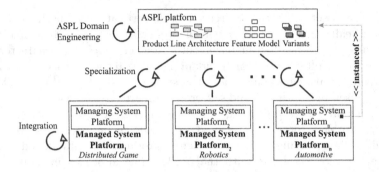

Fig. 1. The ASPLe Processes

2   An Extended Architectural Reasoning Framework

Strategic reuse offers improved quality combined with reduced effort, which would contribute to self-adaptive software engineering practices. However, little or no work in this direction has been conducted in the self-adaptive software systems domain [24].

We have developed the Autonomic Software Product Line (ASPL) [1], an approach that supports both vertical and horizontal reuse [22] of assets across domains of self-adaptive software systems. The ASPL is a multi-product line approach involving three principle components and three development processes as shown in Figure 1. The first principle component is the ASPL platform, which is a horizontal platform for managing systems. It includes reusable assets that target cross-domain reuse, that is, it is independent from the managed system domain. The second principle component is the Managing System Platform, which is a vertical platform for a managing system domain. It is derived from the horizontal platform and specialized for a specific Managed System Platform, which is the third principle component.

The framework also defines three processes. The first process is a domain engineering process for the managing system domain. It is responsible for managing the horizontal ASPL platform and its reusable assets. Then in the middle, we have multiple instances of a specialization process. Each specialization process derives a vertical managing system platform for a specific application domain by specializing the horizontal ASPL platform. The third process integrates a specialized vertical managing system platform with a domain specific managed system platform. This approach is similar to a multi-product line strategy where the ASPL platform is reusable across products and product domains, which reduces complexity for both domain and application engineers.

Architects will reason about self-management properties and additional quality attributes in the three ASPL processes, thus we identified a need for adequate reasoning support, primarily due to the complex interactions of properties, attributes, variability, and uncertainty. A reasoning framework encapsulates quality attribute knowledge and techniques required to understand and analyze

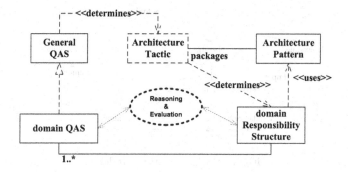

Fig. 2. Building Blocks of the eARF

a system's behavior for a specific quality attribute [7] and provides support for modeling, analysis, evaluation and interpretation [8]. We found that none of the existing reasoning frameworks provide sufficient reasoning support for realizing self-management properties. To that end, we have developed the extended Architectural Reasoning Framework (eARF).

The extended framework's structure is based on the architectural concepts defined by Diaz-Pace et al. [11]. Figure 2 outlines the extended framework and its elements: (1) Quality Attribute Scenarios (QAS), (2) domain QAS, (3) domain Responsibility Structure, (4) Architecture Tactics, and (5) Architecture Patterns. As compared to the reasoning framework proposed by Diaz-Pace et al. [11], the domain QAS and domain responsibility structure elements are the extended forms of a general QAS and responsibility structure, respectively, whereas the element "architecture patterns" is a new addition to the extended framework. We use an illustrative example to explain all these elements.

2.1 Illustrative Example

The PhotoShare Software Product Line (PSPL) contains service based products that allow users to upload, edit, and share photos. As shown in the feature model depicted in Figure 3, "uploading" and "sharing" are mandatory features, whereas "editing" is an optional feature. In addition to the mandatory features, the products are also required to guarantee performance from self-optimization. For example, a general self-optimization scenario is: *"From time to time, a PSPL product experiences increase in the number of picture upload requests that it can not handle adequately. The product can detect unacceptable latencies and adapt to self-optimize its performance"*. More details on PSPL may be found on the case study home page http://homepage.lnu.se/staff/janmsi/casestudydRS/.

Figure 4 depicts a workflow for how the eARF elements assist architects to realize self-management properties. The eARF artifacts used and produced are described below. We illustrate a scenario from the specialization process that prepares assets from the horizontal ASPL platform for integration with the vertical PSPL platform.

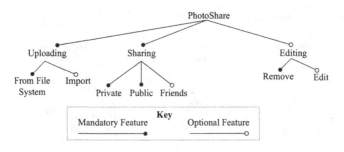

Fig. 3. PSPL – Feature Model

2.2 Domain Quality Attribute Scenarios

The identification and characterization of domain requirements and their variability is a prerequisite for architecture reasoning and design. The eARF uses quality attribute scenarios dQAS [3], an extension of QAS [6] with support to characterize domain variability, to specify a domain's requirements for self-management.

In ① in Figure 4, the domain requirements for self-optimization are elicited and specified. The requirements are analyzed for domain variability in activity ② and specified as domain scenarios. The ASPL platform provides a repository of reusable scenarios that may be adopted and reused. The PSPL architects reuse and adapt scenarios to reduce or expand their scope. For example, PSPL always schedule subscription users first; this domain specific constraint is specified by adapting scenarios from the ASPL platform. The domain analysts define new QAS and dQAS, if the platform contains no matching assets. We continue and design a domain Responsibility Structure when the dQASs are defined.

2.3 Domain Responsibility Structure

A domain Responsibility Structure (dRS) is an architectural model that consists of a responsibility part and a variability part. The first step, activity ③ in Figure 4, analyzes domain scenarios and identifies domain responsibilities [28] and variation points. The responsibilities and variation points are further analyzed for structure, associations and variants in activity ④. The responsibility part of a dRS is defined by mapping responsibilities to responsibility components. In this process, architects use tactics and patterns to support reasoning and decision making. Activity ④, completes the dRS by defining its variability part, i.e., variation points with variants, and connecting variation points to corresponding responsibility structures. The architects reuse and adapt features, variants, and variability points from ASPL into PSPL.

Self-management properties are similar to regular quality attributes. Their system-wide nature with tight coupling makes them difficult to modularize, which is also a known characteristic for quality attributes [6]. To assist the architects in reasoning about alternatives and decision making, the framework

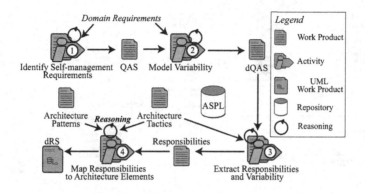

Fig. 4. Analysis and Design Workflow Using the eARF

provides design reasoning strategies, patterns and tactics for self-adaptive software systems. Examples of design strategies include "attribute driven design" [6] and "responsibility driven design" [28]. For the PSPL example we use the latter.

An architectural tactic encapsulates design decisions that may influence behavior of a system with respect to a particular quality attribute [6]. The framework promotes architectural tactics for the self-managing property. For the PSPL, we have several performance based self-optimization tactics, for example, resource demand, resource management, and resource arbitration [6].

The ASPL platform includes a set of tactics and patterns used to realize self-management properties, for instance, MAPE-K control loop tactic, and tactics for self-healing and for coordinating decentralized self-adaptation [26]. Tactics and patterns together assists architects to analyze and reason about a system's responsibilities and structure. Each tactic represents a design option, i.e., a variant, and the platform provides responsibility components and variants for the supported tactics. Tactics assist architects to identify variability and map it to a variability model for the dRS.

Figure 5 depicts a fragment of a dRS for self-optimization in the PSPL domain. Responsibilities and their variability were defined in activity ③. The resource management performance tactic, and the MAPE-K control loop pattern are used to identify and reason about sufficient allocation of responsibilities and possible variants for achieving self-optimization in the application domain.

The resulting dRS in Figure 5 contains a monitor element, the Response Monitor, from the MAPE-K pattern and a variation point with three variants: continuous, periodic, and event based. The PSPL products always include the event-based variant, while the other two variants are optional. The Planner element reuses two strategies from the resource management performance tactic: add threads, and add resources. Both strategies are mandatory for all products.

The Performance Manager subsystem in Figure 5 indicates that the target domain supports two performance manager variants; (1) centralized, and (2) decentralized. This is an example of how architects have used patterns in the process. The detailed design for one of the performance manager variants uses a

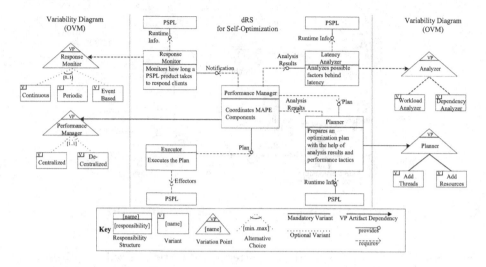

Fig. 5. Domain Responsibility Structure (dRS) for Self-Optimization

decentralization pattern for the managing systems [26], while the other variant uses a centralized feedback-loop.

The initial PSPL domain architecture for the self-optimization is ready. It will be further refined, detailed, and reconciled for additional self-management properties, and integrated with PSPL domain artifacts in the integration process. That is, however, not the focus for the work presented herein.

3   Evaluation

We conducted a case study to evaluate the eARF approach's feasibility. For a full account of the study, we refer to the study home page[1]. The primary goals for the study were: (1) to evaluate the eARF approach in comparison to a state-of-the-art reference approach, and (2) to collect user experiences for improving the eARF approach. For (1), we performed a case study with final year master students as a frame of reference [29]. The primary focus was on reusability [15], and fault density [13]. For (2), we collected qualitative data from interviews and questionnaires to understand the level of support for architectural reasoning.

We used the evaluation in (1) and user experiences from (2) to answer our hypothesis that the proposed reasoning framework provides better support for architectural reasoning and reusability in domains characterized by run-time variability, and reduces the effects of architects' skills and experience, and product's fault-density, in comparison to state-of-the-art practices.

---

[1] http://homepage.lnu.se/staff/janmsi/casestudydRS/

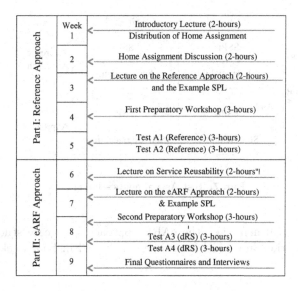

	Week		
Part I: Reference Approach	1	<	Introductory Lecture (2-hours)
			Distribution of Home Assignment
	2	<	Home Assignment Discussion (2-hours)
	3	<	Lecture on the Reference Approach (2-hours) and the Example SPL
	4	<	First Preparatory Workshop (3-hours)
	5	<	Test A1 (Reference) (3-hours)
			Test A2 (Reference) (3-hours)
Part II: eARF Approach	6	<	Lecture on Service Reusability (2-hours"!
	7	<	Lecture on the eARF Approach (2-hours) & Example SPL
	8	<	Second Preparatory Workshop (3-hours)
		<	Test A3 (dRS) (3-hours)
	9	<	Test A4 (dRS) (3-hours)
			Final Questionnaires and Interviews

Fig. 6. Overview of the Nine Weeks Course in which the Case Study Took Place

3.1   Design and Planning

We follow a planning template suggested by Wohlin et al. [29]. The objective of the study is defined above. The eARF framework and a reference approach are the two cases studied. The reference approach consists of state-of-the-art practices for self-adaptive software system design, centered around MAPE-K feedback loop [18]. The Monitor, Analyze, Plan, Execute, and Knowledge (MAPE-K) loop was first introduced by IBM [18] to add self-managing properties to software systems. It monitors and controls one or more underlying managed elements. The managed element might be a hardware or a software system. The reason for selecting the MAPE-K as a state-of-the-art reference approach is that, at present, it is the most widely used approach to realize self-adaptive software systems.

Test assignments, questionnaires and interviews are used as methods of data collection. We match the case study's objective and research questions with data collection methods to decide which data units we would use in our analysis, i.e., our selection strategy. Given our setting with a small number of subjects we adopt an "analyze-all" strategy, that is, data collected from all subjects is investigated and analyzed.

The case study was performed as a part of a nine weeks course, involving three researchers and 13 subjects. Most of the preparatory work, data collection, and analysis were performed by a doctoral student assisted by two senior lecturers, primarily in the role as reviewers and advisors. The subjects were final-year students on a two year master program in software engineering. As depicted in Figure 6, the case study was conducted in two parts, one for each case studied. The first part was concerned with the reference approach, and the second

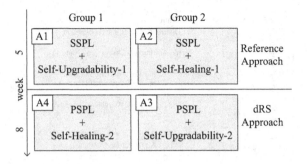

Fig. 7. Test Assignments - Design

introduced the treatment, i.e., the eARF approach. The case study was completed with questionnaires and interviews conducted in final week of the part two.

3.2 Data Collection

The case study involves four test assignments that are performed by dividing subjects into two groups randomly based on blocked subject-object study classification [29]. A blocked subject-object study analyzes two or more objects (cases or units of analysis) using two or more subjects per object. In this type of study, each subject receives both treatments, i.e., the reference and the dRS approach. This allows paired comparison of the two approaches.

The test assignments target first two of the three variability dimensions addressed by the ASPL approach. Domain variability, the first dimension, comes from the product line engineering domain. Thus, two example SPLs, (1) Soft-Phones Software Product Line (SSPL) and (2) PhotoShare Software Product Line (PSPL) were designed for the test assignments. Details about these example SPLs are given at the case study home page. To cater for the second dimension, run-time variability, requirements for self-upgradability and self-healing were added to the product lines' scope. For each test, Figure 7 depicts a combination of an example SPL and a self-management property, for example, test A2 uses SSPL with self-healing as problem domain.

Each test assignment first introduces a problem domain followed by three tasks. Tasks 1 and 3 are design tasks. Task 1 has two parts: *a* and *b*. Each part requires subjects to extend an initial product design to support a given self-management property, either self-upgradability, or self-healing. Task 2 requires subjects to extend the core assets base by adding reusable artifacts from the Task 1. This represents the third variability dimension, which originates from reuse across multiple domains, i.e., horizontal reuse. Task 3 requires subjects to use the extended core assets base from Task 2 and design a new product. All tests were conducted as regular class assignments. No feedback was given to subjects on the first part prior to the completion of the second part.

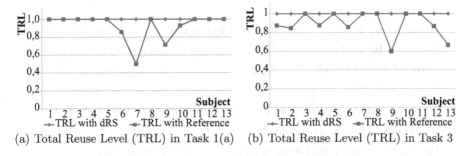

(a) Total Reuse Level (TRL) in Task 1(a)   (b) Total Reuse Level (TRL) in Task 3

Fig. 8. Total Reuse Level Achieved Using the Reference and the dRS Approach

Questionnaires and semi-structured interviews were used to collect data for the study's second objective. There were two types of questionnaires. The first type was a combination of "pre" and "post" test questionnaires designed to identify false positives and false negatives. The second type compares the two approaches with respect to their support for architectural reasoning. Each subject was interviewed at the very end of the data collection phase to clarify responses in questionnaires and collect details. The interviews were conducted after publishing the course result to assure that the subjects did not adjust their responses to get a better grade.

4   Analysis of Results

This section presents the data analysis and pinpoints findings that were observed to confirm or reject our hypothesis. The main objective was to analyze the eARF approach in comparison to the state-of-the-art reference approach with respect to three properties: (1) reusability, (2) fault density, and (3) support for architectural reasoning. We divide the analysis in three parts, one for each property.

4.1   Support for Reusability

To analyze the two approaches with respect to their support for reusability, we use quantitative data from the test assignments. The "reuse level" software metric [15] is used for this analysis. It is defined for hierarchically composed component system, and is well aligned with the way products are designed and composed in the test assignments. The metric is defined as:

$$\text{Total Reuse Level} = \text{External Reuse Level} + \text{Internal Reuse Level}$$
$$\text{External Reuse Level} = E/L$$
$$\text{Internal Reuse Level} = M/L$$

L – the total number of lower level items in the higher level item.

E – the number of lower level items from an external repository.

I – the number of lower level items not from an external repository.

M – the number of items not from an external repository but used more than once.

All reuse levels will be between 0 and 1, here 0 indicates no reuse. We assume that the products designed in the tests are the higher level items and compute the value of L by counting the number of lower level items used in a product. The core assets base from the example SPLs provides lower level items. We compute E by counting the number of items from the core assets, and I by counting items developed specifically for a product. M is computed by counting the items not belonging to the core assets base but used more than once.

We calculate total reuse level for task 1 and task 3 as depicted in Figure 8. There is no significant difference in the total reuse level for task 1(a). This is because this task presents subjects with an initial product design and asks them to extend it to support a self-management property. The approach is, however, at least as good as the reference approach for all subjects and sometimes the total reuse level is better. The results are similar for task 1(b), thus excluded for space consideration.

The difference between the two approaches in terms of the achieved total reuse level becomes more clear in task 3. In this task, a new product with support for a self-management property is designed from scratch. All subjects achieve maximum total reuse level of 1 with the eARF approach. In comparison only 46% were able to achieve the maximum total reuse level with the reference approach.

4.2   Fault Density

Fault density is the number of known faults divided by product size [25]. It is a de-facto measure of user perceived software quality [13]. We use it to analyze the eARF approach's support for producing high-quality architectural designs. We used quantitative data from task 1 and task 3 to calculate the fault density.

$$\text{Fault Density} = \text{Faults} / \text{Size} \tag{1}$$

To compute fault density using equation 1, we need to compute values of two input variables: *faults*, and *size*. As the tasks selected for this analysis resulted in design level artifacts, we were restricted to use methods at design level. We estimated faults for each task of each subject by comparing subjects' solutions (designs) with a reference solution, and counting one fault for each missing or

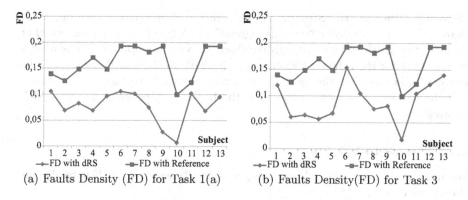

(a) Faults Density (FD) for Task 1(a)   (b) Faults Density(FD) for Task 3

Fig. 9. Faults Density Comparisons Using the Reference and the dRS Approach

incorrect element. The missing or incorrect element can be a component, service, interface, method, or a method parameter for test assignments A1 and A2 that use the reference approach. In the test assignments A3 and A4 that require the eARF approach, the element can be a responsibility component, responsibility definition, interface, variation point, or a variant.

The size of a software system can be measured in different ways. We used function point analysis (FPA) [4] method to measure size. As the test assignments involve design artifacts so we searched for an FPA based method that could be applied to design level artifacts. We could not find a method that suited the design artifacts created in the selected tasks. However, we found an FPA based high level analysis approach [20] that targets software requirements specification. We decided to use this approach. The approach uses independent assessors to rate each requirement on a scale: low, average, and high. We used three assessors, two doctoral students and a senior lecturer in software engineering. Following the procedure described by the approach, we computed three scores for *size* in terms of function points: minimum, expected, and maximum. We took average of these scores to get a size estimate. For details about the computation procedure, we refer to the original work by Peeters et al. [20] and the case study home page.

Figure 9 depicts the fault density for the approaches. It is clear that for both tasks the eARF approach results in a reduced fault density.

4.3 Support for Architectural Reasoning

We use qualitative data collected with a questionnaire to analyse the approaches with respect to their support for architecture analysis and reasoning. As the data is qualitative, the results are indicative.

In the final questionnaire, subjects were asked to answer six closed questions targeting support for architectural reasoning. A majority of the subjects rated the eARF approach as relatively better for the first two questions. In the remaining questions, we gave a statement and asked to select one of five options from

"Strongly Disagree" to "Strongly Agree", and a "Don't Know" option. More than 90% of the subjects "strongly agreed" or "agreed" to a statement that declared the eARF to be more assistive than the reference approach. The results were similar for the other statements, i.e., positive to the eARF approach. The analysis indicates that the eARF contributes positively to the design process and the subjects feel more confident with the support provided by the eARF approach.

4.4   Threats to Validity

We use the classification scheme suggested by Runeson et al. [23] to discuss threats to validity.

Construct validity ensures that a study actually relates to the problem that the study aims to address. The eARF focuses on realization of self-management properties characterized with domain and cross-domains variability. Accordingly, the study selected two SPLs with requirements for self-management properties as problem domains. A possible threat to validity is "use of unclear terminology" that causes subjects and researchers to interpret the used terms or concepts differently. We reduced this threat by dedicating three weeks in both parts of the study to lectures and preparatory workshops. Another possible threat is that subjects may guess what the researchers are looking for and adapt their answers accordingly. This threat was mitigated by presenting the activities as coursework. We also gave feedback and grades prior to the questionnaires and interviews.

Internal validity is a concern for explanatory studies where causal relations are examined [23]. This study is explorative, and thus less sensitive to this type of threat. Other potential threats are increased understanding and maturity of subjects. To mitigate these threats, we took three measures in the case study design: (1) a comprehensive knowledge base in the first part, (2) use of a new problem domain (PSPL) and requirements set in the second part, and (3) use of standards tools and methods such as UML.

External validity is concerned with the extent to which findings can be generalized and are relevant outside the study. This study uses final year master students as subjects [17]. The profile for such students is that they are knowledgeable but lack in professional skills and experience. One of the aspects we were interested in is, "how the experience and knowledge provided by eARF contributes to the design quality". It is important to note that professional architects will exhibit similar differences in knowledge and experience as the group of students usually have, and thereby, the effect of eARF would be generalizable. The size of the study's population is, however, small to generalize the results.

Another potential threat is that the framework and the test assignments are designed by the same group of researchers. There is a risk that the test assignments were designed in a way that favors the eARF approach. To reduce this threat, an independent senior researcher was requested to review the assignments. Moreover, a large portion of data collection and analysis was performed by a single researcher. The data analysis of the test assignments is based on objective data, except for the size measure. External reviewers were involved for that particular data point. With opinions from multiple sources the risk of a biased analysis is mitigated.

Reliability refers to the ability of other researchers to replicate the study. To support replication, a complete documentation for all activities in this study is available online at the case study home page.

5 Related Work

Reusable decision models support architectural reasoning by capturing architectural decisions and exchanging these within and between projects in the same or similar context. Olaf et al. [30] presented a proactive approach to model and reuse architectural knowledge. The approach need to be investigated in the context of self-management properties. Bass et al. [7] proposed use of reasoning framework which encapsulate knowledge and tools needed to analyze behavior of a system such as the modifiability reasoning framework [11]. A reasoning framework may help the architects to evaluate an architecture in its early stages, and save lot of effort and resources in the end. However, none of the existing frameworks target self-management properties and the three variability dimensions targeted in this study. An open source project, DiVA [12], provides a tool-supported methodology and framework for managing dynamic variability in adaptive systems. The project claims to contribute with a reasoning framework that takes a context and adaptation rules as input and does the reasoning to find and rank possible configurations for the given context. However, there are no details for the framework elements, which makes it difficult to compare with our work.

A related research theme that addresses development issues for reusable and dynamically reconfigurable core assets is Dynamic Software Product Lines (DSPL) [16]. The DSPL community has proposed several approaches to deal with run-time variability. The MADAM [14] middleware is one such approach that uses architecture models at run-time to reason about and control adaptations. In its current implementation, it uses a utility function to reason about and select the design options, this can be supplemented by encapsulating knowledge in the form of a reasoning framework. Thus the eARF framework has a potential to be integrated with the MADAM middleware to enhance reasoning support needed to deal with the three variability dimensions investigated in this study.

Liu et al. [19] proposed a dynamically reconfigurable reference architecture based approach to develop systems with evolvable run-time variability. The approach uses a dynamic update mechanism which at run-time updates the reference architecture by adding, removing, and modifying architectural elements. The authors described a process through which such updates are performed, however, there is no discussion about what triggers the dynamic update process, and how the design choices are analyzed and reasoned about at run-time.

Whittle et al. [27] presented RELAX, a requirements specification language for self-adaptive systems. It may help developers to identify variability in the requirements, by specifying requirements that a system could temporarily relax under certain conditions. However, RELAX does not support design and reasoning at the architecture level which is the focus for our work presented herein.

Cetina et al. [9] proposed a Common Variability Language (CVL) for runtime variability modeling. The CVL approach separates variability modeling from the base domain modeling. The split between variability modeling and base domain modeling in the CVL approach is similar to the split between variability part and responsibilities part in the extended responsibility structure presented in this study. However, the authors did not explicitly state and address the architectural reasoning support needed to make decisions and trade off at runtime.

Bachmann et al. [5] called for the provision of special methods that may assist in designing an architecture with quality attribute requirements. The authors require such methods to have three features, (1) knowledge encapsulation, (2) trade-offs, and (3) traceability from requirements to architecture. The eARF provides support for all these features through tactics, patterns, domain scenarios and the responsibility structures.

6   Discussion and Conclusions

Development of self-adaptive software systems with systematic reuse presents architects with the challenge of extensive architectural analysis and reasoning needed to analyze, reason about, and trade-off multiple design choices. The extended architectural reasoning framework supports the architects by providing them with models and techniques for reasoning, mapping, and structuring responsibilities with variability into a reference architecture. In addition, it provides architects with design knowledge and proven best practices encapsulated in the form of tactics and patterns.

We conducted a case study to investigate the feasibility of the proposed architectural reasoning framework. We conclude that the results from the study indicate that the framework offers better support for reuse and reduces fault density in comparison to the reference approach. We also collected qualitative data that indicates that the architects appreciate the structure and guidance provided by the eARF framework. This is also supported by the quantitative data where we see that skills and experience have less impact on the measured properties with the eARF approach.

The proposed extensions are the first steps towards a comprehensive design framework that leverages on reuse to engineer self-adaptive software product-lines across multiple domains. However, much work remains. For instance, the framework must include better support for reasoning. We have plans to further investigate tactics and patterns with the aim to establish a core of best practices for engineering self-adaptive software systems and include the practices as design advices for further increase of reusability and reuse levels.

Acknowledgments. Acknowledgments The research was funded by VINNOVA, the Swedish Agency for Innovation Systems and Innovative Product Development (Grant No. 2013-03492).

References

1. Abbas, N.: Towards autonomic software product lines. In: Proceedings of the 15th International Software Product Line Conference, SPLC 2011, vol. 2, pp. 44:1–44:8. ACM, New York (2011)
2. Abbas, N., Andersson, J.: Architectural reasoning for dynamic software product lines. In: Proceedings of the 17th International Software Product Line Conference Co-located Workshops, pp. 117–124
3. Abbas, N., Andersson, J., Weyns, D.: Modeling variability in product lines using domain quality attribute scenarios. In: Proceedings of the WICSA/ECSA 2012 Companion Volume, pp. 135–142. ACM, New York (2012)
4. Albrecht, A., Gaffney, J.E.: Software function, source lines of code, and development effort prediction: A software science validation. IEEE Transactions on Software Engineering **SE–9**(6), 639–648 (1983)
5. Bachmann, F., Bass, L., Klein, M., et al.: Designing software architectures to achieve quality attribute requirements. IEE Proceedings - Software **152**(4), 153–165 (2005)
6. Bass, L., Clements, P., Kazman, R.: Software Architecture in Practice, 2nd edn. Addison-Wesley Professional (2003)
7. Bass, L., Ivers, J., Klein, M., et al.: Encapsulating quality attribute knowledge. In: Proceedings of the 5th Working IEEE/IFIP Conference on Software Architecture, WICSA 2005, pp. 193–194. IEEE Computer Society, Washington, DC (2005)
8. Bass, L., Ivers, J., Klein, M.H., et al.: Reasoning frameworks. Tech. rep. (2005). http://www.sei.cmu.edu/library/abstracts/reports/05tr007.cfm
9. Cetina, C., Haugen, O., Zhang, X., Fleurey, F., Pelechano, V.: Strategies for variability transformation at run-time. In: Proceedings of the 13th International Software Product Line Conference, SPLC 2009, pp. 61–70. Carnegie Mellon University, Pittsburgh (2009)
10. de Lemos, R., et al.: Software engineering for self-adaptive systems: a second research roadmap. In: de Lemos, R., Giese, H., Müller, H.A., Shaw, M. (eds.) Software Engineering for Self-Adaptive Systems. LNCS, vol. 7475, pp. 1–32. Springer, Heidelberg (2013)
11. Diaz-Pace, A., Kim, H.-W., Bass, L.J., Bianco, P., Bachmann, F.: Integrating quality-attribute reasoning frameworks in the ArchE design assistant. In: Becker, S., Plasil, F., Reussner, R. (eds.) QoSA 2008. LNCS, vol. 5281, pp. 171–188. Springer, Heidelberg (2008)
12. DiVA: Diva-dynamic variability in complex, adaptive systems. http://sites.google.com/site/divawebsite
13. Fenton, N.E., Neil, M.: Software metrics: roadmap. In: Proceedings of the Conference on The Future of Software Engineering, pp. 357–370. ACM, New York (2000)
14. Floch, J., Hallsteinsen, S., Stav, E., et al.: Using architecture models for runtime adaptability. IEEE Software **23**(2), 62–70 (2006)
15. Frakes, W., Terry, C.: Software reuse: Metrics and models. ACM Computing Surveys **28**(2), 415–435 (1996)

16. Hallsteinsen, S., Hinchey, M., Park, S., et al.: Dynamic software product lines. IEEE Computer **41**(4), 93–95 (2008)
17. Höst, M., Regnell, B., Wohlin, C.: Using students as subjects-a comparative study of students and professionals in lead-time impact assessment. Empirical Software Engineering **5**(3), 201–214 (2000). http://dx.doi.org/10.1023/A:1026586415054
18. Kephart, J., Chess, D.: The vision of autonomic computing. Computer **36**(1), 41–50 (2003)
19. Liu, J., Mao, X.: Towards realisation of evolvable runtime variability in internet-based service systems via dynamical software update. In: Proceedings of the 6th Asia-Pacific Symposium on Internetware, Internetware 2014, pp. 97–106. ACM, New York (2014)
20. Peeters, P., van Asperen, J., Jacobs, M., et al.: The application of Function Point Analysis (FPA) in the early phases of the application life cycle A Practical Manual: Theory and case study, 2.0 edn. Netherlands Software Metrics Association (NESMA) (2005)
21. Pohl, K., Böckle, G., Van Der Linden, F.: Software product line engineering: foundations, principles, and techniques. Springer-Verlag New York Inc. (2005)
22. Prieto-Diaz, R.: Status report: software reusability. IEEE Software **10**(3), 61–66 (1993)
23. Runeson, P., Höst, M., Rainer, A., et al.: Case Study Research in Software Engineering: Guidelines and Examples, 1st edn. Wiley Publishing (2012)
24. Weyns, D., Iftikhar, M., Malek, S., et al.: Claims and supporting evidence for self-adaptive systems: a literature study. In: 2012 ICSE Workshop on Software Engineering for Adaptive and Self-Managing Systemsm, pp. 89–98 (2012)
25. Weyns, D., Iftikhar, M.U., Söderlund, J.: Do external feedback loops improve the design of self-adaptive systems? a controlled experiment. In: Proceedings of the 8th International Symposium on Software Engineering for Adaptive and Self-Managing Systems, pp. 3–12. IEEE Press, Piscataway (2013)
26. Weyns, D., Schmerl, B., Grassi, V., Malek, S., Mirandola, R., Prehofer, C., Wuttke, J., Andersson, J., Giese, H., Göschka, K.M.: On patterns for decentralized control in self-adaptive systems. In: de Lemos, R., Giese, H., Müller, H.A., Shaw, M. (eds.) Software Engineering for Self-Adaptive Systems. LNCS, vol. 7475, pp. 76–107. Springer, Heidelberg (2013)
27. Whittle, J., Sawyer, P., Bencomo, N., et al.: RELAX: a language to address uncertainty in self-adaptive systems requirement. Requirements Engineering **15**(2), 177–196 (2010)
28. Wirfs-Brock, R., McKean, A.: Object design: roles, responsibilities, and collaborations. Addison-Wesley Professional (2003)
29. Wohlin, C., Runeson, P., Höst, M., et al.: Experimentation in Software Engineering, 1st edn. Springer, Heidelberg (2012)
30. Zimmermann, O., Gschwind, T., Küster, J.M., Leymann, F., Schuster, N.: Reusable architectural decision models for enterprise application development. In: Overhage, S., Ren, X.-M., Reussner, R., Stafford, J.A. (eds.) QoSA 2007. LNCS, vol. 4880, pp. 15–32. Springer, Heidelberg (2008)

Towards a Framework for Building Adaptive App-Based Web Applications Using Dynamic Appification

Ashish Agrawal[✉] and T.V. Prabhakar

Department of Computer Science and Engineering,
Indian Institute of Technology Kanpur, Kanpur 208016, Uttar Pradesh, India
{agrawala,tvp}@cse.iitk.ac.in

Abstract. Appification, the process of building app-based web applications, can help in improving various quality attributes of the application and reduce consumption of resources at server side. A major challenge in ensuring quality attributes of such applications is run-time variations in availability of client resources like battery power. A generic architecture-based approach for building applications that can not only accommodate the dynamic environments by ensuring multiple quality attributes but can also opportunistically exploit the client resources, is missing in the literature. This paper presents a technique called *Dynamic Appification* using which an application can manage its expectations on the environment at run-time. Findings of our investigation on building adaptive applications using this technique are formulated as a methodological framework called *Appification Framework*. Using our framework, we implemented an application that can not only handle the scenarios of low client resources but can also opportunistically exploit the client resources to improve its capacity by more than 100% of the initial capacity.

Keywords: Mobile apps · Dynamic architecture · Adaptive applications

1 Introduction

Appification, the process of building app-based web applications, can also be seen as an opportunity to exploit resources available at the mobile clients. However, mobile devices operate in dynamic environments and availability of resources at client devices can vary with time like battery level, network connectivity, etc [7]. Such environmental changes cause issues in ensuring quality attributes of the application and also limit the application's ability to exploit client resources. For example, if an application is designed with light computation on client devices, it will not be able to fully use the client resources when possible. Existing approaches in the literature to handle dynamic environments at run-time (e.g., *Cyber Foraging* [1] and *Fidelity Adaption* [8]) are focused towards ensuring only a specific set of quality attributes. Also, these solutions accommodate the dynamic environments only from the client perspective (low availability of client

© Springer International Publishing Switzerland 2015
D. Weyns et al. (Eds.): ECSA 2015, LNCS 9278, pp. 37–44, 2015.
DOI: 10.1007/978-3-319-23727-5_3

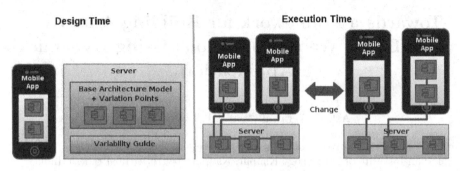

Fig. 1. An example of application adapting using our methodology

resources) and do not consider the server perspective of exploiting the client resources when possible.

Aim of this work is to provide a generic architecture-based approach that can accommodate the dynamic environments while considering both client and server perspectives. Our focus is on investigating the architecture-level decisions that are specific to the appification process. In this process, an important architectural decision is to divide the application components into two groups, one to be executed on the client device and the other to be executed on the server. This decision has an impact on the quality attributes of the application. We call this design decision as *"Appification Strategy (AS)"* for that application. An application can have several possible *ASs* which have different impacts on quality attributes. In current approaches, an *AS* is decided during the design phase. This leads to a one-time selection of what the quality attribute trade-offs are likely to be.

We present a technique called *Dynamic Appification* where the *AS* of the application is not fixed at design-time and can vary at run-time. This technique can help in handling dynamic environments from both client and server perspectives. From the client perspective, an application can select an *AS* more suitable for a particular type of client at that time. From a server perspective, among possible *ASs* for a particular client at a given time, an application can choose the one with maximum reduction in operational load on the server. Thus, at run-time, the application can have different *ASs* for different clients and can migrate from one *AS* to another *AS* for any client. Figure 1 depicts an example of adaptation in the application using our methodology. It shows that *AS* for a particular client can be changed by executing more components on the client device.

Findings of our initial exploration to realize *Dynamic Appification* for building adaptive applications are formulated as a methodological framework called *Appificaton Framework*. We have also implemented a simple application as a proof of concept for the *Appification Framework* and conducted experiments to accommodate scenarios of low battery power, intermittent network connectivity and high load on the server. Rest of the paper is structured as follows: Section 2 describes *Appification Framework* in detail. Section 3 explains implementation

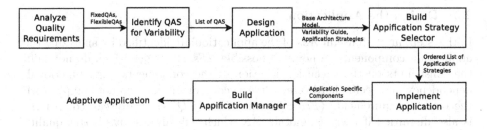

Fig. 2. Steps of the Appification Framework

of our prototype and results of the experiment conducted for handling changes in the environment. Section 4 concludes the work with directions for future work.

2 Appification Framework

This section presents a methodological framework for building applications with the ability to adapt in a dynamic environment at run-time using *Dynamic Appification*. The framework abstracts out the responsibilities involved in building such applications, and provides guidelines for architectural design, implementation and deployment of the application. Figure 2 depicts steps involved in the framework that are further explained in the following subsections.

2.1 Analyze Quality Requirements

The first step is to analyze the application requirements to identify the quality attributes that can be changed at run-time during adaptation. An application may have freedom in parameters of some quality attribute requirements like performance (response-time) may vary between 0 to 10 seconds. Thus, there can exist multiple *ASs* for that application which comply with the restrictions imposed by the quality attribute requirements. In this step, quality attributes desired from the application are categorized into two sets: 1) *FixedQAs* contains quality attributes for which variations are not allowed; 2) *FlexibleQAs* contains quality attributes for which application can have some variations.

2.2 Identify QAS for Variability

In this step, we need to identify the scenarios for which application needs to adapt. The main idea of our approach is to achieve variability quality attribute [4] in the application architecture and requirements for the same are captured through *Quality Attribute Scenarios (QAS)* [3] for variability. Documenting QASs for variability helps in identifying in what situations application needs to adapt and what should be the desired result after adaptation. For example an application can have the following QAS: "If client battery is less than 30%, reduce the energy consumption of the application on that client device".

2.3   Design the Application

In this step, first, all useful *ASs* of the application are identified by analyzing the application components. Among all possible *ASs*, strategies which do not fulfil the constraints on the execution location of the components (e.g., functional, dependency on specific hardware/software components), or do not comply with the quality requirements (*FixedQAs* and *FlexibleQAs*), are discarded. An *AS* is also discarded if there is another *AS* which will always give better quality attributes compared to this one.

Finally, a base architecture model of the application is designed which represents execution location of the components. If a component has same execution location (client or server) in all useful *ASs*, it has a static execution location in the base model. If a component has different execution location in any two useful *ASs*, its execution location is modeled as a variation point. Such a variation point has two choices, either to execute that component on the client device or on the server. This base architecture model will have a set of possible reconfigurations (*ASs*) for run-time execution. Details of variation points (e.g., choices, variation-time, etc.) are stored in the variability guide. These strategies are also evaluated in terms of their impact on quality attributes. Such evaluation results will be used in the process of selecting the best possible *AS*. In case it is not possible to fully quantify such an impact, it is captured in relative terms.

2.4   Build Appification Strategy Selector

In this step, we build a component to facilitate selection of an *AS* for given quality attributes. This component will be used to decide initial *AS* of the application and which *AS* to be used during adaptation. Such selection is a complex problem as there may be a situation in which no single strategy is giving better values for all quality attributes. For example, one *AS* may provide poor performance and better security and another may provide better performance but poor security. We have formulated this problem as a multi-criteria decision making problem and used *Technique for Order of Preference by Similarity to Ideal Solution (TOPSIS)* [5] framework as it selects the solution closest to the best possible solution. Due to page limitation, details of our TOPSIS model are omitted here and the readers are referred to [2].

Output of the TOPSIS model is an ordered list of *ASs*, let's say *ASOrderedlist*, where the *AS* at the top is most preferable (most closest to the desired quality attributes). The application maintains a copy of *ASOrderedlist* for every client and initially, the topmost strategy is selected for current execution. On the occurrence of a QAS, the application selects an *AS* with the highest rank that fulfills the desired QAS response. Such selection will have the minimum adverse effect on other quality attributes. In case the adaptation is requested by the server environment (e.g., load on the server), then the application might have to change *ASs* for a set of client devices. Depending on the desired quality improvement, the number of client users, for whom *ASs* have to be changed, is defined using methods like stress-testing.

2.5   Implement the Application

In order to have the ability to dynamically change the *AS* at run-time, application components having variation points, have to be implemented in a way such that their execution location (client or server) and communication pattern (local or remote) can be changed at run-time. Our technique for building such components is based on the following tactics:

1. **Code Redundancy:** Deploy such components on both server and mobile device to reduce the overhead of transferring components on the fly. It may increase implementation cost as such components may have to be built in both the technology stacks of server and client.
2. **Encapsulate:** Provide an explicit interface of the components such as application programming interface (API). It is required for easy interaction with other components.
3. **Defer Binding:** As the exact execution flow of the application will be decided at run-time, components have to be designed in such a way that they can dynamically decide whether to make a remote call or a local call. Thus, to change the *AS*, application just need to change the call graphs of the components.

2.6   Build Appification Manager

In this step, we implement the functionality of dynamically changing the *AS* for client devices. The application should be able to monitor the environment to trigger a QAS, select *ASs* for clients, and migrate the client(s) to their selected *AS*. For handling these issues, we present a conceptual architecture of such component, *Appification Manager*. Architecture of *Appification Manager* is based on MAPE-K control loop [6] for adaptive systems which clearly abstracts out the responsibilities of an adaptive system. Following describes components of *Appification Manager* in detail.

1. **Context Monitor**: This component monitors the contextual variables (e.g., CPU load) and reports the data to the *Analyzer*.
2. **QAS Analyzer**: By analyzing the data provided by the *Context Monitor*, this component checks if any variability QAS has occurred in the system. For example, it notifies the *Planner* component if CPU load on the server becomes more than 80% continuously for 15 minutes.
3. **Strategy Planner**: This component decides what changes should be incorporated in the application. By using the results from *Appification Strategy Selector*, it identifies the number of users and their new *ASs*.
4. **Executor**: This component is responsible for finally changing the *ASs* of the clients identified by *Planner*. For each user, depending upon the *AS*, it selects the call graph (stored in the *Knowledge Base*), and updates both server and client with this information.
5. **Knowledge Base**: This component maintains a repository of architectural information used by other components of the manager.

3 Case Study

We have implemented a simple application as a proof of concept for the *Appifica-tion Framework* and conducted experiments to show the feasibility of two kinds of adaptations: 1) *Server-driven adaptation* in which server changes *ASs* of a set of clients to handle high operational load, and 2) *Client-driven adaptation* in which a single client adapts its *AS* to handle low availability of resources at the client-side. Our application facilitates image-based searching of products and has mainly three components; **TakeImage** for capturing an image, **ImageToText** for extracting text from an image, and **Search** for searching the textual content in a product database. We identified two *ASs* for the application as:

- as_1: Component **TakeImage** executes on mobile client; **ImageToText** and **Search** execute on server.
- as_2: Components **TakeImage** and **ImageToText** execute on client; **Search** executes on server.

For client devices, components are implemented in Java for the Android platform. For server, components are implemented in Python using Django framework. **ImageToText** is build using Tesseract-OCR library [9] for both the Android platform and the server. The server part is deployed on a virtual machine with 1 CPU core and 2 GB RAM. Here, the application can have some variations in performance, energy-efficiency on the clients, and capacity. However, the average response-time of requests should not be more than 10 seconds. Following sections explain the two kinds of adaptations investigated by us:

3.1 Server-Driven Adaptation

We demonstrate the ability of the application to accommodate dynamic changes in server environment (user-load) by opportunistically exploiting the resources available at the client devices. QAS for such adaptation is:

- **QAS1**: "If the server reaches 85% of its capacity, reduce the load on the server".

In our case, capacity is represented as the number of clients the application can serve while maintaining the average response-time to less than 10 seconds. We selected as_1 as the initial *AS* for the application in order to minimize the energy consumed on client devices. Without dynamic appification, the server has a capacity to handle around 46 simultaneous users. Compared to as_1, strategy as_2 has less operational load on the server as **ImageToText** is executed on client. Thus, to accommodate high user-load, the application changes the *ASs* for a set of clients. In order to identify the number of such clients for a given user-load, we performed profiling of the application. For a given user-load, average response time is calculated with varying number of users moved to as_2, as shown in Figure 3(a) and 3(b). For example, in case of 60 users, for reducing average response time to less than 10 seconds, at least 10 users should be moved to as_2.

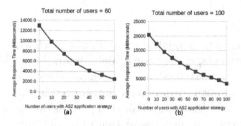 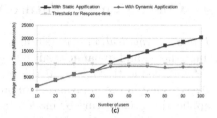

Fig. 3. Experimental results: (a) & (b) depict profiling results for different user-load. Here, average response-time is depicted with varying number of users appified to as_2 strategy. (c) depicts application behaviour with and without dynamic appification

Figure 3(c) presents results of dynamically varying capacity of the application to 100 users. Here, with static appification (with strategy as_1), average response-time goes more than 10 seconds after 46 users. With dynamic appification, the application behaves similar to static appification till 40 users. After 40 users, the application dynamically scales to increase its capacity. In case of 100 users, application changes ASs of 50% users to maintain the average response-time to less than 10 seconds. This adaptation has an adverse impact on energy consumptions of the client devices. By changing AS dynamically, an application can increase its capacity only up to a limit. For example, in our case, the application can not handle more than 165 users even by using as_2 strategy for all users. Here, contrary to the traditional/cloud approach, capacity is improved without adding new server-side resources. Thus it does not increase operational-cost of the application. One thing to note here is that the improvement in the capacity will directly depend upon the amount of computation off-loaded to the client devices. Aim of this experiment was to show feasibility of our approach. Exact improvement in capacity may vary with application.

3.2   Client-Driven Adaptation

Here, to handle the environmental changes, a client adapts its AS at run-time. The QASs for such adaptations are:

- **QAS2**: "If the battery power at a client is less than 30% of full power, reduce energy consumption at the client device". To test this scenario, initially the client is configured with as_2 strategy. By moving to as_1, client can reduce the energy consumption by removing the overhead (0.95 seconds of execution time) of executing component **ImageToText**.
- **QAS3**: "If the client is having intermittent network connectivity, reduce response-time from the server so that the dependency on a stable network is narrowed". To test this scenario, initially the client is configured with as_1 strategy. By moving to as_2, the application can reduce server part of response-time from 0.24 seconds to 0.11 seconds.

4   Conclusion and Future Work

Dynamic Appification can help in solving various quality related issues such as; unpredicted and dynamic quality requirements, energy constraints, intermittent network connectivity, etc. In this paper, we explored how to realize *Dynamic Appification* in the application. In our approach, variability is introduced in the application architecture by modeling the appification-specific design decisions as variation points. Such architecture supports multiple variants that differ in terms of their impact on the quality attributes and consumption of resources. Thus, depending upon the environmental context, an application can adapt at run-time by migrating to a suitable variant. Selection of the best suitable variant is done in a manner such that the adverse effects on other quality attributes are minimum. We presented a methodological framework, called *Appification Framework* to provide guidance on building adaptive applications with *Dynamic Appification*. Experiments conducted on a prototype implementation showed that the application can not only handle scenarios of low client resources, but can also dynamically scale by exploiting resources available at the client devices. In the future, we would like to explore on automating the framework activities in order to reduce the design and development overhead.

Acknowledgments. Acknowledgments The authors gratefully acknowledge the financial support from Tata Consultancy Services and MHRD, Govt. of India for this work.

References

1. Avgeriou, Paris, Zdun, Uwe (eds.): ECSA 2014. LNCS, vol. 8627. Springer, Heidelberg (2014)
2. Agrawal, A., Prabhakar, T.V.: Using topsis for decision making in software architecture. http://www.cse.iitk.ac.in/users/agrawala/topsis.html (retrieved June 2015)
3. Bachmann, F., Bass, L., Klein, M.: Deriving architectural tactics: A step toward methodical architectural design, technical report, CMU/SEI-2003-TR-004 (2003)
4. Bass, L., Clements, P., Kazman, R.: Software Architecture in Practice, 3rd edn. Addison-Wesley Professional (2012)
5. Hwang, C., Yoon, K.: Multiple Attribute Decision Making: Methods and Applications. Springer, New York (1981)
6. Jacob, B., Lanyon-Hogg, R., Nadgir, D.K., Yassin, A.F.: A practical guide to the to the ibm autonomic computing toolkit, April 2004
7. Messer, A., Greenberg, I., Bernadat, P., Milojicic, D., Chen, D., Giuli, T.J., Gu, X.: Towards a distributed platform for resource-constrained devices. In: Proceedings of the 22 nd International Conference on Distributed Computing Systems (ICDCS 2002), p. 43 (2002)
8. Noble, B.D., Satyanarayanan, M., Narayanan, D., Tilton, J.E., Flinn, J., Walker, K.R.: Agile application-aware adaptation for mobility. In: Proceedings of the Sixteenth ACM Symposium on Operating Systems Principles, SOSP 1997 (1997)
9. Smith, R.: An overview of the tesseract ocr engine. In: ICDAR, vol. 7, pp. 629–633 (2007)

Meta-Adaptation Strategies
for Adaptation in Cyber-Physical Systems

Ilias Gerostathopoulos[✉], Tomas Bures, Petr Hnetynka,
Adam Hujecek, Frantisek Plasil, and Dominik Skoda

Faculty of Mathematics and Physics, Charles University in Prague, Prague, Czech Republic
{iliasg,bures,hnetynka,plasil,skoda}@d3s.mff.cuni.cz

Abstract. Modern Cyber-Physical Systems (CPS) not only need to be dependable, but also resilient to and able to adapt to changing situations in their environment. When developing such CPS, however, it is often impossible to anticipate all potential situations upfront and provide corresponding tactics. Situations that lie out of this "envelope of adaptability" can lead to problems that range from single component malfunctioning to complete system failure. The existing approaches to self-adaptation cannot typically cope with such situations as they still rely on a fixed set of tactics, which in case of complex systems does not guarantee achieving correct functionality. To alleviate this problem, we propose the concept of meta-adaptation strategies, which extends the limits of adaptability of a system by constructing new tactics at runtime to reflect the changes in the environment. The approach is demonstrated on an existing architecture-based self-adaptation method and exemplified by two concrete meta-adaptation strategies.

Keywords: Meta-adaptation strategies · Adaptation tactics · Cyber-Physical systems

1 Introduction

An important feature of efficient and dependable CPS is self-adaptivity, i.e., the ability to change their behavior or structure in response to changes in their environment. Self-adaptation in software systems is usually achieved in three fundamental ways: (i) by relying on a detailed application model, e.g., Markov Decision Processes (MDP), and employing simulations or other means of state-space traversal to infer the best response of the system, (ii) by identifying control parameters and employing feedback-based control techniques from control theory, and (iii) by reconfiguring architecture models, typically with the help of Event-Condition-Action rules – *architecture-based self-adaptation*.

Existing approaches. A common denominator for all these three fundamental ways is that they monitor the state of the environment and select an operation to perform from a pre-designed fixed set of actions. In (i), a model of the environment is assumed to be available (either known or learned) and the self-adaptation selects an action (e.g., "go

© Springer International Publishing Switzerland 2015
D. Weyns et al. (Eds.): ECSA 2015, LNCS 9278, pp. 45–52, 2015.
DOI: 10.1007/978-3-319-23727-5_4

straight", "turn left", "turn right") to maximize future reward. In (ii) a fixed set of control parameters is given and the actions consist of setting (increasing/decreasing) a parameter value (e.g., Java heap size). In (iii), self-adaptation rules are expressed as actions involving particular architecture reconfigurations applicable under certain conditions in the presence of certain events or situations [1, 2]. The combination of Rainbow framework with the Stitch language is representative of (iii). In Stitch, a *tactic* is a specification of an activity with a pre- and post-condition and an associated action. The self-adaptation in (iii) can be thus seen as selecting one or more tactics from a fixed set.

These three ways have also been used both combined and together with learning-based approaches. For example, control theory has been employed in the runtime modification of the probabilities of a MDP [3]. Learning-based approaches have been proposed to deduce the impact of adaptation actions at runtime [4], and to mine the application model from system execution traces [5].

In the realm of CPS, where we deal with large complex distributed systems, the high level view of architecture-based self-adaptation (i.e., (iii)) is generally favored [1, 2, 6, 7]. At the same time, due to external uncertainty [8] (e.g., hardware failures, temporary network unavailability), anticipating all potential situations upfront is not an option. As a result, adapting by switching between available tactics applicable in different situations is problematic, as the CPS may arrive in a situation where no combination of tactics applies. A similar problem of selecting only from fixed actions and parameters applies also to (i) and (ii).

Goals. As a remedy, focusing specifically on architecture-based self-adaptation, we propose to generate new tactics at runtime to reflect the changes in the environment and increase the overall system utilities, in particular safety, performance, and availability. We do so by introducing the concept of meta-adaptation strategies (MAS). MAS allow us to enrich the adaptation logic of the system (thus the "meta" prefix) by systematically generating new tactics. This provides a dynamic space of actions and effectively extends the limits of adaptability of the system.

In particular, we present the idea of MAS and define their structure similar to design and adaptation patterns. On top of this basis, we show two examples of MAS and demonstrate their applicability. The two MAS examples of course do not cover the whole space of potential MAS, however, we believe that by introducing the idea of MAS as means for dynamically extending the limits of systems adaptability, we provide helpful inspiration for future research on self-adaptive systems.

2   Running Example and Background

To demonstrate the concept of MAS, we briefly overview below the running example and the IRM-SA self-adaptation method along with the DEECo component model, which serve as the model and technological basis we use to exemplify MAS.

Running Example: Firefighter Coordination System. Firefighters belonging to tactical groups are deployed on the emergency field and communicate via low-power nodes integrated into their personal protective equipment. Each of these nodes is configured at runtime depending on the task assigned to its bearer. For example, a hazardous situation might need closer monitoring of a certain parameter (e.g., temperature).

In the setting of the complete case study [9], firefighters have to communicate with the officers (their group leaders), who are equipped with tablets; the software running on these tablets provides a model of the current situation (e.g., on a map) based on data measured at and aggregated from the low-power nodes. Parameters measured at each low-power node are *position*, external *temperature*, *battery level*, and *oxygen level*. The data aggregation on the side of the group leaders is done with the intention that each leader can infer whether any of his/her group members is in danger and take strategic decisions. Such a coordination system has increased safety and performance requirements. It needs to operate on top of opportunistic ad-hoc networks, where no guarantees for end-to-end response time exist, with minimum energy consumption, and without jeopardizing its end-users. It also needs to respond to a number of challenging situations: What if the temperature sensor starts malfunctioning or completely fails at runtime? What if firefighters are deployed inside a building where GPS readings are not available? What if the communication between members and their leader is lost?

In all these situations, each node has to adapt its behavior according to the latest information available. For example, if a firefighter node detects that it is in the situation "indoors", it has to switch from the tactic of determining the position via the GPS to the tactic of using an indoors tracking system. Other tactics include increasing the sensing rate in face of a danger or even relying on the nearby nodes for strategic actions when communication with the group leader is lost.

Obtaining an *exhaustive* list of situations that trigger adaptations in the firefighter coordination system is not a realistic option, as the environment is highly dynamic and unpredictable. We rather need to be able to build a system that would dynamically change its behavior by (i) generating new tactics on demand, and (ii) using them in the adaptation actions in order to deal with unanticipated situations.

IRM-SA and DEECo. The Invariant Refinement Method for Self-Adaptivity (IRM-SA) [9, 10] is a requirements-oriented design method tailored for the CPS domain. IRM-SA captures goals and requirements of the systems as *invariants* that describe the desired state of the system-to-be at every time instant. For example, consider invariant (1) in Fig. 1, which specifies that the leader of each firefighter group should have an up-to-date view (encapsulated in the positionMap field) of his/her group members. This "necessity" is AND-decomposed into invariants (2) and (3), which specify the necessities of propagating the position from each member to the leader and determining the position on the side of each member, respectively. The refinement is finished when each leaf invariant of the refinement tree is either an *assumption* or is a computation activity corresponding to a *process* or *knowledge exchange*. Alternative designs are captured by the OR-decomposition pattern, where each variant is guarded by an assumption capturing the state of the environment. For example, invariant (3) can be satisfied either by determining the position through an indoors tracking system – invariant (5) – or a global positioning system – invariant (7). At runtime, the system monitors the satisfaction of assumptions (4) and (6) and activates the activity corresponding to the chosen branch in the tree.

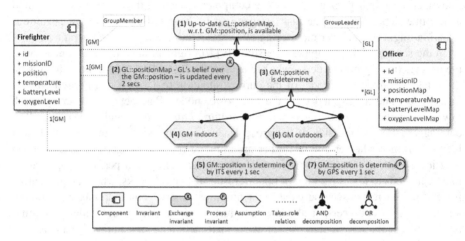

Fig. 1. Excerpt from the IRM-SA model of the running example.

Although IRM-SA is a method that can be used independently, it is very well aligned with the DEECo component model [11]. DEECo features autonomous components forming dynamic goal-driven collaboration groups – *ensembles*. Components contain knowledge (their data) and processes, whose periodic execution results in periodic updates in their knowledge. Components are not bound to each other; they can only indirectly communicate within an ensemble. The communication takes the form of mapping a component's knowledge field into another component's knowledge field – *knowledge exchange*. Membership of a component in an ensemble is not static, but periodically evaluated at runtime based on a condition specified over ensemble-specific interfaces that provide partial views over the components' knowledge.

In the IRM-SA–to–DEECo mapping, IRM-SA components correspond to DEECo components; process invariants to component processes; exchange invariants to ensembles; and assumptions to DEECo runtime monitors. The IRM-SA graph corresponds to the adaptation logic that DEECo applications use in order to switch on and off certain features (according to the branches selected at runtime on the IRM-SA graph). In this frame, an adaptation action is choosing an applicable configuration by choosing among the branches in the IRM-graph, whereas a tactic corresponds to an individual leaf invariant. An adaptation action thus consists of selecting a set of tactics.

3   Meta-Adaptation Strategies

As already discussed in the previous sections, a system, even a self-adaptive one, can be designed to handle a limited number of runtime situations. Interestingly, the number of new distinct tactics that can be devised in response to an unanticipated situation is in principle infinite. Hence, apart from being able to devise new tactics, it is important to be able to rank them according to their effect on the system, in order to be able to select the most promising one, or, at least, to select the ones that are worth trying. (Here, we assume the general adaptation loop in which the adaptation mechanism activates a tactic, observes its effect on the system and, depending on its impact, either keeps it or tries another tactic.)

To systematize the creation of new tactics, we rely on the concept of meta-adaptation strategies (MAS). MAS serve as patterns for extending the limits of adaptability of the system, with each strategy extending the limits in a certain way. The goal of such a strategy is twofold:

1. *To provide an algorithm to systematically generate a set of tactics at runtime.*
2. *To provide a metric on the generated set according to which the tactics can be ranked.*

In the rest of the section, we exemplify our proposal by describing two MAS. Note that the two strategies can be applied sequentially or in parallel in the running system, since they are by design orthogonal to each other. Due to space constraints, we omit a third strategy that we have so far developed – details on that can be found in [12].

Tactics Generated by Data Classification. In CPS, exploiting the interdependencies between sensed data is an opportunity for introducing specific meta-adaptation strategies. A particular case is the location-dependency of data, i.e., the fact that the value of certain measurable system attributes depends on the physical location of the sensors that provide the data. Below we describe a strategy providing a way to automatically create knowledge exchange specifications (*ensemble specifications* in DEECo) that introduce "collaborative sensing" (when direct sensing is not possible anymore) and feed them into the running system. Hence, such new ensembles represent new tactics.

Strategy Name: Knowledge Exchange by Data Classification

Intent: To increase the robustness of the system, prolong its acceptable functioning, or achieve graceful degradation in face of data unavailability and outdatedness.

Context: The strategy targets the case when values of a knowledge field of a component become outdated to the extent that they cannot be relied upon in terms of correct behavior of the component. For instance, there is a sensor malfunction that prevents value updates.

Behavior: To make up for losing the ability to obtain the actual value of an outdated knowledge field, create a new ensemble specification through which the field is assigned an approximated value based on the up-to-date related knowledge values of other components. This specification consists of (i) a membership condition, which prescribes the condition under the components should interact, and (ii) a knowledge exchange function, which specifies the knowledge exchange that takes place between the collaborating components. (For simplicity, we consider the knowledge exchange that just copies the data without manipulating them in any other way.)

To be able to construct the membership condition when the situation targeted by the strategy happens, observe first the system when it is healthy and log components' knowledge (as a time series of the knowledge evolution). Analyze (typically offline) the logged knowledge and find conditional correlations indicating that when values of some knowledge fields $A_1, B_1, \ldots, A_n, B_n$ are pairwise "close" then other values of other knowledge fields C, D are "close" as well. Formulate an ensemble (to be instantiated when the situation targeted by the strategy happened), which uses the pairwise "closeness" of $A_1, B_1, \ldots, A_n, B_n$ as the membership condition and has the assignment $D := C$ as the knowledge exchange.

Generate a number of possible membership conditions corresponding to different tactics. Then, select a tactic by applying the metric of selecting the tactic which provides the most general condition given the target confidence level.

Contraindications: The analysis of the collected time series can be very resource demanding and therefore a dedicated hardware infrastructure should be used. Similarly, the data collection may be a rather resource-intensive process, especially when components' knowledge is big or changes frequently. Also, introducing superfluous new ensembles can overload the system with unnecessary replicated data.

Example: In the firefighter coordination case study, each firefighter component features the knowledge fields of position and temperature. Suppose that the temperature values are used to control the suit cooling system. Obviously, when the temperature sensor breaks, a real-life threat arises. Since firefighters are usually moving in groups so that those close to each other obtain similar temperature readings, the temperature value of one component can be approximated based on the temperature values of the others, when their positions are close. Technically, the threshold of temperature proximity can be set (e.g., 20°C).

Tactics Generated by Period Adjusting. A CPS typically brings real-time requirements that are reflected in schedulability parameters of component processes. The schedulability parameters can be typically inferred by real-time design via schedulability analysis. However, when schedulability parameters influence the systems in a complex manner (e.g., when there is a tradeoff between CPU utilization, battery, network utilization), it is not possible to infer them by systematic analysis. Rather, the schedulability parameters are set manually, based on the experience of the system's architect. The strategy below addresses the case when the manually set schedulability parameters cannot cope with an unanticipated situation.

Strategy Name: Process Period Adjusting

Intent: To optimize the scheduling of processes with respect to overall system (application-specific) performance in a system where processes are scheduled periodically.

Context: The strategy targets situations when the system starts failing due to violated timing requirements and the schedulability parameters cannot be inferred a priori because they influence the system in a complex manner.

Behavior: Let R be the set of all active real-time processes in the system. To be able to identify the situation when a requirement for a process r_i in R with period p_i is not satisfied anymore, equip each r_i with a runtime monitor returning a fitness value f_i (real number in [0-1]). Generate tactics that correspond to a new real-time processes r_i' created from r_i by adjusting (reducing or enlarging within pre-defined permissible bounds) p_i to p_i', when f_i drops below an acceptable threshold. To explore the search space of possible period adjustments, employ the genetic algorithm (1+1)-ONLINE

EA [13]. Changing p_i can be interpreted as generating a new tactic r_i' and using it to substitute the tactic r_i in the system. Terminate the period adjusting procedure when the adjustment of each p_i has been exercised in both directions and there is no further benefit.

In this strategy, tactics (new processes) are compared by substituting them to the running system and calculating the overall system fitness as a function of f_i's.

Contraindications: Reducing periods (a usual action) may have a negative impact on other resources (CPU, battery, network). In such a case, the impact would have to be modelled and taken into consideration in the state-space search.

Example: Consider extending the design of our running example by a root invariant that specifies that "battery consumption should be kept minimized". In order to satisfy this invariant, the system will try at runtime to tweak the processes' periods to invoke them as scarcely as possible. At the same time, when there is high inaccuracy in the GPS readings (e.g., less than 3 satellites in sight), the GPS process may need to be invoked more often to make sure the cumulative inaccuracy of the estimated position of a moving firefighter is within certain bounds. (The cumulative inaccuracy is essentially the sum of the initial inaccuracy of the GPS reading and the distance a firefighter has moved since the last GPS reading.) It is thus a dynamic trade-off between availability and dependability that has to be resolved at runtime.

4   Experimental Evaluation and Conclusion

In order to evaluate the feasibility of the proposed MAS, we implemented them as extensions of the IRM-SA jDEECo plugin[1]. Our evaluation scenario consisted of three firefighters moving in a building, periodically monitoring their battery level, position, and external temperature. The objective of the system was to obtain accurate enough values of position and temperature, while keeping battery consumption minimal. Two malfunctions were introduced: (i) the GPS of one of the firefighters became inaccurate, and (ii) the temperature sensor of the firefighter was broken completely.

The MAS described in the paper were able to successfully cope these unanticipated malfunctions – the "Process Period Adjusting" reduced the inaccuracy stemming from knowledge outdatedness thus compensating the inaccuracy of the GPS reading; the "Knowledge Exchange by Data Classification" created and deployed a new ensemble, which provided a temperature estimation to compensate for the broken sensor. The evaluation, together with all the measurements, is described in detail in [12].

Conclusion. In this paper, we suggested a way to address the problem of limited adaptability caused by a fixed set of tactics. To this end, we have introduced the concept of meta-adaptation strategies (MAS) as a means for creating new tactics by observing the behavior of a system at runtime. In addition to laying out the general concept of MAS, we have exemplified the concept by two instances of MAS. Generally, if a

---

[1] https://github.com/d3scomp/IRM-SA/tree/ECSA2015

system is subject to environment uncertainty, the extent of the problem space that should be covered by systems adaptability is unknown. This makes it impossible to devise all adaptation tactics at design time. It of course makes it also impossible to presume all necessary meta-adaptation strategies, as each strategy covers only a certain sub-space of the problem space. However, compared to pre-designed tactics, the meta-adaptation strategy involves observation of system's and environment's evolution at runtime and utilizes this to formulate new tactics. As such, it has the potential to carry through higher expressive power than pre-designed tactics and consequently achieve significantly higher coverage of the problem space.

Acknowledgements. The work on this paper has been supported by Charles University institutional funding SVV-2015-260222.

References

1. Cheng, S.-W., Garlan, D., Schmerl, B.: Stitch: A language for architecture-based self-adaptation. J. Syst. Softw. **85**, 1–38 (2012)
2. David, P.-C., Ledoux, T., Léger, M., Coupaye, T.: FPath and FScript: Language support for navigation and reliable reconfiguration of Fractal architectures. Ann. Telecommun. **64**, 45–63 (2009)
3. Filieri, A., Ghezzi, C., Leva, A., Maggio, M., Milano, P.: Self-adaptive software meets control theory: a preliminary approach supporting reliability requirements. In: Proc. of ASE 2011, pp. 283–292. IEEE (2011)
4. Elkhodary, A., Esfahani, N., Malek, S.: FUSION: a framework for engineering self-tuning self-adaptive software systems. In: Proc. of FSE 2010, pp. 7–16. ACM (2010)
5. Yuan, E., Esfahani, N., Malek, S.: Automated mining of software component interactions for self-adaptation. In: Proc. of SEAMS 2014, pp. 27–36. ACM (2014)
6. Garlan, D., Cheng, S.-W., Huang, A.-C., Schmerl, B., Steenkiste, P.: Rainbow: Architecture-Based Self-Adaptation with Reusable Infrastructure. Computer **37**, 46–54 (2004)
7. Hirsch, D., Kramer, J., Magee, J., Uchitel, S.: Modes for software architectures. In: Gruhn, V., Oquendo, F. (eds.) EWSA 2006. LNCS, vol. 4344, pp. 113–126. Springer, Heidelberg (2006)
8. Esfahani, N., Kouroshfar, E., Malek, S.: Taming uncertainty in self-adaptive software. In: Proc. of SIGSOFT/FSE 2011, pp. 234–244. ACM (2011)
9. Gerostathopoulos, I., Bures, T., Hnetynka, P., Keznikl, J., Kit, M., Plasil, F., Plouzeau, N.: Self-Adaptation in Cyber-Physical Systems: from System Goals to Architecture Configurations. Department of Distributed and Dependable Systems, D3S-TR-2015-02 (2015)
10. Keznikl, J., Bures, T., Plasil, F., Gerostathopoulos, I., Hnetynka, P., Hoch, N.: Design of ensemble-based component systems by invariant refinement. In: Proc. of CBSE 2013, pp. 91–100. ACM (2013)
11. Bures, T., Gerostathopoulos, I., Hnetynka, P., Keznikl, J., Kit, M., Plasil, F.: DEECo – an ensemble-based component system. In: Proc. of CBSE 2013, pp. 81–90. ACM (2013)
12. Gerostathopoulos, I., Bures, T., Hnetynka, P., Hujecek, A., Plasil, F., Skoda, D.: Meta-adaptation strategies for adaptation in cyber-physical systems. Department of Distributed and Dependable Systems, D3S-TR-2015-01 (2015)
13. Bredeche, N., Haasdijk, E., Eiben, A.E.: On-line, on-board evolution of robot controllers. In: Collet, P., Monmarché, N., Legrand, P., Schoenauer, M., Lutton, E. (eds.) EA 2009. LNCS, vol. 5975, pp. 110–121. Springer, Heidelberg (2010)

Design Approaches

Revisiting Architectural Tactics for Security

Eduardo B. Fernandez[1]([⊠]), Hernán Astudillo[2], and Gilberto Pedraza-García[3,4]

[1] Florida Atlantic University, Boca Raton, FL, USA
ed@cse.fau.edu
[2] Departamento de Informática, Universidad Técnica Federico Santa María, Valparaíso, Chile
hernan@inf.utfsm.cl
[3] Universidad de Los Andes, Bogotá, Colombia
g.pedraza56@uniandes.edu.co
[4] Programa de Ingeniería de Sistemas, Universidad Piloto de Colombia, Bogotá, Colombia

Abstract. Architectural tactics are design decisions intended to improve some system quality factor. Since their initial formulation, they have been formalized, compared with patterns and associated to styles, but the initial set of tactics for security has only been refined once. We have examined this tactics set and classification from the viewpoint of security research, and concluded that some tactics would be better described as principles or policies, some are not needed, and others do not cover the functions needed to secure systems, which makes them not very useful for designers. We propose here a refined set and classification of architectural tactics for security, which we consider more appropriate than the original and the previously refined sets. We also suggest how to realize them using security patterns.

Keywords: Architecture tactics · Secure architectures · Security patterns · Secure software development

1 Introduction

Secure systems are notoriously hard to build; like most global system quality criteria, a piecemeal approach based on securing system elements is simply inappropriate. Design decisions have a global effect on other quality attributes, e.g. availability, and thus local optimizations are not possible. From a security research standpoint, lacking quantitative measures, a secure system is one that can be shown to withstand a variety of attacks; although many approaches to build secure systems have been proposed [25], they usually focus on some specific aspect, e.g. authorization, and address only one type of threat.

The security research literature describes many ways to secure specific parts of a system, to build secure systems, or to stop specific attacks, but few studies exist about how to make a whole system secure [8, 17, 25, 30]. On the other hand, the software architecture literature addressed security as one of several global quality properties, and proposes using "architectural tactics" [2, 3]; however, the specific proposed tactics are not justified on coverage or parsimony grounds, thus largely ignoring the existing research work on security. Also, security tactics give general guidance but

© Springer International Publishing Switzerland 2015
D. Weyns et al. (Eds.): ECSA 2015, LNCS 9278, pp. 55–69, 2015.
DOI: 10.1007/978-3-319-23727-5_5

not detailed construction advice; in fact, tactics are not mentioned in any of the best-known secure development methodologies [25].

Since their initial formulation, tactics have been formalized [1], compared with patterns [19], associated to the Common Criteria [18], and associated to styles [15]. However, the initial set of tactics for security [2, 3] has been refined only once [21]. This article presents a reasoned examination, pruning and reclassification of architectural tactics for security, considering both the original set and the refined set and applying security knowledge. We also consider a possible realization using security patterns; tactics require a convenient realization to provide detailed guidance to architects. *Patterns* are encapsulated solutions to recurrent problems in specific contexts, *security patterns* define solutions to handle threats or to fix a vulnerability [10]. Patterns are considered a good way to build secure systems and several methodologies based on them exist [7, 10, 25]. Patterns include several sections that define in addition to a solution, their use, applicability, advantages, and disadvantages. Other software architecture quality factors such as reliability, availability, and safety are also important, but we concentrate on security in this paper.

This article contributions include:

- A discussion of the correspondence of some security and software architecture concepts to understand them better. The security and software architecture communities are rather disjoint and we attempt to help bridge their gap.
- A revised set of tactics, based on security knowledge, which is our main contribution
- A detailed consideration of the use of security patterns as a way for realizing tactics.

The remainder of the article is organized as follows: Section 2 describes architecture tactics; Section 3 discusses security patterns; Section 4 defines security principles and policies, and other terms used for secure systems design; Section 5 examines the initial (and still used) tactics tree and indicates its problems; Section 6 presents some new tactics based on security knowledge; Section 7 proposes a realization for tactics using security patterns; Section 8 discusses related work; and Section 9 summarizes and concludes.

2   Architectural Tactics to Build Secure Systems

Architectural tactics, originally introduced in 2003 [2], are "measures" or "decisions" taken to improve some quality factor, a definition later refined to "architectural building blocks from which architectural patterns are created" [3]. Each tactic corresponds to a design decision with respect to a quality factor; i.e., tactics codify and record best practices for achieving that factor.

Rozanski and Woods [30, 31] defined architectural tactics as architectural design guidance, i.e. strategies or advice on how to drive a general design issue related to improving required quality attributes without imposing a particular software structure. They also suggest (but give little operational detail) that the application of security tactics may be expressed in the software architecture as adding, modifying, or deleting architectural elements with specific responsibilities, introducing security technologies, or describing new operational procedures to support secure operation.

The literature records a few approaches to use architectural tactics to build secure systems [15, 16]. Harrison and Avgeriou [15] proposed (see Figure 1) that the architecture be first defined using architecture patterns to determine the structural aspects of the functional requirements, and then apply tactics to introduce non-functional aspects such as security and reliability. Their article does not attempt to evaluate the actual level of security or reliability thus obtained, or whether different realizations may yield unnecessary security mechanisms. In fact, this work does not indicate any realization of the selected tactics. They do not consider specific threats either. However, this is a comprehensive treatment of how security tactics can be applied and as such is an important paper for software architecture security.

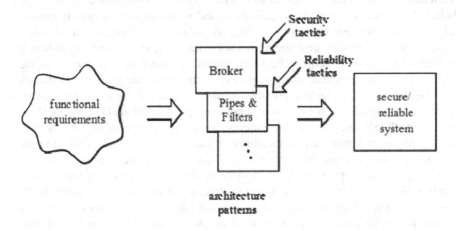

Fig. 1. Producing secure or reliable architectures from tactics.

In Woods and Rozanski [30], security tactics are part of a wider framework to improve quality attributes, which defines a set of activities, checklists, tactics and guidelines. They also suggest that the impact of security tactics in software architecture may be described on architectural views (context, functional, information, concurrency, development, deployment and operational). In order to achieve security quality attribute in software architecture, they propose to identify sensitive resources, define the security policy, identify threats to the system, design the security implementation and assess the security risks. These steps correspond to a security methodology such as the one described in [26]. Although they do not describe how architects can apply the security tactics catalog, this work is be a good basis for a more complete security methodology.

3   Building Secure Systems with Patterns

An extensive literature exists on how to build secure systems using patterns, formal methods, and other approaches [25]. A recent approach [26] uses patterns for incorporating security solutions but also for modeling threats; patterns are applied using security solution frames, which are groups of related patterns. This methodology is the only one which explicitly uses tactics.

There has been also a good amount of work on finding appropriate realizations for tactics. An attempt to make tactics more precise is by formalizing them [1]. Formalizing a vague concept is misleading since there can be many ways to do it and the formalizer needs to make many assumptions. Real systems need to be designed and design is not a mathematical or formal process but it requires experience and intuition from the designer. Often, system designers are not experts on security, and selecting precise solutions is too hard for them; thus, premature formalization is not a good practical idea. However, we can formalize specific parts separable from the rest of the system; for most of them, a semi-formal approach like UML is enough, and heuristics like patterns are a promising direction.

Patterns are encapsulated solutions to recurrent system problems and define a vocabulary that concisely expresses requirements and solutions without getting prematurely into implementation details [4]. *Security patterns* are a type of architecture pattern in that they usually describe global software architecture concepts, although some consider security patterns to be a type of design pattern as well. Finally, some security patterns are a type of analysis pattern in the sense that security constraints should be defined at the highest possible (semantic) level of the system where no implementation details are present to obscure conceptual solutions [11]. While there is no "official" template for security patterns, we use a variation of the POSA template [4], which is composed of a thumbnail of the problem it solves (a threat to the system), the context where the pattern is applicable, a brief description of how it solves the problem (stops or mitigates the threat), the static structure of the solution (usually UML class diagrams), the dynamic structure of the solution (usually UML sequence diagrams or possibly activity or state diagrams), and guidelines for the implementation of this pattern. The contents of all the sections of the template are fundamental for the correct use of the pattern. Patterns are not just solutions and are not plug-ins. However, their solutions require some level of concreteness to be useful, vague or too general concepts are not much guidance to designers.

The effect of a pattern on security, performance, or any other factor depends on how it is used; for example, applying authentication in many places in a system may increase security but reduces performance if users or processes need to re-authenticate themselves each time they access resources. There are tradeoffs when improving any quality factor. "Encrypt data" is a tactic that can be realized in more than one way, i.e. symmetric or asymmetric encryption. Depending on the application, one is more convenient than the other. If the architect is not experienced or knowledgeable about security, it is important to provide him with more detailed guidance.

Good security design requires that security is enforced at the system (platform) level. Several applications may be sharing a common platform. Policies about access must cover all applications sharing system resources. This means that, if there are several applications sharing the same platform, all of them should share intrusion detection, authentication, authorization enforcement, and logging; i.e., all the available defenses. When a user of the application attempts to access some resource the system functions enforce that this access satisfies the security constraints of the whole system. Additional security constraints may be placed in applications but a base set of security mechanisms controls the execution of all applications. Even if there is only one application using the platform, this separation is important because of the need to decouple those aspects which are not intrinsic to a specific application. This was the same motivation that lead to aspect-oriented design [19]. All this means that a software architect only needs to verify that the system implements some tactics and does not need to include them in her design; only calls to those functions are needed so they are enforced during the application execution. If the platform is designed on its own, all these tactics would be implemented there. An architect should make sure that all the corresponding tactics are in place and can support all applications.

4 Security Principles and Policies

Security differs from other quality factors, like availability or scalability, in its close tie to the application or system semantics; e.g., "only the owner of an account can withdraw money from it", or "a process cannot write outside its own virtual address space". Also, external regulations may prescribe (directly or indirectly) specific information protection needs, leaving little space for possible tradeoffs among tactics.

To be able to analyze tactics we need to discuss first some related concepts.

Principles are general statements that define ways to produce good designs, they are fundamental laws or assumptions. The classical paper of Saltzer and Schroeder [22], defined a set of *security principles* that included among others: least privilege, separation of duty, and least common mechanism. Later, more principles have been added, including "Defense in depth", "Start from semantic levels", and others [23]. Principles are very general and have many possible realizations; they are guidelines that must be explicitly or implicitly followed when building systems if we want these systems to be of high quality.

Policies are high-level guidelines defining how an institution conducts its activities in its business, professional, economic, social, and legal environment [14]. The *institution security policies* include laws, rules, and practices that regulate how an institution uses, manages and protects resources. *Regulations* are legal or government policies that must be reflected in the implemented system.

More concretely, policies are management instructions indicating a predetermined course of action or a way to handle a problem or situation. Every institution has a set of policies, explicit or implicit, some of which are security policies. *Security policies* are essential to build secure systems since they indicate what to protect and how much effort to invest in this protection. In general, policies come from regulations, institution practices, or just good principles of design, i.e., prescribing some quality aspects for the final product.

Policies are also used to indicate a way to avoid or mitigate threats; for example, a mutual authentication policy avoids impostors from either side. Each system uses a combination of policies according to its objectives and environment. As an example, two of the most common security policies used in practice are:

- *Open/closed systems* —in a closed system, nothing is accessible unless explicitly authorized, whereas in an open system everything is accessible unless explicitly denied. Institutions where information security is very important, such as banks, use a closed policy (e.g. "only an account's owner can access it"); institutions whose objective is disseminating information, such as libraries, use an open policy (e.g. "all books are accessible except rare books").

• *Least privilege (need to know)* —people or any active entity that needs to access computational resources must be given authorization only for those resources needed to perform their functions; e.g. "a secretary should only have access to employees' addresses"; it also applies to the institution (e.g. "it should not collect more information than strictly necessary about its members"). This policy can be considered a refinement of the closed system policy as well as a principle.

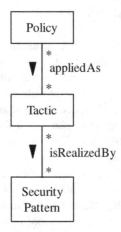

Fig. 2. From policies to security patterns.

Policies are prescriptive, and can be thought of as directions for designers. Policies can be structured into hierarchies, and more specific policies apply to the components of a system. It is possible to express individual policies using UML class diagrams with constraints.

In software architecture terms, policies are guidelines to apply tactics, which in turn may be realized using for example security patterns, as shown in Figure 2. The associations are many-to-many: a policy may be applied using several tactics, which in turn can be realized using several security patterns; conversely, a security pattern may realize more than one tactic, and a tactic may come from several policies. For example, Figure 3 indicates a policy which prescribes that "only owners of accounts can access their accounts", which is translated into two more specific policies, for *Authentication* and for *Content-Dependent Authorization*, which can be realized by corresponding security patterns. In this example, the "content-dependent authorization" policy can prescribe the use of the tactic "Authorize actors", which would be realized by a "Content-dependent Authorizer" security pattern [12]. Broad policies or tactics are usually obtained by applying several patterns; e.g. "Authorize actors" can be obtained combining the patterns *Authenticator, Authorizer, Identity Management* and *Security Logger/Auditor* [10].

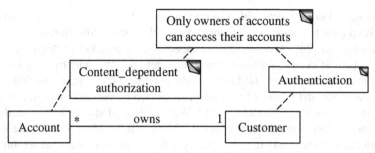

Fig. 3. Hierarchies of policies.

5   Evaluating the Current Tactic Set from Security Standpoint

The original list of tactics is structured as a classification tree (see Figure 4); the tactics are the tree leaves and most of them are at the same level. Although security patterns can be classified [28, 29] to cover all concerns, all the architectural levels

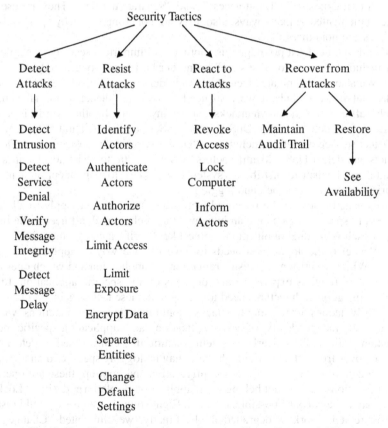

Fig. 4. Classification of security tactics according to Bass et al. [3].

of a system, and other facets with a multidimensional matrix, tactics are simpler and we will keep their tree structure. The branches of the current tree correspond to one of the dimensions in [28]. And we have changed "Resist attacks" to "Stop or mitigate attacks", which is closer to what security designers do. We start by removing some tactics considered not useful and later we add some new ones. This selection is based on our experience and security knowledge, supported by concepts introduced in Section 5 and our security methodology [26]. We also looked at a variety of methodologies for secure design to see what concepts they use in building their secure systems [25]. There is no formal way to prove that ours is an optimal or minimal set, but based on our survey (which is quite comprehensive) we can have some level of confidence that our set is appropriate [25]. We do not indicate how to perform the operations to realize tactics now; security patterns, discussed later in the paper, indicate possible ways of realizing for example, "authenticate users".

Some security tactics are really security *principles*. As indicated in Section 3, principles are not specific enough to become patterns or even tactics; there may be millions of solutions that satisfy a given principle. Thus, tactics that correspond to principles are not useful; they are good recommendations, but the designer has no concrete guide about their realization. In the tactic set of Figure 4 we can then eliminate tactics "Limit exposure", "Limit access", and "Separate entities". They are useful but can be implemented in many ways; also, they are not complete: Why apply only these principles and not others?

"Need-to-know (least privilege)" is another very important security principle, but it is not included, "use a closed system" is another basic security principle not included either. We also can eliminate "Detect message delay", which is a way to detect some attacks, but if we include it we also need to include "detect abnormal behavior", "match traffic events to known attacks", and many others. In other words, it is really a specific way to detect attacks. DoS (Denial of Service) is just another type of attack, so "Detect service denial" is included in "Detect intrusion"; most Intrusion Detection products can detect DoS. "Identify actors" is not a tactic to resist attacks, it is a fundamental mechanism in distributed systems, necessary to implement authentication, authorization, secure channel, and logging.

As indicated, some of the proposed tactics are functions that apply to all applications, not to specific application architectures; as such, they don't need to be incorporated in each individual application. Some like "Verify message integrity" could be left in the set if the application needs to have its own way of applying verification checks. Which security mechanisms remain in the application and which ones are left to the system requires experience and depends on the specific application; to imply that all application architectures need to incorporate these tactics is inappropriate.

Similarly, tactics for reacting to attacks should include system functions, which are implemented independently of any application, and application-specific policies. "Maintain audit trail" is clearly a system function that can be used to detect attacks and to recover from attacks, although there may be logging specific to an application. "Change default settings" is about reconfiguration and boot up; these are operational system functions, and do not belong in an application or platform design. "Lock computer" may not always be possible, e.g., in a flight control system we would instead to reconfigure it to work in degraded mode. Finally, we eliminated "Change default settings" because it is a system-operational function.

6   New or Modified Tactics

As a design principle, a tactic should not be too general or too specific. If too general, the designer is confused because of the variety of alternatives, which is the reason we eliminated principles to start with; if too specific, the designer gets mechanisms instead of tactics and their options are restricted.

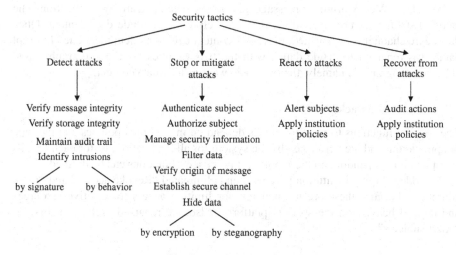

Fig. 5. A new set of tactics.

Figure 5 describes the modified set of security tactics, which are organized in four branches, similarly to the original set [2]: detect attacks, stop or mitigate attacks, react to attacks, and recover from attacks.

6.1   Detect Attacks

The tactic "Verify message integrity" was left, but we added "Verify storage integrity" to indicate the need to define checks to ensure that data have not been modified. "Maintain audit trail" was moved from the branch "recover from attacks" because it allows identifying an attacker. We also split "Identify intrusions" into "by signature" and "by behavior", the two standard ways to apply intrusion detection, in order to replace "Detect intrusion".

6.2   Stop or Mitigate Attacks

According to standard security terminology [14], a subject is an active entity that can request resources and includes humans and executing processes; thus, we changed the words "user" and "actor" for "subject" in "Authenticate actor" and "Authorize actor", and eliminated "Identify actors". To enforce the rules defined in "Authorize users (subjects)", we introduce a "Control access" tactic for the security concept of

Reference Monitor [14], which enforces authorization rules. We assume here that authorization enforcement is part of Authorize subjects.

We eliminated "Limit exposure", "Limit access", and "Separate entities" as tactics because these are security principles. We added "Manage security information", which includes the management of keys for cryptography, the secure storage of authorization rules, and other ways to handle security information. Also, "Filter data" is necessary to avoid attacks based on abnormal inputs or from untrusted sources.

We added "Verify origin of message", a form of data authenticity verification. The tactic "Establish secure channel" is required before we can hide data content. Once the secure channel is established, messages content can be hidden; the tactic "Encrypt data" was renamed to "Hide data", with the two varieties "Use cryptography" and "Use steganography", namely, the two basic ways to hide data content.

6.3   React to Attacks

The specific functions to react to attacks depend on institutional policies and the type of application, and are performed by the system for all applications or for each specific application, depending on these policies; no general functions can be defined.

We added "Apply institution policies", and eliminated "Revoke access" and "Lock computer" because these are mechanisms for limiting access to sensitive resources and depend heavily on the specific platform. Also, we renamed "Inform actors" as "Alert subjects".

6.4   Recover from Attacks

We moved "Maintain audit trail" from this branch to "detect attacks" because it is related to tracing and identifying attackers. We also added "Audit actions" (to indicate the recovery system task) and "Apply institution policies". Finally, we eliminated "Restore" because this action is not related to security.

7   Realizing Tactics with Security Patterns

The previous discussion shows that patterns and tactics are not equivalent: patterns are well-defined structured entities, whereas tactics are recommendations without prescribed implementation. This are complementary rather than alternative concepts. We propose to see tactics application as a step previous to patterns', but selecting the right pattern takes more detailed knowledge, represented in the contents of the pattern itself and some in the pattern classification; in fact, several methods exist to help designers use them appropriately [25].

Other realizations for tactics are possible, e.g., generic security architectures and components [16], aspects [19], and S&D patterns [13]. Our own experience leads us to believe that the most convenient realization of tactics is by using security patterns, but more experience with their use is needed to prove this point. To illuminate this point, [10] and [27] show examples of complete applications implemented using patterns.

Also, Table 1 shows a correspondence between tactics and security patterns indicating possible realizations of the new tactics. Some of those patterns have not been yet written, and are ongoing work. Note also that detailed design is required; e.g. it is not enough to select Authenticator, but also its type (password, biometric, etc.); existing techniques like [25] and [26] can guide the designer.

Since tactics do not prescribe any realization, several researchers have introduced their own realizations. Kim at al. [16] reified tactics as reusable UML building blocks that can be plugged in the architecture according to a list of non-functional requirements (NFRs). A similar approach was used by Bagheri et al. [1] to detect faults, with tactics like "ping echo", which is clearly a specific mechanism (realizable using patterns). These approaches are in line with [19] and rely on plug-ins or templates to apply realizations, whereas security patterns are generic solutions that stipulate conditions to apply as well as consequences.

Tactics also have value for other purposes besides design. Cañete [5] used tactics to annotate Jackson's problem frames; the annotations provide arguments for satisfaction of quality factors. Harrison and Avgeriou [15] also used tactics for annotations about design decisions.

Table 1. Security pattern realizations of tactics

Tactic	Security pattern realization
Verify message integrity	Secure Channel
Verify storage integrity	Authenticator and Authorizer
Maintain audit trail	Security Logger/Auditor
Identify intrusions by signature	Signature-based IDS
Identify intrusions by behavior	Behavior-based IDS
Authenticate subject	Authenticator (Remote), credential
Authorize subject	Policy, Role and Attribute based Access Control
Manage security information	Authorizer, Generation and distribution of public keys
Filter data	Filter, Packet Filter Firewall
Verify origin of message	Digital Signature with hashing
Establish secure channel	Secure Channel
Hide data by encryption	Symmetric and Asymmetric Encryption
Hide data by steganography	Steganographic Encoding
Alert subjects	Abstract IDS
Apply institution policies	Policy-based Enforcement
Audit actions	Security Logger/Auditor

8   Related Work and Validation

As indicated earlier, several authors have found relationships among security tactics and security patterns, in particular [15, 16, 17, 20].

Thus, Kim et al. [16] proposed architectural tactics as reusable UML architectural building blocks that offer generic solutions to specific problems related to quality attributes. Tactics are represented as feature models to support decision making for non-functional requirements through a set of explicit solutions. Unfortunately, this approach introduces rigidity and does not give the designer the freedom provided by patterns. The choice of blocks is also limited, since no extensive catalogs of these building blocks exist.

Ray et al. [19] proposed tactics as an intermediate architectural concept between high-level decisions and patterns of architecture, so architectural patterns implement architectural tactics.

Ryoo et al. [20] defined a methodology to extract tactics from security patterns through activities such as reclassification of architectural patterns, decomposition of patterns, derivation of tactics hierarchies applying reasoning and intuition over patterns, and realization or instantiation of existing tactics. It evaluated several sets of security architectural patterns and applied a Delphi technique to yield a new security tactics hierarchy, shown in Figure 6. It includes tactics "Limit exposure" and "Limit access", which we argued for removal, and redundancies like "Maintain confidentiality" (shown as a separate tactic, but which requires Authentication and Authorization, which are also tactics).

Fig. 6. Classification of security tactics according to [20]

How should tactics be validated? The original proposal [2] did not explicitly validate the initial set of tactics (it did not include published examples), and indeed to formal or argued parsimony and completeness arguments have been given; conversely, mentioning support from a Delphi approach seems too weak a rationale. The proposed modified set of tactics rests on our combined experience on security and software architecture, as well as background knowledge on security requirements, like the NFR Framework [6].

In particular, we surveyed [25] several best known methodologies to build secure systems to determine which concepts are secured as part of the whole system design; we have already [26] used these techniques in two non-trivial examples.

The modified set of tactics also gets some validation from the fact that it covers all assets that need to be protected in a system, as shown in Figure 7 at several architectural levels. The use of operations in the application can be controlled by Authentication and Authorization, and similarly access to data in the database system. Data in an application could be sent out to another application through a channel; this can be protected by encryption. The database usually includes the authorization rules and related system procedures, which are also protected by protecting the database system. As further verification, we point that in [26] we used a different system decomposition, along functional instead of architectural layers, and arrived to a similar tactic set.

Although there is no formal way to prove that this is an optimal or minimal set, our recent work lends us some confidence that it is appropriate [25, 26]. Acknowledging that ultimate validation can only come from practice, we remark that have not seen any report of practical systems being built using security tactics but several examples have been produced using security patterns [10, 26].

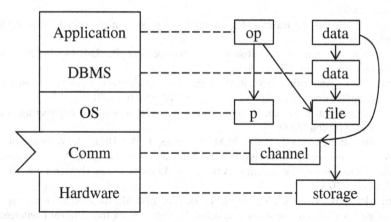

Fig. 7. Assets that must be protected (op=operation, p=process) in security tactics

9   Conclusions

Building secure systems demands an approach where security can be specified from the start of software development, considering the semantics of the application, and iterating between requirements and design. Architectural tactics and security patterns are among the many proposed approaches (in [25] alone we identified 17).

We addressed some confusion in terminology, definitions, and relationships among security patterns and tactics, which has led to methodologies that are difficult to combine with each other and with unclear impact on security. In time, precise definition of these concepts should lead to better architectural knowledge and better methodologies to build secure systems. We have tried here to clarify these concepts by examining the original set of tactics according to established security knowledge, and showing some well-reasoned ways to realize them. A modified set of tactics was derived by combining architectural and security knowledge; we do not claim they are complete or optimal, but we believe that they are more useful than previous sets, especially when complemented with a catalog of security patterns like [10]. In particular, unlike previous tactic sets, these can be directly realized with existing security patterns.

Acknowledgements. This work was partially supported by CONICYT (grant FONDECYT 1140408 and CCTVal FB0821). We thank the anonymous referees for their comments that improved the paper quality.

References

1. Bagheri, H., Sullivan, K.: A formal approach for incorporating architectural tactics into the software architecture. In: Procs. of SEKE, pp. 770–775 (2011)
2. Bass, L., Clements, P., Kazman, R.: Software architecture in practice, 2nd edn. Addison-Wesley (2003)
3. Bass, L., Clements, P., Kazman, R.: Software architecture in practice, 3rd edn. Addison-Wesley (2012)
4. Buschmann, F., Meunier, R., Rohnert, H., Sommerland, P., Stal, M.: Pattern-oriented Software Architecture. Wiley (1996)
5. Cañete, J.M.: Annotating problem diagrams with architectural tactics for reasoning on quality requirements. Information Proc. Letters **112**, 656–661 (2012)
6. Chung, L., Nixon, B.A., Yu, E., Mylopoulos, J.: NFRs in software engineering. Kluwer Acad. Publ., Boston (2000)
7. Fernandez, E.B., Larrondo-Petrie, M.M., Sorgente, T., VanHilst, M.: A methodology to develop secure systems using patterns. In: Mouratidis, H., Giorgini, P. (eds.) Integrating Security and Software Engineering: Advances and Future Vision, chapter 5, pp. 107–126. IDEA Press (2006)
8. Fernandez, E.B., Yoshioka, N., Washizaki, H., VanHilst, M.: An approach to model-based development of secure and reliable systems. In: Procs. Sixth International Conference on Availability, Reliability and Security (ARES 2011), Vienna, Austria, August 22–26
9. Fernandez, E.B., Astudillo, H.: Should we use tactics or patterns to build secure systems? In: First International Symposium on Software Architecture and Patterns, in conjunction with the 10th Latin American and Caribbean Conference for Engineering and Technology, Panama City, Panama, July, 23–27, 2012
10. Fernandez, E.B.: Security patterns in practice - Designing Secure Architectures Using Software Patterns, Wiley Series on Software Design Patterns (June 2013)
11. Fernandez, E.B., Yoshioka, N., Washizaki, H., Yoder, J.: Abstract security patterns for requirements specification and analysis of secure systems. In: Procs. of the WER 2014 Conference, a Track of the 17th Ibero-American Conf. on Soft. Eng. (CIbSE 2014), Pucon, Chile, April 2014

12. Fernandez, E.B., Monge, R., Carvajal, R., Encina, O., Hernandez, J., Silva, P., R.: Patterns for Content-Dependent and Context-Enhanced Authorization. In: Proceedings of 19th European Conference on Pattern Languages of Programs, Germany, July 2014

13. Gallego, B., Muñoz, A., Maña, A., Serrano, D.: Security patterns, towards a further level. In: Procs. SECRYPT, pp. 349–356 (2009)

14. Gollmann, D.: Computer security, 2nd edn. Wiley (2006)

15. Harrison, N.B., Avgeriou, P.: How do architecture patterns and tactics interact? A model and annotation. The Journal of Systems and Software **83**, 1735–1758 (2010)

16. Kim, S., Kim, D.-K., Lu, L., Park, S.: Quality-driven architecture development using architectural tactics. Journal of Systems and Software (2009)

17. Neumann, P.G.: Principled assuredly trustworthy composable architectures. Final SRI report to DARPA, December 28, 2004

18. Preschern, C.: Catalog of Security Tactics linked to Common Criteria Requirements. In: Procs. of PLoP (2012)

19. Ray, I., France, R.B., Li, N., Georg, G.: An aspect-based approach to modeling access control concerns. Inf. & Soft. Technology **9**, 575–587 (2004)

20. Ryoo, J., Laplante, P., Kazman, R.: A methodology for mining security tactics from security patterns. In: Procs. of the 43rd Hawaii International Conference on System Sciences (2010). http://doi.ieeecomputersociety.org/10.1109/HICSS.2010.18

21. Ryoo, J., Laplante, P., Kazman, R.: Revising a security tactics hierarchy through decomposition, reclassification, and derivation. In: 2012 IEEE Int. Conf. on Software Security and Reliability Companion, pp. 85–91

22. Saltzer, J.H., Schroeder, M.D.: The protection of information in computer systems. Procs. of the IEEE **63**(9), 1278–1308 (1975)

23. Shapiro, J.S., Hardy, N.: EROS: A Principle-Driven Operating System from the Ground Up. IEEE Software, January/February 2002

24. Taylor, R.N., Medvidovic, N., Dashofy, N.: Software Architecture: Foundation, Theory, and Practice. Wiley (2010)

25. Uzunov, A.V., Fernandez, E.B., Falkner, K.: Engineering Security into Distributed Systems: A Survey of Methodologies. Journal of Universal Computer Science **18**(20), 2920–3006

26. Uzunov, A.V., Fernandez, E.B., Falkner, K.: ASE: A Comprehensive Pattern-Driven Security Methodology for Distributed Systems. Journal of Computer Standards & Interfaces (2015). http://dx.doi.org/10.1016/j.csi.2015.02.011

27. Uzunov, A.V., Fernandez, E.B.: Cryptography-based security patterns and security solution frames for networked and distributed systems (submitted for publication)

28. VanHilst, M., Fernandez, E.B., Braz, F.: A multidimensional classification for users of security patterns. Journal of Res. and Practice in Information Technology **41**(2), 87–97 (2009)

29. Washizaki, H., Fernandez, E.B., Maruyama, K., Kubo, A., Yoshioka, N.: Improving the classification of security patterns. In: Procs. of the Third Int. Workshop on Secure System Methodologies using Patterns (SPattern 2009)

30. Woods, E., Rozanski, N.: Using architectural perspectives. In: Procs. of the 5th Working IEEE/IFIP Conference on Software Architecture (WICSA 2005)

31. Rozanski, N., Woods, E.: Software systems architecture: working with stakeholders using viewpoints and perspectives, 2nd edn. Addison-Wesley Educational Publishers (2012)

Improving the Quality of Architecture Design Through Peer-Reviews and Recombination

Mojtaba Shahin[(⊠)] and Muhammad Ali Babar

CREST – The Centre for Research on Engineering Software Technologies,
The University of Adelaide, Adelaide, Australia
{mojtaba.shahin,ali.babar}@adelaide.edu.au

Abstract. Software architecture reviews help improve the quality of architecture design decisions. Traditional reviews are considered expensive and time-consuming. We assert that organizations can consider leveraging peer-reviews and recombination (i.e., promoting design improvement through sharing design ideas) activities to improve the quality of architectures and getting staff trained. This paper reports a case study aimed at exploring the potential impact of combining peer-review and recombination on the quality of architecture design and design decisions made by novice architects, who usually have limited practical experience of architecture design. The findings show that the use of peer-review and recombination can improve both the quality of architecture design and documented decisions. From the decision-making perspective, this study also identifies the main types of challenges that the participants faced during architectural decision making and reasoning. These findings can be leveraged to focus on the types of training novice architects may need to effectively and efficiently address the types of challenges identified in this study.

Keywords: Software architecture design · Design quality · Peer-review · Recombination · Architectural design decision

1 Introduction

With the increasing size and complexity of software-intensive systems, the role of software architecture (SA) as a means of understanding and managing large-scale software intensive systems is considered very critical. The high level design description of a large system can help a system's stakeholders to understand and reason about the designed architecture with regards to architecturally significant requirements (ASRs) of a software-intensive system [23]. Software architecting is a knowledge-intensive activity, in which a large amount of knowledge is being continuously consumed and produced. A poor quality architecture can lead to project failure that usually costs an organization dearly. Software development organizations pay significant attention and allocate resources to design an appropriate architecture that can help achieve the functional and quality requirements expected of a system by all the stakeholders. That is why organizations focus on building their competencies in designing and evaluating architectures before committing substantial resources to build-

© Springer International Publishing Switzerland 2015
D. Weyns et al. (Eds.): ECSA 2015, LNCS 9278, pp. 70–86, 2015.
DOI: 10.1007/978-3-319-23727-5_6

ing a system [12, 13, 15]. Software architecture reviews are usually performed informally by architects themselves or formally by quality assurance teams [13].

An architecture review is considered as an effective way to ensure the quality of software architecture design [12, 15]. However, the current architecture review methods and processes have not been widely adopted by industry due to a large number of limitations [12, 14]. Historically, (formal) architecture review processes rely on time-consuming, tedious and expensive face-to-face meetings [12, 14]. Given the increasing trend to leveraging crowdsourcing in knowledge-intensive activities, we assert that software architecture community should explore the potential role of crowdsourcing as an alternative method in designing and evaluating software architectures and getting novice architects to gain the required knowledge, skills, and experience by soliciting the contributions from the online communities [16]. We argue that two concepts peer-review and recombination can be leveraged simultaneously to improve the quality of architecture design. Peer-review is a reciprocal process, in which people working in groups comment on the work of peers and provide feedback on the reviewed work [9]. Peer-reviews have been applied to several disciplines for identifying the potential defects and improve the quality of the final product [9]. It is demonstrated that crowdsourcing can help reduce development cost, faster time to market and increase the quality through soliciting diverse expertise and creativities from a large workforce [16].. In the recombination process, a specific type of crowdsourcing, the designers should share their designs to others and then they are encouraged to use the ideas from the shared designs if appropriate for revising their own design [3]. The recombination can be interpreted as an indirect collaboration [25]

The main goal of this study is to investigate the role of peer-review process in combination with recombination on the quality of architecture design and design decision. We were also interested in identifying and classifying the types of challenges that the participants faced when asked to deign an architecture for a non-trivial system to be developed using state-of-the-art technologies of mobile cloud computing. We have conducted a case study involving students in an academic context. The findings provide preliminary evidence to support our assertion that combining peer-review and recombination can help improve the quality of architecture design and design decisions as the participants took inspirations and borrowed ideas from designs of their peers and got engaged in intense design reasoning discussions. We have also identified four main categories of challenges that the participants of our study faced. The findings are expected to encourage further studies of leveraging crowdsourcing in software architecture design and guide the future training programs that can prepare the future architects to effectively and efficiently address the types of architecture design challenges faced by the participants of our study.

The rest of the paper is organized as follows: section 2 gives a summary of background and motivation. Section 3 provides the details of the case study. The quantitative and qualitative results of the study are described in Section 4. The section 5 reports a discussion on findings. Finally, we present our conclusions with future work in Section 6.

2   Background and Motivation

Whilst there has been significant research on improving the quality of software architecture through architecture evaluation (i.e., reviews) [12], there has been little work on exploring the impact of peer-reviews on software design quality. Other design disciplines have devoted significant amount of efforts to investigate how feedback, (self) critique, and peer-review can improve design [1, 2]. Dow et al. [1] studied the impact of feedback on the quality of web advertisement designs when created in parallel and serially. They found that the parallel feedback on design led to better quality and more divergence in design. Dow et al. [2] showed that designing and sharing multiple designs for group discussion increases the quality of design rather than sharing the best design for discussion. Moreover, they also found that sharing and discussing multiple designs can also lead participants to explore more concepts.

Mao et al. conducted a survey of using crowdsourcing to support software engineering activities [24]. The results of the survey reveal that although crowdsourcing has been widely employed for supporting coding and maintenance activities, it has been rarely used for software design. TopCoder[1], as one of a few commercial crowdsourcing platforms, supports crowdsourcing software design in which competitors are allowed to provide software design specification based on given user requirements [24]. However, very little research exists on how architecture design, review and evolution can be performed by multiple designers' solutions (i.e., crowd) [3, 24]. To the best of our knowledge, there has been only one paper [3], recently published, that reports a study similar to our line of research. LaToza et al have investigated the role of "recombination" in software design by Crowd [3]. In the "Recombination" process, designers are encouraged to share their designs with others and take ideas and inspiration through such sharing of design for improving their own. LaToza et al studied the impact of "Recombination" on the quality of two types of software design, user experience design and architecture design, through a design competition in which the participants (i.e., graduate students) were asked to share their initial design. The authors organized two separate studies of user experience design and software architecture design. Each of the participants was asked to produce an initial version and a revised version design. For the revised design, the participants were encouraged to take inspiration from other designs and the lessons learned from the crowd (i.e., other participants). The study concluded that the quality of software design can be improved through competitions and "Recombination" as almost all the participants borrowed at least one idea from other participants, who are considered "Crowd" in the study. One of the most interesting findings of the study was that even the strong designers used the ideas from the weak designs and improved their designs.

We came across the work of LaToza et al. [3], while analyzing our data. That study increases our confidence in the importance of exploring the potential benefits of crowdsourcing in design and training architects how to leverage the power of peer review and recombination for improving the quality of software design. Our study investigates the roles of peer-reviews and recombination together on the quality of

---

[1] http://www.topcoder.com/

architecture design. We are especially interested in comparing the quality of design decisions documented by novice architects before and after peer review and recombination. Thirdly, our study design promoted extensive discussions involving technical arguments in favor and against the reported design and counter justifications. These discussions provided huge amount of qualitative data that helped us to discover the types of challenges novice architects can face when designing architectures.

3   Research Design and Logistical Details

Our long term goal is to empirically build a body of knowledge about the dynamics and potential benefits involved in applying crowdsourcing for improving software architecture design when traditional architecture review have been proven too expensive to be widely adopted [12]. Based on the body of knowledge, we were also interested in training future software architects by identifying and classifying the types of common challenges they face during architecture design. This particular study purported to empirically study and understand the potential impact of crowd level reviews and discussions on the quality of design using peer-reviews and recombination. We identified two research questions for this work.

RQ1. How do peer-review and recombination affect the quality of architecture design? We planned to answer this question by analyzing the quality of the architecture design decisions and architecture designs submitted by each group of the participants before and after the peer reviews and recombination phases. The quality of the architecture designs and decisions has been quantified by applying the evaluation criteria (see sections 4.1.1 and 4.1.2). We also analyze the qualitative data from the discussions and the feedback of the teaching assistant who had observed the whole process and assessed the architecture designs.

RQ2. What challenges do the novice architects experience in architectural decision-making and design reasoning? We envisioned to answer this question by analyzing the discussions on the design decisions made available for review, students' reflections summaries in the submitted design reports, and the feedback of the teaching assistant on the students' performance on design decisions before and after the peer-review and recombination phases and the recurring challenges reported to her.

3.1   Research Method

An empirical study should be carried out using a suitable research method chosen based on the nature of the studied problem and the research questions to be answered. Since there has been scant research on the impact of peer-reviews and recombination on the quality of software design, we decided to carry out an exploratory case study in an academic setting. Case study is considered a suitable research method to investigate a contemporary phenomenon within its real-life context. Our study was an exploratory case study as it mainly deals with the "What" questions. Apart from the guidelines provided by Yin [8], we followed the checklist provided by Kitchenham et al. on case study research [27]. The unit of analysis is group consisting of 4 participants.

3.2   The Participants and The System

This study was carried out through the software architecture design and evaluation activities and submitted artifacts of 31 students who doing a senior level semester long (i.e., 14 weeks) software architecture course in 2014 at the University of Adelaide. Designing and evaluating architecture of a non-trivial software intensive system, healthcare emergency support, were the major assessment tasks (i.e., 50% of the final grade). The design activities were supposed to be carried out by groups of 4 members (one consisted of 3 members). The main training topics included quality attributes, architectural personas, concepts, principles, methods, and best practices of software architecture design, and documentation approaches.

The main goal of the system is to support Australian healthcare workers when responding to emergency situations away from the hospitals. The emergency response team can consist of paramedics, doctors and medical staff located at hospitals. The system is supposed to provide mobile and reliable access to the required information about the patients. The system was to be designed to leverage mobile cloud computing technologies using Service Oriented Architecture (SOA) principles. Security and privacy were identified as the most important quality attributes. The system is expected to be able to integrate with other systems of Australian health care system to become a part of a healthcare ecosystem.

3.3   Case Study Process

The case study process (i.e., shown in Figure 1) consisted of following steps:

1. Each group was given a set of requirements of a distributed emergency healthcare system and asked to design and document software architecture. Each group was supposed to provide following materials at the first phase:

    a. Concrete scenarios and reasons for the key quality attributes.
    b. A set of services to support different features of the system. The decisions made for identifying the services along with the rationale.
    c. Documented design decisions using suitable architectural styles and patterns along with the rationale for the choices made (in a given template). Table 1 shows the decision template along with an example of the documented design decision by group B.
    d. Model the Service Oriented Architecture (SOA) of the system by using SoaML [17] and show the use of patterns. The designed SOA was expected to contain the Service (including composed services) and Component layers.

2. The research team evaluated the quality of software architecture designs and design decisions made by each group in the first phase based on predefined criteria. The submitted architecture designs were evaluated by a senior Teaching Assistant (TA) who had more than 10 years of industry experience. The TA did not know about the study. Later the two authors evaluated the quality of the documented design decisions.

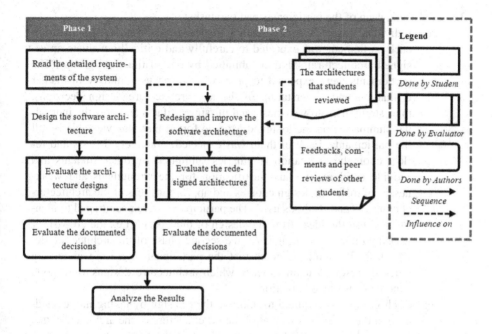

Fig. 1. The steps of case study

Table 1. A design decision captured using the template by group B.

Concern		How to develop the application to adapt to different devices?
Ranking criteria		1. Portability 2. Modifiability
Option(s)	Name	MVC pattern
	Description	MVC pattern divides an interactive application into three components and separates the data from presentation. The model contains the core functionality and data. Views display information to the user. Controller handle user input.
	Status	This option is decided
	Relationship(s)	-
	Evaluation	1. Portability is achieved by making the View an independent part and the system. GUI is not interwoven with functionality, so to adapt to different devices; we only need to change the View. 2. Modifiability is achieved by separating Model, View and Controller. Each part is independent and can be modified without affecting other parts.
	Rationale of decision	This option is decided because it provides a good solution to the quality attributes required.

3. In phase 2, each of the participants had two tasks:

    a. Individual task (i.e., participating in peer-review and recombination): each participant was expected to carefully and critically evaluate an assigned architectural solution submitted by one of the eight groups. The participants were expected to prepare a 1-2 pages summary of his/her evaluation and understating of the key architecture design decisions, their strengths, and weakness, and missing artifacts and post the individual summaries on the assigned Moodle forum that was viewable by all the participants. Each of them was expected to actively discuss and reflect upon the evaluation summaries submitted by other students and provide solid reasons and justification for the strengthens and weaknesses of different design choices and appropriateness of the architectural concepts and methods used. The participants were encouraged to identify and use the ideas from the design of their peers (i.e., the crowd) for revising their group designs for the second phase of the architecture design task. It should be noted that the participants were not given any clues by research team to learn which architecture designs were good candidates for recombination.

    b. Each group was required to improve their design by taking into consideration their own assessment of their architecture or the architecture that they would have found more suitable, and the feedbacks provided to them by other students through Moodle discussion forum and teaching assistant.

4. Like step 3, the TA and the authors again evaluated the quality of architecture designs and documented decisions submitted in the second phase.

5. The authors analyzed the quantitatively data based on all the evaluations of the architectures submitted in two phases for answering the RQ1 and qualitatively analyzed the students' discussions and reflections and feedback by the TA to answer the RQ2.

4   Results

Following sections report the results from the analysis of different types of data gathered for answering the two research questions that motivated this study.

4.1   Findings from Analyzing Quantitative Data

4.1.1   The Quality of Architecture Design

We quantitatively evaluated the quality of architecture design submitted by each group. We asked all the groups to submit two versions of their architecture designs. We expected that the second version submitted in second phase has been influenced by (i) the groups' assessment on their architecture; (ii) the architecture that they would have reviewed and (iii) the feedback and critiques provided to them by their peers through Moodle discussion forum and teaching assistant. For commenting and critiquing other's designs, we encouraged the participants to follow the sequential critiquing framework [4] that is expected to help improve the quality of the critique. We had an independent evaluator (i.e., TA) to score the quality of architecture designs submitted in phase 1 and 2 separately. It is worth nothing that the evaluator did not know about this study. The submitted architectures were evaluated based on the following criteria; any group could have received 10 points if they satisfied each criterion (i.e., the maximal score can be 60 points)

1. Description of the Personas of doctors, paramedics, and other members of an emergency response team located at a hospital.
2. Three concrete scenarios and associated rationale for 2 quality attributes.
3. Five design decisions and rationale for achieving the identified quality attributes by applying suitable architecture and/or design patterns.
4. SOA models using SoaML to show different services, their interactions.
5. Provide components/service diagrams using any 3 views of the 4+1 views.
6. Provide the details of some services by showing the class diagrams (application of design patterns) and the sequence diagrams.

Table 2. The summary of architecture design scores

Groups	Score of Phase 1	Score of Phase 2	Changes in scores
Group A	47	50	3
Group B	60	62	2
Group C	47	48	1
Group D	49	51	2
Group E	38	41	3
Group F	48	50	2
Group G	58	60	2
Group H	47	49	2
Mean	49.25	51.38	2.13

A comparison of the two architecture designs provided by each group is shown in Table 2 that clearly shows that all of the groups got better score in the second phase. It is interesting to note that the increment obtained after peer review and recombination could be between 0 and 3 points (i.e., 3 as the largest improvement). Each group's score on architecture design improved by approximately 2.2 points on average. We applied Wilcoxon signed-rank test as a nonparametric statistical method to assesses whether or not the improvement was statistically significant [5]. We chose this type of statistical method as the outputs of those participants had to be evaluated twice [10]. The dependable variable is the quality of architecture designs before and after peer-review and recombination process. The application of the Wilcoxon signed-rank test revealed that the quality of the architecture designs submitted in phase 2 was significantly better than the quality of the architecture designs submitted in the first phase at the level of confidence of 95% (see Table 3). These findings provide the evidence that the peer-review and recombination help improve the quality of architecture design. The feedback and critique provided by the participants to each other helped the participants to fix their decisions, reasoning and design flaws, but also it encouraged them to explore broadly design space and think more critically [1, 2].

Table 3. Descriptive statistics of the results on quality of architecture design

	Phase 1		Phase 2		p-value
	Mean	SD	Mean	SD	
	49.25	6.92	51.38	6.72	**p=0.011**

4.1.2 The Quality of Design Decisions

Previous section reports the findings from our investigation of the impact of peer review and recombination activities on the quality of all the artefacts submitted as part of architecture design, i.e., all sorts of decisions and documentation. This section reports the findings from particularly investigating whether or not the peer review process has an impact on the quality of design decisions. The participants had been asked to document each of the key design decisions using a given template along with the rationale for that design decision. We noticed that the participants documented the design decisions using the template (i.e., see Table 1, we name them as template-based decision) as well as without using the template (i.e., unstructured decision). In order to evaluate the quality of both types of design decisions, we extended the criteria proposed in [11] by adding three elements, which are expected to reflect architectural decision's quality. The quality of each decision was evaluated by the first author and the doubtful situations were discussed and agreed upon with the second author. Each criterion used a three points Likert scale: "Yes"=1, "No"=0 and "Partially"=0.5. The accumulated quality score for each decision was expected to range from 0 and 7. The following criteria have been employed:

- C1: Is the decision stated clearly?
- C2: Is the rationale of the decision stated clearly?
- C3: Is the documented decision is a viable solution with regard to the described?
- C4: Are multiple design options considered?
- C5: Are the pros and cons of decision compared?
- C6: Does the documented decision reuse any patterns/tactics /reference architectures?
- C7: Are quality attribute, constraints and business goal considered during decision making process?

We found that the number of template-based design decisions increased from 31 to 42 decisions from first phase to second phase and an average quality score per decision improved by 0.5 point. A comparison of the number of documented decisions along with the average quality score in phase 1 and phase 2 is shown in Table 4. It is clear from Table 4 that the average quality score for unstructured decisions increased by 0.3 point. Since we wanted to find out if the improvement in the quality of design decisions before and after the peer-reviewing process was statistically significant, we used the Wilcoxon signed-rank test. Two paired tests (e.g., Wilcoxon signed-rank test) need the same number of samples in each condition. That was why we randomly selected 31 template-based decisions from phase 2 in order to make the samples equal (i.e., the number of decisions) with phase 1. Tables 5 and 6 contain the p-values for the template-based and unstructured decisions respectively. With a p-value of 0.003, we conclude that applying the peer-review process led to statistically significant improvement in the quality of template-based decisions. The investigation of the used criteria revealed that the design decisions documented by the participants in both phases 1 and 2 satisfied the criteria C1, C3 and C7 to a very large extent. The improved quality of the design decisions in phase 2 compared to phase 1 was mainly due to the increased scores in C2, C5 and C6. It appears that the peer review forced the novice architects (i.e., study's participants) to better justify their decisions in the second step. During the peer review phase, most of the participants were challenged by their peers with such kinds of questions: *"what was your rationale for this given decision"*. These questions encouraged the participants to document the positive points of their decisions in the revised version of architecture documents (i.e., C5). However, the novice architects rarely talked about the drawbacks of the choices they made. In phase 2, the students applied more architectural patterns and tactics for satisfying the architectural issues. One possible reason for this trend could be that the participants learnt how to employ architectural patterns for architectural problems and understood that justifying the design decision with architectural patterns is easier. There was no statistical significance in the improvement over criterion C4 between phases 1 and 2.

Table 4. The summary of the number of and quality scores of template-based and unstructured decisions

	Phase 1	Phase 2
Number of template-based decisions	31	42
Number of unstructured decisions	11	18
Average quality per template-based decision	4.64	5.19
Average quality per unstructured decision	3.50	3.83

Table 5. Descriptive statistics of the results on quality of template-based decisions

Phase 1		Phase 2		p-value
Mean	SD	Mean	SD	
4.64	1.03	5.19	0.88	**p=0.003**

Having done the same analysis for the unstructured decision, we could not find a significant deference between the quality of the unstructured decisions before and after the peer reviewing process (i.e., p-value>0.05). Similar to the template-based decisions, the unstructured decisions positively fulfilled the criteria C1 and C3 in both phases 1 and 2. The scores of other criteria except C4 improved from first phase to the second one, however, it was not sufficient to have a statistical significance.

Table 6. Descriptive statistics of the results on quality of unstructured decisions

	Phase 1		Phase 2		p-value
	Mean	SD	Mean	SD	
	3.50	1.09	3.86	0.83	p=0.29

4.2 Findings from Analyzing Qualitative Data

Our study design and execution also included several means of collecting qualitative data, which is considered an important source of evidence and can supplement the findings from analyzing quantitative data. We gathered qualitative data from dozens of pages of design decisions discussions by students on Moodle forum, students' reflections notes in the submitted design reports, and teaching assistant's feedback. For analyzing the qualitative data, we employed thematic analysis [6], a qualitative data analysis method for identifying, analyzing, and reporting patterns (themes) from the collected data. We decided to analyze the data to identify the challenges that the participants faced and shared with their peers. Following are the main categories of challenges that were reported through discussions.

Service Decisions: One of the key tasks was to decide and reason about the types of services required of the system to be designed. Our analysis revealed that the participants found it quite challenging to determine what services and sub-services were required. It was also difficult for the participants to decide about the levels of abstractions to be used for describing the identified services and justifications for them. This situation made it difficult for others to easily understand the reported service. One of the participants described this challenges: *"This report should give more detail of the connections of each service. One of the important thing is they should give the details of the task manager service. How can this service integrated with other service, and how the services communicate in the system?"*

Design Decisions: Our analysis revealed that the participants faced many problems in making and documenting design decisions as well as in understanding the decisions made by other groups. It was also revealed that the participants did not consider and reasoned about more than one design option when making the design decisions; nor did they document all the decisions made. There was a significant difference between the number of documented decisions in architecture document (AD) and that of we derived from the discussion forum. This situation changed during the peer review process as the participants frequently asked questions like *"what your rationale is for decision X or pattern Y"*. This types of questions and peer critiques of the reported design decisions and the rationale provided resulted in detailed and intense discussions about design decisions, rationale and the design options that could have been considered. The simulants for such discussions were questions like *"what is your rationale for this decision?"* and *"how can you ensure that your decision reaches quality X?"* *"how the system can avoid attacks such DDoS attacks?"*

These types of questions made the participants talked about the design options that they thought about, their pros and cons, and why those design options had been rejected. One participant shared that *"We can also add some measures which can help reduce the impact of DoS attacks, such as using 2-factor authentication and rejection of any further requests from a device until it has been confirmed. With the rejection being done on a separate cluster with redundancy to reduce the chance that this service will be taken down from such an attack."* Another participant replied, *"The main concern that I see with using 2-factor authentication is that in the high-pressure environment of an emergency accident scene or in a hospital emergency room, authentication can be time consuming and stressful for emergency staff. As such, it is very important to ensure that the authentication methods chosen are as simple to use as possible. One idea would be to use a staff member's NFC access card....our group is considering the option of having the device itself as a possible token, where that device is registered to the system for approved access by a specific user"*

Despite the participants complaining about not having sufficient documented information about design decisions shared for peer review, the situation did not improve in the second phase either. Albeit the quality of the overall design and design decisions improved, but most of the documented design decisions lacked sufficient rationale. Compared with the phase 1, some students did mention about the difficulty in ranking different design options and selecting the best solution based on the required quality attributes, constraints, and patterns' forces. We found that participants had more difficulty to justify the decisions related to the whole structure of the system (i.e., architectural decision [20]) than those used to meet component-level design issue (i.e., low-level decision [20]). Our analysis also revealed that the participants found it hard to maps the individually reported design decisions onto overall architectural views. For example, they frequently asked *"where we can find the impact of this decision on architecture design"*. It became clear that a general lack of established traceability between the architectural decisions and the overall architecture designs submitted by different groups made it difficult to gain a good understanding of the designed architectures. Moreover, a large majority of the groups did not document execution decisions (i.e., tool, technology, process, organization as per Kruchten's classification of decisions [7]) using decision template. However, some of the participants did mention such decisions in their comments. For example, one participant commented, *"It is sure that we need more work on the multi-platform. As we use MVC design pattern and SOA software architecture, it is just an easy work move to other platform, we will use HTML 5 to design the GUI, So that all the devices can access to the system. We will make the description more clear and specific."*

Quality Attributes Decisions: Our analysis revealed that most of the groups did not provide any details about the trade-offs among quality attributes in the documented design decisions in the phase 1, however, they demonstrated a reasonable understanding of considering tradeoff decisions among quality attributes when prompted. For example, one participant remarked, *"... the design decision of data encryption is significantly correct and necessary here. However, the performance issue that may be caused by encryption is not taken into consideration in this decision"*. The response to this comment was: *"You're right that we didn't mention anything about performance*

here. We were aware of the issue, but we'll make sure to put it in writing for phase 2".
On another group's submission, a participant commented, *"... you put a central serv-er, which is the cloud in one location, and it only handles the logic process. It needs to retrieve data from data servers distributed in different locations. If this is the case, ... it increases the data communication between central server and data servers a lot. Latency may increase here".* The response was, *"As you can see, we did not mention this decision in the design decision section which we definitely should. The problem you raised, the latency, is a problem indeed... we pay more attention to the security part than the latency... we shall document this design decision in the next phase... we will regard it as a trade-off point and further discuss it in detail".*

Pattern Challenges: the analysis of the qualitative data also indicated that the partic-ipants were having challenges in understanding the goals and suitability of patterns reported to be used in software architecture design diagrams. One reason for that situ-ation appeared to be missing information about the names of the patterns used. For example, one participant commented, *"...What is the name of the design pattern or patterns being employed in this design?..strictly the Model-View-Controller (MVC) pattern or is it a hybrid of MVC and the repository pattern. This was not clearly stated and looking at their diagrams and architectural design I would make the as-sumption of the Model-View-Controller pattern but it is not always easy to tell."*

5   Discussion and Limitations

Peer Review and Crowdsourcing in Architecture Design and Review: The find-ings from our exploratory case study provide preliminary evidence to support the assertion that peer-review and recombination approaches can improve architecture design and decisions quality. Such an improvement can possibly be examined as fol-lows: (i) Once the novice architects participated in the peer review process, they were motivated to justify the rationale of their architecture design and the decisions made; (ii) most of the feedback and critique provided by the participants to each others were constructive; (iii) reviewing and looking at the architecture designs of peers enabled the participants to explore broadly the design space and consider the possible design alternatives. Since designing and reviewing an architecture of a complex software systems heavily rely on knowledge and expertise from different fields as well as expe-rience and intuitions, which is usually beyond the possession of a given organization, we believe that organizations can employ the peer-review and recombination through crowdsourcing for improving the quality of final architecture design. Linus's law (i.e., "given enough eye balls, all bugs are shallow" [18]) has shown the effectiveness of a peer-review process and it has been adopted as an effective practice for quality im-provement by Open Source Software communities [19]. Since a peer-review through crowdsourcing can leverage the experiences and expertise of a large number of indi-viduals, we assert that it can result in better architecture design quality. An organiza-tion can use the method as an effective approach to reviewing software designs. It is different to traditional architecture review, which involves formal, time-consuming and expensive meetings. It can also reduce the tension raised during the face-to-face meetings. There needs to be more research to examine the opportunities and perils of a design peer-review process by crowdsourcing.

More Training and (Semi) Automated Decision Making Support: The results have revealed that novice architects, who are supposed to be the next generation of architects, had many problems during decision-making process. Although they were successful in capturing and documenting the design decisions and their rationale to a satisfactory extent, but they experienced many challenges in other steps of the decision making process such as proposing design alternative, evaluating the alternatives, tradeoff analysis between conflicting quality attributes and selecting the best solution. We can assert these challenges may partially stem from lack of enough expertise and experience. These findings are similar to the results reported in [20], which revealed that the personal experience is a major influencing factor in making and documenting architectural decisions. It can be said that there needs to be more focus on providing the future architects with sufficient training and experience in different aspects of designing and evaluating design decisions and providing appropriate support for (semi) automate decision-making to improve the efficiency and effectiveness of the architecture design and evaluation activities. In a recent study, it was found that most of the existing design decision tools just focus on modeling, capturing and documenting decisions without providing sufficient automation support for decision-making [11]. We assert that the areas for automation support can be ranking design options, generating design alternatives, and supporting quality attributes trade-off analysis.

Limitations: One of the key limitations of this study can be the process and evaluators of the architecture design and decisions. Albeit the external evaluator was not aware of the study when evaluating the submitted artifacts, it would be better to apply double-blinded evaluation process to reduce the impact of potential bias in the evaluation of architecture design and decisions. We tried to alleviate this threat by intensive discussions between the two authors to reach a consensus on different evaluations performed on the artifacts used in this study. The other validity threat could be the participants of this study and system (i.e., healthcare emergency support system) being studied. Since there has been a little research on the impact of peer-review and recombination on the quality of software design and decisions, we decided to start this exploratory research by studying students' design and evaluation activities in an academic context as those students can be considered the future generation of software architecture professionals [21]. Researchers have found that students are suitable replacements for industry professionals if performing small tasks of judgment [22]. We plan to extend this research in a number of ways including the possibility of conducting a study with software architects from industry.

The third validity treat is how to ensure the improved quality of architecture designs and decisions in phase 2 was indeed due to peer review and recombination, not simply because of knowledge acquired by the participants (i.e., learning factor) through the study. We agree that the learning factor has the potential to be a confounding factor in our study as well as it is closely intertwined to peer-review and recombination techniques, but we argue that the participants as novice architects did not have the tendency to self-question and self-critique on their own designs and they preferred to start self-question and self-critique after getting external feedbacks and comments from the teaching assistant and peers (i.e., crowd). We assert that our suggested techniques and particularly peer-review process can challenge *"Law of Least Effort"* [26].

6 Conclusion and Future Work

We have carried out an exploratory case study to investigate how peer-review and recombination affect the quality of architecture design. The quality of designed architectures and documented decisions by software architecture students, as novice architects, before (as a first version) and after the peer-reviews and recombination (as second version) were examined and the results have enabled us to conclude that: (1) the peer-review and recombination activities can potentially improve quality of software architecture design and decisions (i.e., particularly decisions documented by template). (2) The novice architects can face specific types of challenges in design decision making process: (i) determining the required levels of abstractions to be used for describing the identified services and justifying them. (ii) Reporting the rationale for decisions made and proposing and ranking design options. (iii) Performing tradeoff decisions among conflicting quality attributes. (iv) Understanding the goals and suitability of patterns reported to be used software architecture design diagrams. We conclude that these findings can lead to design and execution of better training programs for novice architects to help them to gain the required knowledge and experience in relatively short amount of time as the technological advancement and increasing complexity require software development organization to have highly skilled and experienced architects.

Our ongoing future work can be outlined as follows: (1) we plan to replicate our case study in different settings and different sizes of population and with practitioners to explore if similar findings can be achieved with different contexts attributes. (2) We plan to further investigate the qualitative data from the Moodle forum to find out the types of design decision that were mentioned and discussed in the forum.

References

1. Dow, P.S., Glassco, A., Kass, J., Schwarz, M., Schwartz, D.L., Klemmer, S.R.: Parallel Prototyping Leads to Better Design Results, More Divergence, and Increased Self-efficacy. ACM Transactions on Computer-Human Interaction **17**(4) (2010)
2. Dow, P.S., Fortuna, J., Schwartz, D., Altringer, B., Schwartz, D.L., Klemmer, S.R.: Prototyping dynamics: sharing multiple designs improves exploration, group rapport, and results. In: The SIGCHI Conference on Human Factors in Computing Systems, pp. 2807–2816 (2011)
3. LaToza, T.D., Chen, M., Jiang, L., Zhao, M., van der Hoek, A.: Borrowing from the crowd: a study of recombination in software design competitions. In: 37th International Conference on Software Engineering (2015)

4. Xu, A., Bailey, B.P.: A crowdsourcing model for receiving design critique. In: CHI 2011 Extended Abstracts on Human Factors in Computing Systems, pp. 1183–1188 (2011)
5. Armitage, P., Berry, G.: Statistical Methods in Medical Research, 3rd edn. Blackwell (1994)
6. Braun, V., Clarke, V.: Using Thematic Analysis in Psychology. Qual. Res. Psychol. **3**(2), 77–101 (2006)
7. Kruchten, P.: An ontology of architectural design decisions in software intensive systems. In: 2nd Groningen Workshop on Software Variability, pp. 54–61 (2004)
8. Yin, R.: Case Study research: Design and methods, Sage Publications, Inc. (2003)
9. Nicol, D., Thomson, A., Breslin, C.: Rethinking Feedback Practices in Higher Education: a Peer Review Perspective. Assessment & Evaluation in Higher Education **39**(1), 102–122k (2014)
10. McCrum-Gardner, E.: Which is the Correct Statistical Test to Use? British Journal of Oral and Maxillofacial Surgery **46**(1), 38–41 (2008)
11. Lytra, I., Gaubatz, P., Zdun, U.: Two Controlled Experiments on Model-based Architectural Decision Making. Information and Software Technology **63**, 58–75 (2015)
12. Ali Babar, M., Gorton, I.: Software Architecture Review: The State of. Practice **42**(7), 26–32 (2009)
13. Tang, A., Lau, M.F.: Software Architecture Review by Association. Journal of Systems and Software **88**, 87–101 (2014)
14. Tang, A., Kuo, F.-C., Lau, M.F.: Towards independent software architecture review. In: Morrison, R., Balasubramaniam, D., Falkner, K. (eds.) ECSA 2008. LNCS, vol. 5292, pp. 306–313. Springer, Heidelberg (2008)
15. Maranzano, J.F., Rozsypal, S.A., Zimmerman, G.H., Warnken, G.W., Wirth, P.E., Weiss, D.M.: Architecture Reviews: Practice and Experience. IEEE Software **22**(2), 34–43 (2005)
16. Klaas-Jan Stol, K., Fitzgerald, B.: Two's company, three's a crowd: a case study of crowdsourcing software development. In: 36th International Conference on Software Engineering, pp. 187–198 (2014)
17. Service Oriented Architecture Modeling Language (SoaML) Specification, OMG. http://www.omg.org/spec/SoaML/1.0.1/PDF
18. Raymond, E.S.: The Cathedral and the Bazaar: Musings on Linux and Open Source by an Accidental Revolutionary. O'Reilly (2001)
19. Wang, J., Shih, P.C., Carroll, J.M.: Revisiting Linus's Law: Benefits and Challenges of Open Source Software Peer Review. International Journal of Human-Computer Studies **77**, 52–65 (2015)
20. Weinreich, R., Groher, I., Miesbauer, C.: An Expert Survey on Kinds, Influence Factors and Documentation of Design Decisions in Practice. Future Generation Computer Systems **47**, 145–160 (2015)
21. Kitchenham, B., Pfleeger, S., Pickard, L., Jones, P., Hoaglin, D., El Emam, K., Rosenberg, J.: Preliminary Guidelines for Empirical Research in Software Engineering. IEEE Transactions on Software Engineering **28**(8), 721–734 (2002)
22. Host, M., Regnell, B., Wohlin, C.: Using Students as Subjects - A Comparative Study of Students and Professionals in Lead-time Impact Assessment. Empirical Software Engineering **5**(3), 201–214 (2000)
23. Bass, L., Clements, P., Kazman, R.: Software Architecture in Practice, 3rd edn. Addison Wesley, Boston (2012)

24. Mao, K., Capra, L., Harman, M., Jia, Y.: A Survey of the Use of Crowdsourcing in Software Engineering. Technical Report RN/15/01, Department of Computer Science, University College London (2015)
25. Jiang, L.: Recombination Contest: Crowdsourcing Software Architecture and Design. Master Thesis, University of Amsterdam (2014)
26. Kahneman, D.: Thinking, Fast and Slow. Penguin (2011)
27. Kitchenham, B., Pickard, L., Pfleeger, S.L.: Case Studies for Method and Tool Evaluation. IEEE Software **12**(4), 53–62 (1995)

Modeling RESTful Conversations with Extended BPMN Choreography Diagrams

Cesare Pautasso[1], Ana Ivanchikj[1]([⊠]), and Silvia Schreier[2]

[1] Faculty of Informatics, University of Lugano (USI), Lugano, Switzerland
c.pautasso@ieee.org, ana.ivanchikj@usi.ch
[2] innoQ Deutschland GmbH, Monheim, Germany
silvia.schreier@innoq.com

Abstract. RESTful Web APIs often make use of multiple basic HTTP interactions to guide clients towards their goal. For example, clients may get redirected towards related resources by means of hypermedia controls such as links. Existing modeling approaches for describing RESTful APIs expose low-level HTTP details that help developers construct individual requests and parse the corresponding responses. However, very little attention has been given to high-level modeling of RESTful conversations, which abstracts the structure of multiple HTTP interactions. To address such issue in this paper we introduce an extension of the notation used in BPMN choreography diagrams. Its purpose is to represent concisely all possible interaction sequences in a given RESTful conversation.

Keywords: RESTful web services · Conversations · BPMN choreography · Modeling notation extension

1 Introduction

In traditional messaging systems, conversations involve a set of related messages exchanged by two or more parties [1,2]. Web services borrowed the notion of conversation [3] to indicate richer forms of interactions going beyond simple message exchange patterns [4]. As more and more Web services [5] adopt the constraints of the REpresentational State Transfer (REST) architectural style [6], conversations remain an important concept when reasoning about how clients make use of RESTful Web APIs over multiple HTTP request/response cycles [7].

In this paper we introduce an extended version of the choreography diagrams of the Business Process Model and Notation (BPMN) 2.0 standard [8, Chap.5]. Our goal is to provide a concise and yet expressive visualization of all possible interactions that may occur in a given RESTful conversation, in order to facilitate the communication among RESTful APIs' architects and developers. The extension emphasizes details found when using the HTTP protocol, such as hypermedia controls [9], headers and status codes. They are all relevant for defining the salient properties of the request and response messages composing a

© Springer International Publishing Switzerland 2015
D. Weyns et al. (Eds.): ECSA 2015, LNCS 9278, pp. 87–94, 2015.
DOI: 10.1007/978-3-319-23727-5_7

RESTful conversation. To illustrate the expressiveness of the proposed notation we model an example of a frequently reoccurring conversation.

The BPMN for REST [10] extension we have proposed earlier in 2011 targeted the modeling of RESTful Web service invocations from business process models and the invocation of resources published from within business processes. In this paper we target a different viewpoint focusing on the interactions between clients and resources, while abstracting away the processes that represent the internal logic of the two (or more) parties involved in the conversation.

The rest of the paper is structured as follows. In Section 2 we define the main properties of RESTful conversations. We survey related work in Section 3. We introduce the extension for BPMN choreography diagrams and use it to model a well known conversation in Section 4 and conclude in Section 5.

2   RESTful Conversations

REST is a hybrid architectural style, which combines the layered, client-server, virtual machine and replicated repository styles with additional constraints (i.e., the uniform interface, statelessness of interactions, caching and code-on-demand) [6]. As a consequence, interactions within a RESTful architecture are always initiated by clients. They send request messages addressed to the resources hosted on servers which are globally identified by Uniform Resource Identifiers (URIs). Requests are always followed by response messages, whose representation may change depending on the current state of the corresponding resource. Relationships between resources can be expressed and resources can refer clients to related resources. This way, URIs are dynamically discovered by clients. The mechanism whereby hyperlinks (or resource references) are embedded into resource representations or sent along in the corresponding meta data [11] is one of the core tenets of REST, known as Hypermedia.

RESTful conversations thus can be seen as a specific kind of message-based conversation defined by the following characteristics: 1. Interactions are client-initiated; 2. Requests are addressed to URIs; 3. A request message is always followed by a response, however there may be different possible responses to the same request message; 4. Hypermedia: responses embed related URIs, which may be used to address subsequent requests; 5. Statelessness: every request is self-contained and therefore independent of the previous ones; 6. Uniform Interface: there is a fixed set of request methods a resource can support. Furthermore, it is possible to distinguish safe or idempotent requests from unsafe ones.

These characteristics make it possible to share the responsibility for the conversation's direction between clients and servers. Servers guide the client towards the next possible steps in the conversation by choosing to embed zero, one or more related URIs as hyperlinks in a response. Clients may choose which hyperlink to follow, if any (they may decide to stop sending requests at any time). This way, clients decide how to continue the conversation by selecting the next request from the options provided by the server in previous responses. In general, clients can accumulate URIs discovered during the entire conversation or may remember them from previous conversations. Zuzak et al. call this the *Link Storage* in their finite-state machine model for RESTful clients [12]. Additionally, responses may be tagged as cacheable and thus clients will not need to contact the server again when re-issuing the same request multiple times. The discussion so far assumes that servers are available and always reply to client's requests[1]. In case of failures, either due to loss of messages or the complete unavailability of servers, an exception to the response-request rule must be made.

3   Related Work

The necessity of conceptual modeling of interactions has resulted in different modeling language proposals such as Let's Dance [13] or iBPMN [14], and has led to the introduction of the Choreography Diagram in version 2.0 of the BPMN standard [8, Chap.5]. Since the main targeted domain of these languages is modeling interactions involving traditional Web services, their capability of depicting effectively and efficiently RESTful interactions is limited, which has motivated our work on extending the BPMN choreography. RESTful Conversations have been introduced in [7], where they are used as an abstraction mechanism to simplify the modeling of individual RESTful APIs making use of them. In this paper we model the conversations themselves, which in some cases, may span across multiple APIs. Whereas in [7] UML sequence diagrams are used to visually represent the selected sample of conversations, in this paper we use extended BPMN choreography diagrams, following the fast-growing adoption of the BPMN standard which became an ISO standard in 2013 (ISO/IEC 19510).

4   Extension for RESTful BPMN Choreographies

The graphical representation of all the possible interactions, that may occur as part of a RESTful conversation, facilitates its comprehension. While UML sequence diagrams can be a good starting point when dealing with simple conversations [7], they are limited in concisely presenting conversations that can follow alternative paths. Therefore we propose using BPMN choreographies to visualize RESTful conversations. They focus on the exchange of messages with the purpose of coordinating the interactions between participants [15, pg. 315], while at the same time showing the order in which the interactions may occur.

As Lindland et al. [16] claim in their framework for understanding the quality in conceptual modeling, a very important aspect of a modeling language is its domain appropriateness. Cortes-Cornax et al. [17] emphasize the same when evaluating the quality of BPMN choreographies. They state that "the language must be powerful enough to express anything in the domain but no more". Therefore, to render the BPMN choreography diagrams more concise when targeting the modeling of RESTful conversations, we propose minor changes to their notation.

---

[1] Servers may indicate their unavailability by sending responses carrying the 503 Service Unavailable status code.

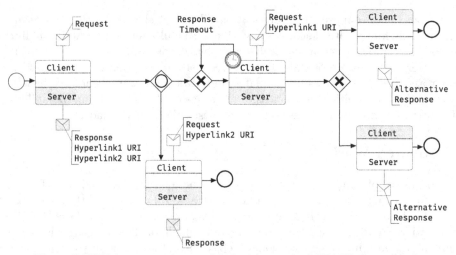

Fig. 1. RESTful conversation modeled with standard BPMN choreography

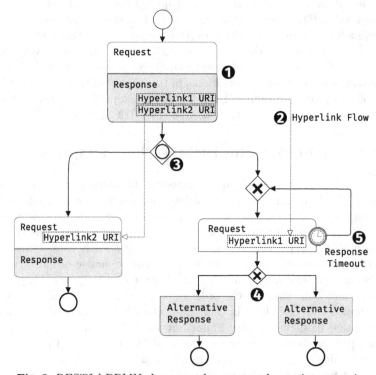

Fig. 2. RESTful BPMN choreography: proposed notation extension

As it happens often in high-level conceptual modeling [18, pg. 93], various assumptions and simplifications need to be introduced in order to avoid over-whelming the reader with too many visual elements. This usually results in the exclusion of certain details from the models. We introduce the following list of assumptions and simplifications for the RESTful BPMN choreographies: 1. While a hyperlink that has been discovered by the client can be used at any time in the future, to avoid decreased readability due to line-crossing we only take into consideration the hyperlink from the last received response; 2. While clients may decide to stop sending requests at any time, we model a path as finished (by using an end event), only if an initially intended goal has been achieved; 3. While servers may send responses that include many different HTTP status codes, we only include the status codes which are relevant for the specific conversation. For example, 5xx status codes can occur at any time. The client will need to decide how to react to such errors depending on the domain and error details; 4. While clients may choose to resend idempotent requests an arbitrary number of times, we only model situations where the client retries sending non-idempotent request (POST, PATCH) after a *response timeout* event occurs.

Figures 1 and 2 show the same generic conversation in order to illustrate the proposed extension of the notation and its conciseness. In contrast to business processes where it is important to highlight which participant is responsible for initiating the interaction, in a RESTful conversation the initiator is always the client, and there is no one-way informative interaction. The content of the messages is of a particular interest, because it defines the action to be taken by the server and the future direction of the conversation. To comply with these differences, we replace the BPMN activity comprised of an optional incoming/outgoing message with a text annotation to depict the message content and a three band choreography task containing the names of the participants, with a two band request/response element with embedded message content (Fig. 2, no. 1). Moreover, since in RESTful conversations the focus is not on the activities but on their request/response content, we consider a vertical flow direction more intuitive to follow, with a starting event leading directly to client's request and the server's response leading directly to the following request or an end event.

The remaining extensions that we propose capture distinct tenets of RESTful APIs. The *hyperlink flow* indicates how URIs are discovered from hyperlinks embedded in the preceding response to clarify how clients discover and navigate among related resources (Fig. 2, no. 2). In RESTful conversations it is important to distinguish between: 1. Path divergence due to client's decisions, e.g., to navigate to a given resource or to end the process, in which case any type of gateway (exclusive, inclusive, parallel or complex) can be used (Fig. 2, no. 3); and 2. Path divergence due to different possible responses from the server to a given client's request, in which case only exclusive gateway can be used, since the server always sends exactly one response (Fig. 2, no. 4). In the latter case, the exclusive gateway is introduced between a given request and the alternative response messages. This is the only situation in which a request and its response are not aggregated in the same element. Response timeouts may occur when the server takes too long to respond and thus the client decides to resend the request. To model them we use an interrupting boundary timer event attached to

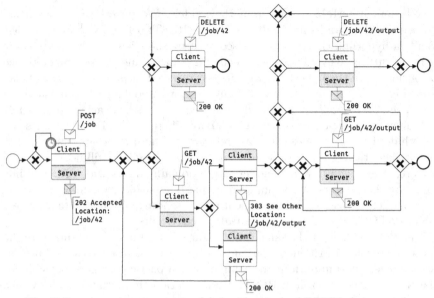

Fig. 3. Long running request modeled with standard BPMN choreography

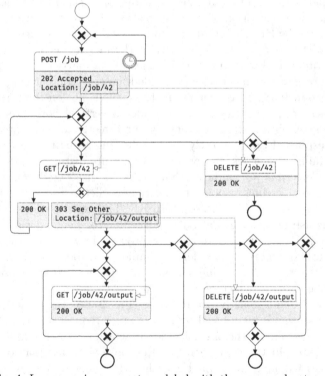

Fig. 4. Long running request modeled with the proposed extension

the request element. Such an event breaks the normal request-response sequence by introducing a request-timeout-request-response sequence (Fig. 2, no. 5).

In addition to the generic conversation shown in Fig. 1 and 2, in Fig. 4 we have applied our notation to a conversation that can be found in many RESTful APIs, e.g., Amazon Glacier's API for long term storage of infrequently used data[2]. Retrieving such data can take several hours (usually 3 to 5 hours [3]). Therefore to avoid having the client wait for such a long time, the operation is turned into a job resource, which is created using the original request. Assuming that creating the job twice has no side effects and the client does not receive a response to the job creation request within a given time frame, it can decide to send the POST request again. Once the job has been created the client may poll the job resource to GET its current progress and will eventually be redirected to another resource representing the output, once the long running operation has completed. Since the output has its own URI, it becomes possible to GET it multiple times, as long as it has not been deleted. Additionally, the long running job can be cancelled at any time with a DELETE request, thus implicitly stopping the operation on the server or deleting its output if it had already completed in the meanwhile. Fig. 3 and 4 show the conversation covering the whole lifecycle of a long running operation using the standard BPMN and our proposed extended BPMN notation, respectively. They illustrate how concisely this conversation can be visualized with our extension by emphasizing the important REST tenets.

5   Conclusion

Conversations are relevant in the context of RESTful Web APIs because multiple basic HTTP interactions are combined by clients navigating through the API's resources guided by the hyperlinks provided by the server. Thus, the design of RESTful APIs always consists of conversations and not only, for example, of the URI patterns and supported media types of its resources. Giving a visual representation of RESTful conversations is an important first step towards understanding and improving how RESTful APIs are designed.

The contribution of this paper is the graphical representation of RESTful conversations by proposing minimal extension to the standard BPMN choreography diagrams. The goal is to render the conversations more precise by focusing on the specific facets of RESTful APIs (e.g., hyperlink flow, request-response sequencing). We have illustrated the expressiveness of the proposed notation by modeling a typical conversation found in many RESTful APIs.

In the future we plan to design and conduct a survey among both designers of RESTful APIs and developers of client applications consuming them, to validate that the proposed notation enhances the understandability of RESTful conversations. Furthermore based on our experience and existing literature we plan to model a collection of frequently used RESTful conversation patterns and

---

[2] http://docs.aws.amazon.com/amazonglacier/latest/dev/job-operations.html
[3] http://aws.amazon.com/glacier/

to explore how to compose together individual reusable patterns to simplify the modeling of larger conversations.

Acknowledgments. The work is partially supported by the Hasler Foundation (Switzerland) with the Liquid Software Architecture (LiSA) project.

References

1. Hohpe, G.: Let's have a conversation. IEEE Internet Computing **11**(3), 78–81 (2007)
2. Barros, A., Dumas, M., ter Hofstede, A.H.M.: Service interaction patterns. In: van der Aalst, W.M.P., Benatallah, B., Casati, F., Curbera, F. (eds.) BPM 2005. LNCS, vol. 3649, pp. 302–318. Springer, Heidelberg (2005)
3. Benatallah, B., Casati, F., et al.: Web service conversation modeling: A cornerstone for e-business automation. IEEE Internet Computing **8**(1), 46–54 (2004)
4. Völter, M., Kircher, M., Zdun, U.: Remoting patterns: foundations of enterprise, internet and realtime distributed object middleware. Wiley, Chichester (2013)
5. Richardson, L., Amundsen, M., Ruby, S.: RESTful Web APIs. O'Reilly, Sebastopol (2013)
6. Fielding, R.T.: Architectural Styles and the Design of Network-based Software Architectures. PhD thesis, University of California, Irvine (2000)
7. Haupt, F., Leymann, F., Pautasso, C.: A conversation based approach for modeling REST APIs. In: 12th WICSA, Montreal, Canada, pp. 1–9. ACM, May 2015
8. Weske, M.: Business Process Management: Concepts, Languages, and Architectures, 2nd edn. Springer, Heidelberg (2012)
9. Amundsen, M.: Building Hypermedia APIs with HTML5 and Node. O'Reilly, Sebastopol (2011)
10. Pautasso, C.: BPMN for REST. In: Dijkman, R., Hofstetter, J., Koehler, J. (eds.) BPMN 2011. LNBIP, vol. 95, pp. 74–87. Springer, Heidelberg (2011)
11. Nottingham, M.: Web linking. Internet RFC 5988, October 2010
12. Zuzak, I., Budiselic, I., Delac, G.: A finite-state machine approach for modeling and analyzing RESTful systems. J. Web Eng. **10**(4), 353–390 (2011)
13. Zaha, J.M., Barros, A., Dumas, M., ter Hofstede, A.: Let's dance: a language for service behavior modeling. In: Meersman, R., Tari, Z. (eds.) OTM 2006. LNCS, vol. 4275, pp. 145–162. Springer, Heidelberg (2006)
14. Decker, G., Barros, A.: Interaction modeling using BPMN. In: ter Hofstede, A.H.M., Benatallah, B., Paik, H.-Y. (eds.) BPM Workshops 2007. LNCS, vol. 4928, pp. 208–219. Springer, Heidelberg (2008)
15. Jordan, D., Evdemon, J.: Business process model and notation (BPMN) version 2.0. OMG (2011). http://www.omg.org/spec/BPMN/2.0/
16. Lindland, O., Sindre, G., Solvberg, A.: Understanding quality in conceptual modeling. IEEE Software **11**(2), 42–49 (1994)
17. Cortes-Cornax, M., Dupuy-Chessa, S., Rieu, D., Dumas, M.: Evaluating choreographies in BPMN 2.0 using an extended quality framework. In: Dijkman, R., Hofstetter, J., Koehler, J. (eds.) BPMN 2011. LNBIP, vol. 95, pp. 103–117. Springer, Heidelberg (2011)
18. Robinson, S., Brooks, R., Kotiadis, K., Van Der Zee, D.J.: Conceptual modeling for discrete-event simulation. CRC Press Inc., Boca Raton (2010)

(Automated) Software Modularization Using Community Detection

Klaus Marius Hansen[(⊠)] and Konstantinos Manikas

Department of Computer Science (DIKU), University of Copenhagen,
Copenhagen, Denmark
{klausmh,kmanikas}@di.ku.dk

Abstract. The modularity of a software system is known to have an effect on, among other, development effort, change impact, and technical debt. Modularizing a specific system and evaluating this modularization is, however, challenging. In this paper, we apply community detection methods to the graph of class dependencies in software systems to find optimal modularizations through communities. We evaluate this approach through a study of 111 Java systems contained in the Qualitas Corpus. We found that using the modularity function of Newman with an Erdős-Rényi null-model and using the community detection algorithm of Reichardt and Bornholdt improved community quality for all systems, that coupling decreased for 99 of the systems, and that coherence increased for 102 of the systems. Furthermore, the modularity function correlates with existing metrics for coupling and coherence.

Keywords: Software architecture · Module structure · Software modularity

1 Introduction

The way a software system is designed and structured influences both the system's development and runtime qualities. In particular, modularity is the quality that encapsulates interdependence within parts (modules) of a system and independence among parts of the system. Good modularization also provides abstraction, information hiding, and specify interfaces [1]. Software modularity provides more benefits than mere logical structuring. It can arguably reduce development effort, minimize impact of change, and reduce technical debt [2,3]. In particular low coupling among modules and high coherence within modules is important.

An optimal (automated) modularization of object-oriented software systems is perceived as a challenge. In this paper, we use community detection methods both for optimising module structure and also for measuring modularity. We apply these methods to a set of open source systems and compare them with existing validated modularity metrics [3,4] . Our findings show that using community detection (in particular Newman modularity with an Erdős-Réyni null model) optimises the modularity of systems and (tentatively) that community detection metrics may be used to measure modularity.

© Springer International Publishing Switzerland 2015
D. Weyns et al. (Eds.): ECSA 2015, LNCS 9278, pp. 95–102, 2015.
DOI: 10.1007/978-3-319-23727-5_8

2   Background and Related Work

Abdeen et al. [4] define a module as "a group of programs and data structures that collaborate to provide one or more expected services to the rest of the software". Moreover they define a set of modularity principles for object-oriented systems and propose metrics for quantifying whether the principles are fulfilled. Li et al. [3] apply the metrics proposed by [4] as a measure of architectural technical debt.

Several authors have investigated automated modularization. Abdeen et al. [5] investigated how to automatically improve modularization of a software system while preserving original design decisions by through a genetic programming approach. Praditwong et al. [6] similarly described modularization as a multi-objective search problem and empirically demonstrated improvements over a single-objective optimisation strategy. Barros et al. [7] used a heuristic search approach to investigate a restructuring of Ant, but found that optimising according to commonly used coupling and coherence metrics led to complex designs.

Finally, to our knowledge none have addressed modularization as a community detection problem. We discuss this and the existing modularity metrics we apply in the following two sections.

2.1   Software Modularization Metrics

While a large number of metrics for object-oriented software deal with coupling and cohesion at the class level, there are few defined metrics that work on the module or package level [4]. Martin [8], Sarkar et al. [9], and Abdeen et al. [4] present metrics that do work on package level.

Abdeen et al.'s metrics fulfill Briand et al.'s properties of coupling and coherence metrics [10]. Furthermore, Li et al. [3] showed that one coupling metric of Abdeen et al. (Index of Package Changing Impact (IPCI)) and one coherence metric (Index of Package Goal Focus (IPGF)) correlated with a measurement of architectural debt in a set of open source project. We thus chose IPCI and IPGF as metrics for coupling and coherence respectively in our study.

In the following, we will briefly review these. Here P is the set of packages of a system, $clients(p)$ for a package $p \in P$ is the set of packages that contain classes with use/extend dependencies on p, $inint(p, q)$ is the set of classes in $p \in P$ that classes in $q \in P$ have use/extends dependencies on, and $inint(p)$ is the set of classes in $p \in P$ that classes in other packages use/extend.

Index of Package Changing Impact (IPCI). IPCI measures coupling as the average proportion of packages that do not change if a package changes. A value close to 0 implies a high degree of coupling among packages while a value close to 1 indicates the opposite. IPCI can be calculated as 1 minus the density of the graph in which each vertex represent a package and edges represent dependencies among packages (induced by use/extends dependencies among classes):

$$IPCI = \begin{cases} \frac{\sum_{p \in P} 1 - \frac{clients(p)}{|P|-1}}{|P|} = 1 - \frac{\sum_{p \in P} |clients(p)|}{|P|(|P|-1)} & \text{if } |P| > 1, \\ 1 & \text{if } |P| = 1. \end{cases} \tag{1}$$

Index of Package Goal Focus (IPGF). IPGF measures cohesion as the average package focus where the package focus for $p \in P$ is the average proportion of classes in $inint(p)$ that other packages use/extends. A value close to 0 indicates that $q \in clients(p)$ tend to use different sets of classes in p whereas a value close to 1 indicates that $q \in clients(p)$ tend to use the same set of classes in p. Given

$$role(p, q) = \begin{cases} \frac{|inint(p,q)|}{|inint(p)|} & \text{if } |inint(p)| > 0, \\ 1 & \text{if } |inint(p)| = 0. \end{cases}$$

IPGF may be calculated as

$$IPGF = \frac{\sum_{p \in P} \frac{\sum_{q \in clients(p)} role(p,q)}{|clients(p)|}}{|P|} \tag{2}$$

2.2 Community Detection

Many graphs/networks describing real-life phenomena exhibit *community structure* [11]. The structures are partitions of the graph into groups in which there are many edges among vertices in the group, but few edges to vertices outside the group. Community detection methods for finding community structures have been applied in many domains of graph analyses including literary networks, voting patterns, and biology [11,12]. Recently, Gentea and Madsen applied community detection to automated architectural recovery [13], showing improvements over specialized automated software architecture recovery methods.

Community detection algorithms often combine a *quality function* that score a partition and an *optimisation method* that heuristically finds partitions where the quality function is optimal [14]. Our initial idea was to use the Louvain algorithm [14] to find optimal modularizations optimising IPCI and IPGF respectively. However, this is not appropriate since both IPCI and IPGF are degenerate in the sense that they yield a maximum score of 1 for a modularization with all classes in one package (or in one package and with one empty package). We thus focus on more general community detection methods within the Louvain algorithm framework.

Newman's original modularity quality function [15] counts edges within a community and compares this to what would be expected at random:

$$Q = \frac{1}{2m} \sum_{i,j} (A_{ij} - P_{ij})\delta(g_i, g_j) \tag{3}$$

Here, m is the number of edges in the graph, A is the incidence matrix for the graph (i.e., $A_{ij} > 0$ if there is an edge between node i and j), P_{ij} is the expected number of edges between i and j and represents a *null model*, g_i is the community that node i belongs to, and $\delta(g_i, g_j)$ is Kronecker's δ (i.e., $\delta(g_i, g_j) = 1$ if $g_i = g_j$, 0 otherwise). Thus, Q becomes high (close to 1) if communities have many intra-edges compared with the random model.

In our study, we consider an Erdős-Réyni null model in which random graphs $G(n, p)$ with n vertices are created by linking pairs of vertices, i, j, with probability p. This is a simple null model that essentially models that vertices within a community are linked at random. If d is the density of a graph and n is the number of vertices in the graph, then the null model of the graph is $G(n, d)$.

3   Experimental Design

In the following section we explain the design of our study. We conducted a technology-oriented quasi-experiment [16].

3.1   Research Questions

The aim of this study can be summarized by the following research questions:

> *RQ1: How can we modularize an object-oriented software system in an automated way such that this modularity is optimised?*

To address this, we find communities that optimise Newman modularity given an Erdős-Réyni null model (NMER; cf. Section 2.2) and compare this to IPCI and IPGF (cf. Section 2.1). Our second research question builds on this use of community detection methods:

> *RQ2: Can community detection quality functions be useful as software modularity metrics?*

To address this research question, we test to which extent NMER correlates with IPCI and IPGF and to which extent changes in NMER correlates with changes in IPCI and IPGF.

3.2   Data Collection

To study modularity, we chose to study the software systems contained in the *Qualitas Corpus* [17], a collection of curated, open-source Java systems. The reason we chose this is that it is a curated set of open-source systems for which well-defined versions are available for download and because the systems are medium- to large-sized and thus, arguably, modularity is important for them. We studied the latest release 20130901 containing 111 systems The 111 systems have a median NCLOC of 51,860 and standard deviation of 307,473 NCLOCs.

3.3   Analysis Procedures

We first used the Java ASM byte code manipulation and analysis framework [18] to *extract dependencies* in Rigi Standard Format (RSF; [19]) using the binary version of each system in the Qualitas Corpus. Classes recorded were classes defined in the system or depended upon by the system. Dependencies were found in .class files (superclass, implemented interface, accessed attribute types, classes defining invoked method etc.) using a modification of ASM's org.objectweb.asm.depend.DependencyVisitor.

From the RSF file, we created a *dependency graph* using Igraph with classes as vertices and dependencies as edges. The package structure, i.e., the original modularization, was used to create an original partitioning of the graph. Since the system architects only have control over the modularity of classes included in the system, we included only those classes in the graph. The classes belonging to the system were determined as being the ones that were defined in the source folder.

We next computed an *optimised modularization* of the system. The optimised modularization was detected using the Louvain framework[1] for Igraph. We used the Reichardt-Bornholdt quality function [20] with an Erdős-Réyni null model. This is a generalization of Newman modularity that includes a resolution parameter. We set the resolution to 1, thus effectively optimising a Newman modularity function with an Erdős-Réyni null model.

For the original and optimised modularization, we calculated the quality of the modularization using a Newman modularity function with an Erdős-Réyni null model (NMER) using the Igraph Louvain framework and the IPCI and IPGF metrics using our own Python implementation.

To answer Research Question 1, we used three Wilcoxon paired signed-rank test to determine if there was a statistically significant difference between the original and optimised NMER, IPCI, and IPGF measures respectively. We used a Wilcoxon test because measurements on software is not usually normally distributed. We used a paired test because the original and optimised modularizations are paired. For the statistically significant differences, we computed an absolute effect size (i.e., difference in means) and a relative effect size using Cohen's *d*.

To answer Research Question 2, we computed correlation between original NMER and original IPCI, between original NMER and original IPGF, between optimised NMER and optimised IPCI, and between optimised NMER and optimised IPGF. To do this, we used Spearman's ρ. We used Spearman's ρ (instead of, e.g., Pearson's r) again because data is not expected to be normally distributed.

4   Results

Table 1 shows the *p* value of Wilcoxon, indicating that the population mean ranks of NMER, IPCI, IPGF respectively differ highly significantly. The differences in

---

[1] https://github.com/vtraag/louvain-igraph

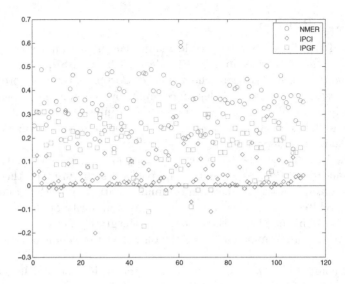

Fig. 1. Plot of the delta of NMER, IPCI, and IPGF after and before optimisation.

mean are 0.3259 for NMER, 0.0529 for IPCI, and 0.1631 for IPGF. Thus, the NMER, IPCI, and IPGF values improve in general even though there are deltas that are negative. Figure 1 shows this as the plot of the delta for NMER (NMER optimised minus NMER original), IPCI, and IPGF. We note that there are some systems with negative delta IPCI (12) and delta IPGF (9). In terms of effect size, calculated as Cohen's d, as can be seen in Table 1, the effect of optimisation is high. In total, we have answered Research Question 1 affirmatively.

To address Research Question 2 we investigate how the IPCI and IPGF metrics correlate with NMER for the original and optimised values. We measure the correlation using Spearman's rank correlation coefficient. The results are shown in Table 2. Except for correlation for original NMER–IPGF, the correlations are highly significant. In terms of the original intent that NMER can be used to measure coupling and coherence, the optimised values are the most relevant and here the correlation is significant.

4.1   Threats to Validity

The software systems that we studied may not be representative samples of the whole population (i.e. all object-oriented open source systems). Moreover, while

Table 1. Significance and effect evaluation for NMER, IPCI, and IPGF.

Score	Wilcoxon p	Mean of original	Mean of optimised	Cohen's d
NMER	5.9863×10^{-20}	0.4301	0.7560	1.6438
IPCI	5.3375×10^{-14}	0.9008	0.9537	0.5150
IPGF	3.2317×10^{-18}	0.7251	0.8882	1.5006

Table 2. Spearman's evaluation for NMER–IPCI, and NMER–IPGF for original and optimised values

Score	Spearman's for original		Spearman's for optimised	
	ρ	p-value	ρ	p-value
IPCI	0.2310	0.0147	0.7116	2.0686×10^{-18}
IPGF	0.1316	0.1685	0.4055	1.0103×10^{-05}

IPCI and IPGF have been validated (for correlation with technical debt in a set of open-source C# software systems [3]), these may not correlate with externally interesting measures for the software systems in the Qualitas Corpus.

5   Conclusion

The modularity and the module structure is an important part of the software architecture of software systems. It has an effect on, among other, development effort, change impact, and technical debt. In this paper we investigate means of optimising software modularity by automated partitioning the classes of object-oriented software systems using community detection methods. Moreover, we investigate the use of quality functions of community detection methods to measure software modularity.

In particular, we propose the use of Newman modularity with an Erdős-Rényi null-model for measuring software modularity and the Reichardt and Bornholdt community detection algorithm that propose a convenient framework for community detection and thus for optimised software modularity. We investigate this in the context of 111 systems contained in the Qualitas Corpus. Our results reveal that our optimisation improved Newman modularity for all systems, that coupling decreased for 99 of the systems, and that coherence increased for 102 of the systems.

References

1. Baldwin, C.Y., Clark, K.B.: Design Rules: The Power of Modularity, vol. 1. MIT Press, Cambridge (2000)
2. Wilkie, F., Kitchenham, B.: Coupling measures and change ripples in C++ application software. Journal of Systems and Software **52**(23), 157–164 (2000)
3. Li, Z., Liang, P., Avgeriou, P., Guelfi, N., Ampatzoglou, A.: An empirical investigation of modularity metrics for indicating architectural technical debt. In: Proceedings of the 10th International ACM Sigsoft Conference on Quality of Software Architectures, QoSA 2014, New York, NY, USA, pp. 119–128. ACM (2014)
4. Abdeen, H., Ducasse, S., Sahraoui, H.: Modularization metrics: Assessing package organization in legacy large object-oriented software. In: 2011 18th Working Conference on Reverse Engineering (WCRE), pp. 394–398, October 2011
5. Abdeen, H., Sahraoui, H., Shata, O., Anquetil, N., Ducasse, S.: Towards automatically improving package structure while respecting original design decisions. In: 2013 20th Working Conference on Reverse Engineering (WCRE), pp. 212–221. IEEE (2013)

6. Praditwong, K., Harman, M., Yao, X.: Software module clustering as a multi-objective search problem. IEEE Transactions on Software Engineering **37**(2), 264–282 (2011)
7. de Oliveira Barros, M., de Almeida Farzat, F., Travassos, G.H.: Learning from optimization: A case study with apache ant. Information and Software Technology **57**, 684–704 (2015)
8. Martin, R.C.: The tipping point: Stability and instability in OO design. Dr Dobb's, March 2005
9. Sarkar, S., Kak, A.C., Rama, G.M.: Metrics for measuring the quality of modularization of large-scale object-oriented software. IEEE Transactions on Software Engineering **34**(5), 700–720 (2008)
10. Briand, L.C., Daly, J.W., Wüst, J.: A unified framework for cohesion measurement in object-oriented systems. Empirical Software Engineering **3**(1), 65–117 (1998)
11. Newman, M.E.J., Girvan, M.: Finding and evaluating community structure in networks. Phys. Rev. E **69**(2), 026113 (2004)
12. Mucha, P.J., Richardson, T., Macon, K., Porter, M.A., Onnela, J.P.: Community structure in time-dependent, multiscale, and multiplex networks. Science **328**(5980), 876–878 (2010)
13. Gentea, A., Madsen, T.: Using community detection methods for automated software architecture recovery. Master's thesis, Department of Computer Science, University of Copenhagen, September 2014
14. Blondel, V.D., Guillaume, J.L., Lambiotte, R., Lefebvre, E.: Fast unfolding of communities in large networks. Journal of Statistical Mechanics: Theory and Experiment **2008**(10), P10008 (2008)
15. Newman, M.E.: Finding community structure in networks using the eigenvectors of matrices. Physical Review E **74**(3), 036104 (2006)
16. Wohlin, C., Runeson, P., Höst, M., Ohlsson, M.C., Regnell, B., Wesslén, A.: Experimentation in software engineering. Springer (2012)
17. Tempero, E., Anslow, C., Dietrich, J., Han, T., Li, J., Lumpe, M., Melton, H., Noble, J.: Qualitas corpus: A curated collection of java code for empirical studies. In: 2010 Asia Pacific Software Engineering Conference (APSEC 2010), pp. 336–345, December 2010
18. Bruneton, E., Lenglet, R., Coupaye, T.: ASM: A code manipulation tool to implement adaptable systems. In: Adaptable and Extensible Component Systems, Grenoble, France, November 2002
19. Wong, K.: Rigi Users Manual. Department of Computer Science, University of Victoria, July 1996. http://www.rigi.cs.uvic.ca/downloads/rigi/doc/user.html
20. Reichardt, J., Bornholdt, S.: Statistical mechanics of community detection. Physical Review E **74**(1), 016110 (2006)

Decisions and Social Aspects

Software Designers Satisfice

Antony Tang[1(✉)] and Hans van Vliet[2]

[1] Swinburne University of Technology, Melbourne, Australia
atang@swin.edu.au
[2] VU University, Amsterdam, The Netherlands
hans@cs.vu.nl

Abstract. The software architecture community has advocated design rationale in the last decade. However, there is little knowledge of how much reasoning is performed when software design judgments are made. In this study, we investigated the amount of design reasoning performed before making a decision. We recruited 32 students and 40 professionals to participate in this software architecture design study. We found that most subjects needed only a few reasons before making their decisions. They considered that giving a few reasons were good enough to judge despite that more reasons could be found. This result shows a satisficing behavior in design decision making. We explore the implications of this common behavior on software architecture design.

Keywords: Satisficing · Design judgment · Design reasoning · Behavioral software engineering

1 Introduction

Software teams often employ software engineering methodologies and processes during development. While the use of methodologies and processes can help, they do not ensure that good design decisions are made. Curtis suggested that the impact of behavior on software productivity is greater than the use of tools and methods [1]. As Donald Schön eloquently said: "We [professionals] are bound to an epistemology of [design] practice which leaves us at a loss to explain, or even to describe, the competences to which we now give overriding importance" [2]. His observation that we cannot explain how a designer thinks is still an accurate description of the state of software design. Software architecture design as a series of design decisions and design rationale have been recognized by many in the software architecture community [3, 4]. Many studies and methods promoted the capture of design rationale [5, 6]. However, we know little of how much reasoning is performed to create design rationale for making decisions. This issue has become clear in a recent workshop on software design [7]. The amount of reasoning software designers perform is an important issue to explore as the presence of design rationale is insufficient to ensure that a design decision is well reasoned.

Software architecture design is a complex business. Architects and designers often face uncertainties as they explore the problem space and the solution space. Decisions

© Springer International Publishing Switzerland 2015
D. Weyns et al. (Eds.): ECSA 2015, LNCS 9278, pp. 105–120, 2015.
DOI: 10.1007/978-3-319-23727-5_9

are made and reasoning is performed with many unknowns. Simon argues that due to bounded rationality, i.e. the limitations of our cognitive ability, the idea of maximisation in design is untenable. Realistically, we cannot consider all possible design options to achieve an optimal design. As such, complete design exploration by traversing the entire problem and solution spaces is impossible. Instead, such design approach should be replaced by the idea of statisficing [8]. Satisficing indicates that a decision maker makes a decision that is good enough to satisfy the goals [9].

If design optimization is not possible, how much reasoning and explorations do designers do before making decisions? How much satisficing is good enough? On the other hand, we know that missing information can potentially cause design flaws [10, 11]. In order to gain some insights on these questions, we set up an experiment to test how professionals and students reason and judge. In this study, we found no significant differences, in terms of the number of reasons and the judgments, between the students and professionals. We found that our subjects typically stopped reasoning and made judgment after finding few reasons.

In order to understand why both groups provided so few reasons, we did a follow up study and asked professional participants when and why they stop reasoning. They said that they chose to stop as soon as they were convinced that they had enough reasons. This is a satisficing behavior. However, a minority group of professionals are the exceptions to this reasoning behavior. We call them non-satisficing designers. They reasoned more thoroughly than most of the students and professionals. They had a different way of reasoning and we found three judgment characteristics.

2   Software Design Judgment

Design judgment and decision making involves reasoning, but other psychological elements such as motivation and cognitive limitation also influence reasoning activities. Software architecture design methodologies typically assume that software designers reason rationally. That is, if a process or a standard is followed and rationale is provided, the quality of the rationale is not questioned [12, 13]. Several studies, however, have found that software designers behave opportunistically [14, 15]. These studies show software designers do not use systematic reasoning to arrive at a design. In this study, we explore software design reasoning from different perspectives:

- How much reasoning do designers give before making design judgments? Why?
- Do professionals and students reason differently?
- What are the characteristics of designers' reasoning behavior?

To study these aspects of design decision making, we prepared vignettes, or scenarios, to describe software system scenarios. Reasoning with scenarios is one of the things that software designers do, and more so for software architects. Software designers and architects are often presented with functional and quality requirements, use cases, system goals and other information. From this information, they have to explore the problem space, reason with the situations and synthesize solutions [16]. In this study, each scenario describes a software system, its requirements and context at a high level. A conclusion is provided to allow the participants to reason with the scenario. The conclusion is worded in a controversial way to provoke reasoning and argument. For example, in one scenario (*scenario 5*), we described a proposed smart-card ticketing system to be built in Pakistan. We provided a controversial conclusion that says: "*It is viable to implement this system in Pakistan*". The participants were asked to do two things. First, they were asked to provide written reasons for disagreeing or agreeing with the given conclusion. The controversial conclusions were worded such that many reasons can be found to object them. The number of reasons, the nature of the reasons and the judgments given by the participants on software design scenarios allowed us to study how a participant uses reasoning and make judgments with software scenarios.

Second, the participants were asked to indicate their level of agreement with the conclusion. A seven-point Likert-like scale was used to indicate their level of agreement. As the conclusions are controversial and deliberately contain many arguments against them, the experiment setup allows us to examine the relationships between reasoning and disagreement conviction. We expected issues to be found in each scenario, and we wanted to observe what reasons the participants would give. The data also allowed us to analyse the given reasons, and relate them with their judgments, i.e. the level of disagreement. An online survey tool was used to gather the data.

2.1 Research Approach

In this research, we provided design scenarios as stimuli to gather designers' responses. The use of vignette to do this kind of study is a valid approach in the fields of social and cognitive psychology [17]. For our research goals, this research approach is appropriate as it would allow us to measure reasoning responses of participants using the same stimuli that are relevant to software architecture design.

In the experiment, we asked our participants to write down those reasons, to simulate the process stipulated by many rational design methods where designers are required to provide design rationale. We collected the data and encoded all unique reasons given. We counted those reasons and performed statistical analysis. We first tested if professionals would produce more reasons to support their design judgments than students. Second, we investigated their design judgements to compare how much disagreement they had with the conclusions. Third, we used a questionnaire to find out how some of our professionals carried out the exercises.

We did two rounds of study, with 61 participants in the first round comprising 32 students and 29 professionals. They were asked to do the exercises only. In the second round, the 11 participants had to do the exercises and then they were questioned about the process of their reasoning as well. When analysing the data from both rounds, we took a constructivist approach [12] in which we interpreted the data collected to build a theory of how software designers reason.

2.2   Scenario Preparation

We developed ten scenarios based on some actual system development cases. We worded the scenarios to allow issues to be embedded within the scenarios. Due to the controversial conclusions, we anticipated that there would be many reasons to challenge the conclusions, especially in complex cases. We wanted to discover what reasons the participants would find. We devised the scenarios such that possible reasons would be typical of the types of issues identified by Meyer [8]. For each scenario, there is a vignette that describes the scenario. A conclusion is given to stipulate reasoning and argumentation. The participants were asked to judge the conclusions and give reasons/issues for why they (dis)agree. Ten scenarios were developed and six of them were chosen to be used in the study. From these six scenarios, two were considered common (scenario 1 and 10) in that it was possible that the professionals had had a chance to encounter them in the work place; the other four scenarios (scenario 5, 6, 7 and 9) were complex and uncommon in that few people would have had the chance to work with such systems. This means that it is highly likely that these scenarios were new, in terms of making design judgment, to most participants. Uncommon and complex scenarios mean that the participants had to carefully question the scenarios [14].

We used an online survey to show the vignettes and the conclusions. The online survey tool gathered the reasons and the level of agreement given. There was no time limit on how long the participants could take to complete the online survey.

2.3   Pilot Testing

We invited four people to participate in our trials. They were given all ten scenarios. We found ambiguous wording in some scenarios and they were rectified. Out of the ten scenarios, we chose six scenarios for the actual study because we found that these six scenarios already contained all the different types of issues that we might find, and the pilot participants were able to identify them.

2.4   Participants' Demographics

We invited students and software professionals to participate. The first group contained 32 second year Bachelor Computer Science students from the Web-systems Project at VU University Amsterdam. There were 40 software professional participants, 29 in the first round and 11 in the second round. We used availability and snowballing sampling methods to recruit them. Many of the industry participants were either known to the researchers through work-related contacts or were colleagues of software developers known to the researchers. There were 6 architects, 1 academic, 16 software engineers and designers, 6 in IT and software management, 4 analysts, 6 consultants and 1 Database Administrator. This group of software professionals had an average industry experience of 16 years.

2.5 Data Gathering

We analysed the reasons given by the participants and identified unique reasons in each scenario to count them. We call this collection of reasons for each scenario a normative set of reasons. These reasons were typically assumptions, constraints and risks stated to argue against the conclusions. Analogies were also used to reason for or against a conclusion. We call them For-Analogy and Against-Analogy. In the second round, we used a questionnaire to get more information from the participants after they had completed the exercise. The purpose hereof was to find out how they reasoned and when they stopped reasoning.

3   Results and Analysis

3.1   Limited Amount of Reasoning by Students and Professionals

First, we analyzed the total number of issues provided for all six scenarios. Students on average found 6.56 issues for all 6 cases taken together, and professionals found 7.55 issues for the 6 cases. We performed an independent sample t-test to compare the mean issues found between the two groups and the results showed insignificant difference. In conclusion, professionals on average did not provide more reasons than students when they made their design judgments.

Second, the number of issues given by both the students and the professionals in each scenario were low as compared with the normative set. The number of issues given, as a percentage of the normative set, was between 9% to 13% in complex scenarios, and about 18% for scenario 10, and 30% (students) and 40% (professionals) in scenario 1. Scenario 1 has only two issues in the normative set. In most cases, although many reasons could have been given, only a small number of reasons were.

Third, participants found different reasons. Some participants said that they found the important reasons and stopped. However, there are many other valid reasons and it is somewhat subjective and arbitrary to argue that some reasons are more *important* than others. Let us examine the possible reasons for Scenario 5 (see vignettes and normative set of reasons[1]). In Scenario 5, the vignette is *"A new contactless smart-card system is designed to be used in the public transport in Pakistan. Each traveller would need to pay a deposit to obtain a personalized smart-card. Each card costs US$4.50. With the smart-card, a passenger can travel on all public transport system such as bus, train and mini-bus throughout the country. The smart-card can be re-loaded at ATM machines or over the counter at a bank. This system will replace all cash tickets in 18 month"*. The conclusion suggests that *"It is viable to implement this system in Pakistan"*. Issue 1 challenges the affordability of a travel card in a poor country. Issue 1 was found by 6 students and 13 professionals. Issue 2 challenges the viability of building the infrastructure. Identification of this issue requires system construction experience. It was found by 2 students and 12 professionals. Issue 6

---

[1]   http://www.ict.swin.edu.au/personal/atang/documents/Design%20Reasoning%20Experiment-V1.5.pdf

states the limitation of the people having access to bank accounts and ATMs. Issue 6 was found by 11 students and 15 professionals. Many students and professionals found these three popular issues. Other issues were not commonly cited. It is difficult for the researchers to say which issue is more important. However, using this example, we see that all the issues are equally valid but participants found different ones.

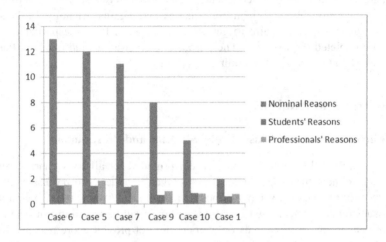

Fig. 1. Average Number of Reasons Identified by Student and Professional Groups Compared with the Total Number of Nominal Reasons

If these are valid issues, why did most participants not continue to find more of them before making their judgments? Table 1 shows the average number of reasons and as a percentage of the normative set of reasons found by the students and the professionals. Both students and professionals found only a fraction of the issues except for the simpler Case 1. A viable explanation was that they had been using the least cognitive efforts [18]. These professionals, and all the students, found some reasons and they decided that these reasons were *good enough* to make their judgments. This is an indication of their satisficing behavior. We verified this result by asking why they stopped reasoning (see Section 3.4).

Table 1. Average Reasons Identified and As A Proportion of Normative Set

	All Cases	Case 1	Case 5	Case 6	Case 7	Case 9	Case 10
Normative Set of Reasons	51	2	12	13	11	8	5
Students Average Reasons	6.56 (12.8%)	0.59 (29.6%)	1.46 (12.2%)	1.5 (11.5%)	1.37 (12.5%)	0.71 (8.9%)	0.9 (18.1%)
Professional Average Reasons	7.55 (14.8%)	0.8 (40%)	1.86 (15.4%)	1.52 (11.7%)	1.47 (13.4%)	1.05 (13.1%)	0.85 (17%)

3.2 Judgment Conviction

We expected that professionals having more experience than students would have been more convicted about their disagreement. This is because they could see the many issues in the given conclusions. Instead, the professionals did not totally object the conclusions. They objected to the conclusions in three cases and they were not totally convicted to the disagreement (see Table 2).

The two groups had very similar level of agreement in all scenarios. We performed a non-parametric test of significance on the median of agreement between the two groups and found no statistical difference between them in any of the cases. As discussed earlier, the level of agreement and the number of reasons of both groups in each of the cases shows no statistical difference. Thus, the two groups judge these cases in the same way. They found similar number of reasons to support their decisions and made similar judgments.

Table 2. Median Level of Agreement

	Case 1	Case 5	Case 6	Case 7	Case 9	Case 10
Students : Median Level Agrmnt	4.0	2.0	2.0	4.0	5.0	5.0
Professionals: Median Level Agrmnt	2.0	2.0	2.0	5.0	4.5	5.0

3.3 Amount of Time Spent on Reasoning

We tested the difference in time spent between students and professionals using Independent Sample t-Test. We found that there is no significant difference in the time spent by the students and the professionals in any of the cases (see Table 3).

Table 3. Average Time Spent by Subjects

	Case 1	Case 5	Case 6	Case 7	Case 9	Case 10
Students Avg Time	4.68m	4.87m	5.03m	4.43m	4.68m	4.68m
Professionals Avg Time	4.23m	4.23m	4.41m	3.70m	4.46m	3.84m

Almost all of the participants did not have hands-on experience with any of the scenarios. This precludes the chance that someone could reason with the scenarios based on intimate working domain knowledge. Despite the lack of domain knowledge, participants only spent a small amount of time on reasoning and judging. This could mean that reasoning is a function of time. After our participants spent a certain amount of time which they consider as *enough* and found what they thought were *reasonable* reasons to judge, they stopped.

3.4 Questionnaire Results

Following the first round of experiments, we found that professionals reasoned similarly to students. They stopped reasoning after finding few reasons. They had similar judgments with the students and the judgments were non-convicting despite that more reasons could have been found. The professionals also spent a similar amount of time as the students. In order to understand these phenomena, we invited more professionals to participate in this experiment in the second round. In addition to the design reasoning exercises, these professionals had to answer some questions afterwards. In the questionnaire, we asked them if they had an urge to complete the task quickly. The median in a 7-point Likert scale is 5, indicating a tendency wanting to complete the task quickly. We asked the professionals if they wanted to complete the task thoroughly. The median in a 7-point Likert scale is 5.5, meaning they wanted to do a thorough job.

We checked if any of the professionals had hands-on experienced in the domain in any of the cases. There was only one developer who did some work with Case 10. There were no domain familiarities with any of the other cases by any professionals. This helps to reduce the risk that hands-on development experience and prior domain knowledge might have biased the results in that judgments are based on prior knowledge rather than explicit reasoning. We asked the professionals to estimate the number of possible reasons for each case. The results were mixed. For professionals who had guessed that there are more reasons, why did they not find more of them? The following are some of the answers they gave.

- "I stopped when I found the main reasons. I did not need to find more reasons."
- "I drew a line at the time I spent in each case."
- "Gut feeling, based on experience and projects I have seen."

We asked the professionals if they were to find more reasons, would they have been more disagreeable with the conclusions. The following are the answers they gave.

- "YES. I would need to do more analysis. If I did, I would come up with more reasons. But when I saw a red flag, that was enough for me to disagree."
- "POTENTIALLY YES. If I spent more time, I would come up with more information to argue against the conclusion."
- "YES. I would have gone into more depth. The reasons I gave were important."
- "YES. To explore more techniques and to measure their feasibility according to risk and trade-offs."

These answers basically show that (a) the professionals knew that they could have found more reasons; (b) they stopped because *there is no need*; (c) they said they would have been more disagreeable had they found more reasons.

4   Satisficing Behavior

Software design is said to be a wicked problem [19] because it is complex and the situations that a designer faces are often new and unfamiliar. In a complex environment, the solutions, the problems and the reasoning behind them are not obvious. We designed the scenarios to be complex and so they require careful reasoning. The results of this study show that (a) students and professionals provided few reasons before judging; (b) students and professionals spent a similar amount of time before judging; (c) the level of agreement of students and professionals on the conclusions was similar and their judgments were non-convicting; (d) some professionals said that they could have found more reasons but they stopped because they thought it was enough. Given these results, we examined a number of theories to explain our results.

4.1 Explaining the Results

First, designers might behave in an opportunistic way when designing [15]. Instead of analysing a design systematically and thoroughly, they use information that is readily available. This behavior could be due to the limited cognitive capacity of designers to process all requirements and design information simultaneously, but there is no extra information from our study to support the theory of cognitive overload. Comments by some participants partially supported the opportunistic behavior, like *"solution that pops up in the mind"*.

Second, psychologists have suggested two modes of thinking: System 1 and System 2. System 1 operates automatically and quickly with little effort. System 2 allocates attention and effortful mental activities. In one experiment, it was shown that more than 50% of Harvard, MIT and Princeton students used intuitive thinking to solve a problem but they gave the wrong answer [20]. Other studies have shown that as people become more skilled in a certain task, the mental efforts they spend on that task are reduced. The *Law of Least Effort* asserts that people will gravitate to the least demanding course to accomplish the same goals. This law applies to cognitive efforts as well, it shows that people are inclined to use less of System 2, even in a situation that demands analysis [18]. In our experiment, we cannot show which system our participants used. But there were hints, based on the comments made by our participants, that participants engaged in both intuition (System 1 thinking) and effortful analysis (System 2 thinking).

Klein suggests "we need to blend systematic analysis and intuition. Neither gives us a direct path to the truth. Each has its limitations" [20]. Hammond suggests that judgments is an exercise to cope with uncertainty [21], and if judgment is a rivalry between intuition and analysis, then if a person's uncertainty is somewhat satisfied, by intuition or by analysis or both, the cognitive process stops and a judgment is made. Zannier et al. found a similar blend of Rational Decision Making (RDM) and Naturalistic Decision Making (NDM) when studying software designers [14]. These two theories point to the same decision making process: intuition vs. analysis. Our participants told us that they did some analysis, but they also used their intuition.

Third, Simon suggested that it is not possible to find an *optimal solution*. Instead, designers design systems incrementally and if a design appears to work, that design is selected and a designer moves on. Therefore, designers do not maximise or optimise a design. S/he chooses a good enough design. Simon suggested that maximisation is untenable and should be replaced by the idea of satisficing. That is, we cannot have a perfect solution, but instead we have a good enough solution [8, 9].

Finding as many reasons as one can achieve is maximization or optimization behavior. Our participants clearly opted to find just-enough reasons before judging. Although there is enough evidence to demonstrate designers are *satisficed* with their judgments, we do not know why *satisfaction* occurred, whether it was due to using System 1 thinking, or a laziness in System 2 thinking, or bounded rationality, or cognitive overloading. With the establishment of the satisficing behavior of software designers and software architects, we examine its implications on software architecting.

4.2 Satisficing in Software Architecture Design

Using the results that we gathered, we triangulate the evidence to conclude that software designers use satisficing when making decisions. We summarise our arguments below and discuss their implications:

Student and Professionals Satisfice to the Same Degree. There is no statistically significant difference to how much students or professionals reason or when they stop finding more reasons. This shows that, irrespective of experience, software designers are satisficed at similar points. *Implications*: As satisficing is a natural thing for most software designers, it is important to recognize such and train software architects and designers to investigate a problem deeper when dealing with complex issues.

Satisficing and Time Bounded Decision Making. All professionals who participated in the second round said they had an urge to complete the tasks quickly, even though they wanted to do a thorough analysis. We don't know where that urge to complete the tasks came from. A number of these professionals commented that they could have spent more time but they did not. *Implications*: This result seems to indicate that satisficing behavior and time bounded decision making are intertwined. Judgments are made quickly because of finding good-enough reasons or a designer has judged that enough time has been spent. Ward interprets satisficing as "choosing among a subset of behavior when information processing or time constraints limit the ability of a decision maker to make an optimal decision" [22]. There is no explicit time constraint in the experiment, but the designers implicitly considered time as a factor. Time is shown to be a cost factor in the study of purchasing behavior [23]. As such, time is like cost, it is spent in order to gain something. In software decision making, the perception of how much time spent on a problem becomes a cost function that is a trade-off with the potential gains of spending that time.

Satisficed Reasoning. Many issues had been identified in the normative set of issues in the experimental scenarios. However, most participants typically found few of them before judging. Out of the 51 unique issues identified for all 6 scenarios, students found an average of 6.5 and professionals found an average of 7.5 issues. Some participants commented they had found the main reasons and so they stopped, and yet they were not convicted to their judgments. This seems to indicate they knew they did not have all the reasons to make judgments but they thought that it was good-enough. *Implications*: The potential issue of such satisficing behavior is that the resulting judgments based on partial reasoning may be incomplete and flawed. As software designers often face new and unfamiliar situations, like the scenarios provided in the experiments, and if these situations require careful analysis in order to consider the many intricate and interrelated scenarios and requirements, then the reasoning before judgment is inadequate. If the result of this study is a general reflection of the way software designers make decisions, then there is a potential software design thinking issue to consider. Satisficing may work fine when a designer is experienced and familiar with the domain, but it may be risky in complex and unfamiliar design situations that require thorough analysis [24]. The question is how we may recognize satisficing, and that it may be causing design risks?

5   Non-Satisficing Professionals

In the student group, the number of issues found was evenly distributed, and there were no outliers (see Figure 2). However, in the professional group, we discovered a sub-group of 4 professionals who reasoned differently. These are the outliers who appear not to use satisficing judgments. We contrast these non-satisficing professionals with satisficing software designers by comparing the following evidence: number of reasons given, judgment conviction, time spent and the use of analogy. The existence of this group of designers is a contrast to the satisficing designers, and the ways they differ help to characterize satisficing behaviors.

5.1   Non-Satisficing Professionals Reason More

Non-satisficing professionals cited many more reasons than the other two groups. They found almost double the number of reasons. They also considered a broader context of the design situations to challenge the given conclusions. The reasons that these professionals identified were not very obvious and they could not have been found without careful thinking. They were also more thorough in their analysis.

As shown in Fig. 2, the average number of reasons this non-satisficing group identified is double that of the student group and the rest of the professionals. We ran an independent samples Kruskal-Wallis test to compare the number of reasons found between the three groups. We found that the non-satisficing group found significantly more reasons than the other groups ($p=0.004$).

We further analysed these four professionals in the non-satisficing group for each of the six scenarios, and found that they were clearly outliers in every scenario. In each scenario, the average number of reasons they found was typically double that of the students and the other professionals. This result highlighted that they reason different from the rest of their peers and the students. We found statistical significant difference between this group and all the other participants. However, with such a small number, the power of the statistical tests is limited.

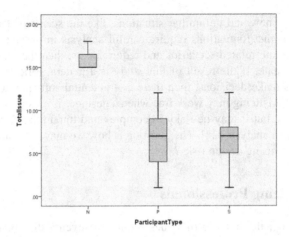

Fig. 2. Reasons Identification by Non-Satisficing Group (N), Satisficing Professional Group (P) and Student Group (S)

5.2   Non-Satisficing Professionals Use Less Analogy

Examining the reasons given by the participants, we noticed that analogies were often used to support or refute the conclusions. Typical arguments were "*XXX is successful, so it should also be applicable to YYY*". But often software design is situated within particular contexts [25], so analogy as an argument would work only when the situations of the cases are very similar.

Analogies are patterns that are used to simplify learning [26]. It is an intuitive way to allow matching solutions to problems that are similar. The use of analogies by students and some professionals suggest that intuitions were used in their design thinking style. Non-satisficing professionals appeared to use far fewer analogies than the other two groups. Table 4 summarizes the number of reasons by analogies given by the three groups. The number in each cell indicates (a) the number of analogies given; and (b) the average number of analogies (within brackets) given by the participants in a group. Let us examine a couple of example analogies found by the participants in Case 5: "*There are some good examples of smart-card systems implemented in other countries' public transport. I don't see why there should be any more difficulties in a country such as Pakistan.*" and "*The description of the system is very similar to London's Oyster card. However, Pakistan's economy is less developed than that of Great Britain. It is very likely that equipment will fail to work after a while and so travellers will be forced to find ways to circumvent the ticket barriers.*"

The analogies given were somewhat relevant to the reasoning and argument of the Pakistani situation. However, one could point out many differences between Pakistan, London and The Netherlands. If we examine them we see they are not very good reasons. Non-satisficing professionals hardly used analogy in their argumentation. When they used analogy, they gave reasons to support them. On the other hand, the other two groups used more analogies on average in 4 different scenarios. Many were not substantiated by sound arguments. The use of unsupported analogy is a characteristic of satisficing reasoning.

Table 4. Analogies per Participant (analogy counts and averages within brackets)

	Case 5	Case 7	Case 9	Case 10
Students	12 (0.375)	8 (0.25)	1 (0.03)	1 (0.03)
Satisficing Professionals	6 (0.24)	7 (0.28)	0 (0)	2 (0.08)
Non-Satisficing Professionals	2 (0.25)	0 (0)	0 (0)	0 (0)

5.3   Non-Satisficing Professionals are More Convicted to their Judgments and Spend More Time Reasoning

We note that the non-satisficing professionals are more convicted to their judgment. This contrasts with the average results reported in Table 2. We argue that non-satisficing professionals disagreed more because they found more reasons to support their arguments and refuted the conclusions. They were also more confident with their judgments. Dörner studied the habits of good and bad decision makers. One observation he made was that a good decision maker asks many why questions to explore reasons, challenges the assumptions, and poses different scenarios [27]. Non-satisficing professionals have these traits as well. They identified more issues and were more certain of their judgments.

The non-satisficing professionals spent significantly more time than the other professionals (Table 5). The cost of time did not appear to affect them as they focused on the reasoning tasks. In every case, they spent more time and found more reasons to support their judgment conviction.

Table 5. Average Time Spent by Professionals

	Case 1	Case 5	Case 6	Case 7	Case 9	Case 10
Satisficing Professionals	3.87m	3.76m	4.07m	3.44m	4.21m	3.64m
Non-Satisficing Professionals	6.75m	7.5m	6.75m	5.5m	6.25m	5.25m

6   Threats to Validity

There are a number of limitations in our study. One might argue that, in a real-life situation, one would do more reasoning but many of the professionals we surveyed after the experiment said that they stopped because they felt that there were enough reasons to convince them (Section 3.4). The results obtained here could reflect how these participants reason and judge.

Second, one potential construct validity issue is that the participants might not want to spend a lot of time to work on the scenarios, and inadvertently limited the amount of reasons given. However, many professionals indicated they stopped because they felt they had identified enough reasons, and did not say that they ran out of time.

Third, this experiment had a limited number of scenarios. The scenarios are short and the participants knew that they were dealing with an experiment albeit that they did not know its purpose. This is potentially a construct validity issue and limits our ability to generalize the results. We only conducted the survey with the second round of 11 participants, the number of responses was limited and as such it limits what we can generalize from these responses. Fourth, the way vignette is used in this study is similar to how information is communicated with software designers although in real-life there are often opportunities for further questioning, and other environmental factors such as time-allowance and presence of expertise that may influence designer reasoning behavior. As such, we cannot claim general representativeness.

Finally, we interpret the experimental results using the theory of satisficing. In the experimental construct and the interpretation of the results, we assume that (a) the kind of reasoning embedded in the scenarios are close to real-life; (b) there is little familiarity of our participants with the domains; (c) our participants are motivated to provide us good information. In these regards, the evidence that we gathered appear to be consistent based on the results that we collected: the reasons given, the judgments and the time-spent. The comments made by the second round of professionals clearly point to satisficing behavior. We found an outlier group, and use their behavior to contrast the behavior exhibited by the student group and most of the professionals.

7   Conclusions

In this work, we study how much reasoning designers do when they are asked to provide design rationale in different design scenarios. We asked designers to provide design reasons before making design judgements. We had 72 participants in our experiment. We provided six scenarios for them to reason with. The results show that most students and professionals provided few reasons before they make a judgment. Their judgments were non-convicting, i.e. they did not totally disagree with the conclusions. They told us that when they found enough reasons, they stopped looking for more reasons and made their judgments. This result shows general satisficing behavior in design reasoning. A small portion of professionals are non-satisficing designers. We identify three characteristics that contrast with the behaviour of satisficing designers: (a) these professionals seldom used analogy; (b) they provided twice as many reasons than the others before judging; (c) when they judged, they were more convicted to their judgments and willing to spend more time to reason before judging.

This study has shown that software designers and architects use satisficing in judging design scenarios. If this practice is representative of the everyday practice of software architecting, then it has significant implications. The software architecture community generally assumes that the presence of rationale is good enough to improve design quality. This study shows that designers only provide a fraction of design rationale. The amount of reasoning and the level of their satisficing could impact on the quality of design decisions, especially in unfamiliar design situations [24]. In a different situation, satisficing could work if the design complexity is low. As such, it is important to recognize satisficing behavior and its potential risks to design quality. Potential solutions to address the issue of premature satisficing lie in the recognition of this human behavior during design. Reflective design thinking [28], better design time management, reasoning techniques [29], architecture design and analysis techniques that include recognition and critical appraisal of satisficing behavior, debiasing [30] and managing design complexities [24] are some of the related approaches that could improve software design practice, and all of them need further exploration.

Acknowledgments. We thank Patricia Lago for her initial contribution to this work. We thank Alice Yip for encoding the data. We also thank our participants.

References

1. Curtis, B., Krasner, H., Iscoe, N.: A field study of the software design process for large systems. Commun. ACM **31**, 1268–1287 (1988)
2. Schön, D.A.: The reflective practitioner : how professionals think in action. Basic Books, Nueva York (1983)
3. Falessi, D., Briand, L.C., Cantone, G., Capilla, R., Kruchten, P.: The value of design rationale information. ACM Transactions on Software Engineering and Methodology (TOSEM) **22**, 21 (2013)
4. Jansen, A., Bosch, J.: Software architecture as a set of architectural design decisions. In: Proceedings 5th IEEE/IFIP Working Conference on Software Architecture, pp. 109–120 (2005)
5. Dutoit, A., McCall, R., Mistrik, I., Paech, B. (eds.): Rationale Management in Software Engineering. Springer (2006)
6. Tang, A., Barbar, M.A., Gorton, I., Han, J.: A Survey of Architecture Design Rationale. Swinburne University of Technology (2005)
7. Petre, M., Van Der Hoek, A. (eds.): Software Designers in Action: A Human-Centric Look at Design Work. CRC Press (2013)
8. Simon, H.A.: The Sciences of the Artificial. The MIT Press (1996)
9. Simon, H.A.: Satisficing. The New Palgrave: a Dictionary of Economics **4**, 243–245 (1987)
10. Meyer, B.: On Formalism in Specifications. IEEE Software **2**, 6–26 (1985)
11. Tang, A., Lau, M.F.: Software architecture review by association. Journal of Systems and Software **88**, 87–101 (2014)
12. Perry, D.E., Wolf, A.L.: Foundation for the Study of Software Architecture. ACM SIGSOFT Software Engineering Notes **17**, 40–52 (1992)
13. ISO/IEC/IEEE: ISO/IEC/IEEE 42010:2010 Systems and software engineering - Architecture description, March 2010
14. Zannier, C., Chiasson, M., Maurer, F.: A model of design decision making based on empirical results of interviews with software designers. Information and Software Technology **49**, 637–653 (2007)
15. Guindon, R.: Designing the design process: exploiting opportunistic thoughts. Hum.-Comput. Interact. **5**, 305–344 (1990)
16. Kruchten, P.: What do software architects really do? Journal of Systems and Software **81**, 2413–2416 (2008)
17. Tversky, A., Kahneman, D.: The framing of decisions and the psychology of choice. Science **211**, 453–458 (1981)
18. Kahneman, D.: Thinking, fast and slow. Penguin (2011)
19. Rittel, H.W.J., Webber, M.M.: Dilemmas in a general theory of planning. Policy Sciences **4**, 155–169 (1973)

20. Klein, G.: Streetlights and shadows: Searching for the keys to adaptive decision making. The MIT Press (2009)
21. Hammond, K.R.: Human judgement and social policy: Irreducible uncertainty, inevitable error, unavoidable injustice. Oxford University Press (1996)
22. Ward, D.: The role of satisficing in foraging theory. Oikos **63**, 312–317 (1992)
23. Fasolo, B., Carmeci, F.A., Misuraca, R.: The effect of choice complexity on perception of time spent choosing: When choice takes longer but feels shorter. Psychology & Marketing **26**, 213–228 (2009)
24. Tang, A., van Vliet, H.: Design Strategy and Software Design Effectiveness. IEEE Software **29**, 51–55 (2012)
25. Gero, J.S., Kannengiesser, U.: The situated function–behaviour–structure framework. Design Studies **25**, 373–391 (2004)
26. Clement, J.: Using bridging analogies and anchoring intuitions to deal with students' preconceptions in physics. Journal of Research in Science Teaching **30**, 1241–1257 (1993)
27. Dörner, D.: The Logic Of Failure: Recognizing And Avoiding Error In Complex Situations. Basic Books (1996)
28. Babb, J., Hoda, R., Norbjerg, J.: Embedding Reflection and Learning into Agile Software Development (2014)
29. Tang, A., Lago, P.: Notes on Design Reasoning Techniques (V1.4). Swinburne University of Technology (2010)
30. Kahneman, D., Lovallo, D., Sibony, O.: Before you make that big decision. Harvard Business Review **89**, 50–60 (2011)

Opening the Ecosystem Flood Gates: Architecture Challenges of Opening Interfaces Within a Product Portfolio

Slinger Jansen[✉]

Information and Computing Sciences, Utrecht University, Utrecht, The Netherlands
slinger.jansen@uu.nl

Abstract. Technology firms are increasingly opening up their products to develop an active ecosystem of developing partners around it. Both opening up products and organizing a developer ecosystem around an organization are non-trivial. In this paper we provide a case study of a leading communications technology firm that opened up and platformized 11 product lines. First, we identify and describe four architecture patterns that are applied multiple times across these product lines. Also, the software ecosystems initiative is centralized in one central department, which has created a central knowledge hub for the creation of a software ecosystem. We highlight the guidelines collected by the central department, to assist technology firms in the platformization process and support them in their own software ecosystem creation efforts.

Keywords: Software platforms · Software ecosystems · APIs · Case study · Extendible product lines · Extension patterns

1 Introduction

The creation of partner and developer ecosystems around IT companies is gaining interest rapidly. IT companies observe the successes that can be achieved with app stores, hackathons, open source developer communities, and other initiatives that drive software ecosystems. The creation of an ecosystem around a traditional IT product, however, is far from trivial and IT companies are looking for approaches to open up their products and have them adopted by communities of active developers who wish to co-innovate and share in the wealth created by the products and its auxiliary materials.

IT companies aim to create active developer communities and ecosystems around their products. We define developer ecosystems as a set of software developers functioning as a unit and interacting with a shared market for software artefacts. We ask the reader to observe the parallels between the definition on developer ecosystems and the definition on software ecosystems: a software ecosystem is a set of actors functioning as a unit and interacting with a shared market for software and services, together with the relationships among them [7].

© Springer International Publishing Switzerland 2015
D. Weyns et al. (Eds.): ECSA 2015, LNCS 9278, pp. 121–136, 2015.
DOI: 10.1007/978-3-319-23727-5_10

We also state that the term (open source) developer ecosystem is a synonym for (open source) developer community [2].

The research domain of software ecosystems is still in its infancy [10]. Researchers and IT companies are curious about new theories, methods, and techniques for the initiation, development, and grooming of software ecosystems. As such, there is an urgent need for examples and case studies that exemplify excellent practices, for theory formation and for teaching practitioners lessons.

Large IT companies are currently launching and running developer ecosystems. The challenges for a large IT company compared to a web start-up, however, are much larger, as large IT firms typically have many products organized in product lines, whereas a small web start-up will only have one or two domain APIs that need to be opened up. From this crucial difference, many new challenges arise. First, a small web start-up will start with a blank slate, whereas a large IT company has different product lines that may already be involved in supporting a software ecosystem of its own, with varying success and stages of maturity. Furthermore, due to the large range of different technologies that are adopted by a large IT firm over time, different entry points are required for each product, different types of participants are active in the ecosystem, and different business models need to be applied over those different products.

In this paper a case study is presented of an IT firm with a large product portfolio that with one initiative is hoping to open up ecosystems around a large set of its products. The lessons provided stem mostly from the software architecture domain: we illustrate how a product portfolio can be opened up using a generic platformization approach. Enabling an ecosystem requires a level of openness for a platform: without any extension mechanisms for third parties it is practically impossible for a software ecosystem to exist [1,6]. The openness level of a software platform is also a powerful tool for platform owners, as their choices determine the flexibility and extendibility of the platform, and subsequently of the ecosystem. A platform that is too open runs the risk of giving away its competitive uniqueness for free, whereas a platform that is too closed risks not being interesting enough for platform extenders in the ecosystem. The platformization approach is explained using four architectural extension patterns that were applied 21 times across 21 products.

We continue this paper with a description of the case study and the use of grounded theory for explorative research in Section 2. In Section 3 the case of NetComp is described. A detailed description is provided of the implementation of the software ecosystems initiative at NetComp: the managerial approach, the technical approach, and the developer ecosystem approach are discussed. In Section 4, four product extension patterns are described and details are provided of the historical background of the technologies provided at NetComp and on how the patterns were influenced by technological and strategical advancement of NetComp. To illustrate the observed patterns, NetComp's Telepresence product line is used to illustrate the observed patterns in Section 5. In Sections 6 and 7 we analyze the efforts at NetComp and identify the challenges of undertaking such an initiative: both from the architecture and managerial perspective.

Finally, we summarize our findings in Section 8 and hint towards a catalog of extensibility patterns that describes the different methods that can be used to extend a software product into a platform.

2   Case Study Method

Context: The context of the case study is NetComp (company and department names anonymized), a relatively young international firm that produces hardware and software products for enterprise and carrier communications. The firm has around 200,000 employees and is growing rapidly. The company has a worldwide presence.

Case Study Type: The case study can be seen as a participant case: the first author has worked alongside the FloodGate Department, a department that is burdened with the ecosystem initiative of the company. The main responsibility of the FloodGate Department is to expose current products to the developer ecosystem of NetComp and to build out the developer ecosystem. Please note that alongside the FloodGate Department are more commercial departments oriented around partnering, business models, etc. The FloodGate Department mostly deals with technical issues, development documentation, and the developer ecosystem. Please also note that the researcher was not involved in any of the decisions described in this paper, as his work focused more on the growth and grooming of the developer ecosystem.

Unit of Analysis: The units of analysis for this study are the architectures and extension points for each of the products in the product lines. Furthermore, the FloodGate Department and its responsibilities have been a unit of analysis as well.

Method: The data about the products and architectures has been collected through interactions with the FloodGate Department and in some cases through direct interaction with the product units. Also, several interviews with extending partners have taken place. The case study has been exploratory: multiple topics for study have been extracted. The current report (i.e., this paper) is the first in a set of reports. The methods followed were document study, interviews, interactions through the in-company chat system, and frequent e-mail interaction. The communication through digital channels helped solve translation issues. In all of the interviews different translators were present. The interviews have been recorded. Through inductive reasoning, topics have been extracted, highlighted, and grouped, using a digital folder system. For the study at hand, document study has been the main source of the material that is presented.

3   Case Report: Studying 11 Product Lines in NetComp

The starting point for this research has been the *FloodGate Department*. The FloodGate Department is a horizontal department in NetComp that is responsible for the ecosystem initiative of NetComp. The FloodGate Department was founded to create one unit within the company that is dedicated towards enabling partners to extend the most successful products of NetComp. As NetComp has a huge product portfolio, the unification of these efforts results in a knowledge hub on the creation of extendible interfaces for software and hardware products. The end goal of the FloodGate Department is to create welcoming and open software ecosystems for partners to participate in.

The FloodGate Department has been built upon several loose initiatives in the product lines to make their products extendible. The product lines for unified communications, for instance, had been creating extendible products and platforms for several years already. Currently, the FloodGate Department opens up capabilities in 11 product lines, in more than 20 products. These product lines have amassed between tens and hundreds of ISV and implementation partners (i.e., extension builders) that are dependent on NetComp products for their revenues.

As the FloodGate Department has executive backing, many product units have found a strategic partner in the FloodGate department: their resources are not influenced by one product's success and they have the knowledge on how to open up any kind of product. Some product lines were reluctant to support the FloodGate initiative at first, but as time progresses, they too see that the FloodGate Department plays an important and strategic role in enabling product units to build their own partner network.

The *FloodGate Components* consist of the different software components that are managed by the FloodGate Department. These components are FloodGate servers, which are typically installed alongside NetComp products, extension libraries (JARs and other SDKs), and controls (like OCX controls). Another important concept in the case study are the *FloodGate Labs*, where partners can remotely test their software against NetComp hardware. These labs are located in one office building and contain hardware test set-ups that can be worked with in a timesharing manner. The FloodGate Labs are described in Section 3.2.

3.1   Joining the FloodGate Initiative

The FloodGate Department supports eight programming platforms (.Net, C(++), Java(script), Ruby, Delphi, JSP, PHP, and Python) and six operating systems (iPhone, Android, Linux, OpenSuse, Windows, and Mac OS X). This variation has mostly been evolutionary: as new product lines join the FloodGate initiative they are bringing in new domain specific technologies. It is important to note that in many cases the FloodGate Department does little more than provide documentation and an open interface for the products. The responsibility for the product and its interfaces remains with the product departments, although in quite some cases the FloodGate Department has inherited the software development of complex extension servers (more on this in Section 4).

NetComp supplies funding to both the product team and the FloodGate Department for each new product that starts creating FloodGate Components. There is no formal procedure for joining the FloodGate initiative, but the process is based on common practices. The process consists of the following steps:

(1) Assess suitability of the product, (2) design new architecture for the product to enable an open extendible platform, (3) publish the products' FloodGate Components (typically an SDK). In the case of some strategic products, the FloodGate Department has initiated the collaboration themselves. The organization does currently not evaluate the financial results of opening up parts of products. The ecosystem initiative is strategic and is assumed to be useful for the whole firm. As it is hard to predict whether some of the products are going to be successful as platforms, NetComp mostly works on feedback from partners and channel managers.

In a typical case, the FloodGate Department is approached by a product unit first. They will explain their needs for extension, the (potential) size of the partner network, and the efforts they think are required to open up their products and platforms. The FloodGate Department assigns a project leader to the product unit, who from then on is responsible for all contact with the product unit. The project is started and an inventory is made of the efforts required to open up the products. Ideally, the FloodGate Department deploys their FloodGate server software next to the products and platforms and uses this server as an abstraction layer between the product unit's products and the extensions built by partners. The FloodGate Department and the product unit develop the capabilities in lock step: first the product is opened up further, and then the FloodGate components (more on these later) are evolved. When the software is considered ready for publication documentation is created on the FloodGate ecosystem hub, a web site where partners are gathered and supported.

As the platform is adopted by partners new responsibilities are introduced. The FloodGate Department remains responsible for the maintenance and development of the extension software, its co-evolution with the products, and partner support. The product units remain responsible for the development and maintenance of the products and the support of partners from a commercial perspective.

The commercial departments of specific products are responsible for managing partners. The FloodGate Department is responsible for solving technical problems that partners face. Unfortunately, there is little to no sharing contact data between the business departments and the FloodGate Department, which leads to two separate databases with partners, i.e., those that collect incentives from the business departments versus those that ask questions to the FloodGate Department. Both the business departments and FloodGate Department are calling for a unified partner management system. The responsibilities are mapped out in Table 1.

The FloodGate Department is responsible for receiving extensibility and product requests from partners. The project leaders in the FloodGate Department forward the product related questions to the product units and implement the extensibility requirements where possible. Product management is in the hands of the product units. The FloodGate Department is responsible for opening up the architecture, but the interfaces have typically been prepared by the product departments. Interestingly, some of the product units are no longer independently

Table 1. Responsibilities divided between product units versus the FloodGate Dept.

	FloodGate Department	Product Departments
Product management		
Release planning	One week after each product release.	The product departments release their versions independently.
Requirements engineering	From the product departments and partners.	From partners and end-customers.
Extendibility requirements	From the product departments.	From partners.
Software delivery	Independently delivers components.	Independently delivers products.
Development and Support		
Architecture development	Gives guidelines in regards to interfaces required.	Develop their own product based architecture.
Error messages	From the FloodGate Components.	From the internal components.
Documentation	About FloodGate Components.	About the product.
Support	To the product departments and to partners.	To the partners (product related) and customers.
FloodGate Labs	Completely responsible.	Helps FloodGate Dept. setting up the products in the labs.
Business aspects		
Partner management	Developer community.	Partner community.
Financial responsibility	Centrally coordinated.	Revenue based.

planning new features for their products, but involve a mixed team with members from the FloodGate Department.

When a new version of a product is released, the FloodGate Department typically responds within one week with an update to the extensible components as well. As the FloodGate Department is kept up to date of a product's progress and release schedule, they are developing the extensibility components parallel to the product development. In many cases they FloodGate Department can release on the same day as the product unit does. The FloodGate Department is somewhat hard to manage because of this: as the product release schedules are not coordinated, the FloodGate Department has different work loads at different times. The FloodGate Department and the product department organize meetings between once and twice per month to coordinate new releases, new development efforts, and ecosystem challenges.

3.2   FloodGate Labs

The ecosystem enablers that may be beneficial for one product are not beneficial for another. For example, some of the products in NetComp, such as IP Cameras and routing equipment, require access to test hardware. NetComp prides itself for providing access to a large laboratory in the cloud, that can be approached by partners at specific times (effectively timesharing the lab). Partners positively evaluate this practice, as they do not need to procure expensive test setups for their own development. NetComp leverages its own IP camera system to show that the hardware controls being called from the lab actually have the desired effect by pointing IP cameras at the hardware, such as servers, switches, and ironically, IP cameras. Please see figure 1 for an example of a movable IP camera that is used to monitor servers in the FloodGate Labs.

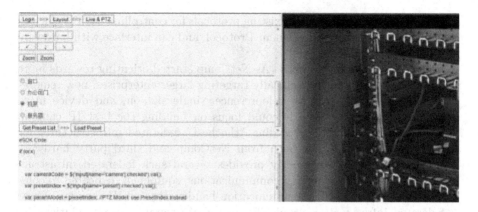

Fig. 1. An IP camera is pointed at a piece of hardware to show API users that the device status changed according to their calls. The IP camera can be moved to look at other adjacent devices as well with simple controls.

For some of the software intensive systems this is not beneficial, however, as it can be less cumbersome to just buy the required hardware or create a virtualized test setup. Partners complain that many of the platforms in the organization can be tested in a virtualized environment or through simulators as well. NetComp is currently building such simulators, to make partners less dependent on FloodGate Labs.

4 Product Extension Patterns

NetComp has always specialized in manufacturing hardware devices, such as routers, switches, and IP cameras. As time progressed and the organization became more mature, multiple abstraction layers have been required over the devices. This can be found in, for instance, the telepresence system that has an advanced management interface that can plan telepresence meetings across a network of telepresence devices, or the abstract datacenter management layer that can control several storage servers simultaneously. In NetComp four levels of abstraction have been observed. The levels of abstraction are found in Figure 2.

- **Server Level -** NetComp has traditionally manufactured servers. The software interfaces to those servers were always of concern, but as in the early years many of the implementation projects were in fact done by NetComp, these interfaces were usually in poor shape in terms of software quality. As the market for software has become more commoditized, however, these interfaces to servers have become better managed, higher quality, and accessible by third parties through APIs.
- **Server Management Level -** As NetComp grew, there was an increasing need for management infrastructures that controlled large numbers of device servers, such as IP cameras, routers, and storage servers. These management

infrastructures typically use existing protocols for controlling devices, such as the Simple Network Management Protocol, and can interface with hardware from other suppliers as well.

– **Federated Servers Level -** As NetComp started orienting towards more advanced markets and specifically targeting larger enterprises, new requirements were introduced for telepresence, single sign-on, and device management. Whereas before it could focus on building the best IP camera, it now has to focus on providing "the best" federated infrastructures for heterogeneous hardware, both from NetComp and third party hardware providers. NetComp currently provides several such federated infrastructures, for instance for unified communications, equipment dedicated to communication in a specific communication bandwidth, and IP cameras. These federated infrastructures typically consist of several software solutions on different servers, but are conceptually unified into one coordinating server.

– **Advanced UIs Level -** At the highest level of abstraction, NetComp enables mobile and other advanced interfaces to the federated infrastructures. This, for instance, enables the creation of NetComp applications for Smart Cities, such as a mobile app that can control a set of federated IP cameras or desktop apps that can control alarms across server federations.

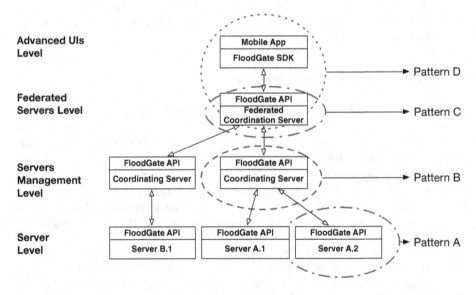

Fig. 2. Three extension patterns are found multiple times in the products of NetComp. The patterns are applied multiple times across different products and product lines.

Figure 2 shows more than just the levels of product abstraction that Net-Comp offers. It also models the four different extension patterns that are employed by the FloodGate Department to open up NetComp's products. In the following overview, each of the extension patterns is described. The overview is summarized in Table 2.

- EXTENSION PATTERN A: SIMPLE SERVER EXTENSION - To provide third parties with opportunities for controlling and interacting with NetComp hardware, many of the hardware products can be extended with a simple server. Several different mechanisms are applied to open up the servers. In some cases a software switch can be flipped, but more frequently, a separate JAR needs to be deployed on the hardware to open up its capabilities.
- EXTENSION PATTERN B: COORDINATING SERVER EXTENSION - In the case of coordinating servers, the patterns and technologies used are similar to that of Pattern A. In many cases, however, this feature is provided and switched on automatically. It is interesting to see that for Pattern A the technologies used are technologically close to the device (i.e., JARs for Java servers, DLLs for Windows based servers, etc.) whereas for Pattern B more abstract technologies are used, such as SOAP and REST.
- EXTENSION PATTERN C: FEDERATED SERVER EXTENSION - Federated servers are powerful mechanisms that can abstractly control heterogeneous devices in a network. These federated servers are even more frequently used for extension by customers and partners, as these are able to control all the customer's devices. These "servers" also are closer to the end-user. An example is the Bring Your Own Device solution, which provides access to different features in that domain, such as a single-sign on server, an asset management solution, and a software repository for mobile devices, also known as enterprise app stores.
- EXTENSION PATTERN D: ADVANCED USER INTERFACE EXTENSION - To provide access to the different infrastructures in the enterprise, NetComp supplies different SDKs and even reference implementations for customers and partners. Examples of such SDKs are the telepresence control SDK for Android and iOS, enabling the development of apps that allow for initiation, planning, execution, and termination of telepresence calls. Many of the apps built by partners are geared towards end-users, even though the SDKs are typically open and allow for much more.

One extra way of extending NetComp products is through third party platforms and products, such as Outlook, VMWare, OpenStack, Microsoft Lync, etc. NetComp supplies software that already extends these platforms. It is interesting to see that as we move up to higher levels of abstraction, more abstract protocols and technology-agnostic extension mechanisms are found. Whereas at the lowest level controls are typically built in highly technologically native environments (Java SDKs, linux libraries, etc.), at the higher levels mechanisms become increasingly abstract (REST, SOAP). This is in part caused by the time at which these higher level abstractions were built, but also because more partners require different types of technologies for integration at higher levels.

Table 2. The observed extension patterns, their occurrences (in a total of 21 extendible components), and the observed technologies at NetComp. Please note that for some product lines multiple extension patterns are observed. In Section 5 all four are observed in one product line.

	Occur.	Extension mechanism	Extension technology
Pattern A: SIMPLE SERVER EXTENSION	6	1. Turn on software switch 2. Deploy server on device 3. Deploy server on another device	Standalone executable, JARs, .so libraries, powershell libs, DLLs
Pattern B: COORDINATING SERVER EXTENSION	3	1. Turn on software switch 2. Deploy server on device 3. Deploy server on another device	Standalone executable, JARs, SOAP, REST
Pattern C: FEDERATED SERVER EXTENSION	4	1. Deploy server on another device 2. Buy secondary dedicated device	Standalone executable, JARs, SOAP, REST, SNMP, Python
Pattern D: ADV. USER INTERFACE EXTENSION	8	1. SDKs for (mobile) apps 2. Provide client controls	Android, iOS, OCX

5   Illustrative Case: The Telepresence Product Line

One of NetComp's most successful product lines is the telepresence. Net-Comp manufactures many different systems for this domain: from HD television mounted cameras to smart microphone and speaker interfaces. These systems are most effective when they integrate well with the infrastructure of a customer organization. Meetings must be planned through office applications such as Outlook, for instance.

Traditionally, managers of telepresence systems performed their operation and maintenance tasks through the NetComp Service Management Center (SMC), a server that is dedicated to the detection and management of telepresence devices. The SMC can directly access features of the telepresence devices and execute device-specific commands, such as start, stop, and record commands.

As customers started developing their systems, however, they also attempt to integrate other NetComp (generic IP cameras) and third party hardware (HD videoconferencing). NetComp added a component to their SMC called the Converged Gateway: a product that enables interaction through a unified interface with other (sometimes non-telepresence) devices.

In the scope of the FloodGate initiative, the capabilities of the devices, the SMC, and the converged gateway are opened up for extension by third parties. This is done through the FloodGate server, which is independently deployed in the IP network. The FloodGate server can be approached directly with SOAP calls. Furthermore, there are JAR libraries available to quick start third parties with the development of the advanced choreographies that are necessary to negotiate advanced telepresence scenarios. The JARs available concern mostly the SMC, but also contain more high-level abstractions, with the most interesting one being the eHealth JAR, containing specific capabilities for remote health care.

The network deployment of the telepresence components is modeled in Figure 3. Extenders have the option to approach the FloodGate server through the SDK or through its direct API, using SOAP. There exists a link between the

FloodGate server and endpoint telepresence devices in the network, but this is no longer documented, as extenders are advised to use the SMC interface. It is interesting to observe that the extension patterns identified in Section 4 are all found in the telepresence product line. First, the SIMPLE SERVER EXTENSION PATTERN is found in the fact that it used to be possible to directly address endpoint devices in the telepresence deployment. Secondly, the COORDINATING SERVER EXTENSION PATTERN is found in the SMC extension possibilities. The SMC controls the whole deployment of telepresence devices and through its FloodGate interface can be controlled by a third party application. Thirdly, the FEDERATED SERVER EXTENSION PATTERN is found in the converged gateway, enabling hardware from others and non-telepresence devices, such as simple IP cameras, to also be controlled by third parties. It must be mentioned that the converged gateway and SMC are no longer deployed separately and are always deployed together. At the highest level we observe the ADVANCED USER INTERFACE EXTENSION PATTERN, as the JARs provided give third parties the opportunity to quick start the development process and develop domain specific solutions, like the telemedicine library offered.

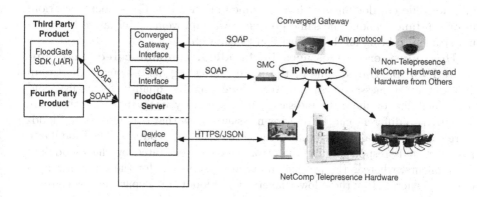

Fig. 3. A typical telepresence network deployment and its extension possibilities. The dotted line indicates that it is still possible to address telepresence devices directly, but it is no longer supported or documented. Lines without a label indicate proprietary protocols that are not visible to third parties.

6   Openness and Architecture Challenges

The FloodGate Department initiative is generally experienced positively by the product departments. Product units get to focus on their product innovations, while extensibility questions and partner support are delegated to the FloodGate Department. Furthermore, as the FloodGate Department has strategic support in the organization, much needed resources in the product units can be used for "regular" product innovation. The centralized approach results into (architectural) challenges that are experienced across different product units.

How open is open enough? There is a constant discussion between partners and NetComp about how open products are. For example, there is a rich tool suite for unified communications, that provides features such as instant messaging, document sharing, voice chat, video chat, and screen sharing. The tool suite is packaged into an extendible client. Partners are calling for modularization, as they do not wish to use the client, but embed smaller features in their own tooling, such as mobile applications. NetComp needs to strategically evaluate such requests: is the call for such modularization going to add value for customers? Will security be compromised? And can profit still be made when partners can replace components so easily? These decisions are typically made by the product lines, with support from the FloodGate department.

How must documentation be standardized for partners? One of the biggest challenges for NetComp has been to standardize across the product units. When looking at the documentation for 3rd parties, for instance, some of the documents are supplied in .chm format (a documentation format that is specific to Microsoft) whereas other documents are supplied through online web content management systems, and as Word documents. Furthermore, the look and feel of the documentation is different across different products and sometimes even for different documents (Java documentation versus C++ documentation, in one instance) about the same product. An improvement initiative has been undertaken to bring all documentation to the web.

How must error messages be handled, communicated, and supported for partners? One of the more interesting discussions at NetComp is about error messages. As we were discussing the quality, findability, and reproducibility of the error messages, it was quickly uncovered that there are actually two different classes of error message: those that come from the FloodGate Components and those that are generated by the products. The FloodGate Department is responsible for the error messages generated by the FloodGate Components, whereas the product units are responsible for the error messages that are generated by these lower layers. The FloodGate Department is running into problems with these: partners call with questions about product error messages, whereas they are only capable of answering questions in regards to the FloodGate Components and their error messages. The FloodGate Department needs a mandate to force product units to regularly update error message documentation and improve them where necessary. Simultaneously, the FloodGate Department is responsible for providing the product units with an infrastructure in which they can publish their error messages and documentation.

How must crashes propagate through the systems? When one of the products crashes, the FloodGate Components, typically a separate server, keeps running. The product units have not been instructed on how to inform the FloodGate Components about crashes and the like. Partners are expected to solve this problem themselves. Should a product crash, it simply becomes unavailable to the FloodGate Components.

How must extensions be secured? In the communications industry security is a major concern. The FloodGate Department architects are responsible for executing and checking security guidelines. These guidelines are well documented and well managed in NetComp. The architects have three levels of security check in place, which we cannot share for reasons of confidentiality. However, we are allowed to illustrate some of the guidelines that are used by the architects. At the first level, the architects look at data leaks, unlawful interception, and privacy protection. At the second level, the architects have more advanced steps, like data encryption, attack and integrity protection, and log auditing. At the third level, the architects apply tools like virus protection, security hardening, protected installations, database hardening, and some guidelines for partners on security. An interesting observation is that NetComp presently shares little of this knowledge with partners, whereas partners can greatly benefit from security audits. There are many ecosystem opportunities here: partners can be audited, certified, and trained in the domain of security. NetComp is evaluating these different options presently.

How must partners be convinced to deploy newer versions? As the hardware running for customers is generally deployed and then left alone, so are the FloodGate Components. This results in situations where the Flood-Gate Components running on extendible hardware is running far behind the most recent version, making it harder to develop against. It is, however, a challenge to convince partners to update the software running on the hardware and its accompanying FloodGate servers without any business incentive. Simultaneously, however, when a customer wishes to acquire extended features through a NetComp partner, all hardware drivers must first be brought up to date. The FloodGate Department is working on a policy to incentivize partners to upgrade software, even when there is no direct need for the partner to do so.

7   Analysis, Discussion, and Related Work

The FloodGate Department is relatively new: many product lines developed similar interfaces before the FloodGate Department was implemented in full. It is impossible to say whether the extension patterns were implemented independently by the product units, although we have good reason to believe this to be the case. It is even more interesting then, that such similar patterns evolved. Parallels must be drawn to other systems for further research, but for now we observe a common theme in software architecture: with the growth and expansion of systems and offerings, so do the abstractions on top of them.

As the challenges are unfolded in this paper, one could even wonder what the advantages are of having one large ecosystem initiative for all different product lines. After all, there are so many challenges, that it may feel like trying to trap all the different animals on earth unwillingly onto an ark. However, the participants in the initiative indicate that their expertise at this point is unparalleled in the company and that none of the product units would have the resources available to undertake the initiative at its current speed. Another trend that keeps surfacing is the "one organization, one ecosystem": if a large partner extends different products from different product lines, NetComp wants to be aware of this, as that partner is playing a strategic role in the ecosystem.

In earlier work, we have conducted similar studies. In the work on the extensibility of mobile operating systems [1] we observed that mobile operating systems are open and extendible, but that restrictions, rules, and abstraction layers protect the inner cores of mobile operating systems. This is true for NetComp to a lesser extent: partners are expected to be 'more responsible' than mobile app developers. Also, as there are simply fewer extending partners than there are mobile app developers, NetComp does not have the resources to test and harden every interface, albeit with an exception for security aspects.

In the work on pragmatic reuse [4,5] in start-up companies, we observed eight different pragmatic extension patterns. The pragmatism is found, for instance, in the fact that these start-ups would sometimes simply hack the database of another product and read and write to it directly to extend it. None of this pragmatism is found in the extension mechanisms provided by NetComp: the extension mechanisms used most are traditional SDKs that communicate with independent "service providers", typically running on the hardware itself. As NetComp is active in the communications industry, this is not surprising: hardware deployments need to be easy to extend, loosely coupled, quick to deploy, easy to manage, and above all secure.

In the work of Kabbedijk [8] he presents a multitude of patterns that enable variability in multi-tenant environments. The pattern catalog created there is an inspiration for the current work on extensible software platforms. In the future we hope to create a similar overview to provide insight into the most common patterns used to enable and support software ecosystems.

Wnuk et al. present several case reports about Axis [12,13], a company that is equally dependent on hardware as NetComp, but where the ecosystem initiative is currently less mature. Parallels that can be drawn are the need for standardization from partners, the need for partners to be informed regularly about platform developments, and the actual response to change requests from partners. Finally, Axis too is having difficulty opening up the platform for several different products, although this is not further specified in the case reports.

A large body of work is available on software product lines. Although seemingly this work focuses on product lines, the real contribution lies in the view on a coordinated effort in opening up products in several product lines. In that sense this work is close to product lines, but perhaps even more about organizational boundaries surrounding product lines, as for instance illustrated by Hanssen [3]. Toft also highlights the challenges of central collaboration between departments in a software product line [11]. Contrary to this work, they propose a decentralized mode of working, that forces departments to collaboratively share architecture and components.

8   Conclusion

The paper provides four contributions. First, four patterns are provided that illustrate typical scenarios for opening up a portfolio of hardware-based software products, with the goal of creating extendible software platforms. The four patterns are SIMPLE SERVER EXTENSION, COORDINATING SERVER EXTENSION,

FEDERATED SERVER EXTENSION, and ADVANCED UI EXTENSION. We provide a background on the history of the creation of the four patterns to illustrate their history and use. Secondly, the (architecture) challenges of doing so in a large company like NetComp, in a centralized fashion, are highlighted and provide interesting insights and challenges. The insights presented illustrate the advantages of centrally coordinating platformization and ecosystem efforts and the division of responsibilities in an organization that has a large product portfolio. Thirdly, several challenges of launching a platform around a hardware and software product portfolio are presented: how to open up different systems, how to document their extendible interfaces, how product and extension error messages must be propagated through the systems and organization, how crashes must be handled, and how extendible interfaces must be secured without becoming useless.

The FloodGate Department still has a large amount of work in front of it. Although the architectures are now ready for extension, the management of the ecosystem and the coordination practices of partners are still immature and varying across product departments. Secondly, the FloodGate Department would like to unify the code bases as much as possible, which is introducing an interesting architectural challenge of supporting different technologies, while keeping all in one code base and collection of software artifacts.

On the academic side, there are challenges as well. First, we plan to create a collection of platform extensibility patterns, i.e., patterns that aim to enable the creation of an ecosystem around a product, similar to our work in multi-tenant patterns [9]. Secondly, we are working on a software ecosystem management maturity matrix (SEM^3) that enables companies to evaluate their ecosystem management practices and advance them based on a set of strategic requirements, based on our earlier work [7].

References

1. Anvaari, M., Jansen, S.: Evaluating architectural openness in mobile software platforms. In: Proceedings of the Fourth European Conference on Software Architecture: Companion Volume, pp. 85–92. ACM (2010)
2. Goeminne, M., Mens, T.: A framework for analysing and visualising open source software ecosystems. In: Proceedings of IWPSE-EVOL, pp. 42–47 (2010)
3. Hanssen, G.K.: Opening up software product line engineering. In: Proceedings of the 2010 ICSE Workshop on Product Line Approaches in Software Engineering, pp. 1–7. ACM (2010)
4. Jansen, S., Brinkkemper, S., Finkelstein, A.: Component assembly mechanisms and relationship intimacy in a software supply network. In: 15th International Annual EurOMA Conference, Special Interest Session on Software Supply Chains (2008)
5. Jansen, S., Brinkkemper, S., Hunink, I., Demir, C.: Pragmatic and opportunistic reuse in innovative start-up companies. IEEE Software 25(6), 42–49 (2008)
6. Jansen, S., Brinkkemper, S., Souer, J., Luinenburg, L.: Shades of gray: Opening up a software producing organization with the open software enterprise model. Journal of Systems and Software 85(7), 1495–1510 (2012)

7. Jansen, S., Cusumano, M.A., Brinkkemper, S.: Software Ecosystems: Analyzing and Managing Business Networks in the Software Industry. Edward Elgar Publishing (2013)
8. Kabbedijk, J.: Variability in Multi-Tenant Enterprise Software. Utrecht University, Department of Information and Computing Sciences (2014)
9. Kabbedijk, J., Salfischberger, T., Jansen, S.: Comparing two architectural patterns for dynamically adapting functionality in online software products. In: The Fifth International Conferences on Pervasive Patterns and Applications, PATTERNS 2013, pp. 20–25 (2013)
10. Manikas, K., Hansen, K.M.: Software ecosystems – a systematic literature review. Journal of Systems and Software **86**(5), 1294–1306 (2013)
11. Toft, P., Coleman, D., Ohta, J.: A cooperative model for cross-divisional product development for a software product line. In: Software Product Lines, pp. 111–132. Springer (2000)
12. Wnuk, K., Manikas, K., Runeson, P., Lantz, M., Weijden, O., Munir, H.: Evaluating the governance model of hardware-dependent software ecosystems – a case study of the axis ecosystem. In: Lassenius, C., Smolander, K. (eds.) ICSOB 2014. LNBIP, vol. 182, pp. 212–226. Springer, Heidelberg (2014)
13. Wnuk, K., Runeson, P., Lantz, M., Weijden, O.: Bridges and barriers to hardware-dependent software ecosystem participation – a case study. Information and Software Technology **56**(11), 1493–1507 (2014)

On the Social Dimensions of Architectural Decisions

Henry Muccini[1]([⊠]), Damian A. Tamburri[2], and V. Smrithi Rekha[3]

[1] DISIM Department, University of L'Aquila, L'Aquila, Italy
henry.muccini@univaq.it
[2] Politecnico di Milano, Milano, Italy
damianandrew.tamburri@polimi.it
[3] Amrita School of Business, Amrita Vishwa Vidyapeetham, Coimbatore, India
v_smrithirekha@cb.amrita.edu

Abstract. An architecture is recognised to be the output of a (group) design decision process. This process typically involves multiple stakeholders composed into a group with a socio-technical connotation.

From a group decision making perspective, the various stakeholders involved in a design decision process analyze a given problem, propose alternate solutions, indicate their preferred alternative, and arrive at a consensus on the best possible solution. From an organisational and social perspective, the various stakeholders involved in a decision process form an organisational social structure (OSS). These structures have a significant impact on project success.

In this work, we explore the overlaps and interconnections between group decision-making dynamics and the corresponding social and organisational dimensions, in the context of architectural knowledge management. We use a meta-model to illustrate these overlaps and interconnections.

1 Introduction

In addition to technical aspects, the ***human and social aspects*** of projects play a significant role in determining the quality of software systems. James Herbsleb, in his keynote at ICSE 2014 the 36th International Conference on Software Engineering), has emphasized the significance of socio-technical coordination in software projects. It is clearly visible through empirical and observational studies that the way people work together, the information they exchange, the number of people interacting and the specific rules they employ has a direct impact on group productivity and outcome [1].

In this context, we have been studying the influence of *Group Decision Making (GDM)* principles on the Software Architecture (SA) decision making process. In the past few years, SA has evolved from being a diagrammatic representation to comprehensive set of *Group Design Decisions* [2,3].

In parallel, along the line of social aspects of software architectures and decision making thereof consists in what we refer as OSS, that is, *organisational social structure*. An OSS is the set of interactions, patterned relations

© Springer International Publishing Switzerland 2015
D. Weyns et al. (Eds.): ECSA 2015, LNCS 9278, pp. 137–145, 2015.
DOI: 10.1007/978-3-319-23727-5_11

and social arrangements emerging between individuals part of the same endeavour [4]. The emerging web of relations, dependencies, collaborations and social interactions they will be part of, is a set of non-trivial patterns (therefore a "structure") which entails people (therefore "social"). These people act as an organised whole, focusing on a particular goal (therefore "organisational") [4]. Empirical software engineering already pointed out the considerable importance of looking at organisational structure as a proxy for software quality [5] avoiding both technical and social debt [6]. Though some of these have been adopted by the Software Engineering community, a large part is yet to be studied and applied when architecting software systems, especially in the industry.

Stemming from these premises, *in this paper we elaborate on the dimensions added by looking at organisational and social structures jointly to group decision-making.*

We found that there are several concepts in GDM that can be further expanded with additional dimensions of complexity if organisational and social structures come into play. For example, how does the social dynamics between formal (or informal) members in a working group change the decision-making process? Similarly, do Problem-Solving Communities [4] assist in the creation of good-quality and resilient architectures? Also, GDM literature typically pivots around internal (i.e., decision internalising factors on software architectures) and external (i.e., decisions to allow architecture to cope with external factors) decisions.

2   Background on Group Decision-Making and Organisational-Social Structures

Group Decision Making (GDM) in management research has received good amount of attention and has found application in several domains including software engineering. GDM involves a group of stakeholders analyzing a given problem, proposing alternate solutions, indicating their preferred alternative through voting or ranking and arriving at a consensus on the best possible solution [7]. Risks, uncertainty and conflicts are inherent to any GDM process. These issues have also been observed when we studied real-world software architects in [3]. Also, in practice it has been observed that as the number of alternatives increases, the uncertainty also increases and this is more so when several stakeholders are involved. Hence minimizing uncertainty is a key aspect of any GDM process [8]. There are several GDM techniques both formal and informal. Some of them include brainstorming, voting, delphi, nominal group technique and consensus based method. As reported in [3], practitioners are used to mix them.

Conversely, our research on *Organisational Social Structures* (OSS) for software engineering is motivated by work such as Nagappan et al. [5] that shows in practice the influence of organisational structure and other "human" aspects on software quality. We started elaborating on the role that organisational and social structures play in software engineering. In [4] we elaborated a Systematic Literature Review (SLR) on OSSs and ways in which they can be detected.

In addition, motivated by works in organisational decision-making (e.g., off-shoring) we found sample arenas in which organisational and social structures can assume sub-optimal forms and social debt emerges [6]. We found that knowing whether the organisational layout of a company is performant (or even compatible) with certain decision is vital, e.g., to measure the social debt [9] for relevant decisions.

3   GDM and OSS: Annotated Metamodels

Inspired by our previous works on GDM in Software Architecture [3] and the General Group Problem-Solving Model [10], we have generated a metamodel for *Group Decision Making* as shown in Figure 1. `Group` represents a collection of

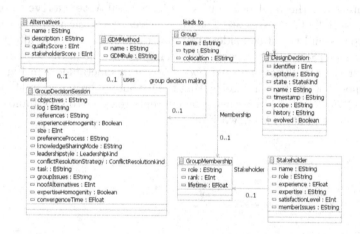

Fig. 1. Group Decision Making Metamodel

stakeholders who are from different hierarchical levels in the organization. The `Group` is defined by attributes *name, type* and *colocation*. `Group Membership` denotes the participation of *stakeholder* in a specific group. Each member of the group has a specific *role* in the group. The *rank* attribute denotes the position of a stakeholder in the group. The period for which the members work together is recorded in *lifetime*. `Stakeholder` denotes the people who are active members of the group and organization. The *role, experience* and the *expertise* attributes are related to the profile of the stakeholder. At the end of the GDM process, the *satisfaction level* of the stakeholder with respect to the various aspects of GDM is recorded with the help of a questionnaire and the responses are summed up. A `GroupDecisionSession` represents a single continuous meeting, or a series of meetings of a *group* of stakeholders. Each group decision session has a set of *objectives*. The *experienceHomogenity* and *expertiseHomogenity* attributes indicate whether the group members have homogeneous or heterogeneous experience and expertise. Group *size* plays a significant role in the performance and efficiency of group. There are different ways that groups use to transfer and share knowledge amongst its members. The *knowledgeSharingMode* attribute is explained in the ensuing section. There are different leadership styles and some popular ones include Directive Participatory, Facilitative, Evocative and Provocative[1]. Each session has a specific *task* to execute and this keeps the group focused on the task. Conflicts and issues are common to the group which are recorded in *groupIssues* and the resolution method is indicated in *conflictResolutionStrategy*. The total number of alternatives in a session is recored under *noofAlternatives*. The time taken to arrive at a consensus varies from session to session and this can be indicated in *convergenceTime*. Each session could use a different GDM method i.e `GDMMethod` depending on the task at hand. If the group prefers, they could use the same method throughout the lifecycle of the project. Each GDM method is associated with a specific *gdmRule* which decides how the preferences are computed and the final decision is made. Several `Alternatives` are generated in a specific GDM session. The alternatives are given a *qualityScore* by domain experts and the stakeholders can also rank/score/vote the alternatives under *stakeholderScore*. These scores play an important role in the final decision.

Consider the *Organisational and Social Structures* metamodel in Figure 2[2]. The metamodel stems from reinterpreting the taxonomy proposed in [4] as seen through a GDM lens, i.e., by focusing on concepts relevant to GDM and within the community definition framework in [4].

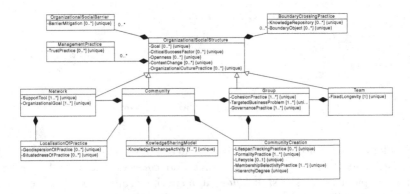

Fig. 2. Organizational Social Structure Metamodel

In essence, an *Organisational-Social Structure* is a super type of four essential community types, namely *Networks, Communities, Groups and Teams*, characterised by a series of attributes common to any OSS as well as attributes peculiar to a type. For example, all *Communities* are made for sharing, especially sharing of knowledge and possibly experience. Also, *Networks* suggest the presence

[1] http://www.co-intelligence.org/leadership-5styles.html
[2] A larger Figure is available here: http://tinyurl.com/ngka39t.

of digital or technological support tools to overcome great distance (geoloca-
tional and/or cultural) however we found this [4] explicitly only for Networks
of Practice [4]. In addition, *Groups* are tightly knit sets of people or agencies
that pursue an organisational goal. The goal/objective is usually dictated by
an *organisational sponsor* who enforces a number of *governance practices* (more
or less formal) e.g., for selecting and appointing *members*. Finally, *Teams* are
specifically assembled (ad-hoc) sets of people with a diversified and complementary set of skills working on a specific mission for a quantified period of time,
i.e., they constitute a community with *fixed longevity*.

This not withstanding, all the above types may be further elaborated into additional levels of granularity. For example, "network" community types may consist (and, in fact, do consist of hybrids of formal networks, informal networks or
networks of practice. Similarly, a "Community" may assume the shape, form and
characteristics of communities of practice, Informal communities, knowledge communities or learning communities. In essence, the challenge lies in striking the right
combination of community attributes such that an equilibrium is reached between
GDM, software development and operations requirements. Frameworks such as
the one we presented in [4] may assume the role of rudimentary compasses to help
managers assess and establish said equilibrium of characteristics (e.g., formality
levels, ROI, competitiveness, knowledge-sharing, knowledge protection, etc.).

Besides the previously mentioned characteristics, any OSS can be exposed to
one or more *organisational barriers*, i.e., impediments, social, organisational or
otherwise that hinder the harmonious operation across the OSS. For example,
formal knowledge exchange protocols constitute a barrier to activities across the
OSS. In overcoming barriers, organisations employ specific *management* or *mitigation* strategies, aimed at resolving or relaxing the limitations and impediments
connected to the barrier.

Finally, all OSS types typically involve a number of boundary crossing practices, i.e., aimed at disseminating to the OSS external environment and context,
whatever practice, knowledge or contribution is produced inside the OSS. Said
knowledge exchange can take place by means of specific *boundary objects*. For
example, IFIP workgroups[3] publish internal proceedings, news or similar.

3.1 GDM-OSS Interconnections as Social Dimensions for Architecture Decisions

We found four essential overlaps revolving around the concept of "Groups",
"Decisions", "Stakeholder" and "Membership". It seems that these overlaps
are essentially new dimensions orthogonal to GDM but extremely related and
impactful w.r.t. relying on resilient GDM practices, e.g. to achieve anti-fragility
at the architecture level. Also, these dimensions seem to suggest the following
points of discussion.

Since "Groups" and "Membership" are social network concepts, it seems
that exploring the use of social network analysis in achieving group fitness, e.g.,

---

[3] http://www.ifip.org/

with the selected GDM approach might be a first step in establishing what social aggregation means is most efficient for decision-making. Since "Decisions" and "Groups" imply a number of social and cognitive concepts (e.g., cognitive distance, cognitive biases, etc.) it is reasonable to start exploring the variables connected to complex organisational structures involved in decision-making since complex structures complicate cognitive processes within [4]. Lastly, "Decision" and "Membership" and the emergent relations in-between, seem to imply some sort of decision ownership and, similarly, accountability. Perhaps GDM dynamics should be studied in combination with OSSs as mechanisms that represent the structure of accountability within development networks [11]. What's more, this problem would assume global proportions in distributed scenarios. In addition, there are at least 3 areas of the extended Architecture Design Decisions meta-model, in which Organisational and Social structures play a major role when combined with GDM, as evident from Figure 3.

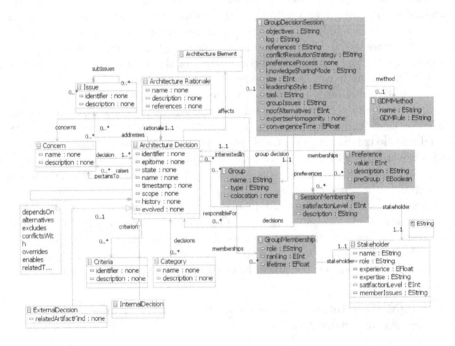

Fig. 3. Extended ADD Metamodel with GDM and OSS

▷ The *Group* metaclass. Looking at the metamodel through the looking glass of organizations research, managers and researchers might wonder: "what kind of group are we talking about?", that is, there are several group layouts that vary considerably in terms of organisational norms, or adopted decision culture and processes. For example, literature summarised in [4] reports at least three such types, namely, "ProfessionalDevelopmentGroup", "WorkGroup" and "Interest-Group". In essence, establishing the best-fitting group structure is key to maximise efficiency in terms of decision-making and/or problem-solving regarding architecture resilience. We observe that the location of group members vary with OSS, while some Communities involve colocated members, Networks involve dispersed members. Hence we have added a colocation attribute indicating Yes/No. Also, in terms of system architecting, there might be group-structures that are best-fit to solving problems (e.g., Problem-Solving Communities, as reported in literature [4]), and for which architecture and system failure is a means to generate new best-practices towards resilience and overall system architecting.

▷ The *GroupDecisionSession* metaclass. Looking at the definition and concerns behind this metaclass from a knowledge-creation standpoint, managers and researchers might wonder: "Does the decision session map onto the typical pattern(s) in knowledge creation? if so, how can the pattern be supported in software engineering? if not, how can conformance be improved?". GDM researchers clearly indicate that the amount and mode of knowledge sharing influences the quality of decisions and hence the resultant systems. How knowledge is transferred from the various quadrants of the Nonaka model [12] and which quadrant yields most effective knowledge passages functional to achieving resilience might be useful in identifying successful GDM patterns. The mode of knowledge sharing will also be impacted by the GDM Method and tools used. For instance, the *Socialization* mode may be more predominant in Brainstorming sessions, *Externalization* may be more seen incase of more structured methods like Delphi technique, *Combination* may be possible while using Group Decision Support Systems (GDDSS) and *Internalization* may be seen in several of these methods. We have also added a size attribute since size of group varies depending on the OSS. The leadershipStyle attribute will highlight the nature of leadership in a particular group decision session. Some OSS requires Strong/Directive style of leadership while some others may require facilitative style. Inorder to account for the *Social Debt* that may occur during group meetings, we have added issueFactors that document the issues that arise in a particular session. We observe that each OSS has different composition and hence taking clues from GDM literature, we have added homogeneous to indicate whether the group is a homogeneous or hetergenous in composition. The number of alternatives is key to the quality of system designed, hence the addition of attribute textttnoOfAlternatives.

▷ The *GroupMembership* metaclass. We found that, in order to assume an organisational perspective, the metamodel needs to include constructs for the experience and expertise of the stakeholder(s). Experience refers to the number of years in the organization or in a particular role. Expertise refers to the skill sets of a stakeholder and domain expertise. Both these are key aspects in differentiating organizational structures adopted. For instance, Strategic Communities and Communities of Practice require high level of experience and expertise from stakeholders. *GroupMembership* will also include lifetime of group to indicate if the group members are together for a specfic task for a short period of time or for a longer period of time. The role and ranking attributes have been expanded to include hierarchical levels depending on the OSS. For example, `Problem Solving Communities` involve organizational sponsors themselves as members.

▷ The *GDMMethod* metaclass indicates the method used by the group. Depending on the OSS, the procedure used to make the final decision varies. Some OSS may use aggregation of votes while some may use pairwise comparison. We have added the `gdmRule` to take care of the rules that are used to make the final decision.

4   Conclusions and Research Roadmap

The objective of this paper was to look ahead at the overlaps and additional dimensions stemming from combining theories on GDM with concepts and findings from organisations and social networks research and how these impact GDM processes.

From our preliminary analysis, we observed that organizations and social-networks research models such as the one elaborated in [4] represent a parallel universe with important overlapping dimensions and restrictions to be applied on GDM. Also, we learned that the four dimensions across which the overlaps were identified, namely, *Groups, Sessions, Decisions* and *Membership*, reflect a number of interesting well-established concepts from social-networks analysis (SNA) such as group cohesion [13] or cognitive distance [14].

In the future we plan to elaborate further on these preliminary insights thorough solid empirical research, e.g., focusing on understanding which group structure from [4] may be more successful in GDM or, conversely, which group structure is more widely adopted in (self-)organised groups for decision-making[4].

In so doing, key research questions may have to be addressed, such as the following:

- *What is the best-fit OSS combination for effective GDM?* Empirically establishing the effectiveness of multiple organisational and social structure types blended together may be critical for showing that certain GDM practices are effective when enacted within those community blends.
- *How can we quantify the efficiency of GDM in certain OSS?* Much study in social networks and organisations research remains qualitative in nature. Managers seldom conduct such expensive studies, relying more on numbers and practical metrics. More research may be needed to find and validate said metrics.

References

1. Saaty, T.L., Vargas, L.G.: Decision making with the analytic network process. Springer (2006)
2. Kruchten, P.: An ontology of architectural design decisions in software intensive systems. In: 2nd Groningen Workshop Software Variability, pp. 54–61 (2004)

---

[4] The work of one of the authors has been partially supported by the European Commission grant no. 610531 (FP7 ICT Call 10), SeaClouds.

3. Rekha, V.S., Muccini, H.: A study on group decision-making in software architecture. In: Proc. WICSA 2014 the 11th Working IEEE/IFIP Conf. on Software Architecture (2014)
4. Tamburri, D.A., Lago, P., van Vliet, H.: Organizational social structures for software engineering. ACM Computing Surveys, 1–35 (2012)
5. Nagappan, N., Murphy, B., Basili, V.: The influence of organizational structure on software quality: an empirical case study. In: International conference on Software Engineering, Leipzig, Germany, pp. 521–530. IEEE (2008)
6. Tamburri, D.A., Kruchten, P., Lago, P., van Vliet, H.: What is social debt in software engineering? In: 2013 6th International Workshop on Cooperative and Human Aspects of Software Engineering (CHASE), pp. 93–96 (2013)
7. Nutt, P.C., Wilson, D.C.: Handbook of decision making. John Wiley & Sons (2010)
8. Marian-Mihai, C.: Collaborative decision-making platform for participatory structures and group decision-making bodies. Business Excellence and Management **2**(1), 31–40 (2012)
9. Tamburri, D.A., Di Nitto, E.: When architecting leads to social debt. In: Proceedings of the 2015 IEEE/IFIP Conference on Software Architecture, WICSA 2015, Washington, DC, USA, pp. 247–250. IEEE Computer Society (2015)
10. Aldag, R.J., Fuller, S.R.: Beyond fiasco: A reappraisal of the groupthink phenomenon and a new model of group decision processes. Psychological Bulletin **113**(3), 533 (1993)
11. de Souza, C.R.B., Redmiles, D.F.: The Awareness Network, To Whom Should I Display My Actions? And, Whose Actions Should I Monitor? IEEE TSE **37**(3), 325–340 (2011)
12. Nonaka, I., Toyama, R., Konno, N.: SECI, ba and leadership: A unified model of dynamic knowledge creation. Long Range Planning **33**, 5–34 (2000)
13. Otte, E., Rousseau, R.: Social network analysis: a powerful strategy, also for the information sciences. Journal of Information Science **28**(6), 441–453 (2002)
14. Gallagher, S.: Introduction: The arts and sciences of the situated body. Janus Head **9**(2), 1–2 (2006)

A Specialised Social Network Software Architecture for Efficient Household Water Use Management

Zhenchen Wang[✉] and Andrea Capiluppi

Brunel University London, Kingston Lane, Uxbridge, Middlesex UB8 3PH, UK
{zhenchen.wang,andrea.capiluppi}@brunel.ac.uk

Abstract. Specialised, or vertical, social networks (SSN) are emerging as a useful tool to address practical issues such as household water use management. Despite the perceived benefits, the design of such systems is still not fully aware of the social interactions or the incentives that could be used to change user's behaviours when engaging with the network and peers. In this work, we propose and demonstrate the software architecture of a social network aimed at the efficient management of water in households, defining and connecting specialised system components. Three aspects are relevant in this work: first, the architecture explicitly defines components that support social interactions, in the context of existing water management instruments. Second, the architecture defines components addressing openness, which enable easy communication with external resources. Third, as part of a gamification ecosystem, universal and transferable rewards are proposed to incentivise the expected online and offline behaviours.

Keywords: Software architecture · Software engineering · Specialised social network · Social interaction

1 Introduction

A system architecture is usually the result of a set of decisions, taking into account multiple factors such as the input of expert knowledge, technical constraints and available resources. Before finalising a system architecture, the designing process can be problematic especially when 1) the software is specialised but needs to target audiences with different expertises and 2) its interfaces may require to be open to heterogeneous systems. SSN (Specialised social network) software is one of such kind. The recent developments of SSN software enables existing specialised software to address the practical issues of niche, specialised groups, addressing broader issues concerning the whole society. As an example, in the FP7 EU Project ISS-EWATUS[1] a SSN software is used to manage the efficient household water use. The SSN allows users to interact with the communities via a range of activities such as i) sharing water bill with friends, ii) monitoring municipal water use statistics, iii) asking and answering water use questions, and iv) entering competitions sponsored by external stakeholders by completing

---

[1] http://issewatus.eu

© Springer International Publishing Switzerland 2015
D. Weyns et al. (Eds.): ECSA 2015, LNCS 9278, pp. 146–153, 2015.
DOI: 10.1007/978-3-319-23727-5_12

specific water conservation tasks offline. While this SSN paradigm is becoming popular, there are also concomitant software design challenges when designing such systems.

1. Aligning User Interactions with System's Objectives: One of the features of a SSN software is that it allows users to interact with other users. The interactions need to be clearly defined, so that the social interactions between users can support the overall system objectives, such as achieving the household water-use efficiency. This task can be tricky especially when considering the SSN system objectives and user preferences or approaches in online social interactions.

2. SSN Ecosystems and Incentives: Since a SSN can be used to help users to positively change behaviours such as in a more efficient water use, the system should define a set of "incentives" to encourage positive change in user behaviours. Existing approaches to incentives for users include obtaining reputation, points, prizes etc., which can be designed and deployed to motivate users to engage more and more often in a SSN. However, planning and delivering these incentives means proposing to the users a set of instruments to support their online and offline tasks, which can be specific to a problem domain. Moreover, these incentives can be SSN specific which makes these problematic to be reused, accumulated or redeemed within other social networks.

3. Interface Openness: Addressing a global issue like the efficient water usage is a concern of the whole society, and it requires the participation of many (if not all) water stakeholders. An SSN, even if specialised, should be designed to reach as many audiences as possible, and part of these audiences can be also using other social network systems, or expertise systems. As a result, the openness of interfaces is required for transparency and integration between social networks. However, this poses an inherent difficulty, in particular when the external system interfaces are unknown or incompatible with the designed SN system interfaces (e.g., when finding a match between user names and identities in the various SNs, etc.).

In this paper, we explore the possibility of a SSN architecture to address the above three challenges, i.e. 1) to model and define the social interactions used in a SSN targeting the efficient water use management at household level; 2) to model and define the incentives that support a user's behavioural change in online and offline water usage; 3) to allow the system to be easily accessed or integrated within an heterogeneous ecosystem.

The presented system architecture is currently being used in the ISS-EWATUS project. We expect that the work presented here can serve as an additional system architecture modelling method, on top of existing software engineering processes. We also expect that our work can be extended and customised for designing and implementing a SNN in other social problem domains.

The rest of the paper is organised as follows. In section 2, related works are reviewed in terms of SSN interactions, social network's implications on user behaviour change and SSN access and openness. The proposed architecture is presented and discussed in Section 3. Section 4 concludes and outlooks the work.

2   Related Works

2.1   Specialised Social Networks and Online Social Interactions

The reasons for why social networks are becoming one of the most popular topics studied by both authorities and researchers can partly be attributed to the growing number of users and different types of features made available for interacting with users [10]. There are privacy regulations and grouping methods specially designed for social network such as in [5] and [1], and there are also implications found from using social networks. For example, users of social network sites are more likely to enact a certain behaviour if they could observe their contacts exhibiting the same behaviour before [2,3]. SSN further extends the common social network to target a niche group of users concerning certain specialised issues. Existing SSNs from related works are more often used as a platform to improve the quality of engineering tasks and to target group of expert users. For example, in [11], a SSN is used to help software developers gaining awareness of relevant software tools by enabling them to learn from their peers. In [4] and [7], the SSN was used to empower communities to discuss and extract high-level design features or design patterns. In this work, we use a newly developed SSN to target common users and specially defined online interactions as a set of instruments supporting the efficient household water use management.

2.2   SSN Incentives and Behaviour Change

Incentives are often used to encourage people to engage in the activities available on social networks. In [8] it was found that behavioural change was more likely to occur if physical (i.e. real) rewards were offered. A virtual reward system (such as scores, stars, reputations and badges), as one of the incentives, is a common practice in many social networks. Gamification is a further recent development of virtual rewards and the gamification here refers to the use of game design elements in non-game contexts [15]. Reasons for why such a reward system is successful can be explained by using the behavioural model proposed in [6], the model argued that activities requiring different difficulty levels, will also correspondingly require different motivation levels for a person to do it.

Another type of reward is the private personal rewards which are strongly dependent upon individuals and they do not have explicit forms. Individual can only expect to receive private personal rewards by participating in social network interactions [12,16] and these rewards cannot be measured objectively. Here, we propose to use universal virtual rewards to be collected, reused and redeemed in an ecosystem of SSNs, in order to encourage more quickly the expected behaviours.

2.3   SSN Access and Openness

The main challenge for SSNs thus is to share content with heterogeneous systems including other social network systems and mobile terminals software. This is difficult when there are a variety of candidate technical options for developing a SSN, e.g. technologies used to build a SSN can include Java, JavaScript, AJAX, PHP, HTML, MySQL, FOAF, SPARQL, RSS, ATOM, etc. Existing solutions are mainly relying on communication protocol specific Web services e.g. SOAP [9] is used to communicate with external systems for service discovery and invocation. In [17] and [18] Restful Service is used for external systems communications. In the proposed system architecture, Restful Web services are chosen to support data exchange between loosely coupled components including infrastructural resources such as smart water meters and external social networks.

3   Towards a SSN Software Architecture for Efficient Household Water Use

There are different ways to create a system architecture. The system architecture presented here is component-based and it supports high cohesions within the components. This allows the system to perform well-defined functions and to loose the coupling between components. A component can be any software package, Web service or module that encapsulates a related set of functions or data [13]. The advantages of using a component based architecture include: Ease of development and deployment, reduced cost (e.g. free third party components) and reusability.

The ISS-EWATUS SSN system architecture consists of a set of components, working together in a distributed configuration. The ISS-EWATUS social media platform also uses resources offered by external components that are not themselves part of the platform, e.g., smart water meters in households to monitor water consumption. Users can interact with the system through application(s) on their mobile phone, or by using a more traditional web browser. The architecture (see Fig. 1) groups the ISS-EWATUS components into three categories, i.e. the ISS-EWATUS social media service, a Web portal, and external resources. After deploying the system, we envision the SSN will be able to provide the following features:

- **Online social interactions for efficient water use:** the social interactions will be used as instruments managing efficient water use and they are defined by referring to the efficient water use theory.
- **Universal Rewards for online and offline behaviours:** the expected interactive behaviours including online interactions and offline water saving activities will be rewarded. The metrics are based upon the data retrieved from external and internal components handling the user activities.
- **Openness:** The platform will make its interfaces open for integration with other social networking applications to share content. And its reward system will also simplify the communication between different social networking applications.

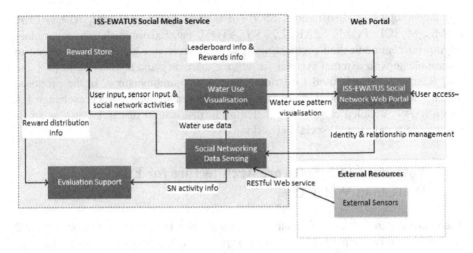

Fig. 1. ISS-EWATUS social media platform system architecture

3.1   ISS-EWATUS Social Media Service

There are four subcomponents within the ISS-EWATUS social media services: the Social Networking Data Sensing, the Reward Store, evaluation support and the Water Use Visualisation.

Social Networking Data Sensing

The Social Networking Data Sensing is primarily used to handle the data from user input and the data from external monitoring systems. These data include user identity, user online activities and those from other social networks. Apart from identifying and validating these data, the component also logs the data and dispenses the validated data to the expected components so that related components within the ISS-EWATUS social media service can always get the expected input.

ISS-EWATUS defines a set of social networking interactions in two steps. The first step is to define them based upon existing popular online social network interactions (including sharing information; getting recommendations; organising social events; playing games and keeping in touch with friends); The second step is to classified and tailored to support the efficient water use by referencing to the WCM (water conservation management) theory [14]. In the WCM, there are five categories of instruments used for efficient water use, they are: a) engineering (i.e. physical WCM equipment); b) economics (i.e. water price related information); c) enforcement (i.e. penalty measurements on water waste); d) encouragement (i.e. endorsement on water conservation behaviour); e) education (i.e. distribution on water conservation knowledge). Table 1 shows a set of social networking interactions defined in the ISS-EWATUS.

Table 1. Social networking interactions in ISS-EWATUS in terms of WCM theory

Instruments	Social Networking Interactions
Engineering	Completing a gamification offline task and win a physical prize
Economics	Sharing water readings with friends
Enforcement/ Encouragement	Reviewing information/recommendations with comments
Education	Sharing tips on water conservation; Take part in discussion; Reviewing information/recommendations with comments; Organising wise water use discussion; Playing water saving educational games

Reward Store

The Reward Store plays a key role in designing the social network tasks for the users. It is responsible for the user task design, rewards definitions, user task monitoring and reward calculations. The system will offer a GUI (graphical user interface) for designing task in terms of a set of task properties and the required time frame to complete the tasks and rewards for the tasks. The rewards can be defined in terms of points, badges and other virtual objects. Upon completion of tasks, the reward store will assign calculated rewards to the users.

In ISS-EWATUS, the rewards are designed to be universally recognised by leveraging the open credit systems such as credly.com[2]. The benefits of doing this are twofold. First, this enables users to further use the rewards gained, e.g. to reuse or redeem the rewards gained from ISS-EWATUS for other services or goods elsewhere. Secondly, this, to an extent, helps promote the integration in an ecosystem consisted of systems of different domains especially if they share the same target users.

Evaluation Support

The Evaluation Support collects data from the reward store and the ISS-EWATUS Data sensing. It can produce the summative results of rewarding and other social network activities occurred within a defined time frame. The Evaluation Support is also designed to facilitate researchers to perform scientific functions such as statistical hypothesis tests. The stats indicators can be defined from inside or outside the ISS-EWATUS systems depending on the system goal. For example if the system goal is to reduce household water consumption lever by 5 %, then the indicator will be the readings of the water meter. There are different options to retrieve the information required by an indicator. Furthering the example above, other than asking a user to input the readings to the social network system, the meter readings can be automatically read by an external system, e.g. as a smart metering system used in ISS-EWATUS where fewer human interventions are required.

---

[2] http://credly.com/

Water Visualisation

The Water Use Visualizer defines the information required for describe water use pattern such as temporal, spatial, activity and cost. Water user visualizer will offer interfaces to receive defined data from other external components, it will also offer interface to end users to allow them to input information that cannot be obtained from external resources.

3.2   Web Portal

The Web Portal allows users with different access terminals such as smart phones, PCs to access the services offered by the platform. Apart from the authentication process provided by the ISS-EWATUS platform, users can also log in with third party social networks credentials, such as Facebook, Twitter etc.

3.3   External Resources

The *External Resources* include the smart water meters and external social networks that the platform will communicate with and they also include the household decision support systems and water companies decision support systems. The user profiles and water use related information can be shared among all these resources. The ISS-EWATUS platform is able to offer anonymous online user profiles and rewarding information to heterogeneous systems. The data exchanges are done via Restful Web services.

4   Conclusion and Further Work

We presented a software architecture with the aim of supporting the design and the implementation of a specialized social network system for managing efficient household water use. We demonstrated how the architecture addresses the related challenges by defining and orchestrating the proposed components. A special attention is given to the openness of the interfaces and the interaction of the proposed architecture with an ecosystem of related platforms, with which our platform will be able to share the results of the interactions between users as well as the points gained in the proposed activities.

The next steps are to implement and to evaluate the proposed approach in the context of the ISS-EWATUS European project. We aim to find out how effective the social interactions and incentives can influence users' behaviours. This will be done via two methods, one is via continuous collecting and analysing the quantitative data from the systems including both within the platform and associated external systems; and the other is to analyse the qualitative data periodically retrieved from questionnaires and focus groups on using the system within and outside the project consortium.

Acknowledgement. This work has been undertaken within the framework of the ISS-EWATUS, Integrated Support System for Efficient Water Usage and Resources Management, FP7 project (grant no. 619228), funded by the European Community.

References

1. Borcea, C., Gupta, A., Kalra, A., Jones, Q., Tftode, L.: The MobiSoC middleware for mobile social computing: challenges, design, and early experiences. In: Proceedings of Mobile Wireless Middleware, Operating Systems, and Applications (2008)

2. Burke, M., Marlow, C., Lento, T.: Feed me: motivating newcomer contribution in social network sites. In: Proceedings of the 27th International Conference on Human Factors in Computing Systems, pp. 945–954. ACM (2009)

3. Centola, D.: The spread of behavior in an online social network experiment. Science **329**(5996), 1194 (2010)

4. Dietrich, J., Jones N.: Using social networking and semantic web technology in software engineering–use cases, patterns, and a case study. In: 18th Australian Software Engineering Conference, ASWEC 2007, pp. 129–136, April 10–13, 2007

5. Directive 2002/58/EC of the European Parliament and of the Council, July 12, 2002

6. Fogg, B.: A behavior model for persuasive design. In: Proceedings of the 4th International Conference on Persuasive Technology (Persuasive 2009), Article 40, 7 p. ACM, New York (2009)

7. Greenwood, P., Rashid, A., Walkerdine, J.: UDesignIt: towards social media for community-driven design. In: 2012 34th International Conference on Software Engineering (ICSE), pp. 1321–1324, June 2–9, 2012

8. Grizzell, J.: Behaviour Change Theories and Models: relating to health promotion and education efforts. American College Health Association (2003)

9. Michlrnayr, A., Leitner, P., Rosenberg, F., Dustdar, S.: Publish/subscribe in the VRESCo SOA runtirne. In: Proceedings of Distributed Event-Based Systems (2008)

10. Miklas, A.G., Gollu, K.K., Chan, K.K., Saroiu, S., Gummadi, K.P., de Lara, E.: Exploiting social interactions in mobile systems. In: Krumm, J., Abowd, G.D., Seneviratne, A., Strang, T. (eds.) UbiComp 2007. LNCS, vol. 4717, pp. 409–428. Springer, Heidelberg (2007)

11. Murphy-Hill, E.: Continuous social screencasting to facilitate software tool discovery. In: 2012 34th International Conference on, Software Engineering (ICSE), pp. 1317–1320, June 2–9, 2012

12. Olson, M.: The logic of collective action: Public goods and the theory of groups. Harvard University Press, Cambridge (1971)

13. Rainer, N.: Software Component Architecture [PDF]. http://congress.cimne.upc.es/cfsi/frontal/doc/ppt/11.pdf

14. Savenjie, H., Van, Z.: Water as an economic good and demand management, paradigms with pitfalls. International Water Resources Association, Water International **27**(1), 98–104 (2002)

15. Sebastian, D., Dan, D., Rilla, K., Lennart, N.: From game design elements to gamefulness: defining "Gamification". In: Proceedings of MindTrek 2011. ACM (2011)

16. Tullock, G.: The paradox of revolution. Public Choice **11**, 89–99 (1971)

17. Zhang, C., Cheng, C., Ji, Y.: Architecture design for social web of things. In: Proceedings of the 1st International Workshop on Context Discovery and Data Mining (ContextDD 2012). ACM, New York (2012)

18. Zhong, Y., Zhao, W., Yang, J.: Personal-hosting RESTful web services for social network based recommendation. In: Kappel, G., Maamar, Z., Motahari-Nezhad, H.R. (eds.) ICSOC 2011. LNCS, vol. 7084, pp. 661–668. Springer, Heidelberg (2011)

Education and Training

An Approach to Software Architecting
in Agile Software Development Projects in Education

Samuil Angelov[✉] and Patrick de Beer

Software Engineering, Fontys University of Applied Sciences, Eindhoven, The Netherlands
{s.angelov,p.debeer}@fontys.nl

Abstract. The architecting activities in agile software development methods are weakly defined and even sometimes neglected. While there is sufficient literature on how software architectures and the architecting activities could be approached in agile projects, there is little information on how this topic should be treated in the education of software engineering students. In this paper, we propose an approach to the architecting activities in agile software projects in a bachelor software engineering course. The approach is inspired by theoretical and industry sources and is tailored to fit our educational goals and context. Our first experiences from the application of the approach show improved and deepened treating of software architectures, clarity on the purpose of the executed architecting activities, and improved student motivation.

Keywords: Software architecture · Agile · Method · Scrum · Teaching · Education

1   Introduction

The potential tension between software architecting and agile development methods has been discussed in numerous publications. A general consensus seems to exist around the value of paying explicit attention to software architectures in agile projects. Various suggestions have been made on how to approach software architecting in agile projects [1–3]. The introduction of software architectures and architecting related activities in educational curriculums has been a topic in several publications and multiple challenges and possible solutions have been outlined [4–6]. The coupling between agile projects and software architectures in education has not yet been sufficiently addressed in the literature. In [7], an approach for treating software architectures in agile projects in education is discussed. The approaches focuses on the architecture design phase in agile projects and specifically on the role of the stakeholders in it but does not address the actual dynamics of an agile project.

In our curriculum, we have a course in which software systems are developed by groups of students using an agile (Scrum-based) method. Among others, the students need to apply and demonstrate in this course competences in system design. In the past, we have required the design and documentation of the system's software architecture but did not provide any further guidance on how this had to be done in an agile project, relying on knowledge on software architectures from a previous course. We

© Springer International Publishing Switzerland 2015
D. Weyns et al. (Eds.): ECSA 2015, LNCS 9278, pp. 157–168, 2015.
DOI: 10.1007/978-3-319-23727-5_13

have observed the lack of motivation among students to deepen on the software architecture aspects, focusing primarily on the development process. The system architecture was hastily and superficially discussed in the teams at the beginning of the
projects and documented at the end of the projects to pass the course, without realizing the purpose and benefits of architecting in an agile project. To improve the educational process, we need to redesign the course in a form where software architectures
receive proper attention from the students in a non-enforced manner, ensuring understanding of the values of software architecting in agile projects. The challenges are,
however, of dual nature. An approach for treating software architecting in agile student projects needs to resolve traditional problems in teaching and applying software
architectures in combination with the challenges introduced by the agile practices
which do not emphasize the architecture topic.

In this paper, we present our approach towards the treatment of software architectures in agile software projects in education. We have reviewed publications in the
area of software architectures, approaches to software architectures in agile software
development, and teaching of software architectures. In parallel, we conducted interviews with practitioners to collect data on how software architecting in agile projects
is treated in the industry. The results from these two sources of information provide us
with the basis for the definition of our approach.

The paper is structured as follows. In section 2, we present our context. In Section 3, we discuss our finding from the sources reviewed. In Section 4, we present our
approach. In Section 5, we discuss our first experiences and lessons learned. We end
the paper with conclusions.

2   Context and Status

Fontys University of Applied Sciences focuses on teaching practice oriented knowledge and skills. Upon completion of their studies, students from the software engineering bachelor school are skilled software engineers. The course with an acronym
PTS4 is 6 ECTS credits (European Credit Transfer and Accumulation System credits)
and is given in the second semester of the second year of the software engineering
study. PTS4 is a project-based course, i.e., knowledge from other courses is applied in
this course for the design and development of a software system. PTS4 focuses on
applying agile practices in a Java-based, software development project. PTS4 is preceded by a project course PTS3[1]. The students work in groups of 5-6 students for 18
weeks. The students are allowed to form the groups themselves, which typically leads
to balanced groups in terms of skills, interests and motivation. Each week, the students work one full day on the project in a dedicated project room. On a weekly basis,
the students are visited in the project room by their Product Owner (PO) and Tutor
(typically both roles are performed by one teacher). Scrum masters are students from

---

[1] In PTS3, a waterfall-based software development method is used. The students follow a path for
requirements elicitation and documentation, architecture elicitation and documentation, implementation, testing. They elaborate an architecture document consisting of use case, class,
sequence, component and deployment diagrams and a list of non-functional requirements.

the teams. A commercial tool for agile project management (which also allows time management) is used by all groups. The project is divided into 4 sprints of 4 weeks with a couple of weeks left as spare. The project is based on a predefined case ("PhotoStore") for the development of an on-line shop for ordering of customized photos optionally printed on a product. In terms of quality attributes, the focus in this project lies mainly on usability, security, and performance. Example architectural choices that student face are: desktop versus web application, type of clients to the main application, communication techniques, security approach, storage and access of photos. The case lacks novelty and is therefore of a somewhat trivial architecture nature: "most projects are not novel enough to require a lot of architectural effort" [8]. Typically, the discussion, evaluation and documentation of a software architecture is a nuisance for the students. They do not perceive any value in performing these activities and prefer to focus on software development. Discussions on the architecture take 5-10 minutes, with no attention being paid to the quality attributes. Although, the students know what quality attributes are, their understanding of the value of architecting and the role of quality attributes is rather limited. The combination of low architecture complexity and little attention on quality attributes and architectural choices often results in functionally satisfactory software products but partially or fully disregarding crucial quality attributes. Low-level designs (class diagram, database model) are made by the students primarily influenced by the way of working in PTS3. Due to the lack of an incentive (no future usages, lack of communication obstacles, and non-demanding POs), the motivation for documenting a software architecture is low and is done only to satisfy the course requirements.

3   Sources of Inspiration

To accumulate knowledge for our course re-design, we have studied literature on software architectures and on approaching them in agile projects and in education. Furthermore, we have interviewed software companies from the region where our students get predominantly employed.

3.1   Literature on Software Architectures and their Usage in Agile Projects

On software architectures: The architecting process involves the analysis, synthesis, documentation, and evaluation activities [15]. The software architecture of a software-intensive system is created in the early development phases and evolves throughout the whole development cycle [16]. An overview of software architecture methods can be found in [17]. The term software architecture has been attributed various definitions. For example: "the set of structures needed to reason about the system, which comprise software elements, relation among them, and properties of both" [9] focuses on the structure aspect. Other definitions view design decision as the focus of software architectures [10], stating that a software architecture reflects "the major design decisions made" [5], and that "the actual structure, or architectural design, is merely a reflection of those design decisions" [11]. Architectural decisions "capture key design issues and the rationale behind chosen solutions" [12]. However, as argued in [9], in agile projects some decisions are made later on throughout the project, and it is hard to justify whether a decision is major. Furthermore, as Kruchten notes, architectural decisions should not be mixed with software design and code decisions [8]. The study in [13] shows that "compared to senior architects, junior architects spend a quarter of the time on making a decision". Documenting decisions may be highly practical in agile projects: "If an architect doesn't have time for anything else, these decisions can provide a concrete direction for implementation and serve as an effective tool for communication to customers and management" [14]. With respect to the documentation of decisions a number of publication propose solutions. The IBM's e-Business Reference Architecture Framework is used in [14] to propose a template for the documenting of decisions. It is suggested that if a system quality is affected by a decision it needs to be documented.

On software architectures in agile development: In [15], the editors predict that "Software architecture will be recognized as a key foundation to agile software development". Few years later, this line is continued in a special issue of IEEE Software focused on the relationship between software architectures and agile practices. In its editorial, Abrahamsson et al. [2] provide a number of advises on the usage of software architectures in agile projects: making the architectural decisions "early enough", defining an architecture owner who is part of the team, usage of architectures for improving communication and coordination in complex projects and settings (e.g. distributed teams). They also state: "If agile developers don't consider software architecture relevant to their day-to-day activities, it would be difficult, even impossible, to convince them to use architectural principles and integrate artifacts in agile development". In [8], Kruchten binds the need for architectural activities and their size with the project context (e.g., project size, criticality, risks). In [16], the authors conclude that practices of software architectures and especially the focus on quality attributes can lead to improvement of projects executed with agile methods. They recommend focus on the overall system structure (shaped by the quality attributes) in the first iteration and subsequently in later iterations when changes are needed. In [17], the value of an architecting team in large-scale agile projects is reported. In [18], a study among IBM professionals reveals that architecting activities are highly relevant for agile developers. Communication, assumptions documentation, validation are supported through architectures. The project complexity also influences the architecture relevance (distribution, size, number of stakeholders).

On documenting software architectures in agile projects: Architecture documentation (and time associated with it) in agile projects is one of the roots of the tension between agile development methods and software architecting: "In an agile process, the team doesn't have time to wait for the architect to completely develop and document the architecture" [14]. In [19], the values and impediments of documenting software architectures in agile projects are discussed. Architecture documentation may serve to: get on board new project members quickly, for future usage (project transfer to another team/phase), quality assurance, or as domain knowledge repository. However, documenting of changing issues can be a wasted effort. Boehm [20] notes that for unpredictable projects decreasing the documentation effort may work, while for projects with predictable requirements this approach may miss useful architectural practices and may have even negative impact by not allowing external reviewers to detect mistakes due to the lack of documentation. An approach to the usage of the SEI method for documenting software architectures in agile methods is proposed in [21]. Initially, the views to be documented and the project stakeholders interested in them are identified. Then, documentation is done on the need-to basis with minimum need for rework. It is advised to document rationale early and throughout the project as postponing this for the end of the project may lead to omissions of choices made, insights, etc. Kruchten considers all possibilities for architecture documentation: documentation in code, with metaphors, diagrams, complete architecture document, etc. depending on the project context [8]. In [22], the documentation was reduced to component diagrams and design decisions published on a wiki.

On architects in agile projects: A study among 10 professionals [22] revealed the existence of three types of architects: one on the client side (software architect), one with management functions (solution architect), and one responsible for the actual implementation in the team (management architect). The first and the latter roles are proposed also in [2,8]. The high-level architecture would be drafted by the software architects and the design decisions and concrete architecture by the implementation and solution architects.

3.2   Literature on Teaching Software Architectures

A course focusing on the analysis and evaluation of software architectures and building a knowledge-base for their design is presented in [4]. The course is targeted at master level students and presents the main ingredients of classical software architecture courses. The authors of [5] classify the courses on software architectures as either focusing on the "tools" to design software systems (patterns, languages, etc.) or focusing on communication aspects of software architectures. They discuss their experiences from two master-level courses focusing on the communication aspects. The objectives of the courses are to teach selection and development of architecture views and architecture assessing and do not incorporate system development activities. The courses follow an architecture-centric approach, where stakeholders should be involved and functional and non-functional requirements are simultaneously addressed during the architecture design process. In [6], the problems of teaching software architectures in academic, non-industrial settings are identified. As main challenges are seen the isolated nature of an academic course and therefore the lack of realistic context (starting from scratch, non-existent stakeholders) and the lack of the inherent fuzziness and complexity of industrial scenarios. Furthermore, as the authors point out, the students lack the experience of solving complex design problems and profound knowledge for the application domain. The authors describe an advanced master-level course designed to teach software architecting as a team effort in a complex problem environment. The architecting team reports to a "Board" (formed by staff members) which considers the solutions and makes choices. The board exemplifies to some extend the multiple stakeholders, working in context challenges delineated above. In [7], a course on tackling software architectures in agile projects is presented. The approach in [7] provides us with valuable directions on architecting in agile projects. However, our course setup leads to different pedagogical goals and challenges (which we discuss in Section 4.1). In [23], an agile software development project course is described, where architecting activities take place in week 3. However, the architecting issues in agile projects are not extensively discussed.

3.3   Industry Study

In total, 12 companies implementing some form of agile software development (predominantly Scrum) were interviewed by students using a standardized questionnaire. The companies were small (3-4 developers), medium, and large (e.g., a bank). Interviews were held with developers, scrum masters, and project leaders. Naturally, the architecting practices varied substantially among the companies, depending on their domain, maturity, size, etc. Ten of the companies spend dedicated time in the beginning of the project to shape the overall architecture. One company does it on the fly and one does not spend time on architecting. One company has a two-step process of architecting. They discuss first a "functional architecture" with the Product Owner and then they elaborate a "technical architecture". Documenting of architectures varies from documenting at the beginning of a project (3 companies), per sprint (5 companies), or at the end if necessary (2 companies). Generally, the aim is to minimize documentation effort. One company stated that documentation effort depended on the project client and the team. As minimum companies document components/structures and their relations. One company stated explicitly that they document the architecture design choices. At one company is made use of a wiki for the architecture documentation. In [24], the experiences of a partner company of our school (among those interviewed) are reported. It is strongly advocated that quality attributes, architecture envisioning and system architecting are paid substantial attention from the beginning of the project, having in mind to only document what needs to be documented.

4   Course Design

Next, we present our main pedagogical considerations, the decisions that we made, rationale behind them, and the course setup.

4.1   Considerations

Our course design was influenced by a set of situational factors (as defined in [25]):

- *General context*: Our curriculum implied the application of an architecture-centric approach in the course (similar to the approaches in [5] and [7]).
- *Characteristics of the learners (second year bachelor students)*:
  - *capabilities:* The Dutch education system predefines the students of applied universities as students predominantly interested in applying knowledge. This opens opportunities for students who are less inclined to reflect on the theoretical aspects of a problem, but it does not exclude students with capabilities for deeper reflections.

- *motivation*: A student needs to be motivated during the course for achieving best learning results. Our students motivation is heavily influenced by the project case (realism, comprehension), degree of challenge (too easy or too difficult projects demotivate students), practical relevance of the course activities, and direct knowledge application.
- *maturity:* As indicated in literature, junior developers (and even more bachelor students in an applied university) have difficulties in reflecting on architectural decisions due to their lack of experience and knowledge [6,13].
- *Nature of the subject (architecting in agile projects):* The project context defines the reasons to conduct architecting activities explicitly and in an organized manner [8,18]. To create an architecting suitable context, a project needs to be of sufficient complexity [6]: big enough, involving several quality attributes and should offer room for taking non-trivial architectural decisions (non-stable architecture) [8,16]. The project needs to be with relatively predictable requirements [20]. A desired contextual factor is team distribution or other communication or coordination hindering factors [2].

4.2   Course Design Decisions and Rationale

Based on the literature and industry input, and the situational factors discussed in Section 4.1, we have taken a number of decisions for our approach.

- *Project case*: We have decided to offer several cases to address the *motivation factor*. Students are allowed to choose the case that motivates them the best. The cases differ in degree of complexity (to address the diversity of student *capabilities*) and in types of architectural challenges offered (team distribution, room for architectural decisions, number of quality attributes, etc.).
- *Process organization:* We have decided to introduce an architecture role (as suggested in [2,22,26]) in order to anchor the architecting activities with clear responsibilities and to stimulate the professional development of students (related to the *general context* factors). This role is assigned to a volunteering student from the group for the project duration.
- *Architecture elicitation:*
  Similar to the approach in [7], we have decided to dedicate explicit time for the architecture design activities in the beginning of the project as there architecting would take place anyway [8] (see Section 4.3, week 1 and 2). In addition, in each sprint, the teams revisit their architecture and if needed adapt it.
- *Documenting*:
  - *When:* We have decided to dedicate time in the beginning of the project for the documentation of the initial architecture design (document rationale early and throughout the project [21]) and to stimulate documentation of architectural changes at the end of each iteration.
  - *What*: As minimum, we require documentation of a list of stakeholders identified, their concerns (based on [27]), a high-level architecture and rationale for the decisions made [14]. This content was selected as it is of direct value for the

Product Owner [8] and is therefore realistic requirement (related to the *motiva-tion* factors). Following the agile principles, the teams could (but not necessari-ly) document detailed design aspects (class diagrams, sequence diagrams, data-base models, etc.) if they perceive this as relevant and useful for the team or needed in the context of the   project.

— *Why*: To motivate documenting in addition to the practical relevance stimuli, we introduced a number of stimulating contextual factors. As part of the school in-ternational activities, one project case involved co-operation on the project with Finish students (introducing team distribution [8]). A second project case stimu-lated the involvement of two or more groups working on it, introducing com-munication and synchronization challenges (which foster documenting). A third case involved a real client, which makes documenting a needed activity. Last but not least, the need was introduced for the PO to be able to quickly look-up architectural choices per group (as the PO has to switch between numerous groups loosing track of the group choices).

— *Where*: We offered the teams to document either in a traditional document or in wiki page in the agile management tool aiming at reducing the risk of decoupl-ing the development process from the architecture document [22,28]. We did not offer to include the stakeholders' concerns in sprint backlogs as concerns live beyond a sprint.

— *How:* The teams were allowed to document minimalistic and efficient (e.g. pho-tos of drawings instead of diagrams) in alignment with the agile lean principles.

• *Backlog content*: To support the team in managing their workload, we allowed them to put in the sprint backlog architecting activities [29]. As students are unex-perienced in having options to consider and in making choices, we encouraged them to plan architecture and technology spikes (related to the *maturity* factor).

4.3   Course Organization for the Architecting Activities

Next, we describe the organization of the architecting activities within PTS4.

1. In week 1 (4h), the students form groups, familiarize themselves with the set of available cases, select a scrum master and an architect. The existing knowledge on software architectures is revisited, focusing on stakeholders, non-functional re-quirements and their interplay with the architectural decisions. After the selection of a case, each group, in a discussion with the PO, identifies and lists the stake-holders and their business goals. Next, in a discussion with the PO, the project backlog is populated with user stories. Throughout the week, the architects in col-laboration with the rest of the team need to elaborate an architectural proposal with rationale for the choices made. The reason to expand this activity beyond the les-son is that students need time to reflect on the problem, to research possible solu-tions and their advantages and disadvantages. Team members may be involved in elaborating detailed designs when a team decides to do so.

2. In week 2 (4h), the architects present their proposals to the PO (the high-level ar-chitecture and the rationale for the choices made). The PO reflects on the proposal.

The discussion is centered around the interplay between the stakeholders' goals and the architecture proposed. In the rest of the lesson time, the team works on the scrum-related activities (e.g., estimates user stories, prepares sprint 1).

3. In week 3, the PO may make certain adaptation to the sprint backlog and the team can begin working on the sprint tasks.
4. During the sprint or at its end, the team is allowed to adapt the architecture if needed. The rationale for a change is recorded and is discussed with the PO.
5. At the end of the sprint and the beginning of the next one, the PO reviews the architecture document (and if there were changes applied to it in the last sprint). The team and the PO reflect on the architecture and the stakeholders concerns - are changes needed, are the architecture choices still in compliance with the goals, etc.

Steps 4 and 5 are repeated for each sprint. The final architecture document/wiki is handed in in week 18 and the architecting process and decisions are revisited in a discussion with the Tutor.

5   Initial Experiences and Lessons Learned

We have applied our approach for the first time in the beginning of 2015. 64 students in 12 groups with 2 teachers acting in the role of PO were involved in the experiment. The students were offered three cases: CIMS (Crisis Information Management System) representing an architecturally complex case, PhotoStore (representing an architecturally less challenging case), and The Hub (a system comparable to the PhotoStore system but requested by an actual client). The international project planned as a distributed effort was not included in the experiment due to organizational problems in it. Five groups have chosen to work on the CIMS case (of which 3 in a collaborative project), 1 group executed a project for a real client and 6 groups selected the PhotoStore case. Currently, the project is in its 10th week.

The explicit focus in week 1 and 2 on the architecting activities had a clear, positive effect. Compared to earlier course executions, the students spent time on the software architecture and the decisions were made in a conscious way in discussions with the PO. Input and questions from the PO resulted in changes of initial choices or in their better argumentation. The students have realized (and stated this) that stakeholders have different perspectives and may have conflicting concerns. One PhotoStore group and 2 CIMS groups needed also week 3 for architecture elicitation activities. Our conclusion is that the work on the major architectural choices may be given space also in week 3 of the project. The CIMS groups left architectural choices open for later sprints where more time would be available to accumulate knowledge and where the context would be better known (e.g., push/pull strategy between certain components). The three collaborating CIMS groups stated explicitly that the architecting activities helped them in coming to a common understanding of the system structure and for the work division among the teams. In Sprint 2, several of the groups needed to revisit their initial choices. For example, in a CIMS group a new type of client application had to be added and in a PhotoStore group, a desktop client needed to be added to the initially envisioned web solution.

In terms of documentation, the needs of the PO and the team needs were the main driving factor to document. Several teams have documented class diagrams and one group has discussed classes but did not document them. The general feeling among students was that class diagrams had little value for them and only one group using the Spring framework needed them. They have acknowledged that they have documented them influenced by previous school requirements. Most groups made ERD diagrams claiming that this was important for the team synchronization and communication. All CIMS and PhotoStore teams had difficulties in communicating their architectural choices to the PO and documenting them. They found it difficult to translate the desired quality attributes into relevant architectural decisions. At the end, all groups used some variant of deployment diagrams accompanied by textual clarifications as a means to communicate their major architectural choices. However, deployment diagrams were unsuitable to express many of their choices which introduced a communication gap with the PO. We conclude that the refreshing lecture needs to focus on the high-level nature of architectures and be extended with information on functional modeling [30] and with architectural patterns that address certain project related quality attributes. In a discussion with the students, they have all approved this conclusion. They have also pointed out that for the PhotoStore case the functional modeling and patterns knowledge would be less crucial. The majority of groups have documented their architecture decisions in a word document. One group used an architecture wiki and one group resorted to photos in combination with diagram pictures. The group working for an actual client did not document any of their decisions in their first sprint. They were focused on making the decisions and discussing them with the stakeholders instead of documenting them. The omission to document their choices led to a misunderstanding with the PO and a delay of their project.

All groups embraced the inclusion of architectural activities in the backlog which they saw as protective mechanism, explicating their work on non-coding activities to the PO. The introduction of the architect role led to the explicit allocation of responsibility in the group on the architecting activities and served as an additional stimuli for the students to focus on architecting. The collaborating CIMS groups decided to have architecting discussion with a limited number of team representatives. They have involved the group architect and a second team member, limiting the discussions to a group of 6 people (instead of 15 they started off with).

The offering of cases of higher and lower architectural complexity has proven a valuable experiment. All groups felt sufficiently motivated. They could also work within the scope of their architectural capabilities and interests. Clearly, the PhotoStore case offers less architectural challenges than the CIMS case. This differentiation in the architecting competences demonstrated by the students in the project would be reflected in their personal development portfolios, currently adapted to reflect differences in competences demonstrated in a course.

6   Conclusions

We present an approach to introducing architecting activities in agile software development projects in education. Our approach is based on industry and academic approaches to architecting in agile projects. The application of the approach has led to an improved and deepened treating of software architectures in the agile projects performed by the students. The strategies selected to introduce and motivate architecting activities in agile projects have proven to be effective and students have performed the activities (e.g., deliberating, designing, documenting) with the realization of their value for the project and in a non-enforced manner. We observed a knowledge gap in our education which hindered the students in producing architectural views relevant for the PO. This omission will be remedied in the next course execution.

The results presented in this paper are of value to other educational institutions where agile software development projects are part of the curriculum. Our approach is targeted to second year, applied study, software engineering students but it can be also used in higher years with minor modifications.

References

1. Breivold, H.P., Sundmark, D., Wallin, P., Larsson, S.: What does research say about agile and architecture? In: 2010 Fifth International Conference on Software Engineering Advances (ICSEA), pp. 32–37 (2010)
2. Abrahamsson, P., Babar, M.A., Kruchten, P.: Agility and Architecture: Can They Coexist? IEEE Software 27, 16–22 (2010)
3. Sharifloo, A.A., Saffarian, A.S., Shams, F.: Embedding architectural practices into extreme programming. In: 19th Australian Conference on Software Engineering, ASWEC 2008, pp. 310–319 (2008)
4. Garlan, D., Shaw, M., Okasaki, C., Scott, C., Swonger, R.: Experience with a course on architectures for software systems. In: Sledge, C. (ed.) Software Engineering Education, vol. 640, pp. 23–43. Springer, Heidelberg (1992)
5. Lago, P., Van Vliet, H.: Teaching a course on software architecture. In: 18th Conference on Software Engineering Education & Training, pp. 35–42 (2005)
6. Mannisto, T., Savolainen, J., Myllarniemi, V.: Teaching software architecture design. In: Seventh Working IEEE/IFIP Conference on Software Architecture, WICSA 2008, pp. 117–124 (2008)
7. Cleland-Huang, J., Babar, M.A., Mirakhorli, M.: An inverted classroom experience: engaging students in architectural thinking for agile projects. In: Companion Proceedings of the 36th Int. Conf. on Software Engineering, pp. 364–371. ACM, Hyderabad (2014)
8. Kruchten, P.: Software architecture and agile software development: a clash of two cultures? In: ACM/IEEE 32nd Int. Conf. on Software Engineering, pp. 497–498 (2010)
9. Bass, L., Clements, P., Kazman, R.: Software Architecture in Practice. Addison-Wesley Professional (2012)
10. Jansen, A., Bosch, J.: Software architecture as a set of architectural design decisions. In: 5th Working IEEE/IFIP Conference on, Software Architecture, WICSA 2005, pp. 109–120 (2005)
11. de Boer, R.C., van Vliet, H.: On the similarity between requirements and architecture. Journal of Systems and Software 82, 544–550 (2009)
12. Zimmermann, O.: Architectural Decisions as Reusable Design Assets. IEEE Software 28, 64–69 (2011)
13. Tofan, D., Galster, M., Avgeriou, P.: Difficulty of architectural decisions – A survey with professional architects. In: Drira, K. (ed.) ECSA 2013. LNCS, vol. 7957, pp. 192–199. Springer, Heidelberg (2013)

14. Tyree, J., Akerman, A.: Architecture decisions: demystifying architecture. IEEE Software **22**, 19–27 (2005)
15. Kruchten, P.: The past, present, and future for software architecture. In: Henk, O., Judith, S. (eds.) IEEE Software, vol. 23, pp. 22–30 (2006)
16. Nord, R.L., Tomayko, J.E.: Software architecture-centric methods and agile development. IEEE Software **23**, 47–53 (2006)
17. Lindvall, M., et al.: Empirical findings in agile methods. In: Wells, D., Williams, L. (eds.) XP 2002. LNCS, vol. 2418, pp. 197–207. Springer, Heidelberg (2002)
18. Davide, F.: Peaceful coexistence: agile developer perspectives on software architecture. In: Giovanni, C., Salvatore Alessandro, S., Giuseppe, C., Paolo, S., Cristiana, D.A. (eds.) IEEE Software, vol. 27, pp. 23–25 (2010)
19. Coram, M., Bohner, S.: The impact of agile methods on software project management. In: 12th IEEE International Conference and Workshops on the Engineering of Computer-Based Systems, ECBS 2005, pp. 363–370 (2005)
20. Boehm, B.: Get ready for agile methods, with care. Computer **35**, 64–69 (2002)
21. Clements, P., Ivers, J., Little, R., Nord, R., Stafford, J.: Documenting Software Architectures in an Agile World. Technical Note CMU/SEI-2003-TN-023, Carnegie Mellon University (2003)
22. Babar, M.A.: An exploratory study of architectural practices and challenges in using agile software development approaches. In: Joint Working IEEE/IFIP Conference on Software Architecture & European Conference on Software Architecture, WICSA/ECSA 2009, pp. 81–90 (2009)
23. Lee, J., Kotonya, G., Whittle, J., Bull, C.: Software design studio: a practical example. In: 37th Int. Conference on Software Engineering (ICSE 2015), pp. 47–55. IEEE (2015)
24. Schoeber, G.: Architecture and agile, friends or enemies? (presentation). In: SATURN 2010, Minneapolis, MN (2010)
25. Fink, L.D.: Creating Significant Learning Experiences: An Integrated Approach to Designing College Courses, 2nd edn. Jossey-Bass (2013)
26. Faber, R.: Architects as Service Providers. IEEE Software **27**, 33–40 (2010)
27. Kazman, R., Bass, L.: Categorizing Business Goals for Software Architectures. Technical Report CMU/SEI-2005-TR-021, ESC-TR-2005-021, Carnegie Mellon University (2005)
28. Clerc, V., Vries, E.D., Lago, P.: Using wikis to support architectural knowledge management in global software development. In: Proceedings of the 2010 ICSE Workshop on Sharing and Reusing Architectural Knowledge, pp. 37–43. ACM, Cape Town (2010)
29. Madison, J.: Agile Architecture Interactions. IEEE Software **27**, 41–48 (2010)
30. Brinkkemper, S., Pachidi, S.: Functional architecture modeling for the software product industry. In: Babar, M.A., Gorton, I. (eds.) ECSA 2010. LNCS, vol. 6285, pp. 198–213. Springer, Heidelberg (2010)

Learning Objectives for a Course on Software Architecture

Arvind W. Kiwelekar[⊠] and Hansaraj S. Wankhede

Department of Computer Engineering,
Dr. Babasaheb Ambedkar Technological University, Lonere,
Raigad 402103, Maharashtra, India
{awk,hswankhede}@dbatu.ac.in

Abstract. Many universities have started to offer a course on the emerging discipline of Software Architecture at either graduate or undergraduate levels. As a result, educators are facing many challenges with respect to which topics to be included in a course on Software Architecture and for which architectural abilities students should be trained and assessed. One way of addressing these challenges is to clearly specify learning objectives for a course on Software Architecture. In this paper, we present a set of learning objectives and its classification using Revised Bloom's Taxonomy (RBT). The analysis brings out the generic cognitive skills required for architecture modeling. One of the potential benefits of classification of learning objectives is that different educational processes such as instruction, learning and assessment can be effectively aligned using the classification of learning objectives presented in the paper.

1 Introduction

Learning objectives play a central role in outcome-based education. A set of learning objectives helps instructors to systematically plan the course delivery. Instructors can also use them to set realistic targets to be achieved during the limited span of an academic semester. In addition to this, demonstrating the achievement of learning objectives is one of the mandatory requirements of accreditation bodies (e.g., National Board of Accreditation in India). Hence, a set of learning objectives needs to be specified during the process of course development. In this paper, we present a course on Software Architetcure (Section 3) along with its learning objectives. The course design, is based on knowledge areas specified in Software Engineering Body Of Knowledge (SWEBOK) [1]. The course includes software architecture related topics from the SWEBOK 's knowledge areas. Further, Bloom's Taxonomy [2] (Section 2) of educational objectives is used to organize the learning objectives. The analysis presented in Sections from 4 to 6 is useful to instructors in two different ways. Firstly, the analysis of learning objectives will help instructors to select an appropriate instructional methodology (e.g. Collaborative Learning, Experiential learning). Secondly, analysis will also be useful to design assessment instruments (e.g., quizzes and examinations) thus co-relating student's performance with learning objectives.

© Springer International Publishing Switzerland 2015
D. Weyns et al. (Eds.): ECSA 2015, LNCS 9278, pp. 169–180, 2015.
DOI: 10.1007/978-3-319-23727-5_14

	Remember	Understand	Apply	Analyze	Evaluate	Create
Factual Knowledge						
Conceptual Knowledge						
Procedural Knowledge						
Meta-Cognitive Knowledge						

Fig. 1. Classification categories in Revised Bloom's Taxonomy

2   Bloom's Taxonomy: Background

Bloom's taxonomy was originally defined by Benjamin Bloom [3] to organize educational objectives. Later it has been revised by Anderson et al. [2] and the taxonomy is referred to as Revised Bloom's Taxonomy (RBT). In the RBT, educational objectives are organized along two dimensions of cognitive processes and knowledge categories. The columns of the table represent cognitive dimension while rows represent knowledge dimension. Six cognitive process categories are: Remember, Understand, Apply, Analyze, Evaluate and Create [2]. The four knowledge categories are: Factual, Conceptual, Procedural and Meta-Cognitive. [2]. Figure 1 shows the organization of educational objectives in a tabular form.

Some of the other alternative taxonomies which can also be used to organize educational objectives are the taxonomies of King and Kitchener [4] and Structure of Observed Learning Outcome [5]. These taxonomies are reviewed and compared with RBT in [6]. In this paper, we use RBT mainly because it is the predominately used taxonomy for specifying learning objectives, course design and assessment activities in the field of Computer Science Education [6].

2.1   Learning Objectives

Learning objectives are typically associated with an instructional activity to make it as an outcome-based activity. Learning objectives are broadly classified based on its scope into three categories namely *global, educational* or *instructional*. Global objectives are broad in its scope such as the objective: *Students will be able to develop architectural thinking and they will apply it to build large and complex software systems.* The time required to achieve a global objective spans over a long period. Educational objectives can be achieved during a semester or a month or a week. For example, the objective: *Students will acquire the knowledge of various approaches to document a software system.* An instructional objective is very narrow in its scope and can be used either to prepare lesson plans or to schedule instructional activities. An example of instructional objective is: *Students will be able to classify requirements into functional and non-functional categories.* Most of the learning objectives described in this paper fall in the categories of instructional and educational objectives. They are formulated with an intention to schedule instructional activities and to design examinations.

Learning objectives essentially capture two aspects of educational processes. First, a learning objective specifies behavior to be developed in a student out of an educational activity. This behavioral aspect is known as *cognitive dimension* in RBT. Second, a learning objective captures the type of content to be acquired during an educational activity. This content aspect is referred to as knowledge dimension in RBT. Grammatically speaking, a verb in a learning objective captures the cognitive dimension and corresponding noun captures the knowledge dimension. For example, in the learning objective *Students will be able to classify requirements into functional and non-functional categories*. The verb *classify* captures the cognitive dimension and the noun-phrase *functional and non-functional requirements* represent knowledge dimension.

2.2   Cognitive Processes in RBT

The cognitive process dimension in RBT is broadly organized in six different categories namely Remember, Understand, Apply, Analyze, Evaluate and Create [2]. The category *Remember* captures the activity of retrieving knowledge from long-term memory. The activities of recognizing and recalling information, objects and events belong to the *Remember* category. The category *Understand* means to construct the meaning out of the learning material presented in the form of either lectures or notes. The acts of interpreting, exemplifying, classifying, summarizing, inferring, comparing, and explaining belong to the category *Understand*. The third category *Apply* refers to carry out or use a procedure in a given situation and it includes the acts of executing and implementing. The fourth category of *Analyze* refers to breaking down the learning material into its part and to relating parts to establish overall structure. The acts of differentiating, organizing and attributing are considered as analytic processes. The fifth category *Evaluate* means the acts of checking and making judgments based on some criteria. The last cognitive process category from RBT is *Create* and it means the acts of generating, planning and producing some product.

2.3   Knowledge Dimension RBT

The knowledge dimension in RBT is classified into four categories of *Factual, Conceptual, Procedural* and *Meta-cognitive* knowledge [2]. The factual information about specific terminologies (e.g., component, modules, views) and basic elements that students must be well versed with are captured under the factual knowledge. The conceptual knowledge category includes the knowledge about classification categories, principles, models and theories. Some examples of conceptual knowledge from software architecture are knowledge about patterns, styles, and design rules. The knowledge about procedures, methods, algorithms are included under the category of *Procedural Knowledge*. Few examples of procedural knowledge are methods for architecture reconstruction and methods for mapping programming elements to architectural elements. The last category *meta-cognitive* knowledge corresponds to knowledge about cognition itself and understanding one's own cognitive abilities.

Table 1. Software Architecture: Course Content

Knowledge Areas	Topics	Subtopics
Requirements Engineering	Requirements Analysis	Architectural Design and Requirements Allocation
Software Design	Key issues in Software Design	Concurrency, Control and Handling of events, data persistence, distribution of components, error and exception handling, interaction and presentation, Security.
	Software Structure and Architecture	Architectural Structures and View-points, Architectural Styles, design patterns, architecture design decisions, families of programs and frameworks
	Software Design Nota-tions	Structural and behavioral descriptions
	Software Design Qual-ity Analysis and Eval-uation	Quality Attributes, Quality Analysis and Evaluation Techniques, Measures
Software Engineer-ing Management	Initiation and Scope definition	Determination and negotiation of requirements, feasibility analysis
	Software Project Plan-ning	Risk and Quality Management

3 Course Design

The course design includes two activities namely defining course content and defining learning objectives. First, Table 1 describes the course content. The course is designed with reference to the Knowledge Areas (KA) described in the SWEBOK. The course includes three different KAs that are relevant to design, document, analyze and evaluate software intensive systems. The selection of a particular KA is based on the criteria that the topics included a KA are also covered by leading conferences on Software Architecture (e.g., ECSA, WICSA) and availability of learning resources in the form of technical papers and books. Being the nature of the course is an introductory one, the course content aims to achieve broad-ness in terms of range of topics. Second, the learning objectives are defined to achieve, in general, ABET's (Accreditation Board of Engineering and Technology) attribute of an engineering graduate [7] and particularly hard-core engineering skills [8] such as problem solving and system design.

4 Requirements Engineering

The topic on *Requirements Analysis* from the Requirements Engineering KA is included in the course. Students require the knowledge of requirements analysis to identify architecturally significant requirements. At the end of this unit, stu-dents are expected to acquire the skills to classify requirements under various

Table 2. Requirements Analysis: Learning Objectives

Identifier	Learning Objectives	Cognitive Category	Knowledge Category
LO1	To detect and resolve conflicts between requirements.	Analyze	Conceptual
LO2	To discover the bounds of the software in terms of organizational and operational environment.	Analyze	Conceptual
LO3	To describe software requirements through conceptual models.	Create	Conceptual
LO4	To classify requirements into functional and non-functional requirements	Understand	Conceptual
LO5	To classify requirements into product requirements and process requirements	Understand	Conceptual
LO6	To classify requirements into volatile and stable requirements	Understand	Conceptual
LO7	To define the scope of requirements i.e. global versus component specific requirements.	Understand	Conceptual
LO8	To prioritize requirements.	Understand	Conceptual
LO9	To allocate requirements to architectural components.	Create	Conceptual

categories such as functional vs non-functional, global vs component specific, volatile vs stable requirements. Students will also be in a position to demonstrate their understanding of software requirements by creating conceptual models for an application. For a given application, students are asked to represent requirements through various models such as use-case model in UML, entity-relationship model, data-flow models, and goal-task analysis in i^* model [9]. Table 2 depicts the learning objectives and their categorization for the course unit on *Requirements Analysis*. Most of the learning objectives are inferred as *Understand* type under the cognitive dimension and as *Conceptual* type under the knowledge dimension. The learning objective *LO*9 is inferred under *Create* category because the task of allocation i.e. resource allocation is normally performed under planning process and it comes under the cognitive category *Create*.

5   Software Design

Four topics from the knowledge area Software Design are included. These are (i) Key issues in software design and design methods, (ii) software structure and architecture, (iii) software design notations, and (iv) software design quality analysis and evaluation. This section describes the learning objectives for software design.

5.1   Key Issues in Software Design and Design Methods

This topic intends to provide knowledge to students about the quality concerns that need to be addressed while specifying architectural solution. The

Table 3. Key Issues in Software Design and Design Methods: Learning Objectives

Identifier	Learning Objectives	Cognitive Category	Knowledge Category
LO10	To decompose a software system in terms of processes, tasks, and threads which will meet the design requirements of efficient, synchronization, scheduling and atomicity.	Create	Conceptual
LO11	To differentiate between information presentation and processing concerns for the given application.	Analyze	Conceptual
LO12	To specify data and control flow through various mechanisms such as implicit invocations and call backs.	Apply	Conceptual
LO13	To specify a scheme of allocation of software components across various hardware platforms handling issues of fault tolerance, heterogeneity and dependability.	Create	Conceptual
LO14	To recognize application domain data elements.	Understand	Conceptual
LO15	To specify interactions between information processing and presentation concerns.	Analyze	Conceptual
LO16	To specify the mechanisms to be used for ensuring security of application specific information such as access controls, and authorization.	Apply	Conceptual
LO17	To apply a design methodologies specific to architecture design such as Attribute-Driven design(ADD), pattern-oriented software architecture, model-driven architecture, and DRAMA.	Apply	Procedural

sub-topic on quality attribute in the topic on Requirements Analysis helps to get an insight about various generic quality attributes that customers expect to be implemented in a software system. This topic mainly covers decomposition of a system considering the issues of performance, synchronization among processes, how to separate business logic from information presentation etc. One way of providing this knowledge is to illustrate various architectural patterns (e.g., Model-View-Controller [10], Active-Object [10]) addressing these design issues. Table 3 depicts the learning objectives and their categorization for the course unit on *Software Design and Design Methods*. The knowledge category *Conceptual* is assigned to all learning objectives except LO17. The category assigned to the learning objective *LO17* is *Procedural* because it is concerned with the application of design methodologies which are procedural in nature.

5.2   Software Structure and Architecture

In this unit, students are introduced with the abstractions to capture the structure of software systems. These abstractions include views, styles and viewpoint frameworks (e.g., SEI's Viewpoint framework, Kruchten' 4+ 1 Framework). The main purpose of this course unit is to emphasize the fact that high-level architectural abstractions achieve design reuse across various applications. They also

Table 4. Software Structure and Architecture: Learning Objectives

Identifier	Learning Objectives	Cognitive Category	Knowledge Category
LO18	To differentiate between high-level architectural design vs detailed design.	Analyze	Conceptual
LO19	To create architectural description in multiple viewpoints.	Create	Conceptual
LO20	To apply techniques of recovering design information from low-level system implementation.	Apply	Procedural
LO21	To acquire the knowledge of various architectural styles.	Understand	Conceptual
LO22	To apply the knowledge of various architectural tactics and styles in given scenario.	Apply	Procedural
LO23	To comprehend an architectural style described in a pattern language.	Understand	Conceptual
LO24	To apply architectural styles for designing software systems.	Apply	Conceptual

allow us to build a complex system by composition of architectural styles. Table 4 depicts the learning objectives and their categorization for the course unit on *Software Structure and Architecture*.

5.3   Software Design Notations

The purpose of this course unit is to introduce students with various notations for representing and visualizing the structure of a software system. Notations for representing structure and behavior of a system are covered under this unit. Students will also be able to interpret an existing architectural models described in ADLs (e.g., ACME) and UML. Table 5 depicts the learning objectives and their categorization for the course unit on *Software Design Notations*.

Table 5. Software Design Notations: Learning Objectives

Identifier	Learning Objectives	Cognitive Category	Knowledge Category
LO25	To differentiate between structural and behavioral aspects of a software system.	Analyze	Conceptual
LO26	To create structural and behavioral models in design notations such as ADL and UML.	Create	Conceptual
LO27	To interpret structural and behavioral models of a software system.	Analyze	Conceptual

Table 6. Quality Analysis and Evaluation Techniques: Learning Objectives

Identifier	Learning Objectives	Cognitive Category	Knowledge Category
LO28	To Provide the definitions of various quality attributes such as modifiability, dependability, portability etc.	Understand	Factual
LO29	To classify quality attributes as run-time, non-run-time and intrinsic quality attributes.	Analyze	Factual
LO30	To apply evaluation techniques such as static analysis, simulation and prototyping and design reviews to ascertain design quality.	Apply	Procedural
LO31	To remember and recognize architectural elements in a reference architecture such as CORBA.	Remember	Factual
LO32	To check the compliance of a given software system such as a light-weight implementation of an Object Request Broker (ORB) (eg., Mico) against its reference architecture CORBA.	Evaluate	Conceptual

5.4   Quality Analysis and Evaluation Techniques

The course unit deals with qualitative analysis and evaluation of software system using architectural models. The unit intends to develop analytical abilities among students to recognize the quality instances in software requirement document, map the requirements on architectural models, and to identify trade-off or sensitivity points for quality attributes. Knowledge of definitions of various quality attributes, their classifications as run-time and non-runtime categories is expected to be provided. Table 6 depicts the learning objectives and their categorization for the course unit on *Quality Analysis and Evaluation Techniques*.

6   Software Engineering Management

The main intention of this course unit is to explain the role of software architecture in the broader context of software engineering. One way of achieving this objective is to describe the application of architectural models for doing risk management and requirements traceability. The unit intends to give exposure to students with the standards for managing architectural knowledge (e.g., OMG's KDM [11]). Table 7 depicts the learning objectives and their categorization for the course unit on *Software Engineering Management*.

7   Course Implementation

Two different variants of the course are offered at Under-Graduate (UG) and Post-Graduate levels to the Computer Engineering students at Dr. B. A. Tech. University (DBATU), India. When the course is offered at PG level, students are asked to present a term paper in a specialized area of software architecture.

Table 7. Software Engineering Management: Learning Objectives

Identifier	Learning Objectives	Cognitive Category	Knowledge Category
LO33	To build an architectural prototype for requirements negotiation and feasibility analysis.	Create	Conceptual
LO34	To perform risk management activities(e.g.,Identifications and prioritize of risk factors and risk mitigation strategies.) using architectural models.	Apply	Procedural

Table 8. Organization of Learning Objectives in RBT Framework

	Remember	Understand	Apply	Analyze	Evaluate	Create
Factual Knowledge	LO31	LO28		LO29		
Conceptual Knowledge		LO4, LO5, LO6, LO7, LO8, LO14, LO21, LO22, LO23	LO12, LO16, LO24	LO1, LO2, LO11, LO15, LO18, LO25, LO27	LO32	LO3, LO9, LO10, LO13, LO19, LO26, LO33
Procedural Knowledge			LO17, LO20, LO30, LO34			
Meta-Cognitive Knowledge						

At UG level students are assigned with two case studies as course projects for software architecture design and software architecture documentation.

Table 8 organizes the learning objectives in RBT framework. We can observe from the table that the course offered at DBATU predominantly contains the *Concepual* type of knowledge. As majority of the learning objectives fall in the cognitive domain of *Undersatnd*, *Apply* and *Analysis*, students are mainly trained for these skills. From the initial experience of course offerings, we observe that achievement of some of the learning objectives such as those that falls in the categories *Conceptual* and *Analyze* is comparatively easier. Assessment of these objectives is also comparatively simpler by conducting quizzes and examinations. The learning objectives that fall in the categories of *Evaluate* and *Create* pose challenges in terms of the time taken for achieving the objectives and for creating small-sized learning case studies that will assess student's performance during a 12-week course time.

8   Related Work

This section reviews some of the earlier work in the field of Software Architecture Education in the context of the work presented in this paper. As such Software Architecture is still an emerging discipline and universities have recently started offering a course on Software Architecture.

One of the earliest course content for a course on Software Architecture is reported in the works of Garlan et al. [12]. The course includes the topics such as architectural idioms, module interconnection languages, formal methods for software architectures, domain specific software architecture and tools for architectural modeling. The paper also suggests to put emphasis on enough practice on architectural modeling than mere knowledge of high-level architectural abstractions.

The paper [13] by Lago et al. describe the experiences of offering two varieties of a course on Software Architetcure. The first course referred to as an intensive course emphasize programming in the large aspects of Software Architecture. The second course referred to as a regular course emphasize communication aspect of architecture to various stakeholders. The paper observes that a regular course emphasizing communication aspect is more successful in terms of developing architectural thinking.

Ewan Tempero [14] adopts Quality Attributes Scenarios (QAS) to teach a course on Software Architecture. The paper identifies constructing a valid and useful QAS as one of the challenges faced when one adopts QAS to teach a course on software architecture. The benefits of the approach includes that it emphasize equipping students with concrete theory rather than hands on experiences on some "real-world" problems.

Methodological issues of teaching a course on Software Architecture is addressed by Fraga et al. [15] and Boer et al. [16]. Fraga et al. suggest a teaching methodology based on use of ontology and case based reasoning. The methodology trains the student on how to apply the acquired architectural knowledge in some practical situations. In the methodology adopted by Boer et al. focus on building up architectural knowledge through exchanges in the community of learners rather than reusing and applying architectural knowledge represented through ontologies.

The earlier work discussed in this section mainly focus on either describing the course content for a typical course on Software Architetcure or sharing experiences of adopting a teaching methodology during a course on Software Architecture. We have presented an analysis of learning objectives in this paper using RBT. This activity is usually performed at the time of course design and planning. RBT as an organizational framework of learning objectives is also useful to align other educational processes such as instruction, assessment, and selecting an appropriate teaching methodology.

9   Discussion

This section discusses some of the issues that have been addressed at the time of course design. Firstly, is it appropriate to design a course on Software Architecture using the knowledge areas specified in SWEBOK? This question is important because earlier researchers have raised arguments against SWEBOK. While reflecting on the state of software engineering education [17], Hans van Vliet mentions that to assume SWEBOK represents the state of the practice is one of five assumptions that can trap software engineering educators. It also insufficiently covers software architecture related topics. We think that the latest version of SWEBOK published in the year 2014 covers topics on software architecture in sufficient depth. We have referred SWEBOK to design a course on software architecture owing to the fact that a separate software architecture body of knowledge is yet to be standardized.

Secondly, is it appropriate to adopt the Bloom's Taxonomy to organize the learning objectives for a course on Software Architecture? The Bloom's taxonomy has also been criticized mainly for its ordering of cognitive process categories. We used Bloom's taxonomy in its revised form in which the issue of ordering of cognitive processes has been addressed by changing the ordering of *Synthesis* and *Evaluataion*. In the RBT, all cognitive processes are renamed from *noun* form to its *verb* form. As mentioned in Section 2, the Bloom's taxonomy has been also applied in the field of Computer Science Education.

10   Conclusion and Future Work

We have described the design of a course on Software architecture in this paper. The course content are drawn from the architecture related topics included in SWEBOK. We found that SWEBOK as a useful reference guide to identify and organize the content of a course on Software Architecture considering its emerging nature. A set of learning objectives for a course on Software Architecture is also defined with an intention to plan systematic instruction delivery. The learning objectives are analyzed using RBT. The analysis shows that the nature of the course described in this paper includes mainly *Conceptual* knowledge. The analysis also shows that students need to be trained on diverse cognitive abilities that range from the level of *Undersatnd* to *Evaluate*. The work presented in this paper can be extended to select an appropriate teaching methodology(e.g., Collaborative learning) and to devise small-sized architectural case-studies for collecting evidences for achievements of learning objectives.

References

1. Bourque, P., Fairley, R.E., et al.: Guide to the Software Engineering Body of Knowledge (SWEBOK (R)): Version 3.0. IEEE Computer Society Press (2014)

2. Anderson, L.W., Krathwohl, D.R., Airasian, P.W., Cruikshank, K.A., Mayer, R.E., Pintrich, P.R., Raths, J., Wittrock, M.C.: A Taxonomy for Learning, Teaching, and Assessing: A Revision of Bloom's Taxonomy of Educational Objectives, Abridged Edition, 2 edn. Pearson, December 2000

3. Bloom, B., Englehart, M.D., Furst, E.J., Hill, W.H., Krathwohl, D.R.: Taxonomy of Educational Objectives: The Classification of Educational Goals - Handbook 1: Cognitive Domain. David McKay Company Inc., New York (1956)

4. King, P.M., Kitchener, K.S.: Developing Reflective Judgment: Understanding and Promoting Intellectual Growth and Critical Thinking in Adolescents and Adults. Jossey-Bass Higher and Adult Education Series and Jossey-Bass Social and Behavioral Science Series. ERIC (1994)

5. Biggs, J.B., Collis, K.F.: Evaluating the quality of learning: The SOLO taxonomy (Structure of the Observed Learning Outcome). Academic Press (2014)

6. Fuller, U., Johnson, C.G., Ahoniemi, T., Cukierman, D., Hernán-Losada, I., Jackova, J., Lahtinen, E., Lewis, T.L., Thompson, D.M., Riedesel, C., et al.: Developing a computer science-specific learning taxonomy. ACM SIGCSE Bulletin 39(4), 152–170 (2007)

7. Shuman, L.J., Besterfield-Sacre, M., McGourty, J.: The ABET "professional skills"-can they be taught? can they be assessed? Journal of Engineering Education 94(1), 41–55 (2005)

8. Felder, R.M., Brent, R.: Designing and teaching courses to satisfy the ABET engineering criteria. Journal of Engineering Education 92(1), 7–26 (2003)

9. Yu, E.S.K.: Towards modeling and reasoning support for early-phase requirements engineering. In: 3rd IEEE International Symposium on Requirements Engineering (RE 1997), Annapolis, MD, USA, January 5–8, pp. 226–235 (1997)

10. Buschmann, F., Meunier, R., Rohnert, H., Sommerlad, P., Stal, M.: Pattern-oriented Software Architecture, vol. 1 (1996)

11. Pérez-Castillo, R., De Guzman, I.G.R., Piattini, M.: Knowledge discovery metamodel-iso/iec 19506: A standard to modernize legacy systems. Computer Standards & Interfaces 33(6), 519–532 (2011)

12. Garlan, D., Shaw, M., Okasaki, C., Scott, C.M., Swonger, R.F.: Experience with a course on architectures for software systems. In: Sledge, C. (ed.) SEI 1992. LNCS, vol. 640, pp. 23–43. Springer, Heidelberg (1992)

13. Lago, P., van Vliet, H.: Teaching a course on software architecture. In: CSEET 2005: Proceedings of the 18th Conference on Software Engineering Education & Training, pp. 35–42. IEEE Computer Society, Washington, DC (2005)

14. Tempero, E.: Experiences in teaching quality attribute scenarios. In: Proceedings of the Eleventh Australasian Conference on Computing Education, vol. 95, pp. 181–188. Australian Computer Society, Inc. (2009)

15. Fraga, A., Lloréns, J.: The challenge of training new architects: an ontological and reinforcement-learning methodology. JSW 2(5), 24–28 (2007)

16. de Boer, R.C., Farenhorst, R., van Vliet, H.: A community of learners approach to software architecture education. In: Proceedings of the 2009 22nd Conference on Software Engineering Education and Training, CSEET 2009, pp. 190–197. IEEE Computer Society, Washington, DC (2009)

17. van Vliet, H.: Reflections on software engineering education. IEEE Softw. 23(3), 55–61 (2006)

Collecting Requirements and Ideas for Architectural Group Decision-Making Based on Four Approaches

Iris Groher[(✉)] and Rainer Weinreich

Johannes Kepler University Linz, Linz, Austria
{iris.groher,rainer.weinreich}@jku.at

Abstract. To collect requirements and ideas for architectural group decision-making (GDM), we present and analyze four different approaches to GDM that were developed by master's students in a practical course at our university. The students involved had about five years of practical experience on average, and roughly 80 % of the students were working as software engineers while enrolled. We analyze the four approaches based on the criteria for evaluating approaches to architectural GDM defined by Rekha and Muccini; nearly all approaches fulfilled most criteria. Two criteria – support for conflict resolution and revisiting information – were partly addressed. The criterion of prioritizing group members was not addressed at all. The student-developed approaches provided some new ideas for architectural GDM, such as communication between stakeholders directly in the GDM tool and review of decisions after they have been made.

Keywords: Software architecture · Software architecture knowledge management · Group decision-making

1 Introduction

Group decision-making (GDM) has been extensively studied in the business domain since the 1970s [1,2]. Various existing approaches have been successfully used in practice to collaboratively find solutions by selecting among different alternatives, such as brainstorming, the Delphi method, or the Nominal Group Technique [3]. We recently conducted an international survey on architectural decision-making with software architects and lead developers in Europe and the United States [4], which revealed that architectural decision-making is to a large extent a group effort. Architectural decisions with a high impact, especially, are made in teams. This is in line with another survey among practitioners and researchers [5], which shows that most companies view architectural decision-making as a GDM process. Teams are usually distributed and heterogeneous, and involve people with different roles and responsibilities. Arrival at consensus seems to be more important than individual opinions. Farenhorst et al. [6] define architecting as consensus decision-making, seeking the agreement of most stakeholders.

© Springer International Publishing Switzerland 2015
D. Weyns et al. (Eds.): ECSA 2015, LNCS 9278, pp. 181–192, 2015.
DOI: 10.1007/978-3-319-23727-5_15

Established GDM techniques have not yet found their way into the software-architecture domain, and there is but little research regarding software architecture decision-making as a group process [5]. Only a few existing Software Architecture Knowledge Management (SAKM) tools provide support for GDM [7], even though support for collaboration has been identified as an important property of SAKM tools [6]. Rekha and Muccini [8] analyze how current architectural decision-making techniques support GDM, revealing that the current methods are not fully suitable for GDM because they are missing important aspects like stakeholder preference indication and group decision rules, among others.

To collect ideas and requirements for an approach to architectural GDM, four different prototype approaches to GDM were developed as part of a practical course at our university. After a short introduction, four groups of master's students were assigned the task to develop web-based tools specifically intended for architectural GDM. Nearly all students were working part-time as software developers or project managers. The groups also included very experienced students with several years of experience in professional software development. We asked the students explicitly to develop GDM approaches based on their practical experience. We evaluated the resulting approaches based on the criteria for evaluating architectural GDM approaches defined by Rekha and Muccini [8], revealing that nearly all approaches fullfilled most criteria. Two criteria – provisioning for conflict resolution and revisiting information – were only partly addressed. The criterion of prioritizing group members was not addressed at all. Analyzing the four approaches resulted in a number of new ideas and requirements for architectural GDM, such as communication between stakeholders directly in the GDM tool and rating of decisions after they have been made.

2   Study Setup

In a practical course on Service Engineering for master's students in Business Informatics at our university, students were given the task of developing a prototype GDM approach. The eighteen students enrolled in the course were divided into four teams (two teams of five students each and two teams of four students each).

We questioned the students about their working experience, the domains in which they had worked, technologies with which they were familiar, roles they had had in previous projects, and their current employment status. Over three-quarters of the students were currently working in addition to their studies (14 out of 18 students). They had worked in various domains, such as industrial automation, automotive, finance, insurance, logistics, customs, ERP systems, customer relationship management, mobile development, and voice and image recognition. The students had mainly worked as developers, but some had also worked as project and product managers, operations managers, CEOs, consultants, administrators, testers, and in sales and support.

The students had, on average, about five years of working experience. Two of the groups included very experienced people with 15 and 22 years of professional experience. In Team 1, one student had little experience (up to two years of working experience), one had medium experience (up to five years of experience), and two team members were highly experienced (more than five years of experience). In Team 2, three students had little experience, one student had medium experience, and one student had high experience. In Team 3, two students had little experience, two students had medium experience, and one student had high experience. In Team 4, one student had little experience, two students had medium experience, and one student had high experience. In total, seven students had little experience, six students had medium experience, and five students were highly experienced.

We presented the general idea of GDM and architectural decision-making to the students and provided them with basic literature regarding GDM and SAKM.[1] We explicitly asked them to extend the basic GDM functionality described in the literature with functionality they regarded as useful according to their practical experience. The students were instructed to use a web-based approach but were free in the selection of technologies.

Each team was required to create a project diary and a time account for each team member. They were asked to document the requirements and to create a small prototype to explore the chosen technologies. At the end of the course, the teams created a video[2] presenting their system from a user perspective, as well as documents describing the system architecture and test process.

The teams had bi-weekly meetings with the course instructors (the authors of this paper) and weekly meetings with two teaching assistants. During the meetings, we discussed their progress; the teaching assistants helped in case of technical problems.

3   Four Approaches to Architectural Group Decision-Making

The four approaches to architectural GDM that were developed in the course are called *Decide2Gether* (Team 1), *TeamDecision* (Team 2), *CollaboDecision* (Team 3), *Collaborative Design Decision Support System* or *CDDSS* (Team 4). In the following, we describe the main features of the developed approaches in more detail.

Basic Elements and Relationships. The *Decide2Gether* approach supports projects at the highest level. Projects contain topics and subtopics. Both topics and subtopics can have associated alternatives. Alternatives can require or exclude each other. The main concepts of *TeamDecision* and *CollaboDecision*

---

[1] The list of papers provided to the students during the course is available at: http://www.se.jku.at/wp-content/uploads/2015/06/gdm-papers.zip

[2] The videos of the four approaches are available at: http://www.se.jku.at/wp-content/uploads/2015/06/gdm-videos.zip

are issues, decisions, and alternatives. In *TeamDecision*, requires and excludes relationships can be defined between alternatives and between decisions. If a decision requires other decisions, those decisions have to be made first. In *ColaboDecision*, issues can be tagged. Users can search for issues with matching tags when creating new issues. Similar tags indicate potential relationships between issues. Supported relationships are: depends on, resolved by, and related to. The main concepts of *CDDSS*, finally, are issues and alternatives. Arbitrary types of relationships between issues can be defined. Similar to *CollaboDecision*, issues can be tagged. CDDSS provides a set of predefined tags; new tags can be defined as needed.

Stakeholders. All approaches support basic user and rights management, but the supported roles are different. *Decide2Gether* distinguishes between team members and project managers, where team members can add and rate alternatives, while project managers can make decisions. Additional kinds of stakeholders can be defined if necessary. In *TeamDecision*, issues have associated users and specific users (responsibles) can make decisions. In *CollaboDecision*, issues and decisions have an owner and a set of users. In *CDDSS*, issues have associated users with roles (contributor, viewer) and different rights.

Documents. All four approaches support adding documents to various elements. In *Decide2Gether*, documents can be associated with projects, topics, and alternatives. In *TeamDecision*, documents can be added to issues, decisions, alternatives, and positions. In *CollaboDecision*, documents can be attached to decisions and alternatives. *CDDSS* supports adding documents to issues and provides a set of predefined document types; new types can be added as needed.

Comments and Discussion. In *Decide2Gether*, team members can comment on projects, topics, and alternatives; comments are associated with the respective team member. In *CollaboDecision*, users can comment on decisions and alternatives; other users can also reply to each others' comments. In *TeamDecision*, users can discuss a decision using a chat feature, and the chat is stored and linked to the respective decision.

Lifecycle. All approaches provide a lifecycle for issues; the three main states are open (after creating issues), in progress (creating and rating alternatives), and closed (after deciding for a particular alternative). *CollaboDecision* provides an explicit lifecycle (visible in the UI) with the states of new, in progress (when decisions and their alternatives are created and ranked), resolved (when all decisions are made), obsolete, and rejected. *CDDSS* defines a workflow that guides users through collecting alternatives and criteria, weighting criteria, and rating alternatives.

History. *TeamDecision* logs all actions users perform, such as the creation of new issues and the rating of alternatives, in an activity history. Users can search or filter this history by user, modification date, type of modification, issue, or decision.

Rating Alternatives. All four approaches support the rating of alternatives. In *Decide2Gether*, team members rate the captured alternatives by agreeing or disagreeing with each one. Different colors are used to indicate the percentage of votes already submitted for a specific topic or subtopic. In *TeamDecision*, users can take positions (positive, neutral, or negative) on alternatives. In *CollaboDecision*, alternatives can be ranked (from 1 to n, where n is the number of alternatives). Based on the individual rankings of the users an overall ranking of the alternatives is calculated. *CDDSS* supports the rating of alternatives based on predefined criteria. Each contributor first needs to weight each criterion by how important they believe it is for the issue. Then, each alternative needs to be rated (from 1 to 10) for each criterion. Based on the individual ratings and the weights of the criteria, an overall ranking of the alternatives is calculated.

Reviewing and Rating Decisions. In all four approaches decisions taken can be reviewed afterwards so that stakeholders are able to provide comments on the usefulness and adequacy of the chosen decision later in the development process. This may lead to the development team revisiting and reevaluating decisions. In *Decide2Gether*, stakeholders can rate decisions by agreeing or disagreeing with the chosen alternative. In *TeamDecision*, decisions can be rated as positive, neutral, or negative. In *CollaboDecision*, decisions can be rated from 1 to 10; based on the individual ratings of the stakeholders, an overall rating for the decision is calculated. *CDDSS* also supports reviewing already taken decisions. Each decision allows comments and ratings from 1 to 5. Based on the individual ratings of the stakeholders, an overall rating is calculated.

Dashboard. All four approaches provide a dashboard to present the current state of the decision-making process to users. *Decide2Gether* presents the projects in which a user is involved, including a summary of the current ratings for each topic and its alternatives. The user also gets an overview of all alternatives that he/she has not yet rated. *TeamDecision* shows summaries of all decisions that have been made and all positions taken on the available alternatives. It also supports making a decision by selecting one of the alternatives directly in the dashboard. The dashboard also supports the rating and closing of issues. *CollaboDecision* provides a dashboard that presents issues and decisions assigned to the user, as well as decisions that need to be ranked or rated.

Final Decision. In all four approaches, the final decision is made by manually selecting one of the alternatives. The calculated rating may be used for guidance, but when making the final decision, the responsible persons with the right to make a particular decision can choose freely among the identified alternatives.

4   Evaluation of Approaches

We evaluate the four approaches to GDM presented in the previous section using the evaluation framework of Rekha and Muccini [8]. This framework has been developed to assess how well current software architecture decision-making methods support GDM. It is based on the group-problem-solving model proposed by Aldag and Fuller [9] and has been adapted to suit software architectural decision-making. In the following, we describe the evaluation criteria and how the four approaches address these in detail. Table 1 summarizes the evaluation of the four approaches based on the eight criteria, which are as follows:

1. Problem Identification: This criterion evaluates whether groups are involved right from the problem-identification stage, during which problems are identified, broken into sub-problems, and mapped to requirements. All four approaches support concepts like issues or topics for describing problems. *Decide2Gether* supports the management of projects, topics, and subtopics. *TeamDecision*, *CollaboDecision*, and *CDDSS* support the management of issues and their associated decisions. The hierarchical decomposition into problems and sub-problems is only provided by the *Decide2Gether* approach. *CollaboDecision* and *CDDSS* support tagging issues and establishing relationships between them. Tags and relationships can also be used for structuring the problem space. All approaches provide basic user and rights management in such a way that stakeholders with different rights can be assigned to the identified problems. Typically, one role (e.g., decision owner, project manager) takes the responsibility for a specific issue or problem. While all other stakeholders may propose alternative solutions, comment on issues and alternatives, and rank the proposed alternatives, the final decision is typically made by the responsible stakeholder.

2. Development of Alternatives: This criterion evaluates whether the development and identification of alternatives is integrated into the GDM process. The group should be supported in discussing, identifying, and evolving alternatives. All approaches support the collaborative development of alternatives and the inclusion of additional material, such as uploaded documents. Relationships between alternatives can be established in *Decide2Gether* and *TeamDecision*. Discussing alternatives by adding comments and answering other users' comments is supported in *Decide2Gether* and *CollaboDecision*. The *TeamDecision* approach provides a chat function linked to each respective alternative. Alternatives can be iteratively added and changed in all approaches, which supports their evolution.

3. Preference Indication: This criterion evaluates whether stakeholders can indicate preferences through ranking or scoring. Preferences should be based on the requirements to be fulfilled by the system or on other organizational criteria. All approaches support some form of preference indication. In *Decide2Gether*, stakeholders can agree or disagree with each of the available alternatives and comment on each of them. In *TeamDecision*, stakeholders can take positions (positive, neutral, or negative) on alternatives. *CollaboDecision* supports the ranking of alternatives. *CDDSS* supports adding criteria and weighting them.

4. Prioritizing Group Members: This criterion evaluates whether the approach supports prioritizing decision-makers, as not all group members may be equally important. None of the approaches supports the explicit prioritization of group members. However, all approaches provide basic user and rights management. *Decide2Gether* and *TeamDecision* restrict final decision-making to certain users. *CollaboDecision* provides the concept of decision ownership, where the decision owner makes the final decision by selecting one of the alternatives. *CDDSS* distinguishes between contributors and viewers; viewers are not allowed to edit information.

5. Provision for Conflict Resolution: This criterion evaluates whether an approach provides explicit mechanisms for avoiding or resolving conflicts in the group during decision-making. Avoidance and resolution of conflicts due to divergent views and preferences is supported by different means of communication among stakeholders. *Decide2Gether* and *CollaboDecision* provide means to comment on alternatives and answer comments made by other users. The *TeamDecision* approach provides a chat feature. Conflicts can also occur between decisions and/or alternatives (e.g., because of an excludes relationship). Some approaches support the definition of relationships between decisions that could be used for automatically detecting such conflicts. However, none of the approaches provides explicit conflict detection or resolution mechanisms.

6. Group-Decision Rules: This criterion evaluates how a decision is finally made by taking the preferences of the various stakeholders into account. *CollaboDecision* and *CDDSS* calculate an overall rating for each alternative based on the individual ratings of the stakeholders. *Decide2Gether* and *TeamDecision* present charts for visualizing stakeholders' ratings of each alternative. None of the approaches automatically selects an alternative based on these ratings. Instead, the preferred alternative is presented to the stakeholder making the final decision, who then manually selects one of the alternatives based on the proposed results and comments provided by the other stakeholders.

7. Information Exchange and Recall: This criterion evaluates how the approach supports balanced information exchange and representation so that optimal decisions are made. All four approaches support information exchange and recall. Issues, decisions, and alternatives can be freely described, along with users' rationale. Artifacts that provide additional information can be uploaded and linked to issues, decisions, and alternatives. All approaches provide a dashboard that presents an overview of all information relevant to the current user, including tasks that need completion such as alternatives to rank or decisions to make. Group discussions can occur in comments or chats about issues, decisions, and alternatives. *Decide2Gether* uses different colors to support the visualization of agreement and disagreement regarding alternatives. Color codes also indicate how many stakeholders have already rated the alternatives. Different icons are used to visualize closed and open topics. *CollaboDecision* uses different colors to mark alternatives that need to be ranked and decisions that need to be reviewed by the current user.

8. Revisiting Information: This criterion evaluates how the approach supports later revisiting alternatives, preferences, and decisions made. Revisiting information is partly supported by all approaches, because not all information can be changed at any time. *Decide2Gether* supports the revoking of decisions. *TeamDecision* supports editing information, but the information is locked from changes once a decision has been made. In *CollaboDecision* and *CDDSS*, issues and related information can only be revisited within the same stage of the life-cycle or workflow. It is not possible to go back to an earlier stage.

All approaches support rating and reviewing decisions after they have been made in order to reflect on the usefulness and adequacy of the selected alternative.

Table 1. Comparison of Approaches

Criteria	Decide2Geth.	TeamDecis.	CollaboDecis.	CDDSS
1. Problem Identification	projects, topics, subtopics	issues	issues, relationships, tagging	issues, relationships, tagging
2. Development of Alternatives	alternatives, relationships, comments, attachments	alternatives, relationships, attachments, chat	alternatives, comments, attachments	alternatives
3. Preference Indication	agree/disagree with alternatives	positions (positive, neutral, negative) for alternatives	ranking of alternatives	criteria and their weighting for rating alternatives
4. Prioritizing Group Members	not supported	not supported	not supported	not supported
5. Provision for Conflict Resolution	comments and answers	chat	comments and answers	not supported
6. Group Decision Rules	visualization of individual ratings	visualization of individual ratings	overall rating based on individual ratings	overall rating based on individual ratings
7. Information Exchange and Recall	issues, attachments, dashboard, comments	issues, attachments, dashboard, chat	issues, attachments, dashboard, comments	issues, dashboard
8. Revisiting Information	editing and revoking decisions, review of decisions	editing allowed, but decisions made cannot be changed, review of decisions	editing only allowed within a lifecycle stage, review of decisions	editing only allowed within workflow stage, review of decisions

5   Discussion

In total, seven out of eight criteria from the evaluation framework of Rekha and Muccini [8] are at least partially supported by the students' four approaches.

This result also serves to evaluate the criteria themselves, because the master's students who developed these approaches were not aware of the criteria.

Regarding *problem identification*, the approaches mainly differ with respect to the naming of the provided concepts (e.g., topics versus issues). Hierarchical structuring and tagging of issues and decisions is provided by some of the approaches; these seem to be valuable concepts. The tagging feature, particularly, can be very helpful when establishing relationships and constraints between issues and/or alternatives. *Development of alternatives* is similar in all approaches. *Preference indication* is also supported by all approaches, the simplest form of which is agreement or disagreement with alternatives. A more advanced strategy for preference indication is ranking of alternatives. One approach supports the definition and weighting of criteria. *Prioritizing group members* is not supported by any of the four approaches. This is also the case in the study of Rekha and Muccini [8], in which all evaluated approaches treated stakeholders equally. This could be an indicator that the criterion of prioritizing group members is not that important because, as Rekha and Muccini had already speculated, group members expect fairness during decision-making. *Conflict resolution* in the sense of commenting on and discussing issues and alternatives is provided by most approaches. Conflict resolution in the sense of resolving conflicts between dependent decisions is not provided, perhaps because of the limited time the students had to implement their approaches. *Group-decision rules* in the simplest form are supported by visualizations of results, such as charts. Two approaches also calculate overall ratings based on the individual ratings of stakeholders. Automated decision-making seems not to be desired but would easily be possible based on these rating results. This is in line with our recent survey [4], which revealed that typically a dedicated person or group of people makes a final decision. *Information exchange and recall* is supported by all approaches, but fulfillment of this criterion could surely be improved by spending more development time on UI features. *Revisiting information* is partly supported by all approaches but could definitely be improved. Only one approach supports revoking decisions. Two approaches support editing only within a stage of the lifecycle or workflow. One approach does not support changing decisions that have been made.

An additional feature that is not among the criteria but has been provided by all approaches is a dedicated rating and review of made decisions. This feature can be used for judging the appropriateness of a decision over time, and this feedback may be an input for revisiting decisions as a system evolves, as well as for making decisions in other projects.

In the following, we reflect on our experiences in supervising this project with master's students at our university.

Teams in the course did not see the intermediate results of other teams. This proved valuable because teams developed their own ideas without being influenced by the features or UI design of the approaches developed by the other teams.

As outlined in Section 2, the teams had different levels of professional experience. All in all, it seems that experience did not significantly influence the overall quality and feature sets of the teams' approaches. Still, it is interesting that the approach of the most experienced team, Team 1, provides the fewest features, focusing more on usability than on functionality, while the approaches of the teams with less experience provide a richer feature set with more complex interaction. The most experienced team obviously decided to provide a less restrictive workflow than did the other teams, and it was the only team whose approach allows revisiting and revoking decisions at any time. Having persons with high experience as part of the team also proved to be beneficial in general, since the highly experienced team members drove the project, were respected, and also raised the level of motivation.

We had originally planned to let the teams document their own decisions and later capture them using their own approaches, but this did not work as intended. This was because students needed some time and work on their approach to more deeply understand what to capture and when. They were not motivated enough to capture their decisions without tool support. We plan to use and evaluate the tools in future courses with software-engineering projects and also with our industrial partners.

In general, the project drew student interest on the topic of SAKM and the documentation of decisions and their rationales. Students emphasized that they had already experienced problems due to a lack of decision management in their previous projects and that they would push for systematic decision-making in their future work.

6 Related Work

The Software Architecture Warehouse (SAW) tool [10] provides support for both co-located and distributed design workshops through an argumentation viewpoint and live design documents. The argumentation viewpoint integrates issues, alternatives, and positions, which are subjective opinions of team members on design alternatives. A position can be captured together with a rationale and a weight, which indicates the confidence level of the position. Decisions and alternatives have an associated lifecycle. SAW provides so-called live design documents in which changes are immediately propagated to all team members. Different color codes are used to visualize the state of decisions and positions, and relationships (influence) between issues and/or alternatives can be defined. SAW does not support prioritizing group members or provide tools for conflict resolution. Group-decision rules are partly supported, as SAW provides an overview of all positions for each captured alternative. Review of decisions is not supported in SAW.

The CoCoADvISE approach [11] supports collaborative architectural decision-making based on reusable decision models. Documented, reusable decisions defined for recurring design situations can be instantiated and used as guidance for architectural decision-making. CoCoADvISE integrates consistency constraints that are automatically enforced during decision-making. Roles and permissions are also supported and enforced. The approach only partially supports problem identification and development of alternatives, because it restricts decision-making to already documented, reusable decision models. Preferences cannot be indicated, and group-decision rules are not supported. Prioritizing group members is supported by the roles and permissions features. Conflict resolution is partly supported by an automatic constraint-enforcement feature. In general, the approach more emphasizes a final decision rather than developing, discussing, and rating alternatives as a team.

The Repertory Grid Tool (RGT) [12] is a web-based tool for group decision-making based on the Repertory Grid Technique, a methodology for knowledge capture. RGT supports the capturing of decisions, alternatives, and concerns. Concerns have an associated priority to indicate their importance. Alternative-concern pairs are rated to express how well a concern is addressed by an alternative. RGT enables analysis of each decision, its alternatives, and its concerns in order to support decision-making. RGT is based on a Delphi-like, iterative approach to structuring group interactions, in which decision-makers are shown the priorities and ratings of other decision-makers. In addition, RGT produces viewpoint-based documentation of the captured information. RGT does not support prioritizing group members and does not provide explicit support for conflict resolution. Review of made decisions is also not supported in RGT.

7   Conclusion

Architectural decision-making is a group effort in many organizations [4,5]. However, the domain of software architecture has not yet applied established GDM techniques, and support for GDM has not yet been fully integrated into existing tools for SAKM.

In this paper, we presented four GDM tools developed as part of a practical course at our university, collecting requirements and ideas for architectural GDM by evaluating these approaches using the eight criteria published in [8].

This evaluation suggested that the criteria seem to fit, because seven out of eight criteria are at least partly supported by approaches that were developed without the criteria in mind. One criterion, prioritization of group members, is generally questionable because it is not supported by any of the four approaches, nor was it supported by the approaches reviewed in [8]. Revisiting information during decision-making by returning to previous stages or reverting already made decisions is important but not fully supported by the approaches presented in this paper. More studies are necessary in this case to identify which information should be revisitable and when. Strategies for rating alternatives were quite different among the four approaches. Some provided simple strategies while others supported the definition of weighted criteria. More studies are also necessary in this case to identify suitable strategies for preference indication during architectural GDM. Automated decision-making does not seem to be a desirable feature of GDM tools; in all four approaches, final decision-making is a manual activity.

Some approaches put more focus on UI design than do others by, for example, using color codes and icons to indicate stakeholder preferences and to visualize the status of decisions. As usability is important for GDM tools, more work in this direction is needed.

Acknowledgments. Acknowledgements We would like to thank the master's students who participated in the course and developed the four GDM approaches described in this paper.

References

1. Janis, I.: Victims of Groupthink: A Psychological Study of Foreign-Policy Decisions and Fiascoes. Houghton Mifflin Company (1972)
2. Myers, D., Lamm, H.: The group polarization phenomenon. Psychological Bulletin **83**(4), 602–627 (1976)
3. Van de Ven, A., Delbecq, A.: The effectiveness of nominal, delphi, and interacting group decision making processes. Academy of Management Journal **17**(4), 605–621 (1974)
4. Weinreich, R., Groher, I., Miesbauer, C.: An expert survey on kinds, influence factors and documentation of design decisions in practice. Future Generation Computer Systems **47**, 145–160 (2015)
5. Rekha, V.S., Muccini, H.: A study on group decision-making in software architecture. In: 2014 IEEE/IFIP Conference on Software Architecture (WICSA), pp. 185–194, April 2014
6. Farenhorst, R., Lago, P., van Vliet, H.: Effective tool support for architectural knowledge sharing. In: Oquendo, F. (ed.) ECSA 2007. LNCS, vol. 4758, pp. 123–138. Springer, Heidelberg (2007)
7. Shahin, M., Liang, P., Khayyambashi, M.R.R.: Architectural design decision: Existing models and tools. In: Joint Working IEEE/IFIP Conference on Software Architecture & European Conference on Software Architecture, WICSA/ECSA 2009, pp. 293–296. IEEE (2009)
8. Rekha, V.S., Muccini, H.: Suitability of software architecture decision making methods for group decisions. In: Avgeriou, P., Zdun, U. (eds.) ECSA 2014. LNCS, vol. 8627, pp. 17–32. Springer, Heidelberg (2014)
9. Aldag, R., Fuller, S.: Beyond fiasco: A reappraisal of the groupthink phenomenon and a new model of group decision processes. Psychological Bulletin **113**(3), 533–552 (1993)
10. Nowak, M., Pautasso, C.: Team situational awareness and architectural decision making with the software architecture warehouse. In: Drira, K. (ed.) ECSA 2013. LNCS, vol. 7957, pp. 146–161. Springer, Heidelberg (2013)
11. Gaubatz, P., Lytra, I., Zdun, U.: Automatic enforcement of constraints in real-time collaborative architectural decision making. Journal of Systems and Software **103**, 128–149 (2015)
12. Tofan, D., Galster, M.: Capturing and making architectural decisions: an open source online tool. In: Proceedings of the 2014 European Conference on Software Architecture Workshops, ECSAW 2014, pp. 33:1–33:4. ACM, New York (2014)

Cloud and Green

Characterization of Cyber-Foraging Usage Contexts

Grace A. Lewis[1,2]([✉]) and Patricia Lago[2]

[1] Carnegie Mellon Software Engineering Institute, Pittsburgh, USA
glewis@sei.cmu.edu
[2] VU University Amsterdam, Amsterdam, The Netherlands
p.lago@vu.nl

Abstract. Cyber-foraging is a technique to enable mobile devices to extend their computing power and storage by offloading computation or data to more powerful servers located in the cloud or in single-hop proximity. There are many domains and applications that can benefit from the longer battery life and better application performance on mobile devices that is typically associated to the use of cyber-foraging, such as field operations, sensor systems, and entertainment. However, obtaining these benefits in operational systems requires meeting functional and non-functional requirements that vary depending on the usage context of the cyber-foraging system. This paper presents a characterization of usage contexts for cyber-foraging defined in terms of functional and non-functional requirements for cyber-foraging systems. The goal of the characterization is to provide context for software engineering life cycle activities for cyber-foraging systems, such as requirements engineering, software architecture and quality assurance, with the intent of developing systems that fully realize the benefits of cyber-foraging.

1 Introduction

Cyber-foraging is an area of work within mobile cloud computing that leverages external resources (i.e., cloud servers, or local servers called surrogates) to augment the computation and storage capabilities of resource-limited mobile devices while extending their battery life. There are two main forms of cyber-foraging. One is computation offload, which is the offload of expensive computation in order to extend battery life and increase computational capability. The second is data staging to improve data transfers between mobile devices and the cloud by temporarily staging data in transit.

While computation offload and data staging can be done between mobile devices and cloud resources, this work focuses on offloading computation and data to proximate servers called surrogates, as shown in Figure 1, as opposed to a remote cloud server. The offload operation is synchronous to a surrogate that is in single-hop proximity, over a likely high bandwidth connection. The communication between the surrogate and the cloud resource is multi-hop and either synchronous or asynchronous depending on the quality of the link and mobile

© Springer International Publishing Switzerland 2015
D. Weyns et al. (Eds.): ECSA 2015, LNCS 9278, pp. 195–211, 2015.
DOI: 10.1007/978-3-319-23727-5_16

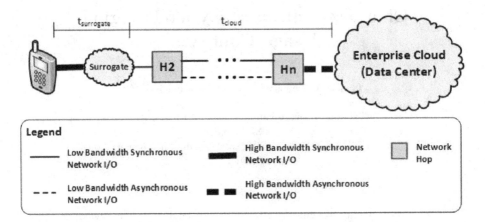

Fig. 1. Surrogate-Based Cyber-Foraging

application needs. If we assume that $t_{surrogate}$ is less than t_{cloud}, nearby surrogates are a better option from an energy consumption and latency perspective [1].

This paper presents the characterization of the usage domains and contexts that benefit from surrogate-based cyber-foraging, defined in terms of functional and non-functional requirements. The goal of this characterization is to provide context for software engineering life cycle activities for cyber-foraging systems, such as requirements engineering, software architecture and quality assurance, with the intent of developing systems that fully realize the benefits of cyber-foraging. The next section describes the analysis that led to the characterization of usage contexts for cyber-foraging. Sections 3, 4, and 5 contain the details of each identified usage context. Section 6 presents the related work in this area. Finally, Section 7 concludes the paper and outlines next steps.

2   Analysis

In previous work we conducted a systematic literature review (SLR) on architectures for cyber-foraging [2] that identified 57 primary studies and 60 cyber-foraging systems. Common design decisions present in the cyber-foraging systems described in the primary studies were codified into architectural tactics for cyber-foraging and then grouped into functional and non-functional architectural tactics [3][4]. For this work we started with the same set of primary studies identified in the SLR. In the first phase, for each primary study we extracted the names of the environments and types of applications that were being targeted in the cyber-foraging systems presented either as examples or case studies. We then clustered these results based on similarity. The results of the mapping between usage contexts and primary studies is shown in Table 1. In the second phase we revisited the primary studies in each usage context extracting functional requirements (FRs) and non-functional requirements (NFRs) explicitly and implicitly stated in each study, with the goal of identifying recurring requirements in each usage context. Each FR and NFR that was stated in at least three of the primary studies was considered a recurring requirement. The exception is the *Mobile Applications in Hostile Environments* usage context which only has two studies, in which case we considered it recurring if it was stated in both.

The identified FRs and NFRs for each usage context are shown in the conceptual model in Figure 2, inspired by UML class diagrams and the inheritance relationship. The rectangles with the rounded top corners represent a *context characterization* and include FRs and NFRs that are common across more than one usage context. The rectangles marked with *UC#* represent the usage contexts derived from Table 1 and include FRs and NFRs that are unique to that usage context. Each usage context inherits FRs and NFRs from context characterizations and other usage contexts, as defined by the inheritance relationship between elements. Some FRs, such as *FR1*, appear in several context characterizations and usage contexts. In this case, the inheriting element is "overriding" the FR with specific details for the context characterization or usage context.

3   Cyber-Foraging Usage Contexts

Cyber-foraging systems in all usage contexts need to satisfy:

- **(NFR1) Energy efficiency**: Offloading computation should consume less energy than local execution based on the premise that offloading is beneficial when large amounts of computation are needed with relatively small amounts of communication [5].
- **(NFR2) Faster response time:** Offloading computation should lead to a faster response time that local execution.
- **(NFR3) Increased computing power:** Offloading computation and data should take advantage of the greater computing power of surrogates.

4   Computation Offload Usage Contexts

Cyber foraging systems that perform computation offload need to satisfy:

- **(FR1) Offload of computation-intensive operations:** A cyber-foraging-enabled application, upon encountering computation-intensive code explicitly marked for offload, the mobile application determines if the conditions are appropriate for offload (e.g., surrogate availability, network conditions, remaining battery). If so, the mobile device locates a surrogate for offload, offloads the computation, and waits for a response from the surrogate.

4.1   Usage Context 1: Computation-Intensive Mobile Applications (Short Operations)

The systems in this usage context are mobile applications that contain computation-intensive operations which if executed on a mobile device would take in the order of tens of seconds, but if offloaded could improve response time considerably. These are typically request-response, synchronous operations such as:

- Image, audio and video processing and manipulation
- Face detection and recognition
- Speech recognition and translation
- Antivirus/Anti-malware
- Gaming (typically AI-based)

Table 1. Cyber-Foraging Usage Contexts: Mapping of Primary Studies

Usage Context	Example Applications and Domains	Systems in Primary Studies
Computation-Intensive Mobile Applications (Short Operations)	- Image, audio and video processing and manipulation - Face detection and recognition - Speech recognition - Speech translation - Antivirus/Anti-malware - Gaming (AI-based)	31 Systems: Chroma [Balan2007], Computation and Compilation Offload [Chen2004a], Cloud Media Services [Cheng2013], CloneCloud [Chun2009], HPC-as-a-Service [Duga2011], OpenCL-Enabled Kernels [Endt2011], Real Options Analysis [Esteves2011], Collective Surrogates [Goyal2011], Virtual Phone [Hung2011], Single-Server Offloading [Imai2012], Android Extensions [Iyer2012], ThinAV [Jarabek2012], Cuckoo [Kemp2012], ThinkAir [Kosta2012], MACS [Kovachev2012], Scavenger [Kristensen2010], AMCO [Kwon2013], MCo [Lee2012], PowerSense [Matthews2011], AIDE [Messer2002], PARM [Mohapatra2003], Resource Furnishing System [Ok2007], SOME [Park2012], SmartVirtCloud [Pu2013], MAPCloud [Rahimi2012], VM-Based Cloudlets [Satyanarayanan2009], IC-Cloud [Shi2013], Heterogeneous Auto-Offloading Framework for Mobile Web Browsers [Zhang2009], Weblets [Zhang2011], DPartner [Zhang2012], Elastic HTML5 [Zhang2012a]
Mobile Applications in Low Coverage Environments	- Resource-challenged environments - Field operations (e.g., researchers, medics, sales and marketing)	7 Systems: Mobile Agents [Angin2013], Edge Proxy [Armstrong2006], Mobile Information Access Architecture for Occasionally Connected Computing [Bahrami2006], MAUI [Cuervo2012], 3DMA [Fjellheim2005], Spectra [Flinn2002]

Continued on next page

Table 1. (*Continued*)

Usage Context	Example Applications and Domains	Systems in Primary Studies
Computation-Intensive Mobile Applications (Long Operations)	- Service-based applications - Workflow-based applications - Search-based applications	4 Systems: Cloud Operating System to Support Multi-Server Offloading [Imai2012], Odessa [Ra2011], SPADE [Silva2008], Offloading Toolkit and Service [Yang2008]
Mobile Applications in Hostile Environments	- Emergency response - Military operations	2 Systems: Cloudlets [Ha2011], Application Virtualization on Cloudlets [Messinger2013]
Public Surrogates	Everyday use	4 Systems: Collaborative Applications [Chang2011], Roam [Chu2004], Trusted and Unmanaged Data Staging Surrogates [Flinn2003], Slingshot [Su2005]
Sensing Applications	- Healthcare - Intelligent transport systems - Ambient intelligence - Environmental monitoring - Context-aware applications - Participatory sensing (Crowdsensing)	8 Systems: mHealthMon [Ahnn2013], C2C [Aucinas2012], Grid-Enhanced Mobile Devices [Guan2008], Feel The World [Phokas2013], Smartphone-Based Social Sensing [Rachuri2012], Large-Scale Mobile Crowdsensing [Xiao2013], Sonora [Yang2012], Mobile Data Stream Application Framework [Yang2013a]
Data-Intensive Mobile Applications	- Mobile cloud applications - Online gaming - Data-rich domains	4 Systems: Kahawai [Cuervo2012], AlfredO [Giurgiu2009], Telemedik [Kundu2007], Cloud Personal Assistant [OSullivan2013]

In addition to FR1, NFR1, NFR2, and NFR3, cyber-foraging systems in this usage context need to satisfy:

- **(NFR4) Maintainability and Evolvability:** Systems may perform a runtime decision to offload. In this case, two versions of the same code (local and remote) need to be maintained and evolved over time.

Benefits: The main benefit of cyber-foraging in this usage context is augmented execution due to computation offload (FR1) to more powerful resources (NFR3). Computation offload also reduces battery consumption (NFR1) which leads to longer battery life and provides better response times (NFR2) due to offload to proximate resources instead of remote cloud resources [1].

Constraints: Systems that make runtime decisions in this usage context to execute locally or remotely have the advantage of additional battery savings because

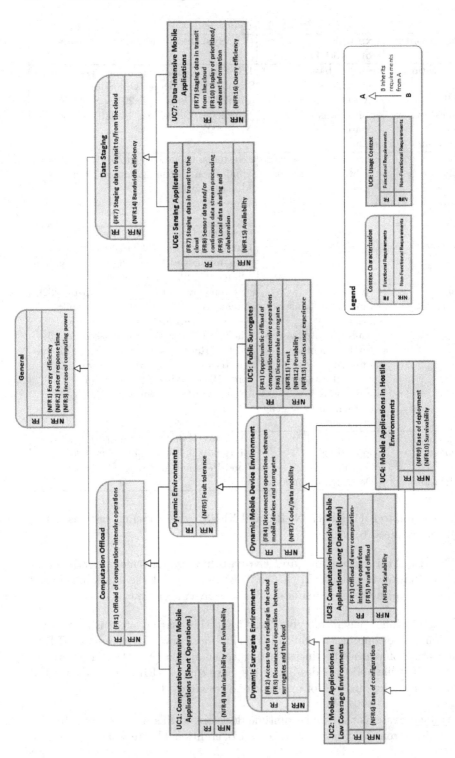

Fig. 2. Conceptual Model for Cyber-Foraging Usage Contexts

offload only occurs when conditions are conducive to battery savings based on code characteristics, surrogate availability, and environment conditions (e.g. network quality, available bandwidth). Also, because operations take seconds to execute, restarting an operation locally due to a disconnected surrogate may not have a large negative effect on user experience if recovering does not exceed an acceptable wait time and user is informed of the situation. However, care has to be given to maintainability and evolvability (NFR4) because it is likely that two versions of the code have to be maintained: one for the mobile device and one for the surrogate. If not managed carefully it can lead to increased effort in parallel code maintenance and evolution.

4.2 Dynamic Environments

Cyber-foraging systems often operate in dynamic environments where connectivity between mobile devices and surrogates, or between surrogates and the cloud, cannot be guaranteed. These systems need to be able to detect and react to periods of disconnection.

- **(NFR5) Fault tolerance:** Mobile devices leveraging surrogates, and surrogates connected to the cloud, should be able to detect and react appropriately to periods of disconnection.

In situations in which connectivity between the surrogates and the cloud cannot be guaranteed (*Dynamic Surrogate Environment*), there is a need for surrogates to continue supporting the computational and data needs of mobile devices even during periods of disconnection.

- **(FR2) Access to data residing in the cloud:** Surrogates serve as caches for data located in the cloud that is required by mobile applications.
- **(FR3) Support for disconnected operations between surrogates and the cloud:** Surrogates should take advantage of available connectivity to the cloud to synchronize with master data sources and cache data that might be required given changes in context, user preferences, or user actions.

In situations in which connectivity between the mobile devices and surrogates cannot be guaranteed (*Dynamic Mobile Device Environment*), there is a need for surrogates to save results of offload operations until connectivity is restored, or where computation can move as mobile devices move.

- **(FR4) Support for disconnected operations between mobile devices and surrogates:** If a mobile device loses contact with the surrogate before it can obtain a result, the surrogate should save the results until the mobile device is reachable.
- **(NFR7) Code/Data mobility:** If multiple connected surrogates are available the system should be able to move code and data to other surrogates to fulfill application needs and continuity of operations.

Usage Context 2: Mobile Applications in Low Coverage Environments.
Low coverage environments are characterized by disconnection, or occasional
connectivity, between surrogates and the cloud, but potentially good connectivity
between mobile devices and surrogates. Examples of applications and domains
include:

- Resource-challenged environments: Less-privileged regions characterized by
  limited Internet access, limited electricity and network access, and potentially low levels of literacy can leverage surrogates, deployed in for example
  kiosks, to obtain information to support their communities.
- Field operations: People that spend time away from their main offices or
  labs, such as researchers, medics, and sales personnel, can leverage portable
  surrogates to support their computation and data needs.

In addition to FR1, FR2, FR3, NFR1, NFR2, NFR3, and NFR5, cyber-
foraging systems in this usage context need to satisfy:

- **(NFR6) Ease of configuration:** Surrogates should contain capabilities
  that enable administrators to load surrogates with the computation and data
  needed to support the mobile applications that will be using it, especially in
  areas where they might not be technical staff available.

Benefits: Mobile applications in low coverage environments can benefit from
cyber-foraging for augmented execution due to computation offload (FR1) to
more powerful resources (NFR3). In the case of resource-challenged environments, surrogates can execute computation-intensive operations such as speech,
image or gesture recognition as alternate forms of input to account for low levels
of literacy. Reduced battery consumption (NFR1) due to offload of computation-
intensive operations leads to longer battery life, especially in environments
where recharging mobile devices is difficult. In addition, applications have better response times (NFR2) as well as lower energy consumption (NFR1) due
to offload to proximate surrogates instead of remote cloud servers. Finally, pre-
provisioned surrogates (FR2) can carry all computation and data that is needed
by surrogate users and can function disconnected from the cloud (FR3).

Constraints: The benefits of cyber-foraging are only possible if surrogates are
properly pre-provisioned, that is, they contain all the data and computation
required by the mobile applications that use them. Processes that predict computation and data usage based on user profiles, workflows, or access history are
necessary to support ease of configuration (NFR6). In addition, cyber-foraging
systems operating in low coverage environments require fault tolerance (NFR5)
mechanisms to be able to detect periods of connection and disconnection between
surrogates and the cloud and seamlessly switch between operating in connected
and disconnected mode. Surrogates should continue supporting mobile applications when disconnected from the cloud, even if in degraded mode.

Usage Context 3: Computation-Intensive Mobile applications (Long Operations). The systems in this usage context are mobile applications that contain computation-intensive operations which if executed on a mobile device would take minutes to hours, but if offloaded could improve response time considerably. In most cases there is not an option for local execution given the computing requirements of the offloaded operations, which are likely greater than what is available locally, or would drain the battery before returning a result. The types of applications that contain long operations — that are also typically asynchronous to avoid blocking — include:

- Service-based applications: Applications that are composed of a number of possibly independent services which may perform long operations.
- Workflow-based applications: Applications that execute a workflow that may include steps that are long-running, such as business applications in which the mobile application initiates a long-running business process.
- Search-based applications: Applications that require searching through large data sets, such as data analytics applications or applications that combine data from different sources. These applications can be composed of discrete tasks or single replicated tasks (i.e., executing the same search against different data sources).

While systems in this usage context still need to satisfy FR1 (computation offload), it would have to be redefined as *Offload of very computation-intensive operations*. What this means is that upon encountering very computation-intensive code marked for offload, the mobile application locates a surrogate for offload, offloads the code, and either waits for a response from the surrogate (synchronous) or is notified by the surrogate that the operation is complete (asynchronous).

In addition to the redefined FR1, FR4, NFR1, NFR2, NFR3 NFR5, and NFR7, cyber-foraging systems in this usage context need to satisfy:

- **(FR5) Parallel offload:** If surrogates are connected to other surrogates and operations are parallelizable, the cyber-foraging system should attempt to leverage the combined computing power of the set of available surrogates.
- **(NFR8) Scalability:** If multiple connected surrogates are available, and offloaded operations are parallelizable, the system should be able to determine the optimal amount of surrogates to utilize for execution of the offloaded computation.

Benefits: Mobile applications that contain long computation-intensive operations can benefit from cyber-foraging from augmented execution due to computation offload (FR1) to more powerful resources (NFR3), and longer battery life (NFR1) due to offload of long computation-intensive operations. In addition, applications have better response times (NFR2) as well as lower energy consumption (NFR1) due to offload to proximate resources instead of remote cloud resources.

Constraints: Very-computation intensive operations may require the resources of more than one surrogate in order to achieve the benefits of cyber-foraging. If possible, due to parallelization of these long computation-intensive operations, multiple connected surrogates would need to implement load balancing for scalability (NFR8, FR5). However, load balancing requires moving computation and data between surrogates, which in turn requires execution containers such as virtual machines that support code and data mobility (NFR7). In addition, given that a mobile device may lose contact with a surrogate before the operation finishes, mechanisms such as caching data until the mobile device is reconnected, or using alternative communication mechanisms to reach the mobile device (e.g., SMS) are necessary (FR4). A user should be informed when this happens so that he/she knows that the results will not be available until reconnection (NFR5).

Usage Context 4: Computation-Intensive Mobile Applications in Hostile Environments. Hostile environments, such as those in which emergency responders or military personnel operate in, are characterized by very dynamic environments in which disconnected operations — or occasionally-connected operations — between surrogates and the cloud, and between mobile devices and surrogates, are highly likely. In addition to FR1, FR2, FR3, FR4, NFR1, NFR2, NFR3, NFR5 and NFR6, systems in this usage context need to satisfy:

- **(NFR9) Ease of deployment:** It should be easy to deploy surrogates in the field to support a mission (e.g., on vehicles, in tents, or in provisional operations centers).
- **(NFR10) Survivability:** Surrogates and mobile applications should be able to continue operating in spite of disruptions caused by the operational environment.

Benefits: Mobile applications in hostile environments can benefit from augmented execution due computation offload (FR1) to more powerful resources (NFR3). Reduced battery consumption (NFR1) due to offload of computation-intensive operations which leads to longer battery life is another benefit, especially in these environments where recharging mobile devices may be difficult. Applications also benefit from better response times (NFR2) as well as lower energy consumption (NFR1) due to offload to proximate resources instead of remote cloud resources. To deal with dynamic environments, pre-provisioned surrogates (FR2) can carry all data that is needed by surrogate users executing a mission and can function disconnected from the cloud (FR3). Offload decisions can be based on a basic algorithm that simply detects surrogate availability such that operations execute locally if a surrogate is not available (FR4). In case of disconnection, surrogates can cache offload operation results (FR4) until the mobile device is reconnected. Finally. if computation is self-contained (e.g., in a VM) and more than one surrogate is available, computation can migrate between surrogates due to mobile device mobility (i.e., mobile device moves beyond the range of a surrogate) and/or surrogate mobility (e.g., in case surrogates reside in vehicles) (FR4, NFR7).

Constraints: The benefits of cyber-foraging are only possible if surrogates are properly pre-provisioned, that is, they contain all the data and computation required by the mobile applications that use them. Processes that predict computation and data usage based on mission profiles, user profiles, workflows, or access history are necessary to support ease of configuration (NFR6). In addition, cyber-foraging systems operating in hostile environments require fault tolerance mechanisms (NFR5) to be able to detect periods of connection and disconnection, and seamlessly switch between operating in connected and disconnected mode. Because of the uncertainty of connections between mobile devices and surrogates, fallback to local execution is required in case of unavailable surrogates or disconnection during offload operations (FR4). Finally, hostile environments require systems to continue operating in spite of the uncertainly of the environment in order to ensure the success of missions. Mechanisms to ensure ease of deployment (NFR9) and configuration (NFR6) such as self-contained capabilities and management consoles can support quick setup of surrogates and capabilities to support a mission. In addition, mechanisms that promote survivability (NFR10) such as multiple discoverable, connected surrogates that can load balance or transfer offloaded computation in case of disconnection (NFR7), are key to reaching the benefits of cyber-foraging in these environments.

Usage Context 5: Public Surrogates. Publicly-available surrogates on which any user can offload computation-intensive operations is a vision for cyber-foraging cited by the studies listed in Table 1 for this usage context. The goal of mobile applications that leverage public surrogates is seamless mobility, that is, the capability to move code (and data) between mobile devices and surrogates with minimal human intervention.

Although this usage context falls under *Dynamic Environments*, it is different from the other usage contexts in this group because computation offload is opportunistic instead of user-triggered. This is why FR1 is redefined as *Opportunistic offload of computation-intensive operations*. What this means is that upon discovery of an available surrogate, running mobile applications that are determined to be computation-intensive migrate their execution to the discovered surrogate (either manually or automatically). When the mobile device leaves the vicinity of the surrogate (or because of termination actions such as expiration time or manual intervention), the computation on the surrogate migrates back to the mobile device.

In addition to the redefined FR1, NFR1, NFR2, NFR3 and NFR5 cyber-foraging systems in this usage context need to satisfy:

- **(FR6) Discoverable surrogates:** Surrogates should broadcast their presence to cyber-foraging-enabled mobile applications for discovery.
- **(NFR11) Trust:** When a mobile device discovers a surrogate it expects a trustworthy surrogate execution environment, meaning that once an offload operation starts, code and data are not maliciously modified or stolen, and that it provides trustful services. In the same way, a surrogate expects that a mobile device is a valid client and that it will not offload malicious code or use it as a vehicle to other code and data offloaded by other mobile devices.

- **(NFR12) Portability:** Offloaded computation should be able to run on a variety of surrogate platforms.
- **(NFR13) Lossless user experience** The migration of computation (and data) between a mobile device and a surrogate should cause minimal disruption to a user, other than what is defined in the migration process or protocol (e.g, authentication, manual disconnection).

Benefits: A benefit of cyber-foraging using public surrogates is augmented execution due to opportunistic computation offload (FR1) to more powerful, discoverable resources (FR6, NFR3). Reduced battery consumption (NFR1) due to offload of computation-intensive operations, which leads to longer battery life, is also a benefit. Finally, faster response times (NFR2) as well as lower energy consumption (NFR1) are expected due to offload to proximate, more powerful resources.

Constraints: Offload to public surrogates implies that the mobile user does not own the surrogate. Trust (NFR11) has to be built into the cyber-foraging system such that the mobile user trusts that code and data offloaded to the surrogate is not going to be compromised, and the surrogate trusts that the user will not use it to install malicious code. In addition, given that the relationship between the mobile device and the surrogate is transient, fault tolerance (NFR5) mechanisms are required to detect when a mobile device is in proximity of a surrogate and when it is not such that it can seamlessly switch between local execution and remote execution (NFR13). Finally, in public surrogates there is likely no control over their configuration. Portability of offloaded code and data (NFR12) is required in order to adapt to multiple execution environments.

5 Data Staging Usage Contexts

Cyber foraging systems that perform data staging need to satisfy:

- **(FR7) Staging data in transit to/from the cloud:** Surrogates should act as intermediate data caches between mobile devices and the cloud.
- **(NFR14) Bandwidth efficiency:** Mobile devices should offload data to surrogates, and surrogates should send data to mobile devices, only when conditions are conducive to bandwidth efficiency, such as when network quality is above an established threshold, when network traffic is below an established threshold, or when cached data reaches an established bundle size for sending.

5.1 Usage Context 6: Sensing Applications

The systems in this usage context are mobile applications that perform context, environment or urban sensing using on-board sensors (e.g., camera, microphone, accelerometer) or connected sensors (e.g. gas, ambient temperature). The sensing applications collect data from these sensors and send to surrogates as these become available. Examples of domains and applications in this usage context include:

- Context-aware applications: A mobile application uses sensors to acquire contextual information and send to surrogates for processing to perform for example complex activity or scene recognition
- Healthcare: A mobile application is used by patients carrying body sensors to gather data from these sensors and send on to surrogates for analysis.
- Intelligent transport systems: A mobile application integrated into a vehicle can obtain readings from multiple sensors and send on to surrogates located at various points throughout the city to for example perform traffic analysis and control, surveillance, or emergency management.
- Ambient intelligence: Ambient intelligence can be supported by mobile applications that sense contextual data and send to surrogates for rapid processing to provide personalized, adaptive and anticipatory services such as ambient control (e.g., lighting, music, temperature) and calendar management.
- Environmental monitoring: Mobile applications equipped with environmental sensors such as gas, pressure or temperature collect data to send to surrogates for processing for disaster prevention, detection and response activities.
- Participatory sensing (Crowdsensing): Crowdsensing refers to individuals using mobile devices with sensors that share information about an event or task of interest such as environmental monitoring, public safety, traffic monitoring, or collaborative searches.

In this usage context, surrogates typically act as intermediaries as sensed data flows from the mobile devices to the cloud, which is why FR7 (data staging) needs to be redefined as *Staging data in transit to the cloud*. This means that data collected on surrogates is stored for upload to the enterprise cloud when possible.

In addition to the redefined FR7, NFR1, NFR2, NFR3, and NFR14, cyber-foraging systems in this usage context need to satisfy:

- **(FR8) Sensor and/or continuous data stream processing:** As surrogates become available, sensor data collected by the mobile device is sent to the surrogate for processing and storage.
- **(FR9) Local data sharing and collaboration:** Surrogates store and process collected data to make it available to mobile devices that it is serving.
- **(NFR15) Availability:** Surrogates should be available for data offload from mobile devices. A corollary to this requirement is that mobile devices need to be able to deal with unavailable surrogates.

Benefits: Offloading data (FR7) to surrogates releases storage space on mobile devices to continue data collection activities (the surrogate storage can be considered an extension to mobile device storage (NFR3)). Data staging on surrogates (FR8) enables data sharing and collaboration (FR9) between mobile devices leveraging the same surrogate and eventual upload of that data to the enterprise cloud (FR7). Similar to computation offload systems, offloading data processing operations to surrogates minimizes battery consumption (NFR1) on the mobile device. Proximate surrogates also enable faster response times (NFR2) for data processing and queries than sending data/queries to remote clouds. Finally, implementing a runtime decision mechanism for offloading data to surrogates optimizes available bandwidth (NFR14) and minimizes data transfers thereby minimizing battery consumption (NFR1).

Constraints: Availability (NFR14) of the surrogate is key to realizing most of the stated benefits of cyber-foraging for sensing applications. In addition to implementing availability tactics on the surrogate, such as fault detection, recovery and prevention [6], a sensing application needs to detect surrogate unavailability, cache data when the surrogate is unavailable, and make decisions on what to do when operating in disconnected mode and storage capacity limits are reached (e.g., perform local data processing, discard data, or stop operations).

5.2   Usage Context 7: Data-Intensive Mobile Applications

Data-intensive mobile applications rely on large sets of data to provide their functionality. Data typically resides in data centers or in the enterprise cloud. Examples of data-intensive applications and domains include:

- Mobile cloud applications: These applications provide a front end to data residing in the cloud, such as social media apps, map and navigation apps, and e-commerce applications.
- Online gaming: Online gaming requires continuous streaming of data to and from the cloud in order to synchronize with other players.
- Data-rich domains: Healthcare and other data-rich domains are characterized by large sets of connected data, which means that queries for one type of data typically trigger queries for other sets of related data.

Data-intensive mobile applications require large amounts of data that resides in the cloud and surrogates serve as intermediaries between mobile devices and the cloud to avoid direct communication to the cloud for every data operation. FR7 (data staging) is therefore redefined as *Staging data in transit from the cloud*. In addition to the redefined FR7, NFR1, NFR2, NFR3 and NFR14, cyber-foraging systems in this usage context need to satisfy:

- **(FR10) Display of prioritized/relevant information:** Mobile devices have small(er) screen sizes that limit the amount of information that can be displayed at a time. Surrogates pre-process data that is retrieved or pushed from the cloud, such that mobile devices receive data that is ready to be displayed, or filtered such that they only receives data of interest or relevance.
- **(NFR16) Query Efficiency:** Queries should be executed against data located proximate surrogates instead of data residing in the cloud.

Benefits: For data-intensive mobile applications, surrogates can cache data from the cloud (FR7) to minimize high latency communication between mobile devices and the cloud, which decreases response time (NFR2); provides extended, proximate data storage for applications (NFR3); and reduces battery consumption (NFR1). Surrogates can perform data filtering and priorization (FR10) so that mobile devices users receive only the data that they need (NFR2).

Constraints: Data-intensive mobile applications only benefit from cyber-foraging if the data that they need is already on the surrogate, in order to avoid direct communication to the cloud. This means that there have to be mechanisms on the surrogate to predict what data will be needed next by mobile applications (NFR16). Data may be pre-fetched based on mobile device context (e.g., location), user profile (e.g., preferences), access history (i.e., data that the user has accessed in the past), or data relations (e.g., querying a purchase order also fetches vendor, product and other data related to that order).

6   Related Work

There is a large amount of work in cyber-foraging, which includes the primary studies identified in the SLR that are listed in Table 1. One of the findings of the SLR reported in [2] is the the lack of focus on system-level concerns such as fault tolerance, ease of configuration and deployment, survivability, and security, that would be necessary to implement operational systems in many of the identified usage contexts. There are also multiple surveys on the future and benefits of mobile cloud computing and cloud-based augmentation such as [7] and [8]. However, to the best of our knowledge we are the first to develop architectural tactics for cyber-foraging and further to characterize usage contexts for cyber-foraging in this manner.

7   Summary and Next Steps

The paper presented a characterization of usage contexts for cyber-foraging defined in terms of functional and non-functional requirements for cyber-foraging systems. Each usage context showed that NFRs can be both benefits and constraints — there are NFRs that enable a system to achieve the benefits of cyber-foraging, and there are other NFRs that if not met will compromise the benefits of cyber-foraging for mobile systems. As cyber-foraging becomes a standard feature for computation- and data-intensive mobile systems, it will become even more important to have models such as the one presented in this paper. These usage contexts combined with the architectural tactics for cyber-foraging identified in [3] and [4] provide a standard language and set of reusable design decisions that will help in developing better and more standard mobile systems that leverage all the potential benefits of cyber-foraging, as well as mobile devices and operating systems that enable and facilitate these benefits.

The goal of the model is to provide context for software engineering life cycle activities for computation- and data-intensive mobile systems, with the intent of developing systems that fully realize the benefits of cyber-foraging.

- Requirements engineers can use the model to determine if cyber-foraging is the appropriate paradigm for reaching desired functional and non-functional requirements
- Software architects and designers can use the model to better understand the requirements that need to be met to realize the full benefits of cyber-foraging, as well as the constraints for realizing those benefits
- Quality assurance personnel can develop scenarios and test cases that can be used to determine if system requirements are being met.

We are in the process of documenting case studies to validate the architectural tactics identified in [3] and [4]. The case studies in combination with the defined usage contexts will be used as input to define a decision model for cyber-foraging systems that will guide system architects and developers to build systems that fully realize the benefits of cyber-foraging now and in the future.

Online Material. The references for the primary studies can be found in [2] and are also available at http://goo.gl/ZLC1to.

Acknowledgments. Acknowledgements. This material is based upon work funded and supported by the Department of Defense under Contract No. FA8721-05-C-0003 with Carnegie Mellon University for the operation of the Software Engineering Institute, a federally funded research and development center. This material has been approved for public release and unlimited distribution (DM-0002352). This research also received partial funding by project SIA RAAK MKB Greening the Cloud.

References

1. Balasubramanian, N., Balasubramanian, A., Venkataramani, A.: Energy consumption in mobile phones: a measurement study and implications for network applications. In: Proceedings of the 9th ACM SIGCOMM Conference on Internet Measurement Conference, IMC 2009, pp. 280–293. ACM, New York (2009)
2. Lewis, G.A., Lago, P., Procaccianti, G.: Architecture strategies for cyber-foraging: preliminary results from a systematic literature review. In: Avgeriou, P., Zdun, U. (eds.) ECSA 2014. LNCS, vol. 8627, pp. 154–169. Springer, Heidelberg (2014)
3. Lewis, G., Lago, P.: A catalogue of architectural tactics for cyber-foraging, Tech. rep., VU University Amsterdam (2014). http://goo.gl/rDCt3V
4. Lewis, G.,Lago, P.: A catalogue of architectural tactics for cyber-foraging. In: Proceedings of the 11th International ACM Sigsoft Conference on the Quality of Software Architectures (QoSA 2015) (2015)
5. Kumar, K., Lu, Y.-H.: Cloud computing for mobile users: Can offloading computation save energy? Computer **43**(4), 51–56 (2010)
6. Bass, L., Clements, P., Kazman, R.: Software architecture in practice, 3rd edn. Addison-Wesley (2012)

7. Fernando, N., Loke, S.W., Rahayu, W.: Mobile cloud computing: A survey. Future Generation Computer Systems **29**, 84106 (2012)
8. Abolfazli, S., Sanaei, Z., Ahmed, E., Gani, A., Buyya, R.: Cloud-based augmentation for mobile devices: Motivation, taxonomies, and open challenges. IEEE Communications Surveys Tutorials **16**(1), 337–368 (2014)

Software Architecture for the Cloud – A Roadmap Towards Control-Theoretic, Model-Based Cloud Architecture

Claus Pahl[1][(✉)] and Pooyan Jamshidi[2]

[1] IC4 & Lero, School of Computing, Dublin City University, Dubin, Ireland
Claus.Pahl@dcu.ie
[2] Department of Computing, Imperial College London, London, UK

Abstract. The cloud is a distributed architecture providing resources as tiered services. Through the principles of service-orientation and generally provided using virtualisation, the deployment and provisioning of applications can be managed dynamically, resulting in cloud platforms and applications as interdependent adaptive systems. Dynamically adaptive systems require a representation of requirements as dynamically manageable models, enacted through a controller implementing a feedback look based on a control-theoretic framework. We argue that a control theory and model-based architectural framework for the cloud is needed. While some critical aspects such as uncertainty have already been taken into account, what has not been accounted for are challenges resulting from the cloud architecture as a multi-tiered, distributed environment. We identify challenges and define a framework that aims at a better understanding and a roadmap towards control-theoretic, model-based cloud architecture – driven by software architecture concerns.

Keywords: Cloud computing · Control theory · Adaptive system · Software architecture · Microservice · Model-based controller · Uncertainty

1   Introduction

Adapting systems to changing requirements is often a necessity to guarantee on-going correct and satisfying performance. Self-adaptive systems are systems that are able to adjust their behaviour in response to their perception of the environment and the system itself [3]. The software engineering community has approached this from the requirements engineering perspective [11], but has recognised the need for software architecture to play a major role in a solution.

Requirements need to have a representation at runtime to allow self-adaptive systems to interact with the environment, i.e., reflect this through models that also link in the decision-making process necessary to change the underlying system itself [1,2,6]. Dynamically adaptive systems require a representation of requirements as dynamically manageable models, enacted through a controller implementing a feedback look based on a control-theoretic framework [5].

© Springer International Publishing Switzerland 2015
D. Weyns et al. (Eds.): ECSA 2015, LNCS 9278, pp. 212–220, 2015.
DOI: 10.1007/978-3-319-23727-5_17

The cloud is moving towards a distributed, often federated architecture of many individual cloud services [10], providing resources as services in a tiered fashion. The configuration, deployment and provisioning of application architectures can be managed dynamically as a response to changes in requirements and changes in the execution platform environment, resulting in cloud platforms and the applications in them as interdependent adaptive systems. Microservices are emerging as a new architectural style, aiming at realising software systems as a package of small services, each deployable on a different platform. These run in their own process while communicating through lightweight mechanisms without any centralized control[1]. We argue that a cloud-specific control-theoretic, model-based architectural framework is needed. While critical aspects such as uncertainty have been investigated [4,8,9] for the cloud, what has not been accounted for are the challenges resulting from the cloud architecture as a multi-tiered, distributed environment for increasingly fragmented application architectures.

We identify the challenges and define a conceptual framework. The target is a roadmap towards control-theoretic, model-based cloud architecture in which software architecture concerns play the central role.

2   Cloud Architecture – Definition and Scenario

Our view on cloud systems from an architectural perspective addresses the key shortcomings of the current discussion of control-theoretic approaches to adaptive systems, and cloud in particular. We will also argue for a model-based approach to controller definition later on as well. The cloud allows the distributed, tiered deployment of software. The underlying architecture links infrastructure and platform providers with the software applications running in them. Software is usually logically architected in a layered format, but in the cloud mapped onto (virtualised) physical tiers.

- Logical layers organise code. Typical layers include presentation, business logic and data management and storage. However, this does not imply that the layers run on different computers or in different processes.
- Physical tiers are about the location of the application execution. Tiers are places where layers are deployed and where layers run.

The cloud services provided as infrastructure-as-a-services (IaaS), platform-as-a-service (PaaS) or software-as-a-service (SaaS) realise these tiers, albeit in a virtualised form accessed through services.

A further complication arises through clouds as distributed, often federated systems, even if providing the same or similar services, will operate differently. Interaction between the layers, but also horizontally is possible and necessary, which we capture in the following architectural scenario in Figure 1.

Let us illustrate a common problem. An infrastructure server might have the capacity to deal with 100 user applications at the same time, but the workload

---

[1] http://martinfowler.com/articles/microservices.html.

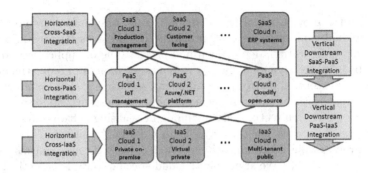

Fig. 1. Tiered and Distributed Cloud Architecture.

might temporarily reduce significantly. Load balancing would allow the system architecture to be adapted and applications relocated to one server, thus scaling down the deployment of servers. Here, the system reacts to external factors – the reduced load – and adapts the configuration to reduce the costs (a non-functional requirement) while still maintaining adequate performance (also a non-functional requirement). Two observations emerge.

- Workload and QoS dictate the adaptation. Cost and quality as drivers for decisions – i.e., decisions are made based on non-functional requirements.
- In the cloud as a tiered architecture, where user applications might run on third-party provided infrastructure servers. Factors that influence here down-scaling as the adaptation include (i) application performance at the user tier/layer and (ii) system workload at the infrastructure tier/layer.

Other scenarios here could involve changing non-functional requirements rather than changing environment factors. The performance requirement might need to be tightened, resulting in an up-scaling of the infrastructure.

Recently, microservice architectures have been discussed, which aim to break up application architectures into independently deployable services that can be rapidly deployed to any infrastructure resource as required. Microservices are independently deployable, usually supported by a fully automated deployment and orchestration framework. They require the ability to deploy often and independently at arbitrary schedules, instead of requiring synchronized deployments at fixed times. The microservice deployment and orchestration across the vertical and horizontal dimensions of the cloud are central architecture concerns. Clouds provide a management tool for their flexible deployment schedules and provisioning orchestration needs, particularly, if these are to be PaaS-provisioned.

3   Dynamic Requirements and Models

As the example above has indicated, both requirements (the user-facing tiers) and the platform (the infrastructure-facing tiers) can change dynamically. What is needed first is a review of modelling concerns for this context. Drivers of change are often requirements to maintain quality-of-service at the user end to maintain within the limits (non-functional requirements) possible stated in a service-level agreement. In [3], a number of model dimensions are identified that help to frame the adaptivity problem:

- Goals as system objectives: evolution, flexibility, multiplicity, dependency
- Change captures causes of adaptation: source, type, frequency, anticipation.
- Mechanism implements adaptation: type, autonomy, organisation, scope, duration, timeliness, triggering
- Effects define adaptation impact: criticality, predictability, overhead, resilience

A challenges here is the mapping of requirements to the underlying architecture. The solution is a control loop, based on control-theoretic foundations [11], but importantly, the layering of the application architecture onto the tiered cloud. The run-time representation of requirements in the form of application requirements and cloud infrastructure models needs to provide model manipulation and access features to allow introspection and reasoning about these models [1,6].

A specific challenge is the uncertainty that arises in the interaction between models and the system architecture – the latter possibly at different tiers/layer, all interacting with one another along their interfaces, cf. Figure 1. Respective models that capture uncertainty and can map this as actions within the control loop are needed. The models themselves need to reflect the adaptation approach, requiring to capture the non-functional properties, but more significantly allow prediction and reasoning to take place in an environment prone to uncertainty.

4   Measurement, Prediction and Uncertainty

The state of a system is characterised by a range of non-functional properties that need to be aligned with non-functional requirements. Due to the layering, mapping and managing these across layers, but also within one layer, is challenging. In general, we need to measure at different layers and map between the different tiers in the cloud.

- The upper level represents the application service-level qualities.
- The lower level are the loads of infrastructure resources that run the service.

Furthermore, there is a mapping of the infrastructure loads into a cost model – which can of course be a major driver of adaptation decisions.

Measurement and Uncertainty. Ideally, system state attributes can be reliably measured. However, the cloud adds a high degree of uncertainty here [11]:

- Uncertainty Level 1: general confidence about the shape of the future, but some key variables do not have precise values.

- Uncertainty Level 2: there are a variety of possible future scenarios, that can be listed and are mutually exclusive and exhaustive.
- Uncertainty Level 3: it is feasible to construct future scenarios, but these are mere possibilities and are unlikely to be exhaustive.
- Uncertainty Level 4: it is not even possible to frame possible future scenarios.

Uncertainty emerges from various sources in cloud systems – as uncertainty from different interpretations and decisions in the adaptation definition process or as uncertainty arising from possible different, distributed monitoring systems resulting in partially unreliable and incomplete data [9]:

- Uncertainty in Adaptation Definition. Adaptation policies need a careful determination of thresholds. This relies on a users knowledge of system behaviour and how resources are managed. Therefore, the accuracy of policies remains subjective, making the effect of adaptations prone to uncertainty. Unpredictable changes in environment or application demand may require adaptation models to be continuously re-evaluated and revised.
- Uncertainty in Dynamic Resource Provisioning. Acquiring and releasing virtual resources in the cloud is not instantaneous. A cloud controller uses the platform services to initiate the acquisition process and has to wait until resources are available. During this time, which may take minutes for VMs, the cloud application is vulnerable to workload increases, causing uncertainty.
- Uncertainty in Monitoring Data. The cloud controller needs to continuously monitor the state of the application as well as of the resources in which the application is deployed in order to timely react to load variations. Monitoring involves a distribution of data collected by measurement-specific probes or sensors, which are not immune to measurement deviations (so-called sensory noise). This sensory noise is another source of uncertainty, as it results in oscillations that may affect how the controller allocates resources.

Formal Models for Uncertainty. Models captures the state, its behaviour and the adaptation rules. Models of different types can reflect how we deal with uncertainty in dynamic systems. The dynamics of a system are often based on state models, describing sequences of possible actions as a protocol. In [1], a Markovian model is used (DTMC – Discrete Time Markov Chains; alternatives could include continuous time models), formalising specific properties in logics such as a probabilistic logics [2] to reason in uncertain spaces – in an uncertain space, the probability of the next state is included in the model.

Others propose fuzzy logic [9], where fuzziness is expressed as a varying, non-binary truth value. This allows the uncertainty of a system situation to be expressed through a membership functions on fuzzy sets. For instance, a fuzzification of adaptation rules [9] can be done. As an example, qualitative values for infrastructure workload and service performance (such as 'very low' or 'very high' for workload) are presented as membership functions in a fuzzy set model, resulting in smoother controller responses.

Analysis and Prediction – Cross-Tier Mapping and Uncertainty. Unreliable or incomplete data causes uncertainty, which can be alleviated to some extent by prediction. Furthermore, the delay in providing resources, as discussed above, also makes prediction a suitable approach. Two aspects emerge:

- Analysing measure system data allows us to predict behaviour, reducing uncertainty and increasing the robustness of the adaptation.
- Prediction also helps to link the layers and tiers in the architecture, as for instance infrastructure tier metrics can be used to predict service-level quality. Prediction captures dependencies and becomes a link between the tiers.

Through predication and analysis of monitored data, we can e.g. identify stable quality utilisation patterns. We can map infrastructure workload patterns for CPU, storage and network utilisation at the infrastructure tier to service-level performance patterns, thus linking models (here pattern-based) across tiers [12].

We can implement a prediction technique for the same workload and performance prediction context, based on simple and double exponential smoothing to smoothen outliers and to anticipate trends. Here the aim is the robustness of the prediction and overall adaptation process (by looking ahead in vulnerable moments when the system is about to change).

5   Control Theory and Controller Architecture

Control theory and control engineering can be applied to build self-adaptive systems. Control theory can help to build the models and the reasoning about them to inform the decision making [3]. Decision making is a multi-objective process [11]. Constructing a utility function that involves all stakeholders (such as end-users and the providers of the various tiers of the system in question) is a challenging task [7]. This utility function is implemented by the cloud controller. This construction of utility function (the model) and the controller is a process involving the following steps [5]: identify goals, identify knobs (measure), devise model and design controller, complemented by validation and verification steps.

A key property of this controller is robustness. Robustness tells how resilient the controller is against noise and uncertainty. Prediction, as discussed above, is in addition to a proper calibration of the model a contributor to robustness. Prediction across layers has already addressed the challenges arising from the tiered cloud architecture. Techniques such as horizontal scaling can deal with the distribution dimension at each tier.

All concerns need to be managed by a control loop. Often, the MAPE-K model is utilised [1], cf. Fig. 2, as the structure of a controller: *M*onitor application and environment (in control-theoretic terms disturbances such as workload). *A*nalyse the input data and detect any possible violation. *P*lan corrective actions in terms of adding resources or removing existing unutilized ones. *E*xecute the plan according to a specific platform. Utilise a shared *K*nowledge (model).

It is the task of the controller to synchronise models with run-time architecture [11]. The model part of the controller needs to be implemented and

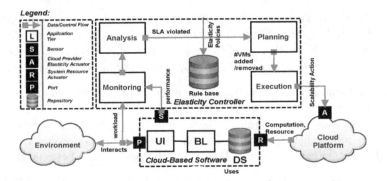

Fig. 2. MAPE-K Control Loop for the Cloud.

integrated with the cloud architecture in order to allow a model-driven cloud control of non-functional aspects [5].

Controller construction still faces a number of problems [4], including uncertainty, synthesize controllers, heterogeneity, unpredictable workloads, resource bottlenecks, multi-tier applications, multi-cloud resources and scalability. We have already discussed uncertainty and unpredictability. The last few points indicate the importance of the cloud as a problem from the software architecture perspective, i.e., an architecture onto which the concerns need to be projected:

– Measurement: the controller integrates different models representing the application and infrastructure models at the different tiers – vertical dimension.
– Actuating/executing: typically within a tier, but across services, e.g., based on scalability actions as adaptations – the horizontal dimension.

Uncertainty [5,8] could also be addressed by reducing the dependency on human stakeholders. Here, machine learning can serve to learn adaptation rules rather than relying on uncertain, possibly erroneous or inconsistent user input. Again, the software architecture perspective can clarify this. A suitable architecture would add a meta-model layer on top of the MAPE-K control loop, representing the learning loop on the models. Models can provide prediction and the feedback loop can correct it, e.g., a queuing model provide how much resources are needed to guarantee an SLA. Since the model is not precise, then it can be augmented with a feedback to correct the error, called feedforwarding.

6   Conclusion

The cloud is a distributed, multi-tiered platform onto which layered, modular software application architectures are mapped. The virtualisation of the cloud resources causes this to be an adaptive system, that is, however, subject to uncertainty and other challenges. Our contribution is the discussion from a software architecture perspective and to propose a roadmap towards a model-based control-theoretic solution that defines some core contributors to future solutions:

- models for uncertainty, allowing prediction and enforcing robustness in a control-theoretic framework,
- a model-driven multi-tier cloud controller to manage layered built from easily deployable microservices,
- adapting the architectural configuration in the cloud, but also re-architecting the application for the cloud.

There is a need for a controller framework that addresses the layered architecture of an application mapped onto tiered cloud resource services through a set of linked models for robust control-theoretic uncertainty management. Challenges for this framework include big data and real-time analytics for the a dynamic adaptation as well as stream processing.

Acknowledgments. This work was supported by Science Foundation Ireland grant 13/RC/2094 to Lero (www.lero.ie) and by the Irish Centre for Cloud Computing and Commerce (IC4), a Technology Centre funded by Enterprise Ireland and the IDA.

References

1. Baresi, L., Ghezzi, C.: A journey through smscom: self-managing situational computing. Computer Science - Research and Development **28**(4), 267–277 (2013)
2. Chan, K., Poernomo, I.H., Schmidt, H., Jayaputera, J.: A model-oriented framework for runtime monitoring of nonfunctional properties. In: Reussner, R., Mayer, J., Stafford, J.A., Overhage, S., Becker, S., Schroeder, P.J. (eds.) QoSA 2005 and SOQUA 2005. LNCS, vol. 3712, pp. 38–52. Springer, Heidelberg (2005)
3. de Lemos, R., Giese, H., Müller, H.A., Shaw, M., Andersson, J., Litoiu, M., Schmerl, B., Tamura, G., et al.: Software engineering for self-adaptive systems: a second research roadmap. In: de Lemos, R., Giese, H., Müller, H.A., Shaw, M. (eds.) Software Engineering for Self-Adaptive Systems. LNCS, vol. 7475, pp. 1–32. Springer, Heidelberg (2013)
4. Farokhi, S., Jamshidi, P., Brandic, I., Elmroth, E.: Self-adaptation challenges for cloud-based applications: a control theoretic perspective. In: 10th International Workshop on Feedback Computing 2015 (2015)
5. Filieri, A., Maggio, M., Angelopoulos, K., D'Ippolito, N., Gerostathopoulos, I., Hempel, A., Hoffmann, H., Jamshidi, P., Kalyvianaki, E., Klein, C., Krikava, F., Misailovic, S., Papadopoulos, A., Ray, S., Shariffoo, A., Shevtsov, S., Ujma, M., Vogel, T.: Software engineering meets control theory. In: Intl Symposium on Software Engineering for Adaptive and Self-Managing Systems SEAMS 2015 (2015)
6. Ghezzi, C., Pinto, L., Spoletini, P., Tamburrelli, G.: Managing non-functional uncertainty via model-driven adaptivity. In: Inl. Conf. on Soft. Eng. (2013)
7. van Hoorn, A., Rohr, M., Gul, A., Hasselbring, W.: An adaptation framework enabling resource-efficient operation of software systems. In: Proceedings of the Warm Up Workshop for ACM/IEEE ICSE 2010, WUP 2009. ACM (2009)
8. Iftikhar, M., Weyns, D.: Assuring system goals under uncertainty with active formal models of self-adaptation. In: Companion Proceedings of the 36th International Conference on Software Engineering. ACM (2014)
9. Jamshidi, P., Ahmad, A., Pahl, C.: Autonomic resource provisioning for cloud-based software. In: Intl. Symp. on Software Engineering for Adaptive and Self-Managing Systems, SEAMS 2014 (2014)

10. Pahl, C.: Containers and clusters for edge cloud architectures - a technology review. In: Intl. Conference on Future Internet of Things and Cloud, FiCloud 2015 (2015)
11. Sawyer, P., Bencomo, N., Whittle, J., Letier, E., Finkelstein, A.: Requirements-aware systems: a research agenda for re for self-adaptive systems. In: International Requirements Engineering Conference, RE 2010, pp. 95–103 (2010)
12. Zhang, L., Zhang, Y., Jamshidi, P., Xu, L., Pahl, C.: Workload patterns for quality-driven dynamic cloud service configuration and auto-scaling. In: International Conference on Utility and Cloud Computing, UCC 2014 (2014)

Model-Based Energy Efficiency Analysis of Software Architectures

Christian Stier[1]([⊠]), Anne Koziolek[2], Henning Groenda[1], and Ralf Reussner[2]

[1] FZI Research Center for Information Technology, Karlsruhe, Germany
{stier,groenda}@fzi.de
[2] Karlsruhe Institute of Technology, Karlsruhe, Germany
{koziolek,reussner}@kit.edu

Abstract. Design-time quality analysis of software architectures evaluates the impact of design decisions in quality dimensions such as performance. Architectural design decisions decisively impact the energy
efficiency (EE) of software systems. Low EE not only results in higher
operational cost due to power consumption. It indirectly necessitates
additional capacity in the power distribution infrastructure of the target deployment environment. Methodologies that analyze EE of software
systems are yet to reach an abstraction suited for architecture-level reasoning. This paper outlines a model-based approach for evaluating the
EE of software architectures. First, we present a model that describes
the central power consumption characteristics of a software system. We
couple the model with an existing model-based performance prediction
approach to evaluate the consumption characteristics of a software architecture in varying usage contexts. Several experiments show the accuracy
of our architecture-level consumption predictions. Energy consumption
predictions reach an error of less than 5.5% for stable and 3.7% for varying workloads. Finally, we present a round-trip design scenario that illustrates how the explicit consideration of EE supports software architects
in making informed trade-off decisions between performance and EE.

1 Introduction

Software architects design enterprise software systems to meet quality requirements in multiple dimensions, e.g., performance and reliability. In designing
a software system they have to make trade-off decisions to address contra-
dictory goals of stakeholders. System users are interested in having sufficient
Quality of Service (QoS) at an acceptable price. System providers aim to reduce
the cost incurred from hosting the software system. Power consumption is a
major operating cost factor. It is responsible for over 15% of a data center's
Total Cost of Ownership (TCO) [9].

The power consumption of servers varies strongly depending on the *load*
induced on the servers. If the utilization of a server increases (e.g. because more
software components are deployed to it, or because more users use its services),
its power consumption increases.

© Springer International Publishing Switzerland 2015
D. Weyns et al. (Eds.): ECSA 2015, LNCS 9278, pp. 221–238, 2015.
DOI: 10.1007/978-3-319-23727-5_18

In addition to the amount of power consumed by the servers, the costs induced by power consumption also include the costs of power distribution equipment. The degree by which system operators consolidate load depends not only on QoS requirements but also on the available power distribution infrastructure. Power distribution infrastructure in data centers is organized in a hierarchical manner [1]. Power distribution units (PDUs) distribute power to racks which in turn provide power to the connected servers. As servers rarely all simultaneously reach peak utilization, the power distribution infrastructure is usually over-subscribed [1]. Whether this over-subscription will lead to problems depends upon the workload mix and the deployed software components.

The software system's architecture impacts these power consumption costs: First, design decisions may influence the power consumption directly, for example the decision how to distribute the system to how many servers, or the decision what architecture-level communication style to use [19]. Second, to assess the costs of the expected power consumption, architects additionally need to consider what power distribution infrastructure is needed and when power is consumed. Thus, software architects need to consider the influence of architecture design on power consumption to make informed trade-off decisions between the QoS of offered services and power consumption costs.

Software engineering approaches are yet to reach an abstraction suitable for supporting the design of energy efficient software systems on an architectural level. Seo et al. perform energy consumption analysis for specific architectural styles [19]. Their work cannot be applied to predict the impact of other design decisions on energy efficiency (EE). Brunnert et al. analyze the EE of software systems on the basis of average-case analysis [6]. This is not sufficient to determine the peak power consumption the deployed software causes on the infrastructure. Approaches from the embedded systems and cloud/grid computing domain make limiting assumptions on the behavior of users [12,14] or disregard parametric dependencies between software components [7,12].

In this paper, we propose an approach for analyzing the EE of software architectures. It accounts for variations in user load and allows to identify periods with high power consumption. Thereby it not only enables software architects to determine whether the planned deployment of a software system meets average-case QoS and energy consumption goals, but also whether the system violates QoS and consumption limits during temporary workload spikes.

The contributions of this paper are as follows. First, it outlines an approach for *modeling the power consumption* characteristics of software systems on the architectural design layer. Second, an *analysis methodology for energy efficiency*, i.e. as a trade-off between power consumption and performance, is presented. Our approach extends an architecture-level approach for performance prediction by power consumption predictions. It does not require software component-specific consumption annotations. Rather, it uses component-independent consumption characterizations of the deployment environment and component-specific performance annotations to reason on the consumption characteristics of a deployed software system.

In our evaluation, we investigated the accuracy of the power consumption predictions for a media hosting system (evaluation question Q1). The architectural power consumption predictions reached an average-case error of less than 5.5%. We evaluated whether the approach could accurately predict power consumption trends (Q2). Furthermore, we showcased the potential benefits of applying power consumption analysis as part of the architecture design by investigating a design decision (Q3) and a deployment decision (Q4) that affect both performance and power consumption in a nontrivial manner. Our approach predicted the absolute effect of using an alternative encoder with an error lower than 18.9% (Q3). A deployment decision scenario illustrated the effect that power infrastructure sizing has on the degree by which a system can be horizontally scaled (Q4)).

The paper is structured as follows: Section 2 provides foundations on power models used for power consumption predictions and Palladio. Section 3 presents the state of research and highlights the gaps. Section 4 introduces the architecture of the running example. Section 5 presents our power consumption model and 6 our analysis methodology. Finally, Section 7 presents the evaluation results and Section 8 concludes.

2   Foundations

This section presents methodologies and concepts that our approach is built upon. Section 2.1 discusses models to estimate the power consumption of hardware components. Palladio's Architectural Description Language (ADL) and performance prediction approach are presented in Section 2.2.

2.1   Power Models

Power models estimate the power consumption of hardware components or sets of hardware components. Power models correlate power consumption with measurable metrics. They are constructed based on power measurements, which are collected as part of a benchmark. A wide variety of power models exists. They range from models that rely on system-level metrics [8,11], i.e., CPU utilization, to models that consider performance counters [5] and other hardware internals [10].

Fan et al. [8] propose and evaluate a linear as well as a non-linear regression-based power model for predicting the power consumption of single servers. Their models correlate power consumption solely with CPU utilization. Non-linear power models exceed the accuracy of linear power model across a wide range of different workloads, as is confirmed by Rivoire et al. [18]. Nevertheless, existing power consumption predictions most commonly build upon linear power models [6,7,17].

2.2   Palladio

Palladio [4] supports the analysis of quality characteristics of a component-based software architecture. Software architectures are specified in the

Palladio Component Model (PCM) ADL. Palladio evaluates the performance characteristics of an architecture either using analytical approaches or Discrete Event Simulation (DES) [4].

PCM is a meta-model for modeling component-based software architectures and the factors that influence the performance of a software system. PCM consists of different views that abstract distinct modeling concerns. The central view of PCM is *Component Specification*. In the Component Specification view the interfaces and behavior of services offered by each component are described. The behavior of a service is specified in a *Resource Demanding Service Effect Specification (RDSEFF)*. The RDSEFF correlates the input parameters of a service call with the demands it issues on resources such as CPU or HDD. Furthermore, the RDSEFF specifies parametric dependencies of the service's performance on the performance of service calls to its required components. The *Assembly Model* view defines an assembly of component instances. Figure 1b provides an example Assembly and RDSEFF instance. Besides the description of components and their assembly, the views include the definition of the system's deployment environment and usage context. The *Resource Environment* view describes the deployment environment of components. It describes the performance characteristics of the available compute and network infrastructure. The *Allocation* view maps the components in the assembly to the deployment environment. PCM's *Usage Model* separately models the behavior and arrival rate of users that interact with the system.

The advantage of PCM's performance abstraction over the direct specification of performance models using formalisms such as Queueing Networks (QNs) lies in its composability. The performance model of each component is defined as a set of RDSEFFs of its provided services. The RDSEFFs of a component are parametrized over the component's assembly, deployment and usage, so that it can be reused for different contexts in which the component itself shall be reused (e.g. in a different system, a different deployment, or a different usage profile). Figure 1b shows an example RDSEFF parametrized over the size of the input values in bytes. Once the assembly, deployment and usage of the components in the architecture have been specified, the Palladio tool composes the performance models and analyzes it via simulative or analytical approaches from the domain of queueing theory [4].

3   Related Work

Over the years many design patterns [16] have been proposed to increase the EE of software systems. Little work, however, has been done on quantitatively evaluating the EE of software systems on an architectural level at design time.

Seo et al. [19] evaluate the impact of architectural communication styles on energy consumption. The authors outline consumption models for specific communication styles such as client-server and publish-subscribe. Their approach disregards power consumption resulting from computation as the authors argue that application behavior is independent from the communication style. While the approach proposed by Seo et al. can be applied to compare the power consumption of specific communication styles, it consequently cannot be leveraged to evaluate the overall energy consumption of a software system.

Meedenyia et al. [14] propose a multi-objective architecture optimization approach for embedded component-based systems. The authors focus on the trade-off between energy consumption and reliability. Their approach annotates each component with an estimate of the energy consumption incurred by calling one of its services. Meedeniya et al. assume that all calls to a component consume the same amount of energy. The authors do not differentiate energy consumption for different input parameters. This limits the applicability of their approach to enterprise software systems where the resource demand of services largely depend upon its input parameters.

Brunnert et al. [6] capture performance and power consumption characteristics of software systems for systematic capacity planning. Their approach predicts energy consumption using linear power models [8]. Non-linear power models are not supported. The authors evaluate energy consumption via an average-case system analysis. Their approach does not support identifying peaks in power consumption and the violation of consumption constraints.

The previously discussed approaches [6,14,19] focus on EE analysis of software systems on an architectural level. A number of consumption modeling and prediction approaches have been developed to evaluate the power consumption of cloud and High Performance Computing (HPC) systems.

The cloud data center simulator *CloudSim* developed by Calheiros et al. [7] supports the prediction of power consumption in data centers using power models. Virtual Machines (VMs) and not software components form the central first-level entities. CloudSim does not consider dependencies in the behavior of VMs. The resource demand of each VM is described as a fixed function over time. *DCWorms* by Kurowski et al. [12] is a simulator aimed at performance and energy consumption predictions for HPC systems. Their model assumes that all computational tasks have predetermined durations. This assumption is often violated for systems outside of the HPC domain.

Basmadjian et al. [2] outline a power consumption estimation methodology for servers. Their approach estimates a data center's power consumption by aggregating the consumption of individual resources such as CPUs and fans. Since the authors assume all resources of one type to follow the same power model, their approach is unsuited for evaluating the energy consumption of heterogeneous computer systems.

4   Running Example

Media Store is a reference implementation of a light-weight media hosting service. Users can download and upload media files using its services. Media Store has been used to empirically validate Palladio's applicability for design-time performance predictions [13]. The accuracy of Palladio's performance predictions has also been evaluated for a specification of Media Store in PCM [4].

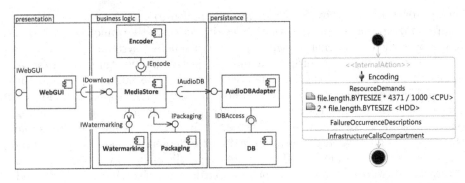

(a) MediaStore architecture   (b) Encoding Service RDSEFF

Fig. 1. Media Store architecture and RDSEFF of Encoding service offered by Encoder

Figure 1 shows the Assembly view on Media Store. The assembly consists of a GUI frontend (*WebGUI*), a business logic layer for organizing users and media files (*MediaStore*), and a persistence layer. For the sake of simplicity, we deploy all three Media Store layers on one high-capacity server.

The *MediaStore* component offers download and upload services. It re-encodes media files to a specific bit rate using the Encoder component. The RDSEFF characterization of the Encoder's download service is depicted in Figure 1. It correlates the file's input size with the number of CPU cycles needed to process one byte.

5   Power Consumption Model

In order to reason on a software system's EE at the architecture level, it is necessary to describe its consumption characteristics on a suitable abstraction level. ADLs like PCM enable the design-time analysis of QoS characteristics such as performance [4]. Quality analysis approaches built upon ADLs rely on a characterization of fundamental factors that impact the system's QoS in the set of considered quality dimensions. Existing ADLs that describe the power consumption characteristics abstract from fundamental characteristics of power distribution infrastructure design [6]. Although more comprehensive abstractions of power distribution infrastructure have been proposed [2,15], they have thus far not been integrated with an architecture-level approach for the design of software systems.

This section outlines our proposed modeling of a software system's power consumption characteristics as part of an ADL. Even though this paper applies the modeling concepts to PCM, the chosen modeling abstraction is independent of it. A detailed description of the models and the integration with PCM is available in [20].

Figure 2 provides an overview of our proposed model of power consumption characteristics as an extension to the PCM ADL. The *Power Consumption* model

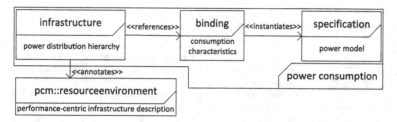

Fig. 2. Overview of the Power Consumption model

annotates PCM's Resource Environment model with the consumption characteristics of the software system. The Power Consumption model is subdivided into three orthogonal model views. These views are presented in the following sections.

5.1 Infrastructure

The *Infrastructure* view describes the power distribution infrastructure of a software system. Its abstraction is based on the power distribution infrastructure of data centers and enterprise-scale software systems. Power distribution infrastructure in data centers is structured hierarchically [8]. For example, data center-level uninterruptible power supplies (UPSs) distribute power to PDUs mounted to racks. UPSs provide backup power and correct irregularities such as voltage spikes. The rack-mounted PDUs then supply the power supply units (PSUs) of individual servers with power.

Figure 3 depicts the Infrastructure's meta-model. *PowerInfrastructureRepository* hosts a set of power distribution infrastructure definitions. The power in each distribution infrastructure originates from a common *PowerProvidingEntity*, e.g. the PDU of a group of racks. The PowerProvidingEntity supplies power to a set of connected *PowerConsumingEntities*. PowerConsumingEntities are distinguished into entities that consume power, e.g. *PowerConsumingResource*, and entities which both consume and provide power (*PowerConsumingProvidingEntity*). This modeling allows to capture the conversion losses that may incur for UPSs. PowerConsumingResource annotates the processing resources in PCM's Resource Environment and puts them into context with the power distribution infrastructure.

Figure 3 shows the Infrastructure instance of our running Media Store example. It enhances PCM's performance-centric Resource Environment model with power consumption and distribution characteristics. The server onto which the Media Store application is deployed hosts a set of CPUs. The CPUs all contribute to the power consumption of the server. Thus, they are modeled as a PowerConsumingResource. All CPUs draw their power from the same PSU.

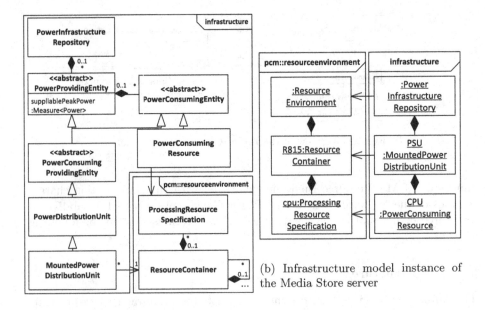

(b) Infrastructure model instance of the Media Store server

(a) Infrastructure meta-model

Fig. 3. Infrastructure meta-model and example instance of the Media Store server

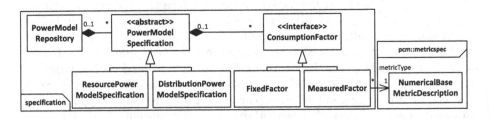

Fig. 4. Specification meta-model used for defining power models

5.2   Specification

The *Specification* view allows to capture power models as introduced in Section 2. Power models are defined in terms of their input parameters. We opted against including the evaluation semantics of power models in the Specification meta-model in order to support the inclusion of power models of arbitrary computational complexity. The evaluation semantics of each power model are specified as part of extensible plugins to our analysis tool.

Figure 4 depicts the Specification meta-model. Software architects can use a common *PowerModelRepository* instance to manage recurring types of power models. Every PowerModelSpecification represents a power model. The model distinguishes between power models of infrastructure elements that distribute power (*DistributionPowerModelSpecification*) and models of resources

(*ResourcePowerModelSpecification*). Power consumption of resources results from their utilization as part of a task. For example, a CPU draws power when it performs mathematical operations. A PDU's power consumption depends solely on the power draw of connected resources.

ConsumptionFactors form the input parameters of each power model. An instance of ConsumptionFactor specifies an input parameter type and not its concrete value. Type and value definition are separated to enable reuse of the power model specifications. Section 5.3 explains how the types are instantiated. A *FixedFactor* represents a fixed consumption characteristic that does not change with the load of a PDU or resource. The power consumption of a CPU under idle load (P_{idle}) falls into this category. A *MeasuredFactor* expresses a dependency of the power consumption to a measured system metric such as CPU utilization. All MeasuredFactors come with semantic information on their type and the unit in which they are measured (*NumericalBaseMetricDescription*). In the context of this paper, MeasuredFactors are gauged on the basis of metrics extracted from simulation. However, real measurements could also be a source of these measurements if the Power Consumption model were to be applied to runtime power consumption evaluations. The right hand side of Figure 5 provides an example on how a linear power model can be defined using the Specification model.

5.3   Binding

PowerBinding links the power consumption characteristics of elements in the Infrastructure with Specification's abstract, type-level definition of power models. A PowerBinding instance specifies how a specific resource type consumes power. Figure 5 shows an example Binding for the Media Store server. The PowerBinding ties the server to the linear power model. The server's consumption is characterized to follow a linear power model with $P_{Idle} = 332$ W and $P_{Busy} = 477$ W. Every FixedFactor in the Specification is matched with a *Fixed-FactorValue*. The PowerBinding of the server binds the values 332 W and 477 W

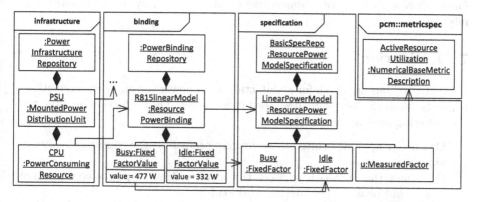

Fig. 5. Excerpt from Specification and Binding instance of the Media Store server

to P_{idle} and P_{Busy}. The utilization parameter u of the linear power model does not need to explicitly get instantiated in the Binding view. It can be implicitly resolved for all servers in the Infrastructure since it does not depend on server-specific consumption characteristics.

6   Evaluating Energy and Power Consumption

In the following, we present our approach for evaluating power and energy consumption of a software system. Section 2.1 outlined that the power consumption of individual servers can be estimated using power models. In order to apply power models to estimate the consumption of a software system, a source for system metrics it depends upon is needed.

System metrics can be extracted from software architectures described in an ADL using analytical or simulation-based approaches. Analytical approaches offer fast evaluation times with a good average-case accuracy. They do, however, make simplifying assumptions to achieve acceptable computational complexity. Analytical approaches commonly disregard temporal effects in user load, such as strong bursts during a specific interval. As we are interested in an analysis that accounts for these effects, we opted to employ Discrete Event Simulation (DES) as the basis of the power consumption predictions presented in this paper. Palladio's DES provides utilization metrics for a specified software system and usage profile. We use these utilization metrics as input for our post-simulation analysis. The implementation is available on our website[1].

Our analysis evaluates the power consumption of the resources in the power distribution infrastructure. It calculates power consumption using the consumption characteristics specified in the Binding view. Subsequently, the analysis aggregates power consumption for the elements provisioning power to the resources. As part of the aggregation, conversion losses can be factored in.

The energy consumption E_s of a software system s between two points in time a and b is calculated by integrating its power consumption P_s over the investigated interval $[a, b]$. Once power consumption predictions are available for a software system, we evaluate energy consumption by means of numerical integration.

7   Evaluation

We evaluated our approach for architecture-level power consumption predictions using the Media Store system described in Section 4. The evaluation investigated the following evaluation questions:

- **Q1:** Is our approach suited to accurately predict energy consumption on an architectural level?
- **Q2:** Does the approach support the identification of power consumption trends and peaks under varying workloads?

---

[1] https://sdqweb.ipd.kit.edu/wiki/Power_Consumption_Analyzer.

- **Q3:** Is the approach applicable to evaluate the energy efficiency (EE) of architectural design decisions?
- **Q4:** Is the approach applicable to evaluate the impact of deployment decisions on EE?

7.1 Deployment Environment

We conducted our evaluation on a Dell PowerEdge R815 server equipped with four Opteron 6174 CPUs. The Media Store implementation used as part of this case study was realized in Java EE. We deployed Media Store on a Glassfish 3.1 server running on an Ubuntu 12.04 VM. The VM was running atop a Xen hypervisor controlled by XenServer 6.2. 16 out of the server's 48 available cores were assigned to the VM. No other VMs besides the Ubuntu VM and the XenServer instance were deployed onto the server. Media Store's *DB* component was realized as a MySQL 5.5 server instance, *Encoder* used LAME 3.99.3 for encoding MP3s. The Vorbis *Encoder* variant introduced in Section 7.4 used *libvorbis* 1.3.2 bundled within the *ffmpeg* framework.

7.2 Power Model Extraction

In order to reason on power consumption we measured the server's power consumption in relation to its load. We derived a power model from the measurements by correlating power consumption and load. The Linux microbenchmarks *stress* and *lookbusy* were used to put varying degrees of load on the server. For each load level a monitoring utility measured power consumption using the server's built-in power meter. The utility collected the measurements through Intelligent Platform Management Interface (IPMI)[1]. While the power meter's accuracy and resolution is limited when compared to a dedicated external meter, it is sufficient to derive a full-system power model. The server was operated in a maximum performance mode for all the experiments to exclude side-effects induced by switching server components into low power states.

First, we investigated how the number of busy cores affected the power consumption of the server. The dots in Figure 6a represent the average-case power consumption when 0 to 16 cores were stressed. The linear function $P_{mult}(u)$ models the relation between power consumption and the number of used cores with an R-squared error of 0.996 for 1 to 16 busy cores (c.f. Figure 6a).

As the idle power consumption significantly deviated from the overall trend we further investigated the power consumption for utilization increments of 10% between zero and one utilized core. Figure 6b shows the power model $P_{single}(u)$ for utilization in this range. Putting both power models together, we derived a piecewise-defined function for the whole utilization domain:

$$P_{full}(u) = \begin{cases} P_{single}(u) & \text{if } u \leq 1 \\ P_{mult}(u) & \text{if } 1 < u \leq 16 \end{cases}, \; u \in [0, 16].$$

---

[1] http://www.intel.com/content/www/us/en/servers/ipmi/ipmi-home.html, retrieved 19.12.2014.

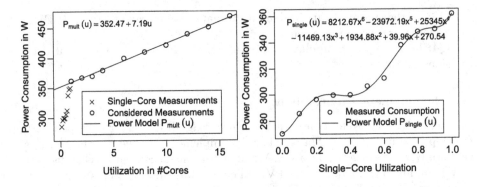

(a) Power measurements with model built on the basis of multi-core measurements

(b) Single-core measurements with polynomial power model

Fig. 6. Power measurements and models based on CPU utilization of the R815 server

Finally, we modeled this function using our Power Consumption model.

7.3   Accuracy of Architecture-Level Consumption Predictions

A power model can only be as accurate as the system metrics with which it is parametrized. In order to warrant sufficient accuracy of the CPU utilization, we calibrated the Media Store performance model using end-to-end service measurements extracted via *perf4j*. We employed a single-user workload to calibrate the performance model.

As expected, performance predictions for the calibration scenario match the performance measurements from the real system. The average response time (RT) prediction error of the calibrated model was 0.05%.

Our analysis derives power consumption predictions from the system metrics that are produced by the simulation, as is discussed in section 6. Due to the low RT prediction error of 0.05% the calibration scenario is well-suited as a benchmark for evaluating the accuracy of the energy consumption predictions. We measured the power consumption of our Media Store server using the built-in power meter while it was processing W_1. Applying the power model to our calibration scenario, we achieved an error of 0.17% for the total energy consumption in the single-user scenario (workload W_1).

Subsequently, we evaluated the accuracy of energy consumption predictions under workloads different from the calibration scenario. In the evaluation workload W_2 16 users repeatedly downloaded a random song from Media Store. The model we had calibrated with a single-user workload managed to predict the RT under the increased load with an error of 2.31%. Energy consumption predictions under the increased load reached an error of less than 5.5% when compared to actual measurements.

Finally, we investigated the accuracy gained from using a piecewise-defined power model P_{full} over strictly linear models as applied by Brunnert et al. [6]. If we were to use a linear power model for the full domain instead of the piecewise-defined P_{mult} the energy consumption prediction error would go up to 1.41% for W_1, and 7.65% for W_2.

In summary, our approach produced accurate energy consumption predictions with an error of less than 5.5%. This indicates that the approach has suitable accuracy (Q1).

7.4   Consumption Peaks and Trends

Besides an average-case energy consumption analysis our approach also supports the evaluation of power consumption under changing user load. This enables software architects to assess the suitability and efficiency of the software system's power distribution infrastructure under changing load.

Instead of the previously examined closed workloads W_1 and W_2 we now compared power consumption measurements with the predictions for a gradually increasing open workload. In W_3 initially no users submitted download requests onto Media Store. For every 160 seconds that had passed, the users' interarrival rate was increased by an additional user request per 16 seconds. Since Palladio's baseline simulative analysis [4] does not support the evaluation of dynamic workloads we used the alternative SimuLizar [3].

The energy consumption prediction error for W_3 amounted to 3.68%. Figure 7 depicts both measured and predicted power consumption for W_3. It can be seen that measured and predicted consumption values differ from each other. However, our prediction managed to identify the power consumption trend with reasonable accuracy (Q2).

7.5   Impact of Design Decisions on Energy Consumption

Encoding is the most resource-intensive service in the Media Store architecture. We thus investigated whether we could save by exchanging the LAME MP3

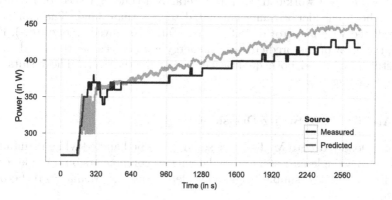

Fig. 7. Power consumption under incrementally increasing load

Table 1. Predicted and measured power consumption for LAME and libvorbis encoder

(a) Workload W_4 with interarrival time of 16s

(b) Workload W_5 with interarrival time of 1s

	Energy Consumption				Energy Consumption		
Encoder	Measured	Predicted	Error	Encoder	Measured	Predicted	Error
LAME	173.77 Wh	171.00 Wh	-1.60%	LAME	215.30 Wh	223.06 Wh	+3.60%
libvorbis	129.11 Wh	133.10 Wh	+2.78%	libvorbis	195.05 Wh	198.97 Wh	+2.01%
Saved Energy	44.67 Wh	37.91 Wh	-15.14%	Saved Energy	20.25 Wh	24.09 Wh	+18.94%

encoder with a Vorbis encoder (*libvorbis*) using comparable audio quality settings. First, we estimated the resource demand caused by encoding a music file based on measurements for the Vorbis encoder. These measurements were conducted in isolation of the original calibration. Second, we modeled the Vorbis encoder in Palladio and integrated it into Media Store's architectural model. We then predicted the effect of using the Vorbis instead of the MP3 encoder using Palladio's simulation in combination with our consumption analysis. Finally, we compared our predictions to actual measurements.

First, we investigated energy consumption under the open workload W_4 with an interarrival time of 16 seconds that was run for 30 minutes. Table 1a compares the energy consumption of the MP3 Encoder component implementation with the Vorbis Encoder. The total predicted energy consumption error was less than 2.8%. To estimate the effect of using an alternative Encoder component on the EE of the Media Store architecture we determined the saved energy as the difference between the predicted consumption for both architecture variants. Our approach was able to predict the saved energy consumption with an error of 15.14% (c.f. Table 1a, Saved Energy row).

Table 1b depicts predicted and measured energy consumption under workload W_5. W_5 is an open workload with an interarrival time of 1 second. Prediction errors of both encoder variants amounted to less than 3.6%. The gained EE was predicted with an error of 18.94% (c.f. Table 1b, Saved Energy row). Even though the error of the predicted saved energy was noticeable, the saved energy could still be assessed both qualitatively and quantitatively. The results thus positively answer Q3.

7.6   Architectural Sizing Decisions

Multi-user load put onto Media Store so far could be handled while maintaining QoS close to a single-user scenario by hosting all components on a single server. When load rises, the simple single-node deployment of Media Store becomes infeasible.

Workload W_6 varies between 5 and 16 users per second. When they are put onto the Media Store system, the system is overloaded. In order to achieve

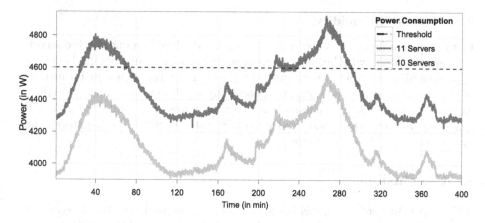

Fig. 8. Aggregate consumption of scaled-out Media Store

performance close to the single-user scenario under W_6, the software architect considers to scale the architecture horizontally and use storage with higher performance. He or she realizes the horizontal scaling by adding a load balancer to Media Store's architecture that distributes the encoding tasks across multiple *Encoder* instances. Now, a possible solution is to balance load between ten *Encoder* components deployed on ten servers. However, the predicted worst-case RT of this solution is more than twice as high as the worst-case RT in the single user scenario W_1. Thus, the software architect might consider to increase the number of *Encoder* instances and servers to eleven. This improves the worst-case RTs to only 23.3% more than in the single user case.

Software architects may consider the cost of adding a new server as a flat fee when evaluating the trade-off between gained QoS and cost. This does not, however, account for the step fixed cost induced by surpassing certain power consumption thresholds. Power distribution infrastructure such as PDUs and UPSs can supply power up to a certain peak power threshold. Once the peak power threshold is surpassed the infrastructure either breaks down or the connected servers are forced into lower power states. Both scenarios result in inferior QoS and should therefore be avoided.

Figure 8 shows that the critical peak power of a UPS supplying 4600 W would be surpassed if eleven *Encoder* instances were deployed. Consequently, the software architect would have to request a larger-scale power infrastructure from the infrastructure operator. An infrastructure upgrade might be warranted if the architect expects a further increase in future load. Otherwise, the architect may favor balancing load between ten *Encoder* instances to avoid a significant additional investment. In summary, the scale-out scenario illustrates effects of power distribution infrastructure sizing decisions on deployment decisions (Q4).

7.7   Threats to Validity

Our evaluation focused on a specific application deployed on one specific server. It does not address whether the proposed energy efficiency analysis methodology applies to different software systems. The use of an internal power meter instead of a dedicated certified power meter potentially results in inaccuracies. Furthermore, the consumption trend analysis experiment was only conducted once. All other experiments were conducted in steady states in which we monitored the system for more than 25 minutes.

8   Conclusions

This paper presents a model-based approach that supports the analysis of energy efficiency (EE) of software architectures. The proposed hierarchical Power Consumption model extends existing architecture models by central power consumption and distribution characteristics of targeted deployment environments. We extend an architecture-level performance analysis to predict the energy consumption of a modeled software system. The evaluation illustrates that our approach accurately predicts the power consumption of software systems in different usage contexts (Q1, Q2). The average energy consumption predictions from our approach reached errors below 5.5% for all experiments. The consumption predictions were accurate enough to assess how individual architectural design decisions affect EE for a specific system and usage context (Q3). We validated this by predicting the effect that the use of an alternative music encoder would have on EE. Our approach predicted the increase in efficiency with an error of less than 18.94%. A horizontal scaling scenario in which we replicated the encoder component illustrated how the explicit consideration of power consumption affects deployment decisions (Q4).

The approach proposed in this paper enables software architects to make systematic trade-offs between EE and other quality dimensions. Software architects do not need to rely solely on best practices and design patterns that have been shown to improve EE. Our approach allows to quantify the effect of design decisions on EE. It uses power models to evaluate the power consumption of software architectures. The power models are extracted via microbenchmarks, and characterize the consumption characteristics of resources independent of specific software architectures. This allows software architects to evaluate the EE of arbitrary software architectures without relying on architecture-specific consumption measurements.

In future work, we plan to extend our approach in three main areas. First, we will integrate our approach with the analysis of self-adaptive software systems to evaluate the effect of energy-conscious self-adaptation tactics (c.f. [16]) on the EE of a designed system. We further intend to include transient performance and energy cost with the analysis. Examples for such costs are the energy consumption and performance degradation caused by VM migration. Second, we aim to reduce the required effort for applying our approach by automating the extraction of power models. Finally, we plan to reduce the effort to identify optimal trade-offs between EE and other quality dimensions using approaches for automated design space exploration.

Acknowledgments. This work is funded by the European Union's Seventh Framework Programme under grant agreement 610711.

References

1. Barroso, L.A., Clidaras, J., Hölzle, U.: The Datacenter as a Computer: An Introduction to the Design of Warehouse-Scale Machines, 2 edn. Synthesis Lectures on Computer Architecture. Morgan & Claypool Publishers (2013)
2. Basmadjian, R., Ali, N., Niedermeier, F., de Meer, H., Giuliani, G.: A methodology to predict the power consumption of servers in data centres. In: e-Energy 2011: Proc. of the 2nd International Conf. on Energy-Efficient Computing and Networking, pp. 1–10. ACM, New York (2011)
3. Becker, M., Becker, S., Meyer, J.: SimuLizar: design-time modelling and performance analysis of self-adaptive systems. In: Proc. of the Software Engineering Conf. (SE 2013), February 2013
4. Becker, S., Koziolek, H., Reussner, R.: The Palladio component model for model-driven performance prediction. Journal of Systems and Software **82**(1), 3–22 (2009)
5. Bircher, W., John, L.: Complete System Power Estimation Using Processor Performance Events. IEEE Transactions on Computers **61**(4), 563–577 (2012)
6. Brunnert, A., Wischer, K., Krcmar, H.: Using architecture-level performance models as resource profiles for enterprise applications. In: Proc. of the 10th International ACM SIGSOFT Conf. on Quality of Software Architectures (QoSA 2014), pp. 53–62. ACM, New York (2014)
7. Calheiros, R.N., Ranjan, R., Beloglazov, A., De Rose, C.A.F., Buyya, R.: CloudSim: A Toolkit for Modeling and Simulation of Cloud Computing Environments and Evaluation of Resource Provisioning Algorithms. Softw. Pract. Exper. **41**(1), 23–50 (2011)
8. Fan, X., Weber, W.D., Barroso, L.A.: Power Provisioning for a Warehouse-sized Computer. SIGARCH Computer Architecture News **35**(2), 13–23 (2007)
9. Greenberg, A., Hamilton, J., Maltz, D.A., Patel, P.: The Cost of a Cloud: Research Problems in Data Center Networks. SIGCOMM Comput. Commun. Rev. **39**(1), 68–73 (2008)
10. Isci, C., Martonosi, M.: Runtime power monitoring in high-end processors: methodology and empirical data. In: Proc. of the 36th Annual IEEE/ACM International Symposium on Microarchitecture. IEEE Computer Society, Washington (2003)
11. Kansal, A., Zhao, F., Liu, J., Kothari, N., Bhattacharya, A.A.: Virtual machine power metering and provisioning. In: Proc. of the 1st ACM Symposium on Cloud Computing, pp. 39–50. ACM, New York (2010)
12. Kurowski, K., Oleksiak, A., Piątek, W., Piontek, T., Przybyszewski, A., Węglarz, J.: DCworms - A tool for simulation of energy efficiency in distributed computing infrastructures. Simulation Modelling Practice and Theory **39**, 135–151 (2013)
13. Martens, A., Koziolek, H., Prechelt, L., Reussner, R.: From monolithic to component-based performance evaluation of software architectures. Empirical Software Engineering **16**(5), 587–622 (2011)
14. Meedeniya, I., Buhnova, B., Aleti, A., Grunske, L.: Architecture-driven reliability and energy optimization for complex embedded systems. In: Heineman, G.T., Kofron, J., Plasil, F. (eds.) QoSA 2010. LNCS, vol. 6093, pp. 52–67. Springer, Heidelberg (2010)

15. Memari, A., Vornberger, J., Marx Gómez, J., Nebel, W.: A Data center simulation framework based on an ontological foundation. In: EnviroInfo 2014 - ICT for Energy Efficiency, pp. 461–468. BIS-Verlag (2014)
16. Procaccianti, G., Lago, P., Lewis, G.A.: Green architectural tactics for the cloud. In: Working IEEE/IFIP Conf. on Software Architecture (WICSA 2014), pp. 41–44, April 2014
17. Raghavendra, R., Ranganathan, P., Talwar, V., Wang, Z., Zhu, X.: No "Power" Struggles: Coordinated Multi-level Power Management for the Data Center. SIGARCH Comput. Archit. News **36**(1), 48–59 (2008)
18. Rivoire, S., Ranganathan, P., Kozyrakis, C.: A comparison of high-level full-system power models. In: Proc. of the 2008 Conf. on Power Aware Computing and Systems. HotPower 2008. USENIX Association, Berkeley (2008)
19. Seo, C., Edwards, G., Malek, S., Medvidovic, N.: A framework for estimating the impact of a distributed software system's architectural style on its energy consumption. In: Working IEEE/IFIP Conf. on Software Architecture (WICSA 2008), pp. 277–280, February 2008
20. Stier, C., Groenda, H., Koziolek, A.: Towards Modeling and Analysis of Power Consumption of Self-Adaptive Software Systems in Palladio. Tech. rep., University of Stuttgart, Faculty of CS, EE, and IT, November 2014. ftp://ftp.informatik. uni-stuttgart.de/pub/library/ncstrl.ustuttgart_fi/TR2014-05/TR-2014-05.pdf

An Energy Consumption Perspective on Software Architecture

A Case Study on Architectural Change

Erik A. Jagroep[1,2]([✉]), Jan Martijn E.M. van der Werf[1], Ruvar Spauwen[1],
Leen Blom[2], Rob van Vliet[2], and Sjaak Brinkkemper[1]

[1] Department of Information and Computing Science,
Utrecht University, P.O. Box 80.089, 3508 TB Utrecht, The Netherlands
{e.a.jagroep,j.m.e.m.vanderwerf,r.a.spauwen,s.brinkkemper}@uu.nl
[2] Centric Netherlands B.V., P.O. Box 338, 2800 AH Gouda, The Netherlands
{leen.blom,rob.van.vliet}@centric.eu

Abstract. The rising energy consumption of the ICT industry has triggered a quest for more sustainable, i.e. energy efficient, ICT solutions. Software plays an essential role in finding these solutions, as software is identified as the true consumer of power. However, in this context, software is often treated as a single, complex entity which fails to provide detailed insight in the elements that invoke specific energy consumption behavior.

In this paper, we propose an energy consumption perspective on software architecture as a means to provide this insight and enable analysis on the architectural elements that are the actual drivers behind the energy consumption. In a case study using a commercial software product, the perspective is applied and its potential demonstrated by achieving an energy consumption saving of 67.1 %.

Keywords: Software architecture · Energy consumption perspective · Sustainability

1 Introduction

The energy consumption of the Information and Communication Technology (ICT) sector is a booming topic of interest. Recent figures indicate that at least a tenth of the world's electricity use is on behalf of ICT [8]; a figure that has kept growing over the years. As a result of the increased awareness on the subject, the term 'sustainability' has emerged which is to "meet the needs of the present without compromising the ability of future generations to satisfy their own needs" [9]. Within the research community this has resulted in much attention going towards increasing the energy efficiency of ICT.

Only recently the role of green software is stressed in finding sustainable ICT solutions [7]. While energy is directly consumed by hardware, the operations are directed by software which is argued to be the true consumer of power [14].

© Springer International Publishing Switzerland 2015
D. Weyns et al. (Eds.): ECSA 2015, LNCS 9278, pp. 239–247, 2015.
DOI: 10.1007/978-3-319-23727-5_19

In current research on the Energy Consumption (EC) of software (cf. [3,4]), the software is often treated as a single, complex entity (i.e. considered on application level) instead of the inter-related elements it actually consists of. A breakdown into hardware components and 'units of work' is made, but this does not provide insight into which modules and functions invoke specific energy consuming behavior. Consequently, a stakeholder can not direct sustainability efforts to where they are needed.

We argue Software Architecture (SA) is able to fill this gap and in this paper we investigate how EC can be positioned within the scope of SA. An Architecture Description (AD) complemented with EC measurements, has the potential to help determine appropriate adjustments, identify where they should be applied and help to simplify the context by limiting the scope. Using a commercial software product, we construct an EC perspective on SA and validate the perspective through a case study. The potential of our research is demonstrated by realizing a reduction in energy consumption of 67.1%.

In this paper we first present related work on energy consumption and SA (Sect. 2). After this brief introduction we continue with constructing the perspective alongside a case study (Sect. 3). Finally, we provide a conclusion, discuss the results and directions for future research (Sect. 4).

2   Green Software and Software Architecture

Our approach to analyze the EC of software on architectural level is not unique. The node map presented in [3] for example, closely resembles what could be labeled as a deployment view which, after including EC figures, provides a 'heat map' of the system. Following this same line [4] presents the 'ME^3SA' model in which again the deployment and functional components of the software are investigated. In relation to green software, a limitation of both approaches is that most recommendations relate to hardware aspects and only provide 'strong clues' on software level.

One of the main issues with respect to green software [7] is to perform detailed EC measurements. Specialized environments, e.g. [4], enable detailed measurements but often lack the ability to expand to more complex environments (e.g. data center) where other approaches, e.g. 'E-Surgeon' [10], are required that have their own limitations. Consequently, the EC of software is often measured by relating the hardware EC to computational resource usage on behalf of the software [3].

To perform EC measurements we expand on the call for sustainability to become a Quality Attribute (QA) with *resource consumption, greenhouse gas emissions, social sustainability,* and *recycling* as subcharacteristics [7]. Continuing on the path of EC we focus specifically on resource consumption which, following the ISO 25010 standard, can be quantified using quality properties and quality measures. From literature [2–6] three potential quality properties can be identified; *Software utilization* (the degree to which hardware resource utilization on the account of software meets requirements), *Energy usage* (the degree to which the amount of energy used by the software meets requirements) and *Workload energy* (the degree to which the EC related to performing a specific task using software meets requirements). In Table 1 the properties are broken down into quality measures complemented with a definition and measurement function. Although further research is required, for now we assume that these quality properties cover the resource consumption subcharacteristic.

Green Architectural Tactics. To address concerns for a software product on the level of the SA, tactics are applied. A tactic is a decision that influences the control of a QA [1] and is a design option that helps the architect in realizing a desired property for a system. In relation to EC, there is still work to be done to find a set of tactics that are able to satisfy EC concerns. Consequently, the presented tactics are by no means definitive and should be considered as a source of inspiration for green software efforts.

Table 1. Quality measures for to the resource consumption subcharacteristic.

Resource consumption

Software utilization

CPU Utilization (CPUU)	Measure of the CPU load related to running the software. $current\ CPU\ load - idle\ CPU\ load$
Memory Utilization (MU)	Measure of the memory usage related to running the software. $\frac{allocated\ memory}{total\ memory} \times 100\%$
Network Throughput (NT)	Measure of the network load related to running the software. $Packages,\ sent/received\ bytes\ per\ second$
Disk Throughput (DT)	Measure of the disk usage induced by running the software. $Disk\ I/O\ per\ second$

Energy usage

Software Energy Consumption (SEC)	Measure for the total energy consumed by the software. $EC\ while\ operating - idle\ EC$
Unit Energy Consumption (UEC)	Measure for the energy consumed by a specific unit of the software. $\left(\frac{Unit\ CPUU}{CPUU} \times \frac{Unit\ MU}{MU} \times \frac{Unit\ NT}{NT} \times \frac{Unit\ DT}{DT}\right) \times SEC$
Relative Unit Energy Consumption (RUEC)	Measure for the energy consumed by a specific unit compared to the entire software instance. $\frac{UEC}{SEC} \times 100\%$

Workload energy

Task Energy Consumption (TEC)	Measure for the energy consumed when a task is performed. $\frac{SEC}{\#\ of\ tasks\ performed}$
Unit Task Energy Consumption (UTEC)	Measure for the energy consumed when a task is performed by a specific unit of the software. $\frac{UEC}{\#\ of\ tasks\ performed}$

In [11] a catalog is presented consisting of three categories, including tactics, that address energy efficiency in the cloud. The energy monitoring category tactics are aimed at collecting power consumption information and estimating infrastructure and software component power consumption. Tactics in the self-adaptation category present possibilities for optimization during run-time. Finally, the cloud federation tactics are aimed at respectively finding and switching to the most energy efficient services to perform a task. Although the tactics are explained specifically in a cloud computing context, they could prove valuable for software in general.

Increase hardware utilization [3]; Ineffective use of hardware is a common source for energy inefficiency and is one of the triggers to consolidate the number of active servers. From an EC point of view less hardware reduces the idle energy consumption.

Concurrency architecture variation [16]; In this specific case the Half Synchronous / Half Asynchronous and the Leader / Followers concurrency architectures are compared and a significant difference was found in the advantage of the first. However, further investigation is required to test the generalizability of this finding.

Increase modularity; In terms of database calls, software consisting of fewer modules could require less calls while significantly more data is transferred per call. When software consists of more modules, an increase in database calls could be observed with the potential that less data is transferred per call, i.e. the calls are more fitted to the process. Assuming that increased disk usage has a marginal impact on the EC figures, less CPU capacity is required for processing the call thereby lowering the EC per call.

Network load optimization; Although modularity can positively affect the EC of software [15], more modules also implies a higher communication load. A positive effect on the EC is expected with a reduced communication load.

3   Energy Consumption Perspective on Software Architecture

To address the EC of software on an architectural level we propose to construct an EC perspective, which is 'a collection of activities, tactics, and guidelines ... used to ensure that a system exhibits a particular set of related quality properties that require consideration across a number of the systems architectural views' [12]. In order to create a comprehensive EC perspective, the perspective catalog [12] (Fig. 1) is used where for each viewpoint a key issue is formulated that addresses the relation to EC and a suggestion is provided on how the AD can be altered to adhere to the perspective. Note that the original catalog contains six viewpoints, but a seventh viewpoint, the 'context view', was added to define societal and economical aspects.

To increase the practical applicability of the perspective, it was created alongside a case study using Document Generator (DG). DG is a commercial software product, used as a service with other commercial software products, to generate over 30 million documents per year by over 300 customers. The case study was performed in a test environment (Fig. 2) that allowed for EC measurements using a WattsUp? Pro (WUP), a device capable of measuring the total power drawn by an entire system with a one second interval between measurements, and performance measurements using Perfmon, a standard performance monitoring tool with Microsoft Windows. As DG was installed on the test server[1] measurements were performed on this system and data was collected with the loggin server. Finally, the client system was used to perform a task with DG.

Perspective Activities. Using a perspective a stakeholder has a means to analyze and validate qualities of an architecture and drive architectural decision making. Following [12], we provide a set of activities (Fig. 3) to apply the EC perspective to the views.

1. Capture Energy Requirements: Requirements form the basis for change in relation to SA [1] and should be considered when strategical, economical or customer motives are present. For the case study we focused on DG's core functionality and investigate an activity encompassing the generation of 5000 documents, where each single document generation is considered a separate task. In relation to EC we formulate the requirement for DG to consume less energy while performing the specified task.

2. Create Energy Profile: An energy profile of the software provides the stakeholder with a starting point and a benchmark to evaluate results. The profile for DG was created with the following protocol; (1) Clear internal WUP memory, (2) Close unnecessary applications and services on the test server, (3) Start WUP and Perfmon measurements, (4) Perform specified task using

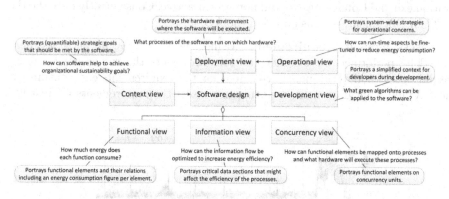

Fig. 1. Viewpoint catalog to apply an EC perspective, after [12], including key issues and AD alteration suggestions.

---

[1] HP Proliant DL380 G5, Intel Xeon E5335 CPU, 800GB local storage (10.000 rpm), 64GB PC2-5300, 64 bit MS Windows Server 2008R2 (Restricted to 2 cores), VMware vSphere 5.1

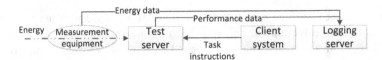

Fig. 2. Setup of the test environment used to perform the case study.

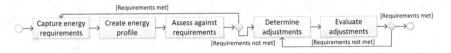

Fig. 3. The activities to apply the EC perspective to software architecture.

client and (5) Collect and check Perfmon and WUP data from logging server. In total 22 measurements were performed divided over six series. After checking, 19 out of these 22 measurements were considered valid. For the energy profile, DG on average required 41 minutes and 49 seconds to generate the documents and with a *SEC* of 17560 Joule (J) (standard deviation 3577 J). An average *TEC* was found of 3.51 J ($\frac{17560}{5000}$) per generated document.

The AD for DG (Fig. 5), including the functional, concurrency and deployment view, learned that DG consists of the Document.exe, Config.exe and Connector.exe processes. The 'Generator' element (Document.exe) is responsible for the actual document generation, 'Utilities' (Config.exe) provides configuration options and the 'Composer', 'Interface' and 'Connector' elements (Connector.exe) handle communications. Mapping the measurements on the AD, performance data shows a 49% *CPUU* of Document.exe, with an average utilization rate of 50.7% and 7.4% for the two available cores, whereas the other processes (Configuration.exe and Connector.exe) did not appear active. Consequently only the the *TEC* for Document.exe was added in the AD.

3. Assess against Requirements: Using the energy profile an assessment should be performed on whether the software meets the requirements. Since we did not formulate a quantitative goal for the requirement, e.g. consume at most *X* Joule per document, we could not assess the requirements against the

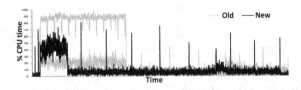

Fig. 4. Comparison of CPU activity of the test server during a measurement.

energy profile. Hence the profile was labeled as benchmark and we proceeded to determining adjustments.

4. Determine Adjustments: Based on the assessment, the adjustments should be determined that are to be applied to the software or its context. From the previous activities we learned that the energy consumption during the activity was mainly caused by the 'Generator' element. Looking at the performance data, we argued that applying the *increase hardware utilization* tactic had the potential to let us meet the requirement. In collaboration with the DG developer the 'balancer' was added, operating according to the broker pattern, changing the SA as shown on the right hand side of Fig. 5.

5. Evaluate Adjustments: After adjustment, an evaluation should be performed to determine whether the requirements are met and assure that no unwanted effects are brought about. After adjustment, 33 (out of 36) valid measurements were obtained (divided over seven series) following the earlier described protocol. On average the new version of DG required 39 minutes and 14 seconds to generate the documents with a *SEC* of 5782 J (std. dev. 1647 J). In this new situation, *TEC* was reduced with 67.1% to an average 1.16 J per generated document and a significant decrease in CPU activity was perceived (Fig. 4). The *CPUU* for Document.exe decreased to an average 19.2%, whereas the utilization rates of the cores appeared evenly divided (12.6% and 15.1% respectively). A note should be made though, as the database server was considered out of scope we did not include any effects on this hardware.

Threats to Validity. With regard to the validity of the case study, an evaluation is performed following the threats as identified in [13]. The *construct validity* considers whether the correct measures were identified for the object under study. With investigating EC, there is little discussion on the relevant measures. To relate these measurements to the software or elements thereof, established performance indicators were used; a common method that is also applied by others in this field of research.

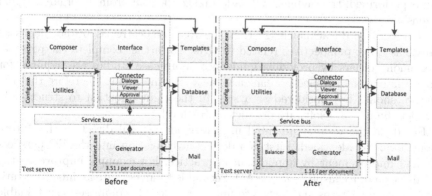

Fig. 5. Functional, concurrency and deployment view of DG for subsequent releases.

In light of the *internal validity*, despite careful preparations, due to the behavior of services we can not be 100% certain that DG was solely responsible for the load on the test server. Therefore each individual measurement was checked for such processes using performance data. Another threat is the lack of experience with configuring DG, e.g. we experienced firewall issues, resulting in a lower number of measurements at the start. For the evaluation we were more familiar with the case and relatively more valid measurements were obtained per series.

A threat to the *external validity* is the fact that the case study was performed in a separate test environment containing specific hardware. Given the relation between hardware and EC, different hardware could provide different findings in absolute terms. However, since an actual commercial software product was used, we argue that the proposed improvement is not specific to our environment.

Finally, *reliability* is concerned with the data and analysis thereof being dependent on the specific researchers. The measurements within the case study were performed by following a strict protocol, of which the activities are openly described. We therefore argue that following the described protocol should yield similar results.

4 Conclusion

In this paper we set out to investigate how EC can be positioned within the scope of software architecture through an EC perspective. In its current form the perspective enables stakeholders to identify, measure and analyze the EC of architectural elements, direct green efforts with regard their software product to where they are needed and verify the results. Using the perspective and the measures presented with the sustainability QA, a stakeholder has a means to quantitatively consider EC during the the design phase.

Alongside constructing the perspective, a case study was performed using a commercial software product (DG). The energy profile for DG directed our efforts and through an architectural change we reduced the energy consumption with 67.1% per generated document. Considering the frequency at which this task is performed, the savings could add up significantly from an organizational dimension.

However, we do acknowledge that the EC perspective is by no means as mature as other perspectives related to QAs. To further complete the perspective, among others by providing guidelines, more case studies are required for which the current perspective can serve as a starting point. Therefore the perspective should be considered as a step in the right direction to structurally consider the EC of a software product on SA level.

Based on the results presented in this paper, several directions for future research can be identified. First is a deeper investigation into the EC perspective and improvement by application in practice. For example improve on the visualization of EC aspects in the AD. Second is to investigate architecture variations, design patterns and tactics to find what actually comprises a sustainable software architecture. A final direction is to investigate, in depth, how insights gained from the architectural perspective can be translated to guidelines for software development.

References

1. Bass, L., Clements, P., Kazman, R.: Software Architecture in Practice. SEI Series in Software Engineering. Pearson Education (2012)
2. Bozzelli, P., Gu, Q., Lago, P.: A systematic literature review on green software metrics. Technical report, Technical Report. VU University Amsterdam (2013)
3. Grosskop, K., Visser, J.: Identification of application-level energy optimizations. In: Proceeding of ICT for Sustainability (ICT4S), pp. 101–107 (2013)
4. Kalaitzoglou, G., Bruntink, M., Visser, J.: A practical model for evaluating the energy efficiency of software applications. In: ICT for Sust. (ICT4S 2014). Atlantis Press (2014)
5. Kern, E., Dick, M., Naumann, S., Guldner, A., Johann, T.: Green software and green software engineering-definitions, measurements, and quality aspects. In: On Information and Communication Technologies, p. 87 (2013)
6. Kipp, A., Jiang, T., Fugini, M., Salomie, I.: Layered green performance indicators. Future Generation Computer Systems 28(2), 478–489 (2012)
7. Lago, P., Kazman, R., Meyer, N., Morisio, M., Müller, H.A., Paulisch, F., Scanniello, G., Penzenstadler, B., Zimmermann, O.: Exploring initial challenges for green software engineering: summary of the first greens workshop, at icse 2012. ACM SIGSOFT Software Engineering Notes 38(1), 31–33 (2013)
8. Mills, M.P.: The cloud begins with coal: an overview of the electricity used by the global digital ecosystem. Technical report, Digital Power Group, August 2013
9. Murugesan, S.: Harnessing green it: Principles and practices. IT Prof. 10(1), 24–33 (2008)
10. Noureddine, A., Rouvoy, R., Seinturier, L.: Monitoring energy hotspots in software. Automated Software Engineering, pp.1–42 (2015)
11. Procaccianti, G., Lago, P., Lewis, G.A.: A catalogue of green architectural tactics for the cloud. In: 2014 IEEE 8th Int'l Symp. on the Maint. and Evol. of Service-Oriented and Cloud-Based Systems (MESOCA), pp. 29–36, September 2014
12. Rozanski, N., E. Woods, E.: Software Systems Architecture: Working with Stakeholders Using Viewpoints and Perspectives. Addison-Wesley (2011)
13. Runeson, P., Höst, M.: Guidelines for conducting and reporting case study research in software engineering. Empirical Software Engineering 14(2), 131–164 (2009)
14. Sun, Y., Zhao, Y., Song, Y., Yang, Y., Fang, H., Zang, H., Li, Y., Gao, Y.: Green challenges to system software in data centers. Frontiers of Comp. Sc. in China 5(3), 353–368 (2011)
15. te Brinke, S., Malakuti, S., Bockisch, C., Bergmans, L., Akşit, M.: A design method for modular energy-aware software. In: Proceedings of the 28th Annual ACM Symposium on Applied Computing, pp. 1180–1182. ACM (2013)
16. Zhong, B., Feng, M., Lung, C.-H.: A green computing based architecture comparison and analysis. In: Proc. of the 2010 IEEE/ACM Int'l Conf. on Green Computing and Communications & Int'l Conf. on Cyber, Physical and Social Computing, pp. 386–391. IEEE Computer Society (2010)

Agile and Smart Systems

A Lean Automotive E/E-System Design Approach with Integrated Requirements Management Capability

Harald Sporer[✉], Georg Macher, Christian Kreiner, and Eugen Brenner

Institute of Technical Informatics, Graz University of Technology,
Inffeldgasse 16/1, 8010 Graz, Austria
{sporer,georg.macher,christian.kreiner,brenner}@tugraz.at
http://www.iti.tugraz.at/

Abstract. Replacing former pure mechanical functionalities by mechatronics-based solutions, introducing new propulsion technologies, and connecting cars to their environment are only a few reasons for the still growing E/E-System complexity at modern passenger cars. Smart methodologies and processes are necessary during the development life cycle to master the related challenges successfully. In this paper, a lean approach for a model-based domain-specific E/E-System architectural design is presented. Furthermore, an integrated requirements management methodology is shown, satisfying the needs for a full traceability between the requirements and design artifacts. The novel model-based language allows domain experts, with limited knowledge of the de-facto system design standard SysML, to describe the mechatronics-based system easily and unambiguously. The lean tool chain orchestration makes the presented approach, especially but not limited to, interesting for small project teams.

Keywords: Automotive embedded E/E-systems · System architectural design · Domain-specific modeling · Requirements management

1 Introduction

The number of functionalities realized through electrical and/or electronic systems (E/E-Systems) at modern cars, and therefore the overall complexity, will keep increasing over the next years. Connecting the cars with their environment, as well as new propulsion technologies will foster this trend. The potential concerning product differentiation between competing companies as well as the possibility to optimize existing E/E-System functionalities is enormous.

High quality standards along the whole product life cycle are crucial to cope with the upcoming challenges. To achieve this, methods and techniques from concepts like Automotive SPICE [1] are strongly recommended. Some of the key aspects of these concepts are bidirectional traceability, as well as consistency between the different development artifacts. Regardless what kind of tool chain

© Springer International Publishing Switzerland 2015
D. Weyns et al. (Eds.): ECSA 2015, LNCS 9278, pp. 251–258, 2015.
DOI: 10.1007/978-3-319-23727-5_20

is chosen to facilitate the product development life cycle, these key concepts must be supported.

In the automotive industry, the E/E-System design models are usually created with techniques based on the *Unified Modeling Language (UML)*. To enable this de facto standard for the embedded automotive system design, either the meta-model is extended or a profile is created. A wide-spread example of an UML2 profile is the *Systems Modeling Language (SysML)*, which reuses many of the original diagram types (*State Machine Diagram, Use Case Diagram*, etc.), uses modified diagram types (*Activity Diagram, Block Definition Diagram*, etc.), and adds new ones (*Requirement Diagram, Parametric Diagram*) [2].

Even if the UML-based methodologies are valuable for projects with emphasis on software, for the embedded automotive system design, sometimes they are too powerful due to the numerous representation options. In particular for domain experts who have no or limited knowledge about software development, the high number of elements available for modeling, turns the system architectural design into an awkward task. However, it is not the intention of this work to decry the SysML approaches created so far. They are a good choice for a multitude of tasks. Instead, this paper showcases an extension to these SysML approaches, which eases the architectural design of embedded mechatronics system designs for UML-non-natives, and provides a comfortable integration of the requirements management processes at the different design abstraction levels. To achieve these goals, a domain-specific modeling (DSM) for the particular needs at the embedded automotive mechatronics-based system development has been created. Moreover, the described design approach has been complemented by a lean requirements management strategy.

In the course of this document, Section 2 presents an overview of the related approaches, as well as of domain-specific modeling and requirements management. In Section 3, a description of the proposed modeling approach with integrated requirements capability is provided. An application of the described methodology is presented in Section 4. Finally, this paper is concluded with an overview of the presented work in Section 5.

2   Related Work

In recent years, a lot of effort has been made to improve the automotive model-based E/E-System design methods and techniques. Traceability, as well as consistency, between the development artifacts has always been an important topic. However, due to the increasing number of electronic- and electric-based functionality, these properties have become vital.

If it comes to safety-critical functionalities, according to the 2011 released international standard ISO 26262, traceability between the relevant artifacts is mandatory [9]. A description of the common deliverables along an automotive E/E-System development, and a corresponding process reference model is presented by the de facto standard *Automotive SPICE* [1]. Neither the functional safety standard nor the process reference model enforces a specific methodology, how the development artifacts have to be linked to each other. However, connecting the various work products manually is a tedious and error-prone task.

In [4] a seamless model-based tool chain orchestration for the automotive system and software engineering domain is described by the authors. As in other contributions in this field ([5], [6], [7]), SysML is utilized for the system architectural design.

To agree with Broy et al. [8], the drawbacks of the UML-based design are still the low degree of formalization, and the lack of technical agreement regarding the proprietary model formats and interfaces. The numerous possibilities of how to customize the UML diagrams, to get a language for embedded system design, drive these drawbacks. This scenario does not provide an optimal base for the engineer who has to design the embedded automotive system from a mechatronics point of view. Ideally, the tool should be intuitive and easily operated also without specific UML knowledge. These findings led the authors to the idea to create a more tailored model-based language for the stated domain. In [3] a detailed description of this domain specific modeling approach can be found.

Regarding the needs for an appropriate requirement handling, Mäder et al. [10] provide evidence that standards like the ISO 26262, which demand full traceability, are not the only argument for implementing a proper requirements management strategy. They conducted an experiment with more than 50 subjects performing maintenance tasks on two projects. Half of the tasks with and the other half without traceability. The result was unambiguous: the subjects with requirements traceability performed on average 21% faster and delivered 60% more correct solutions.

Based on functionality classification, Chemuturi [11] primarily categorize requirements into *Core Functionality Requirements* and *Ancillary Functionality Requirements*, instead of the in the automotive field wide-spread types *Functional Requirements* and *Non-Functional Requirements*. In his opinion, the term *Non-Functional* connotes that the corresponding requirements do not function or do not serve any function. However, even if they may not serve a business process function directly, they are serving a useful purpose in the product. Therefore, he labels requirements corresponding to topics like *Safety*, *Response Time*, and *Memory Constraints* as ancillary functionality requirements. At this approach, the requirements classification of Chemuturi is utilized and adapted to the needs of mechatronics-based systems.

Herrmann et al. [12] depict requirement attributes for different phases during the product development cycle. Additionally, recommendations on their usage are given, supported by the categorization of the attributes into *mandatory*, *reflective*, *optional*, and *not required*. Most of the presented attributes are also used at comprehensive requirements management (RM) tools like *IBM Rational DOORS*[1] and *PTC Integrity Lifecycle Manager*[2]. In this work, the recommen-

---

[1] http://www.ibm.com/

[2] http://www.ptc.com/

dations of Hermann et al. are taken into account and necessary adjustments, evoked by the automotive E/E-System development domain, are made.

3   Approach

In this section, the domain specific modeling methodology for automotive mechatronics-based system development, with a focus on the integrated requirements management capability, is presented. As mentioned in Section 2, details on the domain specific modeling can be found in [3]. Therefore, just a quick overview is given in the following subsection.

3.1   Domain Specific Modeling Approach

The established SysML-based design method from [4] is extended by the newly developed *Embedded Mechatronics System Domain-Specific Modeling (EMS-DSM)* for the automotive embedded system design. The main goal of this methodology is to provide a lean approach for engineers to facilitate an embedded automotive mechatronics system modeling on a high abstraction level. The focus of the approach is on the model-based structural description of the E/E-System under development. Additionally, the signals and interfaces are an essential part of the modeling.

The definition of the newly developed model-based domain specific language is shown in Figure 1. The top node *EMS-DSM Component* is the origin of all other classes at the language definition. Therefore, each of the derived classes inherits the five properties (*ID, Name, Requirement, Verification Criteria*, and *Specification*) from the base class.

The language definition in Figure 1 represents the meta-domain of the model-based language. Subsequently, the EMS-DSM is tailored to the needs of the domain at the particular project or company. That is, design elements of possible types *Mechnical, Compartment, Sensor, Control Unit, Actuator, External Control Unit, Basis Software*, and *Application Software*, are specified for the particular field of application. E.g. the domain of the presented application in Section 4 is *Embedded Mechatronics E/E-System Design for Compressed Natural Gas (CNG) Fuel Tank Systems*.

The EMS-DSM can be supported by a various number of tools, but at the time when the research project was initiated, a highest possible flexibility, as well as full access to the tools source code was desired. To achieve this, an own model editor (***Embedded Automotive System** Design*) has been developed, based on the open source project *WPF Diagram Designer* [13].

3.2   Requirements Classification and Attributes

As mentioned in Section 2, the requirements are primarily categorized into *Core Functionality Requirements* and *Ancillary Functionality Requirements*. Typical

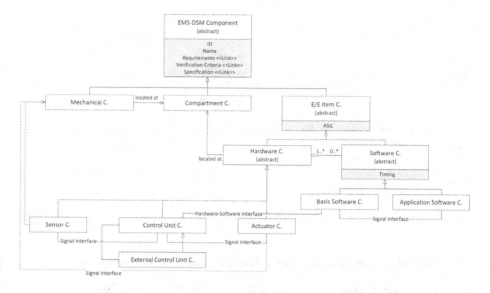

Fig. 1. *EMS-DSM* Definition (UML)

examples for ancillary functionality topics are *Software Footprint, Memory Constraints, Response Time, Reliability,* and *Safety* [11]. By introducing new requirement (issue) attributes, the utilized web-based tool *Redmine*[3] can be adapted to these needs for requirements categorization easily.

The de facto standard Automotive SPICE [1] defines three different types of requirements at the engineering process group: *Customer Requirements, System Requirements,* and *Software Requirements.* Out of the embedded E/E-System view, at least the hardware focus is missing. Additionally, requirements and design items regarding the mechanical components, have to be introduced for the design of an embedded mechatronics-based E/E-System. Similar to the Automotive SPICE methodology on system and software level, engineering processes has been defined for these missing artifacts. Summing up, the available requirement and test case types at this work are: *Customer Req, System Req, System TC, System Integration TC, Software Req, Software TC, Software Integration TC, Hardware Req, Hardware TC, Mechanics Req,* and *Mechanics TC.*

By reconfiguring the project management tool Redmine, all mentioned requirement types have been implemented. The most important attributes which have been added are *Core Functionality* (artifact can be marked as contributing to the products core functionality), *ASIL* (shows the automotive safety integrity level of the artifact), and *Verification criteria.* In Figure 2 a system requirement at Redmine is shown. The link to the corresponding costumer requirement is located at the top of the definition. At *Subtasks* the subsequent requirements, e.g. software requirements are listed and to satisfy the demand for full traceability, a link to the corresponding test cases can be added at *Related issues.*

---

[3] http://www.redmine.org/

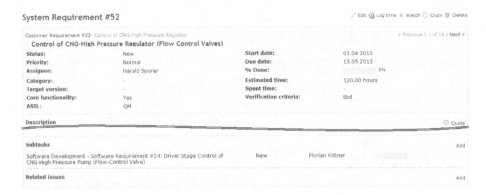

Fig. 2. System Requirement at *Redmine*

3.3 Bridging the Gap between Design and Requirements

Section 3.1 contains the description of how the different types of designs (system level, software level, etc.) are created corresponding to the novel domain specific modeling. To achieve full traceability, these designs, respectively the various components at the designs, have to be linked to the corresponding requirements. This can be done by the *Requirements Linker* at EASy Design, which establishes a connection to the MySQL database, and therefore has full access to the requirements data at Redmine. By utilizing the *ADO.Net driver for MySQL*[4], the Requirements Linker can easily execute all kinds of MySQL commands on the database.

4 Application

In this section, the EMS-DSM approach with integrated requirements management capability, is applied to the development of an automotive fuel tank system for compressed natural gas (CNG). For an appropriate scale of the use-case, only a small part of the real-world system is utilized. The application should be recognized as an illustrative material, reduced for internal training purpose for students. Therefore, the disclosed and commercially non-sensitivity use-case is not intended to be exhaustive or representing leading-edge technology.

In figure 3 the EMS-DSM tool *EASy-Design* including the *System Design Model*, as well as the *Requirements Linker* dialogue is shown. The CNG fuel tank system consists of seven mechanical components, which are blue coloured (Tank Cylinder, Filter, etc.) The medium flow between mechanical components, which is CNG in this use case, is displayed by blue lines with an arrow at the end. Furthermore, five hardware components are placed at the *System Design Model* level, which are yellow coloured (In-Tank Temperature Sensor, Tank ECU, etc.) The signal flow between the components is displayed by yellow lines, ending with an arrow. Between the Control Unit and the External Control Unit component,

---

[4] https://dev.mysql.com/

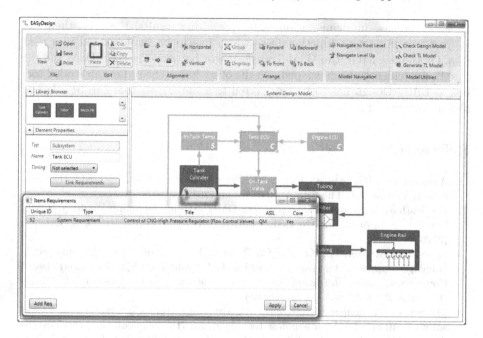

Fig. 3. Self-developed tool *EASy Design* with Integrated Requirements Management Capability

a communication bus is inserted, characterized by the double compound line type and arrows on both ends.

Software Components can not be placed on the System Design Level. With a double-click on a Hardware Component, the next modeling level is opened (named *E/E Item Design Level*). Here, the green coloured *Basis Software Components* and *Application Software Components* are put in place.

By double-clicking a connection between two components, a dialogue is opened and the signal, or in case of a communication bus, the signals can be specified. By selecting a model element and a click on the button *Link Requirements*, the elements requirements dialogue is opened (shown in Figure 3). Already linked requirements from the Redmine database are listed with their ID, Type, Title, ASIL, and Core functionality attribute. By a click on the button *Add Req*, a connection to the database is established as described in Section 3.3 and a new requirement from the database can be added.

5   Conclusions

In the previous sections, a lean method for the design of embedded automotive mechatronics-based E/E-Systems, with full requirements traceability characteristic, was presented. This approach has the potential to bring together the different engineering disciplines along the E/E-System development. Moreover, it's feasible for automotive domain experts with limited knowledge of UML/SysML.

First use case implementations show promising results. However, there are at least two important functionalities which has to be implemented in a next step. On the one hand, the M2M-Transformator between the EMS-DSM and the SysML model has to be developed. On the other hand, the so far hard coded tool box at EASy Design has to be transferred to a library file that can be adapted also during run time.

References

1. Automotive SIG: Automotive SPICE®Process Assessment Model. Technical report, Version 2.5, The SPICE User Group (2010)
2. Friedenthal, S., Moore, A., Steiner, R.: OMG systems modeling language (OMG SysML^{TM}) tutorial. In: INCOSE International Symposium. INCOSE, Orlando (2006)
3. Sporer, H., Macher, G., Kreiner, C., Brenner, E.: A model-based domain-specific language approach for the automotive E/E-System design. In: International Conference on Hardware/Software Codesign and System Synthesis (CODES+ISSS) (2015) (under review)
4. Macher, G., Armengaud, E., Kreiner, C.: Bridging automotive systems, safety and software engineering by a seamless tool chain. In: 7th European Congress Embedded Real Time Software and Systems Proceedings, pp. 256–263, Toulouse, France (2014)
5. Boldt, R.: Modeling AUTOSAR systems with a UML/SysML profile. IBM Software Group (2009)
6. Andrianarison, E., Piques, J.: SysML for embedded automotive Systems: a practical approach. In: Conference on Embedded Real Time Software and Systems, Toulouse, France (2010)
7. Giese, H., Hildebrandt, S., Neumann, S.: Model synchronization at work: keeping SysML and AUTOSAR models consistent. In: Engels, G., Lewerentz, C., Schäfer, W., Schürr, A., Westfechtel, B. (eds.) Graph Transformations and Model-Driven Engineering. LNCS, vol. 5765, pp. 555–579. Springer, Heidelberg (2010)
8. Broy, M., Feilkas, M., Herrmannsdoerfer, M., Merenda, S., Ratiu, D.: Seamless model-based development: from isolated tools to integrated model engineering environments. Proceedings of the IEEE **98**(4), 526–545 (2010)
9. International Organization for Standardization: ISO 26262. Road vehicles - Functional safety. International Standard, Geneva, Switzerland (2011)
10. Mäder, P., Egyed, A.: Assessing the effect of requirements traceability for software maintenance. In: 28th IEEE International Conference on Software Maintenance (ICSM), pp. 171–180. IEEE (2012)
11. Chemuturi, M.: Requirements Engineering and Management for Software Development Projects. Springer Science & Business Media (2012)
12. Herrmann, A., Knauss, E.: Requirements Engineering und Projektmanagement. Xpert.press, Springer (2013)
13. Code Project - WPF Diagram Designer - Part 4. http://www.codeproject.com/Articles/24681/WPF-Diagram-Designer-Part

Distilling Best Practices for Agile Development from Architecture Methodology

Experiences from Industrial Application

Dominik Rost[1(✉)], Balthasar Weitzel[1], Matthias Naab[1],
Torsten Lenhart[1], and Hartmut Schmitt[2]

[1] Fraunhofer Institute for Experimental Software Engineering, Kaiserslautern, Germany
{dominik.rost,balthasar.weitzel,
matthias.naab,torsten.lenhart}@iese.fraunhofer.de
[2] HK Business Solutions, Sulzbach, Germany
schmitt@hk-bs.de

Abstract. Agile development and software architecture are not the enemies any more they seemed to be some years ago. It is agreed that agile development needs some form of architecting, too. However, how this architecting should look like is widely unclear. In this paper, we further characterize the relationship of agile development and architecting. We present our key idea to distill practically applicable and accessible architecture best practices from existing architecture approaches and tailor them for agile development. We describe the identification and template-based documentation of architecting best practices and present an example, which were already successfully applied in industry. Additionally, we share experiences we made in industrial development projects regarding the combination of architecting and agile development.

Keywords: Agile development · Software architecture · Experience report

1   Introduction

In industrial practice, agile development has become the leading software development process in many industries and companies in recent years [1]. In the earlier days of agile development, a lot of discussions were ongoing: are agile development and software architecture contradicting [2]? This discussion seems to be over now: Agile development and software architecture are no opposite ends of a spectrum anymore, both in the perception of practitioners and researchers [3]. However, there is still the question of how to actually do architecting work in agile development projects. The main goal of this paper is to introduce the idea of distilling architecture best practices from established architecture methods to improve agile development. Thus, the next sections look a bit deeper into characteristics of architecture and agile development.

© Springer International Publishing Switzerland 2015
D. Weyns et al. (Eds.): ECSA 2015, LNCS 9278, pp. 259–267, 2015.
DOI: 10.1007/978-3-319-23727-5_21

Characteristics of Architecture

Every software system has an architecture, independent of the development process with which it was developed [4]. That is, the discussion how to combine agile development and architecture has to focus on engineering aspects around architecture, i.e. architecting. We decompose architecting into three main aspects for further discussion:

- *Architecture activities:* operationalization of architecting in engineering activities
- *Architecture documentation:* manifestation of architectural work
- *Architecture responsibilities:* assignment of architecture activities to roles or persons

Characteristics of Agile Development

Agile development approaches like SCRUM are much more rigorous than they appear on a first glance. Rules apply to follow a strictly iterative and incremental development approach that regularly delivers working software. However, neither project management-related agile practices like SCRUM nor implementation-related practices like XP offer engineering-style support for architecting.

Successful agile development projects often share the same characteristics: a small team of experienced and skilled developers build a system of limited size and life time. These characteristics are the foundation of success, since the challenges that are typically addressed by architecting (like complexity of the product and the teams, quality attributes, ...) can be compensated by the skills and experience of the developers.

Agile Development needs more Architecting Practices

Agile development is not only applied when the characteristics described above apply. That often leads to misinterpretations of agile practices [5]. Either agile practices are dogmatically followed (due to the lack of deeper understanding of required customizations) or they are followed in a too informal way (agile rather as an excuse for not following an approach). Since most agile processes do not come with engineering guidance, it has to be added. Our main idea to provide architecting guidance is to distill best practices from the existing body of knowledge (see Section 3).

Contributions of this Paper

- Characterization of the combination of agile development and architecting practices, with a separation of the aspects architecture activities, architecture documentation, and architecture responsibilities (see Section 2)
- Our idea of architecting best practices for agile development, how we document them in a template, and an illustrative example (see Section 3)
- Lessons learned and experiences from the industrial application of the best practices and from architecting in agile development in general (see Section 4)

2   Software Architecture and Agile

In the following, we characterize each of the aforementioned aspects architecture activities, documentation and responsibilities in an agile development setting, as we observed them in many industrial settings. We conclude this section with an overview of related work in the area of architecture and agile.

2.1 Characterization of the Relationships between Agile and Architecture

Architecture Activities in Agile Development

This aspect comprises not only making architectural decisions and documenting them, but also analyzing architectural requirements, evaluating architectural solutions, supporting the derivation of code and checking compliance of the realization. We additionally distinguish two dimensions of characteristics, not meant to be mutually exclusive:

When is the activity performed?
- *Upfront:* A separate "architecting phase" is used to come up with initial architecture.
- *Sprint zero:* An initial sprint or iteration aiming at a coarse-grained architecture.
- *In iteration:* The iteration itself is used to do architecture work, in the form of:
  - *Spikes:* Limited time slots, often considered like special tasks, are used during the iteration to solve issues that have been considered architecturally significant.
  - *Planning:* Existing planning meetings or sprint preparations, where traditionally an upcoming iteration is planned, are used to plan on an architectural level, too.
  - *While coding:* Architectural decisions are made on the fly.
- *Separate team, in parallel:* The architecture work is decoupled from the actual development, for example by having a separate architecture team.

What is the target of the activity?
- *Selected aspects:* Only aspects that are considered as architecturally significant are targeted within the architecture work, e.g. a critical part of an important story.
- *Every story:* Every story is examined from an architectural perspective.
- *Every epic:* Larger epics are targeted with the architecture work.
- *Every delta of a sprint:* All required changes done in a sprint are covered.
- *The overall product:* The architecture work is focused on the overall product.

Architecture Documentation in Agile Development

Architecture documentation is the manifestation of architectural work in terms of decisions, views, and the resulting documentation. We list options of architectural documentation as they occur in agile development projects, typically as a mixture:

How is the documentation done?
- *None:* No explicit documentation of architectural decisions is available.
- *Knowledge of developers* is considered as the only architecture documentation.
- *Whiteboard:* Creating architectures in a collaborative way with the whole team can be done efficiently on whiteboards, but the semantic of these sketches is short-lived.
- *Wiki:* A wiki enables collaboration in the team, but requires continuous maintenance.

- *Architecture document:* An agile architecture document should focus on the main concepts and be accompanied with a lightweight documentation of detailed design.
- *Models* require expertise in creation, maintenance and usage to exploit benefits.

Architecture Responsibilities in Agile Development

This aspect reflects the assignment of architecture activities to certain roles or persons in the development team. They perform these architectural activities or are responsible that the team does it.

Who is responsible for an architectural activity?
- *The complete team:* No dedicated architect role is defined, the team organizes itself by having architectural tasks for potentially many team members.
- *Separate group in team:* There is a group within the team dealing with architectural activities. Having an implicit group is a typical situation in practice if some developers are more interested in architectural considerations than others.
- *Separate role in team:* A dedicated architect role is defined, that works to a major degree on architectural aspects, thus relieving the team from the conceptual work.
- *Separate team*: A separate architecture team works as a kind of consultant for the development team and delivers architectural solutions for it.

2.2   Related Work

Nowadays most practitioners agree that it is possible to combine both advantages from architecture planning and agile development [6]. Nevertheless some approaches are too abstract to be directly applied in practice [7]. On the other side, there are approaches like [8], [9] especially covering architecture responsibilities and activities in large scale development organizations. Works like [10] also aim at changing the development process, but more from a technical perspective, aiming at changing and introducing architectural activities. The intention is to come up with architectural paradigms that are more suited for agile development. A crucial barrier for applying such approaches in practice is the need to invest into an organizational change to clarify architectural responsibilities [11,12] without having a guarantee that the expected benefit will be higher than the investments. A work that explicitly targets self-organizing development teams is [13], aiming to provide directly applicable best practices for solving common issues, mainly in form of architectural activities and documentation practices. We aim at extending this work, especially in a collaborative way with the architecture and agile community, so that experiences from different organizational settings are reflected.

3   Software Architecture Best Practices for Agile Development

In many projects with our customers, we experienced that the integration of software architecture practices and agile development has the potential to significantly improve the achievement of product quality attributes in a more systematic and predictable manner. To package the techniques we applied in projects and make them available to developers in agile projects we have set up the project PQ4Agile (Product Quality for Agile).

It helps us to refine, elaborate and document the practices to create usable support for other developers. PQ4Agile also helps us to create a basis for discussion with the community and provides a frame for evaluation, as illustrated in Fig. 1.

In PQ4Agile, we aim at providing support for developers in agile projects to achieve product qualities in a systematic and predictable manner. This exactly is also the focus of software engineering methods. Many of these methods come with years of experience in practice and are continuously improved. However, compatibility to agile processes is not inherently given. To make this integration possible, software engineering practices need to be adapted to account for the specifics of agile development, like short iteration cycles, close interaction with stakeholders, etc.

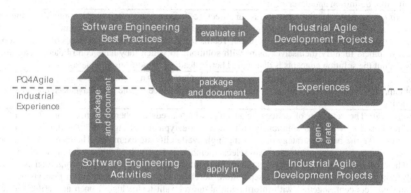

Fig. 1. Creation of Software Engineering Best Practices

Our key idea to tackle this is to subdivide coherent methodologies from software engineering into activity blocks that developers in agile projects can select and apply in an easy and efficient manner. To achieve this, we distill the essence from activities in software engineering methodology to create well packaged best practices, with which agile development processes can be enhanced. The result of this project is a compendium from which developers can select software engineering best practices fitting to their respective project setting.

3.1   Best Practice Development, Documentation, and Evaluation

By analyzing the development processes of our industry partners, we identified similar activities and grouped them into coherent categories. The categories are *requirements, planning and design, evaluation, realization, control,* and *project planning and control*. Activities of these groups are typically performed continuously and iteratively.

The selection of suitable activities to create best practices is mainly based on our experiences from industry projects. The experiences of the respective communities were additional information sources. We generated ideas in workshops and by studying relevant literature (cf. Section 2). Our experiences and lessons learned (cf. Section 4) strongly indicate positive effects on the development of software in agile settings. Quality requirements become more explicit, are addressed with more engagement, rework is reduced and development velocity kept constantly high. To confirm our qualitative experiences and get an additional indication of quantitative effects of practices, we will perform a dedicated evaluation in PQ4Agile.

3.2 Best Practice Examples

In the following, we give an example of an architecture best practice. This is only an excerpt. The full descriptions will continuously be published on http://pq4agile.org.

Collaborative Development of Architecture Solutions in the Team	*Architecture Activities*

Goals: (1) Explicit elaboration of solution concepts, (2) distribution of knowledge in the development team, (3) all team members can identify themselves with the developed solutions, (4) consolidated architecture definition and description

Motivation: In agile development teams, architecture decisions are often made implicitly, which can lead to inconsistency or inadequate solutions. Also, the team members might not know all solutions and therefore lack understanding and be skeptical. Teams can benefit from the experiences of all developers. Team members identify themselves more with solutions to which they have contributed. Also, knowledge about the solution concepts is distributed better, leading to more sustainable solutions.

Inputs: System requirements with a concrete problem, for which an architecture concept is needed.	*Outputs:* An architecture concept for which the experiences of the team have been considered.

| *Description:* The selection of a story or an epic, which needs a coherent concept or arising of new requirements for which the solution is still unclear are typical starting points for this best practice. Questions like the backup strategy or ensuring high availability are examples. The team selects a member responsible for the concept. The team selects members to be involved in the solution development.

The responsible person decomposes the problem into smaller parts that can be worked on as separate architecting tasks. According to this separation, he elaborates solution ideas and a first vision of the architecture concept, together with information about relevant technologies, open and critical aspects, etc. as the basis for the discussion in the team.

As soon as the concept vision has been elaborated, the responsible team member organizes the first meeting in which the selected team members participate. The concept meeting consists of:

- *Presentation*: The responsible developer presents the topic together with its decomposition, the architecture vision, and the elaborated aspects to the team.
- *Discussion*: The team discusses the presented topics. Needs for change, inconsistencies, and improvement suggestions are discussed until a consent is found. The discussed changes are documented and integrated in the initial solution proposal. The result is an aligned concept draft.
- *Task distribution*: According to the topic decomposition, the team distributes the single architecting tasks. The according members are responsible for the further elaboration of the architecture topics.

After the first concept meeting the team members elaborate the detail solutions for their respective subtasks. These solutions should be elaborated to a degree that allows realization. When all team members have completed their respective tasks, the responsible developer organizes the next meeting, in which the contributing members present and discuss their detail solutions for their respective tasks. If certain aspects need to be elaborated further, new architecting tasks are defined and distributed until the architecture concept is sufficiently elaborated. Based on this, realization tasks are defined and carried out.

As a post processing step, the responsible developer consolidates the detail solutions and adds critical aspects to the documentation, so that the solution can be understood by the whole team afterwards. |
|---|

| *Recommendations and Risks:* Acknowledging architecting work as a relevant development activity is a necessary prerequisite. The elaboration of architecture concepts does not result in immediate customer benefit, but is an investment that pays off at a later point in time. Therefore it might be difficult to be able to allocate the necessary time, in particular in situations with high time pressure.

All team members having the same rights can complicate decision making in certain situations. Here, the responsible team member should moderate. Also, the right selection of contributors might be a challenge. Team members with prior experience in a relevant area are good candidates to involve. |
|---|

Duration: Diverse, depending on the complexity of the task and the experiences of the development team. No longer than one iteration, otherwise subdividing into smaller sub-concepts.

4   Lessons Learned

Lessons Learned on Architectural Activities in Agile

Reserve Time for Planning & Architectural Work at the Start of a New Project
Despite a common misconception, agile methodologies do not force you to skip any planning and always jump in at the deep end – they only want you to not try to become a perfect swimmer before going into the water. Therefore concepts like Sprint Zero in SCRUM [14] should be used to define the architectural basis for the new product.

Check Compliance with Architectural Decisions While Doing Code Reviews
Though systematic code reviews are often an integral part of agile setups, in practice they are often solely focused on the code itself and disregard checking the compliance with architectural decisions taken by the team before.

Don't Introduce Too Many Additional Meetings
Agile methodologies are often quite meeting-heavy and this is one of the most heard critiques on them. Though some of our best practices encourage addressing specific topics in meetings, this does not necessarily mean that you have to introduce separate meetings for them, instead existing meetings should be used if possible.

Lessons Learned on Architectural Responsibilities in Agile

The Value of Software Engineering Best Practices Has to Be Conveyed
In agile development, close and constant collaboration between agile teams and stakeholders is indispensable. It's therefore crucial to convince stakeholders or their representatives of the overall benefit of investing some extra effort for applying software engineering best practices. Otherwise they probably always will be postponed.

Make Quality Attributes Explicit by Adding them to Stories or the Definition of Done
Often quality attributes and non-functional requirements are not explicitly defined in agile projects but rather expected that everybody implicitly is aware of them. Making them explicit is crucial to prevent misunderstandings or that they are simply forgotten.

In Multi-team Setups, the Teams Need to Align – Especially on Architecture
The size of agile teams is often restricted by the concrete methodology in use. Thus, typically multiple teams have to work together in bigger software projects. In those cases especially architecture topics have to be aligned very well across all teams. There are different approaches for achieving this (e.g. scrum of scrums), but all of them have shown some issues in practice. Thus we think further research in this area is necessary.

Lessons Learned on Architectural Documentation in Agile

Make Clear that Documentation and Agile Development Are not a Contradiction.
We often were confronted with the belief that agile software development means that documentation is unnecessary and could be ignored. Indeed the Agile Manifesto

states *working software over comprehensive documentation*, but this only emphasizes that too comprehensive documentation should be avoided. An expressive and smart documentation is not only recommendable, but inevitable for a successful software product.

Use Existing and Standard Tools for Documentation
Documentation is often one of the first things disregarded in the course of agile software projects because of the focus on working software. Therefore the hurdles for documentation have to be kept as low as possible. One way to achieve this is to use existing standard tools for documentation whenever possible.

Add "Documentation Created/Adapted" to Your Definition of Done
Another way of encouraging the team to not disregard documentation is to explicitly extend the definition of done with an appropriate check point on documentation. This guarantees that at the end of each iteration the documentation has been extended.

5   Conclusion

In this paper, we described our three contributions to advance the integration of software architecture methodology and agile processes: First, we characterized aspects of the relationship of architecture and agile in three main aspects: architecture activities, documentation and responsibilities in agile development. Secondly, we introduced our idea of creating software architecture best practices by distilling the essence from architecture methods and adapting it to the specifics of agile development. We focus on practices that we successfully applied in industry projects and package them to provide easily selectable and applicable support for developers in agile teams, to achieve product qualities in a systematic and predictable manner. Finally, we provided an insight into experiences we made with applying architecture practices in agile development settings. We hope the lessons we learned provide helpful advice for practitioners and ideas for the community for further research, to shape the integration of architecture and agile development.

Acknowledgement. We would like to thank the German Ministry of Education and Research for funding parts of this work in the program "KMU Innovativ" under grant number 01IS13032.

References

1. VersionOne: The 9th Annual State of Agile™ Survey. http://info.versionone.com/state-of-agile-development-survey-ninth.html
2. Kruchten, P.: Software architecture and agile software development: a clash of two cultures? In: Proceedings of the 32nd ACM/IEEE International Conference on Software Engineering - ICSE 2010, p. 497. ACM Press, New York (2010)
3. Bachmann, F., Nord, R., Ozkaya, I.: Architectural Tactics to Support Rapid and Agile Stability (2012)

4. Bass, L., Clements, P., Kazman, R.: Software Architecture in Practice. Addison-Wesley Professional (1998)
5. Krogmann, K., Naab, M., Hummel, O.: Agile Anti-Patterns - Warum viele Organisationen weniger agil sind, als sie denken (2014)
6. Nord, R.L., Tomayko, J.E.: Software architecture-centric methods and agile development. IEEE Softw. **23**, 47–53 (2006)
7. Eloranta, V.-P., Koskimies, K.: Aligning architecture knowledge management with scrum. In: Proceedings of the WICSA/ECSA 2012 Companion Volume on - WICSA/ECSA 2012, p. 112. ACM Press (2012)
8. Leffingwell, D.: Agile Software Requirements: Lean Requirements Practices for Teams, Programs, and the Enterprise (Agile Software Development Series). Addison-Wesley Professional (2011)
9. Leffingwell, D.: Scaling Software Agility: Best Practices for Large Enterprises. Addison-Wesley Professional (2007)
10. Reenskaug, T., Coplien, J.O.: The DCI Architecture: A New Vision of Object-Oriented Programming. http://www.artima.com/articles/dci_vision.html
11. Abrahamsson, P., Babar, M.A., Kruchten, P.: Agility and Architecture: Can They Coexist? IEEE Softw. **27**, 16–22 (2010)
12. Madison, J.: Agile Architecture Interactions. IEEE Softw. **27**, 41–48 (2010)
13. Toth, S.: Vorgehensmuster für Softwarearchitektur: Kombinierbare Praktiken in Zeiten von Agile und Lean. Carl Hanser Verlag GmbH & Co. KG (2013)
14. Schwaber, K., Sutherland, J.: Scrum Guide. Scrum Alliance. **19**, 21 (2009)

Understanding the Use of Reference Architectures in Agile Software Development Projects

Matthias Galster[1(✉)] and Samuil Angelov[2]

[1] Department of Computer Science and Software Engineering,
University of Canterbury, Christchurch, New Zealand
mgalster@ieee.org
[2] Department of Software Engineering,
Fontys University of Applied Sciences, Eindhoven, The Netherlands
s.angelov@fontys.nl

Abstract. Software reference architectures potentially constrain the flexibility of software design by imposing and sometimes even fixing architectural decisions and structures early. This seems to contradict agile values, principles and practices which acknowledge flexible and changing software requirements and the need to adapt architectural designs accordingly. To increase our understanding of how reference architectures are used in agile software development projects, we conducted an exploratory case study in two Dutch software developing organizations. Both organizations use Scrum as their agile framework. Preliminary findings reported in this short paper indicate that a) some aspects of reference architectures are not specific to using them in agile development projects with Scrum (e.g., types of reference architectures used; limited design choices), and b) reference architectures can support cross-functional and self-organizing teams, and help increase architectural focus in contexts where architectural thinking tends to be neglected.

Keywords: Software reference architectures · Agile · Scrum

1 Introduction

1.1 Background

Agile software development practices have become popular in the software industry. Many, if not most, practitioners follow some sort of agile software development, with Scrum as the most frequently used agile process framework [1]. Agile software development approaches are defined in terms of four basic ideas about values (e.g., individuals and interactions over processes and tools; working software over comprehensive documentation; responding to change over following a plan), twelve basic principles (e.g., highest priority is to satisfy customer through early and continuous delivery of software), and practices depending on specific projects (e.g., XP, pair programming, test-driven development) [2]. All agile approaches (e.g., Scrum, Lean, Kanban, Crystal)

© Springer International Publishing Switzerland 2015
D. Weyns et al. (Eds.): ECSA 2015, LNCS 9278, pp. 268–276, 2015.
DOI: 10.1007/978-3-319-23727-5_22

define their own practices but follow the ideas described in the "Agile Manifesto[1]", e.g., incremental and iterative development, close customer collaboration, empowered and co-located teams, continuous product and process improvement, and frequent delivery of value to customers.

Software reference architectures (RAs) have been utilized in industry to help design concrete architectures in a particular application or technology domain. A RA is not designed for highly specialized requirements, but provides designs and design decisions independent of a particular product. Architects use the RA as a starting point and specialize it for their project context [3]. Therefore, a RA provides partially or completely instantiated design artefacts, designed for particular business and technical contexts, together with support to enable the use of these design artefacts [4]. In this sense, RAs represent reusable architecture knowledge in form of generic artefacts, design guidelines, best practices, standards, architectural styles, domain vocabulary, documentation, etc. [5]. Furthermore, RAs facilitate standardization and interoperability within an application or technology domain since systems within such domain can be based on the same RA. General benefits and problems of RAs have been explored previously [6, 7], including the use of RAs in practice [8].

1.2   Research Problem, Motivation and Contributions

In contrast to a concrete software architecture which emerges and evolves (either explicitly or implicitly) during agile development and subsequent agile iterations ("sprints" in Scrum), a RA already imposes constraints on architectural designs and the development process from the product inception phase and at the very beginning of development. While RAs determine certain design choices at an early stage, agile development defers choices to accommodate changing requirements and maximizing value delivered to customers. On the other hand, RAs may help speed up development by avoiding making the same design decisions for products in a domain over and over again. This may be useful in agile projects that are under pressure to deliver value (in terms of a potentially usable product, rather than system analysis and documentation) to customers. Therefore, in this paper we aim at understanding if the potential conflict of flexibility (agile) and imposed design decisions and constraints (RA) is perceived in practice, or if RA and agile practices are seen as rather complementary. In this paper, we present preliminary results from work-in-progress on improving our understanding of using RAs in agile software development projects. Rather than targeting agile processes and practices in general, we focus on Scrum, the most frequently used agile process framework [1]. The research questions put forward in this paper are the following:

- **RQ1:** *How are RAs used in agile projects that use Scrum?*
- **RQ2:** *What are benefits and limitations of using RAs with Scrum?*

Based on a case study in two Dutch software developing organizations, this paper contributes a) a description of the use of RAs in agile projects in organizations that

---

[1] http://agilemanifesto.org/

use Scrum, and b) preliminary insights into whether RAs can potentially threaten or complement agile values, principles and practices. Note that there are on-going debates in the architecture community about how agile development affects software architecture practice, and vice versa. In this paper, we do not aim to contribute to general discussions of software architecture in agile contexts but focus on RAs and Scrum. The reader may refer to discussions in other works, e.g., [9, 10].

In Section 2, we discuss our research approach. Results are introduced in Section 3 and validity issues discussed in Section 4. We conclude in Section 5.

2   Research Approach

We apply case study research as an "in-the-wild" method, rather than "in the lab" methods (e.g., controlled experiments) since our research is motivated by a practical problem that cannot be studied in isolation from its context. When investigating RAs in agile projects (that use Scrum) in industry, we have little control over all variables (e.g., people, organizational structures). Also, case studies offer an in-depth understanding of practices by allowing "how", "why" and "what" questions [11].

Case Study Design: Our study is a multiple-case study and follows an exploratory approach [12] since it "looks for patterns, ideas, or hypotheses" rather than trying to test or confirm hypotheses [13]. We currently cannot form hypotheses since we lack an understanding of how RAs are used in agile projects. We follow case study guidelines proposed in [14]. Our unit of analysis is an organization and projects.

Case Selection: We selected large software developing organizations based on the availability of individuals and other information sources in these organizations [15]. Furthermore, organizations must use RAs and follow the same agile development framework, i.e., Scrum. This includes implementing Scrum ceremonies (e.g., sprint planning and review, retrospectives, sprints) and Scrum roles (e.g., Scrum team, Product Owner, Scrum Master). Differences in the cases lie in the domains.

Data Collection: We collected qualitative data using semi-structured interviews with lead architects in each organization. Furthermore, we reviewed architecture and process documentation. We took extensive notes (for interviews and documentation reviews) and recorded interviews. We explained to organizations the goal of the study and ensured a common understanding of Scrum and RA. We used open questions to discuss a broad range of issues and answers related to projects and three topic areas: 1) how the RAs are used (related to RQ1), 2) benefits of RAs in agile projects (related to RQ2), 3) limitations of RAs in agile projects with Scrum (related to RQ2). To avoid misunderstandings, we summarized major findings for organizations.

Data Analysis: We transcribed interviews and added manual notes and information from architecture and process documentation to obtain a full record for each case. Then, we used open coding [16] where one code can be assigned to many pieces of text, and one piece of text can be assigned to more than one code [17]. After initial coding, we looked at groups of code phrases and merged them into concepts and related them to the research questions [18]. Since our data was collected within a case study, the data is context sensitive. Thus, we performed iterative content analysis to make inferences from collected data in its context [19]. Analysing qualitative data requires integrating data where different interviewees might have used terms and concepts with different meanings or different terms and concepts to express the same thing [20]. We noticed that this was particularly true for the concept of RA. To address this problem, we use reciprocal translation [20].

3   Results

3.1   Cases

The study included the following cases:

- **Case 1:** Case 1 is a large Dutch organization with more than 500 engineers in the Netherlands and offices overseas. The organization develops embedded systems software for four domains: consumer electronics and telecommunication, life science and health, automotive, and professional equipment manufacturing. Software needs to comply with standards for the quality of medical devices (e.g., ISO 13485). Many projects are done at the customer site to ensure close customer involvement.

- **Case 2:** Case 2 is one of the largest health insurance providers in the Netherlands with offices all across the country. Software is developed for internal (e.g., other departments) and external clients (e.g., health care partners, customers). Most software projects develop web-based applications rather than desktop applications.

3.2   RQ1: How are RAs used in Agile Projects that use Scrum?

We present the answers to RQ1 based on four categories that emerged after open coding and during data analysis:

1. **What Types of RAs Are Used:** A classification of five types of RA was presented by Angelov et al. [7]. This classification was identified independent from agile practices. In both cases of our study, we found that organizations use existing and externally defined RAs (prescribed by the domain, such as AUTOSAR for automotive software), but also define their own company-specific RAs that are used across projects within the organizations. Case 1 stated that the organization developed an internal RA to "avoid reinventing the wheel". In the classification proposed in [7], this would be a classical facilitation architecture implemented in a single organization. Case 2 uses RAs centred on development platforms (Java, .NET) designed by external software providers. According to [7], this would be a classical facilitation architecture designed for multiple organizations by an independent organization with partially concrete implementation artefacts. Case 2 also uses internally defined RAs, supervised by the enterprise architect who defines high-level architectural visions for the domain, including goals and basic design principles. The fact that we are able to classify RAs in case 1 and 2 based on an

existing classification that describes RAs independent of agile implies that the types of RAs are not different in agile projects compared to non-agile projects. Also, organizations not necessarily adapt RAs to make them more suitable for agile development projects.

2. **At What Stage of Development Are RA Applied:** The decision of using a RA may be taken at different stages of a project, i.e., at the very beginning of a project, later after an initial scoping exercise and domain analysis, or even later when evaluating a designed system against domain regulations. In our cases, we noticed that RAs are used from the very beginning of the project. These findings suggest that selecting RAs is a conscious decision made at the beginning of the project and after some initial analysis and architecture envisioning, rather than a decision that emerges based on the needs related to particular sprint goals or sprint backlogs. In case 2, the RA is also heavily used later for compliance checking. In this case, a RA helps identify tasks related to compliance checking when breaking down user stories from the product and sprint backlog during Scrum sprint planning sessions.

3. **Who Is the Driver for Using RAs:** Scrum encourages self-organizing teams empowered to make decisions that they think are best for achieving the sprint goal that has been set together with the Product Owner. Since RAs impose high-level constraints on the software design, there may be different drivers who advocate the use of a RA. We found that in case 1, choosing a RA is a team decision, rather than the decision of a team or product lead, who only suggests the use of the RA. This means, case 1 truly empowers self-organizing teams. This is different to non-agile projects which tend to have team or project leads who decide on the use of RAs. On the other hand, for case 2, the decision about using a RA is not made by the team, but by a software architect. In contrast to case 1, this shows that that in despite of empowered and self-organizing teams in Scrum, some decisions are made by leading roles in an organization.

4. **Why Are RAs Used in Agile Projects:** Based on industrial practice (independent of using agile or non-agile development approaches), a list of more than ten potential reasons for using RAs has been proposed by Angelov et al. [8]. Mapping our findings to items from this list, for case 1 we noted that RAs in agile projects are used because of the following: experience of developers with RA; easy access to best practices; to speed up design work; to ensure reusability of designs; to reduce cost; education and training of engineers; risk reduction. Similarly, for case 2 we noticed the following reasons: standardization in domain; easy access to best practices; to speed up design work; to ensure reusability of designs; to ensure interoperability with other systems; to reduce cost. This diversity indicates that the reasons for using a RA depend on the project context rather than the development method (agile or non-agile). In other words, using Scrum (or agile in general) does not imply reasons for using a RA.

3.3   RQ2: What Are Benefits and Limitations of Using RAs with Scrum?

We identified the following benefits (emerged after categorizing and grouping codes during data analysis):

1. **RAs Simplify Design Tasks:** Some tasks are simplified because of RAs. In case 1, initial architecture setup and design was mentioned as the task that was heavily supported by RAs. In case 2, we found that the RA helps compliance checking in sprint reviews and delivery meetings with customers. Furthermore, in case 2 the RA helps engineers experiment with different design solutions within the scope of the RA (i.e., during sprints, the RA provides a harness for the agile teams to experiment with different design solutions as long as the final solution complies with the RA).

2. **Degrees of Freedom in Development Teams:** In case 1, we found that the RA helps engineers move between different projects or work on more than one project at the same time since the RA is the same across projects. Furthermore, it supports communication within teams since there is a shared understanding of common architectural ideas. This facilitates cross-functional teams, as promoted by agile practices. This benefit, however, was not mentioned in case 2, where RAs may vary per team and project.

3. **Focus on Architectural Aspects:** In case 1, we found that the RA helps focus on architectural aspects which are often neglected in agile contexts. It helps inject architectural thinking into the agile process. This benefit is considered significant and learning about the RA and related efforts are outweighed by these benefits. According to case 2, overheads using the RA are not significant but instead the RA helps avoid a lot of additional and redundant architecture documentation. Similar to case 1, projects benefit from a clear picture that describes core architectural issues and that communicates the shared architectural vision as a "reference point" within a Scrum team during and across sprints.

We identified the following limitations:

1. **Personal Preference of Developers:** In case 1, some developers "do not like" using RAs since they feel restricted in their creativity and freedom in making decision decisions. However, this is a personal or project-related observation and not related to using or not using agile methodologies. This limitation was not found in case 2.

2. **Maintenance of RAs:** In case 1, maintenance and updating the RA is hard due to the required speed and focus on creating a potentially shippable release of the product at the end of each sprint. In case 2, however, the organization applies an initial step to support the "translation" of the RA to a concrete product architecture and creates a so called "solution picture". This step requires some preliminary work to "adjust" the RA for a project before designing a concrete product architecture. In case 2 this is not considered as maintenance of the RA per se. Also, RAs in case 2 are externally defined (see Section 3.2, "What types of RAs are used in agile projects"). Thus, maintenance is not a significant issue in case 2.

We acknowledge that there may be more benefits and limitations of RAs in agile contexts. However, above, we list those that emerged from our case organizations.

4   Validity

Our study is subject to three validity threats [11, 21]. With regards to *construct validity* (did we measure what is intended), our study is limited since we gathered data only from a limited number of sources. However, we obtained insights from different organizations and projects. Also, we used extended semi-structured interviews together with architecture and process documentation. We included control questions and checked the accuracy of data with the organizations. Furthermore, we ensured that all participating organizations shared the same notion of what is a RA (see our notion of RA described in Section 1.1). Also, some companies we discarded for this study used other agile process frameworks. On the other hand, the fact that we studied more than 30 companies but only two resulted in cases for this study (i.e., used Scrum and RAs) could be an indicator that indeed there is a tension between using RAs and agile practices. However, this would be subject to further study. With regards to *external validity* (extend to which findings are of interest outside the investigated cases) we acknowledge that we focus on an analytical generalization (i.e., our results are generalizable to other organizations that have similar characteristics as the cases in our case study and use Scrum, instead of other agile frameworks with even less architecture focus, such as Kanban). In future work, a comparison with similar literature can sharpen generalizability. However, the presented study is a first of its kind. With regards to *reliability* (how data analysis depends on researchers), we recorded interviews and interview data, and reviewed data collection and analysis procedures before conducting the study. *Internal validity* is not a concern since our exploratory case study does not make any claims about causal relationships [22].

5   Conclusions

We investigated the use of RAs in agile projects through an industrial case study in two Dutch software developing organizations. Many findings from do not seem to be agile-specific (e.g., what types of RAs are used in agile projects) but indicate the RAs could complement agile principles and practices (e.g., cross-functional teams; freedom of developers when moving between projects). Furthermore, RAs help focus on architectural aspects despite the need to deliver value fast. Maintenance of internally defined RAs is a potential problem if the organization is heavily agile oriented (case 1) as there may not be enough and explicit resources for RA maintenance. This is because RA maintenance offers no immediate business value for customers, but is more a benefit for the software developing organization.

Future work includes more detailed case studies in industry to increase the validity of the findings presented in this paper. Furthermore, based on the findings from this study, we can conduct a survey to obtain a broad overview of the perception of practitioners about RAs in agile projects. Finally, we need to compare our findings to other studies that investigate agile principles in regulated industries, since many regulated industries (government, medical device industry, or aviation) impose regulations, policies, standards, etc. on software products, often in form of RAs, reference models, or architecture frameworks.

Acknowledgments. We thank the participating organizations and individuals for their support. We thank Patrick de Beer for his help is arranging and performing one of the interviews.

References

1. VersionOne Inc.: 8th Annual State of Agile Survey (2014)
2. Diaz, J., Perez, J., Alarcon, P.P., Garbajosa, J.: Agile Product Line Engineering - A Systematic Literature Review. Software - Practice and Experience **41**, 921–941 (2011)
3. Governor, J., Hinchcliffe, D., Nickull, D.: Web 2.0 Architectures - What entrepreneurs and information architects need to know. O'Reilly Media / Adope Developer Library, Newton, MA (2009)
4. Kruchten, P.: The Rational Unified Process: An Introduction. Addison-Wesley, Boston, MA (2004)
5. Nakagawa, E.Y., Oliveira Antonino, P., Becker, M.: Reference architecture and product line architecture: a subtle but critical difference. In: Crnkovic, I., Gruhn, V., Book, M. (eds.) ECSA 2011. LNCS, vol. 6903, pp. 207–211. Springer, Heidelberg (2011)
6. Martínez-Fernández, S., Ayala, C.P., Franch, X., Martins Marques, H.: Benefits and drawbacks of reference architectures. In: Drira, K. (ed.) ECSA 2013. LNCS, vol. 7957, pp. 307–310. Springer, Heidelberg (2013)
7. Angelov, S., Grefen, P., Greefhorst, D.: A Framework for Analysis and Design of Software Reference Architectures. Information and Software Technology **54**, 417–431 (2012)
8. Angelov, S., Trienekens, J., Kusters, R.: Software reference architectures - exploring their usage and design in practice. In: Drira, K. (ed.) ECSA 2013. LNCS, vol. 7957, pp. 17–24. Springer, Heidelberg (2013)
9. Ali Babar, M., Brown, A., Mistrik, I.: Agile Software Architecture - Aligning Agile Processes and Software Architectures. Morgan Kaufman (2013)
10. Abrahamsson, P., Babar, M.A., Kruchten, P.: Agility and Architecture: Can they Coexist? IEEE Software **27**, 16–22 (2010)
11. Yin, R.K.: Case Study Research - Design and Methods. Sage Publications, London (2009)
12. Robson, C.: Real World Research: A Resource for Social Scientists and Practitioner-researchers. Blackwell Publishers, Oxford (2002)
13. Vogt, P.: Dictionary of Statistics and Methodology - A Non-technical Guide for the Social Sciences. Sage Publications, Thousand Oaks (2005)
14. Runeson, P., Hoest, M.: Guidelines for Conducting and Reporting Case Study Research in Software Engineering. Empirical Software Engineering **14**, 131–164 (2009)
15. Gerring, J.: Case Study Research - Principles and Practices. Cambridge University Press, Cambridge (2006)
16. Strauss, A.C., Corbin, J.: Basics of Qualitative Research: Grounded Theory Procedures and Techniques. Sage Publications, Thousand Oaks (1990)
17. Miles, M.B., Huberman, A.M.: Qualitative Data Analysis. Sage Publications, Thousand Oaks (1994)
18. Adolph, S., Hall, W., Kruchten, P.: Using Grounded Theory to Study the Experience of Software Development. Empirical Software Engineering **16**, 487–513 (2011)
19. Krippendorff, K.: Content Analysis: An Introduction to its Methodology. Sage Publications, Thousand Oaks (2003)

20. Noblit, G.W., Hare, R.D.: Meta-Ethnography: Synthesizing Qualitative Studies. Sage Publications, Newbury Park (1988)
21. Wohlin, C., Hoest, M., Henningsson, K.: Empirical research methods in software engineering. In: Conradi, R., Wang, A.I. (eds.) Empirical Methods and Studies in Software Engineering. LNCS, vol. 2765, pp. 7–23. Springer, Heidelberg (2003)
22. Easterbrook, S., Singer, J., Storey, M.-A., Damian, D.: Selecting empirical methods for software engineering research. In: Shull, F., Singer, J., Sjoberg, D.I.K. (eds.) Guide to Advanced Empirical Software Engineering, pp. 285–311. Springer, Heidelberg (2008)

An Architecture-Centric Approach for Dynamic Smart Spaces

Luciano Baresi and Adnan Shahzada[⊠]

Dipartimento di Elettronica, Informazione e Bioingegneria,
Politecnico di Milano, Piazza L. da Vinci, 32, 20133 Milano, Italy
{luciano.baresi,adnan.shahzada}@polimi.it

Abstract. The development of sound and reliable dynamic smart spaces is a complex task. Many researchers have already addressed the problem from different angles. The autonomic computing community has been focusing on super-imposed adaptation mechanisms by adding further dedicated components to the (software) architecture of the system. In contrast, bio-inspired solutions provide inherent support to self-organization but they fail to guarantee the desired level of reliability and control.

This paper aims to blend the two views and proposes an architecture-centric solution that merges component-based control and bio-inspired (fireflies-based) mechanisms. Suitable abstractions help conceive self-organizing ad-hoc collaborations among the —virtual and physical— components of a space. An example public park is used throughout the paper to explain and exemplify the key features of the proposed solution.

1 Introduction

Pervasive computing has allowed us to move towards technology-augmented intelligent environments, often called *smart spaces*. These spaces provide users with ubiquitous access to contextualized services to ease the interaction with the physical world. Most of the existing solutions are targeted to solve problems related to static and fixed spaces such as smart homes and offices. Dynamic smart spaces such as public parks, train stations, bus terminals and airports, on the other hand, differ in terms of functional purposes, spatial attributes, and offered services [6]. These spaces require pretty dynamic solutions where the actual number and type of components vary while the system is in operation, and different protocols must be blended together to make the whole system work.

Many solutions have been proposed for conceiving highly adaptable service frameworks. The autonomic computing community has been working on solutions which embed adaptation logic within the architecture to monitor

Luciano Baresi is partially supported by project EEB - Edifici A Zero Consumo Energetico In Distretti Urbani Intelligenti (Italian Technology Cluster For Smart Communities) - CTN01_00034_594053.

Adnan Shahzada is funded by the Joint Open Lab S-Cube, sponsored by Telecom Italia S.p.A. - Innovation division, Milan, Italy.

D. Weyns et al. (Eds.): ECSA 2015, LNCS 9278, pp. 277–284, 2015.
DOI: 10.1007/978-3-319-23727-5_23

the changes in the system and to suggest re-configuration (through control loops) accordingly. For example, Gurgen et al. [5] propose an approach for building self-aware cyber-physical systems for smart buildings and cities, while AlfredO [7] and SOCRADES [3] exploit service-oriented infrastructures to provide abstractions over device heterogeneity and configuration alternatives. Unfortunately most of these adaptation solutions are *external*, that is, they are super-impositions over existing systems. Moreover, the spatial information and situatedness, which are core requirements for dynamic spaces, are not first-class abstractions in these solutions. Therefore, adaptation logic would have to be very complex and heavyweight to ensure the capability of adapting to any foreseeable situation, and the extraction of proximity related information would be costly [11].

The inability of the existing frameworks motivated researchers to find alternative solutions that are radically different in their design philosophy. To this end, Agha [1] suggests the use of natural systems as inspiration to re-model the architectural design of these systems instead of complicating existing solutions. The autonomous components of natural systems (e,g., ant colonies [4], or flower pollination [10]) are inherently situated in the space and their behavior is guided through the interaction with other components around them under natural laws. Zambonelli and Viroli [11] highlight that biological metaphors are suitable for modeling the spatial relationships of components and enable both localized and distributed social behaviors. However, these local decision making and self-organization fail to guarantee the desired control over self-* mechanisms to ensure reliable contextualized services to the users.

Therefore, this paper claims the need for —and proposes— an architectural solution that synthesizes the conventional component-based control and the *internal* and inherent self-adaptive capabilities of bio-inspired ecosystems together to exploit the best characteristics of the two paradigms. The architecture must be able to provide: (i) appropriate design abstractions to design a space, (ii) a mechanism to form ad-hoc collaborations, and (iii) self-adaptation mechanisms sufficient to ensure the reliability, self-configuration, and scalability of the system. The proposed solution offers a role-oriented collaboration that groups the heterogeneous components of a space according to user-supplied heuristic functions and lets the components evolve towards more and more efficient topologies of the system. This self-organization process is inspired by and borrows some concepts from fireflies [9]. The architecture also provides mechanisms for re-configuration in case components fail or leave the system unexpectedly. In addition, the support for the co-existence of physical and virtual (simulated) components enables seamless and incremental development of the space.

The rest of the paper is organized as follows. Section 2 introduces the key characteristics of the proposed architecture. Section 3 presents and analyzes our preliminary experiments to design and simulate the park case-study. Section 4 concludes the paper.

2   Proposed Solution

We present an architectural solution that allows the developer to build dynamic smart spaces through abstractions that support both the control loops from autonomic systems and the inherent self-* mechanisms from bio-inspired systems.

We use a public park scenario to illustrate our solution and to evaluate its key features. The park is divided into sections; each section comprises different attractions (e.g., ferris wheel, kids rail, and cafeteria). Thousands of visitors enter the park every day; each visitor carries a mobile device and is interested in different points of interest (POI). The park is equipped with proximity sensors and large interactive screens that also work as access points for the users to connect to the space. The park space groups the visitors with similar interests —within a certain distance— together by exploiting user profiles and contextual information. This special-purpose grouping can enable effective cooperation among the users with similar interests and location by providing efficient data dissemination. Visitors can interact with the screens to receive information about nearby attractions in the park.

Figure 1 shows the proposed architecture. It provides role-oriented abstractions, a collaboration model for integrating components, and fireflies-based self-adaptation mechanisms for the development of dynamic smart spaces.

2.1   Abstractions

The basic architectural unit is a **component**, that is, any physical or virtual entity that provides/requires capabilities to/from other components. The components in our park are thus the interactive screens, which display information, and the users' devices, which interact with each other and with the big screens. Components capture the essential attributes of space entities and maintain their state over time. Sensors, actuators, controllers, devices, and external systems (within layer Physical Space) are all modeled as components. This abstraction allows the developer to concentrate on the properties of interest and define suitable behaviors accordingly. The *same* component can act as proxy of both a physical entity and a simulated one with no external changes. The same architecture is kept throughout the whole development process: it can evolve by both decomposing existing components and replacing simulated behaviors with real ones. **Roles** are scenario-specific behaviors of components. The rationale for employing role-oriented modeling in our framework is the following: roles provide dynamic views on a component (which are typed entities) in a specific context, and thus they are useful for creating contextualized behaviors and specializing data exchange among components. Roles also provide separation of concerns between the component identity (and data) and its behavior and collaborations. They are superimposed on components and can be changed or removed at runtime according to contextual needs. The collaborations set between components on the basis of their roles help control domain dependencies and provided/ required features in a finer-grained manner.

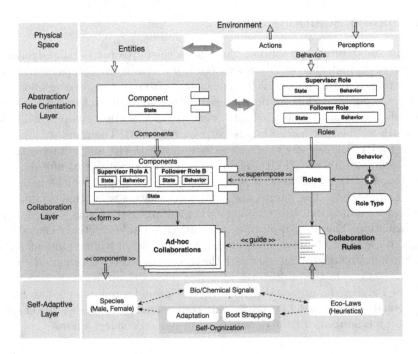

Fig. 1. Proposed architectural framework

A role comprises a *type* and *behaviors*. There are two types: *follower*, which means worker, and *supervisor*, which oversees workers. For instance, there can be a supervisor and a follower role for each POI in the park and they can be played by the user (device) components. Behaviors are application-specific functionality that a component performs in certain situations. A behavior can be either *periodic* (repeated every n time units), or *triggered* (executed when certain events take place). Moreover, a behavior can refer to the *normal* activities carried out by the followers, or to the *control* activities that belong to supervisors.

2.2 Collaboration Model

The Collaboration Layer is responsible for coordinating and integrating heterogeneous components. Components collaborate with each other through **groups** based on their functionality, location, or other logical factors and dependencies. A group acts as a facilitator to integrate various components and forms ad-hoc collaborations. In each group (corresponding to a collaboration), one component is chosen (dynamically by the framework) to play the role of supervisor while the other components are followers [2]. The supervisor component is responsible for managing the group whereas followers act upon the directives they receive from the supervisor. Each component can play different roles in diverse collaborations (groups) and hence enables information sharing across multiple ad-hoc collaborations. To understand this, let us consider the park example where we may have

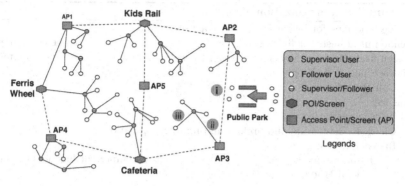

Fig. 2. Example park topology

the following types of collaborations (as shown in Figure 2): (i) screen to screen collaboration, which enables screens to exchange localized data (ii) screen to user collaboration, which enables users to connect to a screen and get personalized information, and (iii) user to user interest-based collaboration, which allows users with similar interests to connect together and exchange helpful information.

To achieve this, first all the smart space entities and their roles are abstracted (as described above), and then, the collaboration layer integrates them in various self-organizing groups according to collaboration rules. These rules define the topological and organizational directives for group management and they comprise collaboration types (along with their role dependencies), space proximity definition, and heuristic functions for ad-hoc group formation. Heuristic functions are used first to bootstrap a newly joined component and later to optimize the topology of the system by finding the best group for each component according to the specific needs. The flexibility of the architecture makes it possible to "plug" heuristic functions for the collaboration policies of these components through any adaptation mechanism; in this paper we describe how we have incorporated fireflies-based self-organization.

2.3   Self-Adaptation Capabilities

The Self-adaptation Layer of the proposed architecture is inspired by the firefly algorithm [9] and mimics the behavior of fireflies to form groups. Fireflies are characterized by the *flashing light* they produce through bio-luminescence. Such flashing light serves as primary courtship *signals* for mating. Females are attracted by behavioral differences in courtship signals and typically prefer *brighter* male flashes. The flash intensity varies with the distance from the source.

Unlike the original firefly algorithm, we consider bi-sex species of flies. Components and roles are mapped to the firefly metaphor as follows: (i) roles are abstracted as flies and role types are male (supervisor) and female (follower) flies, (ii) flies live in nests (components) that are used to represent all the entities of a system, (iii) light flashes, which are generated (as brightness by male flies)

Algorithm 1 Self-organization algorithm

1: Define functions for brightness and attraction
2: Define initial nests for fireflies $N_i, i := 1, 2, \ldots, n$ ▷ define components
3: Assign fireflies (male/female and color) to each nest ▷ define roles for components
4: **for** each nest $n \in N$ **do**
5:     Call BOOTSTRAP(n)
6: **end for**
7: **while** *System.state* := *running* **do**
8:     Check for new nests and fireflies and update population
9:     **for** each nest $n \in N$ **do**
10:        **if** $n[male] := \emptyset$ **then**   ▷ if component has no supervisor
11:           Call BOOTSTRAP(n)
12:        **else**
13:           Call ADAPT(n)
14:        **end if**
15:     **end for**
16: **end while**

---

and perceived (as attraction by female flies), guide the interaction mechanism, and (iv) rules —such as: "brighter fly will be more attractive, and brightness decreases with distance"— provide policies to form ad-hoc collaborations.

The self-organization algorithm (Algorithm 1) consists of two phases: (i) bootstrapping for new or orphan (with no supervisor) components and (ii) adaptation for the components with an active collaboration. The self-organization algorithm requires that the functions for calculating brightness and attraction be defined. We have used the following heuristics for our park scenario:

$$\beta_k(t) = \frac{c1}{\sum_{i=1}^{n} L_{ik}} + c2 \times P_k \tag{1}$$

where $\beta_k(t)$ is the brightness value for supervisor (male fly) k at time t, n is the number of followers (female flies) for node k, P_k is the energy of supervisor k, L_{ik} is the communication load (average no. of messages per unit time) between follower i and supervisor k, and $c1$ and $c2$ are the constants used to assign weights to the corresponding parameters (L and P).

$$\alpha_{ik}(t) = \frac{c3}{d_{ik}^2} + c4 \times \beta_k \tag{2}$$

where $\alpha_{ik}(t)$ is the attraction of supervisor k towards follower i at time t, β_k is the brightness of supervisor k, d_{ik} is the distance between follower i and supervisor k, and $c3$ and $c4$ are constants used to assign weights to distance and brightness.

Whenever a new component joins the system, the BOOTSTRAP procedure is called upon which iterates over the set of roles the component can play. It calculates the brightness for all the supervisor roles and attraction for its follower roles. It then searches for the best possible collaboration for each role according to calculated heuristics (brightness and attraction) values.

The second step of self-organization is the ADAPT procedure. It first checks and if the component is not part of any collaboration, it bootstraps it. Otherwise, it does the following: (i) for each supervisor, it checks whether there is another supervisor available with better suitability, and if it is the case, it changes its role to follower, and (ii) for each follower, it performs the aforementioned procedure and calculates the suitability of the supervisors around. It switches the group if it finds a better supervisor then the current one.

3   Analysis

This section describes and analyzes our preliminary experiments to design and simulate the park case-study. The park is set up and simulated[1] through the Netlogo simulator [8]. The environment in Netlogo is spatially organized in *patches* and the individuals that live in the simulated environment are termed *breeds*. The park is structured around a grid of 30×30 patches, where each patch can be a pathway, a screen, or an attraction. Components (breeds) can be of three types: people, screens and POIs. We started the simulation with a population size of 120 and decided that 5 new people had to join, and 1 person had to leave the system every 25 time units. People move towards the directives received from the screen 50% of the time and take random movements otherwise.

We have run the simulation for the example scenario by considering the role and collaboration types described in Section 2.2. Algorithm 1 is then used to form optimized (in terms of distribution of communication load and energy level for each device) ad-hoc collaborations. The goal is to evaluate the ability of the proposed structure to handle dynamism and mobility of the users within the space while keeping the reliability of the services. Reliability of services refers to the ability of architecture to re-organize the followers (in new groups) when the supervisor component fails or leaves their proximity.

The simulations were run for 1000 time units (simulation cycles) and the population was initialized with 120 components and dynamically increased to 280 elements. We recorded that in case of supervisor failure, all corresponding follower components of the group are re-assigned to a new group within 3 time units. We have also measured the energy and communication load (dependent on the group size) for each (user) supervisor component. The energy consumption of each device is measured as a (constant) penalty for each message sent or received by the device. The proposed solution was able to balance both the energy consumption and the size of different user groups (communication load). Throughout the simulation, we observed that the variability of energy consumption for each device remains within standard deviation of 1% whereas the difference in group size has deviation of less then 1 component across all groups.

The results highlight that the proposed architecture maintains reliable service provision in a scenario with highly dynamic and mobile components. Moreover, it

---

[1] The simulation video is available online at: http://home.deib.polimi.it/shahzada/ ParkSimulation/NetLogo-ParkSim.mov

distributes the communication load uniformly across components by delegating supervision to some users and hence reduces the overall network congestion.

4   Conclusions and Future Work

This paper presents an architectural solution that synthesizes component-based control, from autonomic computing, and fireflies-based self-organization, from self-adaptive biological systems. The architecture eliminates the shortcomings of these approaches, that is, lack of inherent situated awareness and mobility for autonomic approaches, and lack of control over the self-organization in bio-inspired systems. The paper presents a first evaluation of the effectiveness of the solution with the help of a public park case study. As future work, we plan to extend the experiments to have a more comprehensive evaluation of the solution with complex smart spaces.

References

1. Agha, G.: Computing in Pervasive Cyberspace. Communications of the ACM **51**(1), 68–70 (2008)
2. Baresi, L., Guinea, S., Shahzada, A.: SeSaMe: towards a semantic self adaptive middleware for smart spaces. In: Post-Proceeding of the Workshop on Engineering Multi-agent Systems, pp. 169–178 (2013)
3. Cannata, A., Gerosa, M., Taisch, M.: SOCRADES: a framework for developing intelligent systems in manufacturing. In: Proceedings of International Conference on Industrial Engineering and Engineering Management, pp. 1904–1908 (2008)
4. Dorigo, M., Blum, C.: Ant Colony Optimization Theory: A Survey. Theoretical Computer Science **344**(2), 243–278 (2005)
5. Gurgen, L., Gunalp, O., Benazzouz, Y., Gallissot, M.: Self-aware cyber-physical systems and applications in smart buildings and cities. In: Proceedings of the Conference on Design, Automation and Test in Europe, pp. 1149–1154 (2013)
6. Ma, J., Yang, L.T., Apduhan, B.O., Huang, R., Barolli, L., Takizawa, M.: Towards a Smart World and Ubiquitous Intelligence: A Walkthrough From Smart Things to Smart Hyperspaces and UbicKids. International Journal of Pervasive Computing and Communications **1**(1), 53–68 (2005)
7. Rellermeyer, J.S., Riva, O., Alonso, G.: AlfredO: an architecture for flexible interaction with electronic devices. In: Issarny, V., Schantz, R. (eds.) Middleware 2008. LNCS, vol. 5346, pp. 22–41. Springer, Heidelberg (2008)
8. Tisue, S., Wilensky, U.: Netlogo: a simple environment for modeling complexity. In: Proceedings of International Conference on Complex Systems, pp. 16–21 (2004)
9. Yang, X.-S.: Firefly algorithms for multimodal optimization. In: Watanabe, O., Zeugmann, T. (eds.) SAGA 2009. LNCS, vol. 5792, pp. 169–178. Springer, Heidelberg (2009)
10. Yang, X.-S.: Flower pollination algorithm for global optimization. In: Durand-Lose, J., Jonoska, N. (eds.) UCNC 2012. LNCS, vol. 7445, pp. 240–249. Springer, Heidelberg (2012)
11. Zambonelli, F., Viroli, M.: A Survey on Nature-Inspired Metaphors for Pervasive Service Ecosystems. International Journal of Pervasive Computing and Communications **7**(3), 186–204 (2011)

Using Feature Models for Distributed Deployment in Extended Smart Home Architecture

Amal Tahri[1,2](✉), Laurence Duchien[2], and Jacques Pulou[1]

[1] Orange Labs, Meylan, France
[2] INRIA Lille-Nord Europe, CRISTAL Laboratory,
University Lille 1, Villeneuve-d'Ascq, France
amal.tahri@orange.com

Abstract. Nowadays, smart home is extended beyond the house itself to encompass connected platforms on the Cloud as well as mobile personal devices. This *Smart Home Extended Architecture* (SHEA) helps customers to remain in touch with their home everywhere and any time. The endless increase of connected devices in the home and outside within the SHEA multiplies the deployment possibilities for any application. Therefore, SHEA should be taken from now as the actual target platform for smart home application deployment. Every home is different and applications offer different services according to customer preferences. To manage this variability, we extend the feature modeling from software product line domain with deployment constraints and we present an example of a model that could address this deployment challenge.

1 Introduction

Smart Home Extended Architecture (SHEA) expands the Smart Home (SH) deployment environment to the Cloud and mobile personal devices to host the SH applications. Different domains contribute to the SHEA such as home security, comfort and energy efficiency to offer *services* to customers. A service is delivered as a component-based application [11]. The deployment of a SH application is a mapping of a set of components onto a set of deployment *nodes*. These nodes hold computational resources that must satisfy the component requirements deployed on them.

The variability of the SHEA comes from different points of views as it is related to the multitude of involved stakeholders for the SH market and different hardware and software resources. This variability is very challenging and has to be managed to enumerate all the deployment configurations within the SHEA. The effective deployment between the SH and the Cloud is chosen from the analysis results according to specific criteria, e.g., service availability, reduced cost.

Software Product Line (SPL) [9] is a promising methodology to handle the variability. SH applications are defined with Feature Models (FMs) [6], which are tools of SPL principles. FM is a variability modeling technique for a compact

D. Weyns et al. (Eds.): ECSA 2015, LNCS 9278, pp. 285–293, 2015.
DOI: 10.1007/978-3-319-23727-5_24

representation of all possible products, hereafter *variants*, and the definition of compositional and dependency constraints, e.g., implies, excludes, among features. Features are assets describing external properties of a product and their relationships. Constraints clarify which feature combinations are valid, named *valid configurations*, using the Constraint Satisfaction Problem (CSP) solvers [1]. For the deployment purpose, non-functional requirements must be expressed to verify the adequacy of component requirements and node resources. FMs lack tools to express such information. Extended Feature Models (EFMs) [3] overcome the FM limits by introducing non-boolean variables using *attributes*, *cardinalities* and *complex constraints*. Attributes describe non-functional and quantified properties, e.g., CPU, RAM. Cardinalities allow the multiplication of features and thus feature attributes such as CPU, RAM.

However, FM can not represent all *deployment constraints*. Deployment constraints refer to component placement indication among nodes, e.g., collocation, separation, or component requirement adequacy with the deployment node resources. EFMs are not adapted to be used in the deployment purpose as EFMs do not offer enough technical operators to express deployment constraints. Without a clear identification of deployment constraints, EFMs generate huge configuration spaces and often few **convenient** for the deployment purpose.

Our approach uses feature modeling to match the component requirements and the deployment node resources using CSP solver analysis.

The organization of the paper is the following. Motivation behind the distributed deployment across the SHEA is detailed in Section 2. The deployment oriented feature analysis is introduced in Section 3. Preliminary validation is given in Section 4. Related work is described in Section 5. Finally, conclusion and future works are presented in Section 6.

2   Motivations and Challenges

2.1   Motivating Example

A customer purchases a *Control Admittance* application for smart door (un)-locking based on identification mechanisms. Different application variants are available. The basic variant represents the service of door (un)locking using the keypad identification mechanism. The person is asked to enter a pin code in the keypad to open manually the door. The medium variant offers the face recognition service using one recognition algorithm. When the motion detector senses a presence outdoor, the camera forwards images or video frame for face identification. This process matches the camera flow with the customer data base of authorized persons. If the person is recognized, the door opens automatically. The premium variant offers a powerful recognition performance using multiple algorithms. The keypad is available as a degraded mode for all variants, when Internet connection fails as it is deployed in the SH.

Different deployment possibilities are offered to the customers between the SH and the Cloud as in Fig. 1. The Home Automation Box (HAB) is an embedded environment that can host components or even a whole application.

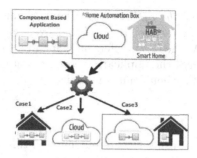

Fig. 1. Deployment possibilities in the SHEA.

We assume that the HAB is the only node in the SH and the Cloud offers one or multiple deployment nodes, e.g., virtual machines on top of the Platform as a Service (PaaS).

Case 1: Deployment on the SH embedded nodes Application deployment in the SH confines all application components into the HAB which may lead to performance degradation because of the HAB limited resources. To satisfy component requirements, a hardware upgrade is required which raises the Bill of Material (BOM)[1] and, therefore, the application acquisition cost.

Case 2: Deployment on the Cloud The Cloud is "a model for enabling convenient and on-demand network access to a shared pool of configurable computing resources that can be rapidly provisioned and released with minimal management effort" [8]. The Cloud offers deployment nodes, e.g., virtual machines with on-demand resource allocation that overcome the limited capacities of the HAB. However, the deployment on the cloud may increase the latency and response time of an application. Connection failure compromises the service availability and user experience.

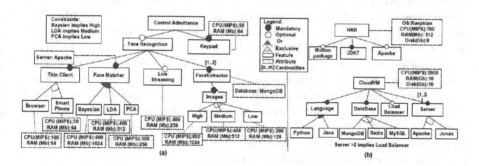

Fig. 2. Control Admittance Extended Feature Model.

---

[1] http://en.wikipedia.org/wiki/Bill_of_materials

Case 3: Deployment across the SHEA nodes The deployment between the HAB and the Cloud offers an attractive trade-off that overcomes the limitation presented in cases 1 and 2. As the Cloud offers on-demand resources that extend the HAB resources and reduces the application cost presented in case 1, the HAB ensures service availability when connection fails.

2.2   Challenges

Two challenges are tackled using feature modeling in this paper:

- *Challenge 1 (C1)* Bridge the gap between feature modeling and deployment analysis by introducing deployment constraints in EFM.
- *Challenge 2 (C2)* Automate the verification of deployment constraints to enumerate all the valid deployment configurations within the SHEA.

3   Feature Analysis Oriented Deployment

3.1   Feature Modeling

We refer to EFM to model the application and each deployment node. In the application EFM in Fig. 2(a), the components are the deployment units and represented as features. This model encompasses all the application variants presented in Section 2.1. In Fig. 2(b), we present all variant for deployment nodes where features are the offered resources. The same ontology is used to declare the requirements and the resources, respectively, in the application and deployment nodes EFMs. **Mandatory** feature, e.g., *face extractor*, represents a core functionality in the application and is always present if its parent is selected in the configuration. **Optional** feature, e.g., *live streaming*, introduces the variability aspect as it may be included or not in a configuration. The **exclusive** group of the *images* feature indicates that only one sub-feature can be selected in a configuration. The **or** group of the *face matcher* feature allows the selection of none, one or several sub-features in the configuration. *Bayesian* **implies** *high* signifies that when the feature *Bayesian* is selected, the feature *high* must be present in this configuration. Attributes (dotted rectangles) are linked to feature to express quantified requirements, e.g., CPU and RAM. Feature cardinality (integer range [m,n], $m <= n$) determines the number of feature instances and thus the corresponding attributes allowed in the product configuration, e.g., *live streaming* can be present up to three times in the same configuration. The root feature *control admittance* and the *keypad* feature are the basic variant. When adding *face recognition* feature and choosing from the *face matcher* group the *PCA* feature, we obtain the medium variant.

3.2   Approach

Deployment Node Feature are a new feature category representing the deployment nodes in the application EFM. This new category allows the separation between component features and deployment node features to declare *Deployment Constraints*. Then, we validate whether a deployment node is a suitable host for application components using feature modeling analysis.

$$HostedBy(\mathcal{NF}, \mathcal{F}) \text{ where } \mathcal{F} \in \mathbb{AF}, \quad \mathcal{NF} \in \mathbb{LNF} \tag{1}$$

$$Colocated(\mathcal{F}, \mathcal{F}'), Separated(\mathcal{F}, \mathcal{F}') \text{ where } \mathcal{F}, \mathcal{F}' \in \mathbb{AF} \tag{2}$$

$$Resource\,Constraint(r_j) := \sum_{l=1}^{k_i} R_{\mathcal{F}_{i_l}}^{r_j} \leq R_{\mathcal{NF}_i}^{r_j} \tag{3}$$

HostedBy constraint, in (1), is a binary relation between the List of deployment Node Features $\mathbb{LNF}$ and the set of Application Features $\mathbb{AF}$. The couple $(\mathcal{NF}, \mathcal{F})$ implies that if the deployment node feature $\mathcal{NF}$ is selected in a configuration, then, the feature $\mathcal{F}$ is deployed on this node.

Colocated and *Seperated* constraints, in (2), are binary relations between two features in $\mathbb{AF}$. When both features $\mathcal{F}$ and $\mathcal{F}'$ are selected in the same configuration, (i) if *Colocated*, they must be on the same deployment node. (ii) If *Separated*, they must be deployed on different deployment node. *Colcated* may be identified between (i) features of the same package that need to be deployed on the same node, (ii) features of different packages but with mutual dependencies and high coupling, (iii) all the features that contribute to the same service and should be deployed in the same network area to ensure high availability of this service in case of connection failure.

Separated constraint can refer to (i) *high availability* when two features duplicate important data that must not be lost during a single node failure, (ii) *potential parallelism* when features operating independently are dispatched among different nodes to improve the throughput of the whole application, (iii) *resource greedy features* when two features require a large amount of resources such as CPU or RAM, they are deployed on different nodes.

The *Resource Constraint*, in (3), ensures that the sum of the attributes for all the selected features to be hosted on embedded nodes does not exceed the node available resources. $\mathcal{F}_i$ is a feature to be deployed on $\mathcal{NF}_i$. k_i is the size of the selected list of features on $\mathcal{NF}_i$ and $\forall r_j \subset R_j$, j is the resource type where $j \in [1, n]$ n being the resource types taken into account. In our example, $n = 2$ as only two resource types are considered: $r_1 = CPU$, $r_2 = RAM$.

These constraints are added in the application EFM and translated to the constraint programming Choco solver [5] to check the configuration validity.

The *PossibleHost* function below finds all $\mathcal{NF}$ that satisfy the feature attributes of $\mathbb{AF}$ and returns the analysis solution set. This function should be preceded by an initialization step that inserts the deployment constraints, i.e., *Hostedby*, *Colocated* and *Separated* predefined by the application developer in $\mathbb{AF}$. The algorithm takes as inputs the $\mathbb{AF}$ and the deployment node EFMs from which it constructs the list $\mathbb{LNF}$ (here $\mathbb{LNF} = \{HAB, CloudVM\}$). The algorithm has two nested *For* loops. The outer loop covers the list $\mathbb{LNF}$. The *addFeature* creates a mandatory feature $\mathcal{NF}$ from $\mathbb{LNF}$ under the root feature of $\mathbb{AF}$. For each node, the inner loop examines successively all the features with attributes in $\mathbb{AF}$. If no predefined *Hostedby* constraint is found for the given $\mathcal{NF}$ and $\mathcal{F}$, the *FindMatch* method searches the $\mathcal{NF}$ related EFM, e.g., Fig. 2 (b), for an equivalent attribute of this $\mathcal{F}$. If match found, the *addConstraint* method introduces a *Hostedby* constraint to $\mathbb{AF}$ between the $\mathcal{F}$ of this attribute and the given $\mathcal{NF}$. If no match found, the *addConstraint* creates *notHostedBy* constraint between the given $\mathcal{F}$ and $\mathcal{NF}$.

The *ResourceVerification* procedure verifies *Resource Constraint* (3) and thus is only carried out for embedded nodes, e.g., in our example only HAB node is involved with the selected features hosted on them. The $\mathbb{AF}$ with these new constraints is translated into constraint programming and introduced to the solver (i.e., addSolver) that automatically outputs the valid configurations from where we feed the *SolutionSet SS*. The outer loop enters a new step and continues to scan the $\mathcal{NF}$ list until its end.

This section tackles the challenges in Section 2.2. The deployment constraints help bridge the gap between feature modeling and deployment analysis of the *C1* and the algorithm automates the verification of these constraints as in *C2* to enumerate the valid deployment configurations within the SHEA.

Algorithm 1 Matching Algorithm

1: REQUIRE *FeatureModel* $\mathbb{AF}$, *list* < *FeatureModel* > LNF
2: ENSURE *PossibleHost*
3: **function** *SolutionSet* PossibleHost($\mathbb{AF}$, LNF)
4:     *SolutionSet SS = empty*
5:     Copy $\mathbb{AF}$ in $\mathbb{AF}'$
6:     **for all** $\mathcal{NF} \in$ LNF **do**
7:         **if** $\mathcal{NF} \notin \mathbb{AF}'$ **then** *addFeature*($\mathbb{AF}'$, $\mathcal{NF}$)
8:             **for all** $\mathcal{F}$ with attributes $\in \mathbb{AF}'$ **do**
9:                 **if** *HostedBy*($\mathcal{NF}, \mathcal{F}$)) $\notin \mathbb{AF}'$ **then**
10:                    **if** *FindMatch*($\mathcal{F}$ with attributes in $\mathcal{NF}$) **then**
11:                        *addConstraint* to $\mathbb{AF}'$ (*HostedBy*($\mathcal{NF}, \mathcal{F}$))
12:                        add $\mathcal{F}$ to $\mathbb{F}_{in\mathcal{NF}}$ ▷ list of $\mathcal{F}$ hosted on $\mathcal{NF}$ used in line 17
13:                    **else** *addConstraint* to $\mathbb{AF}'$ (*notHostedBy*($\mathcal{NF}, \mathcal{F}$))
14:                    **end if**
15:                **end if**
16:            **end for**
17:            **if** *ResourceVerification*($\mathcal{NF}, \mathbb{F}_{in\mathcal{NF}}$) **then**   ▷ check constraint (3)
18:                *addSolver*($\mathbb{AF}'$) to SS ▷ solver invocation
19:            **end if**
20:        **end if**
21:    **end for**
22: **return** SS
23: **end function**

---

4   Preliminary Validation

EFMs of the application and the deployment nodes are defined using the SALOON framework [10], for SoftwAre product Lines for clOud cOmputiNg. This framework relies on SPL principles for selecting and configuring cloud environments according to given requirements. SALOON offers the modeling and analysis tools to manage cloud variability using cardinality-based feature models and relies on the Eclipse Modeling Framework (EMF)[2] to present a meta-model of features. We have extended this meta-model by introducing deployment node features and deployment constraints. We translate the features, attributes and deployment constraints to Choco solver [5] constraint programming to check the configuration validity. The solution evaluation computes the valid deployment configurations of the control admittance EFM on the HAB and the Cloud EFM in Fig. 2. Deployment constraints are introduced as follows: *HostedBy*(HAB, keypad), *Colocated* (Baysien, live streaming), and *Separated* (smart phone, Baysien) and the algorithm 1 is applied to the application EFM. Table 1 shows the results where the valid configuration number is reduced notably for a simple example of 16 features. In the future, realistic application set including several hundred of components will be used to characterize the limits of this method.

Table 1. Valid Configurations for Admittance Control

Feature Model	Features	Config	Config with 1 Colocated	Config with 1 Seperated	Config with 1 Colocated &1 Seperated
Application	16	25	11	16	8
Execution Time (ms)	-	2926	2897	3639	2895

5   Related Work

The authors, in [7], propose an approach for managing and verifying deployment constraints. This approach is based on Model-Driven Engineering to include deployment constraints at earlier stage of application development. The execution context includes the home devices, the mobile phones and the Cloud. The authors introduce FM to manage applications and execution context variability taking into account deployment constraints. Close to this research, our work is an extension with some differences: (i) we only consider deployment time and (ii) use CSP solver to verify the deployment configurations based on deployment constraints in feature modeling. Druilhe et al. in [4] present a deployment model to reduce energy consumption of the home device set (Set Top Box, Gateway). They stand a distribution plan that maps the applications components on the devices considering resources and quantity of resources constraints, e.g., CPU,

---

[2] http://www.eclipse.org/modeling/emf/

RAM. Quinton et al. [10] focus on the deployment on the Cloud considering SPL techniques. They propose an extended feature models framework named SALOON to configure Cloud environments to host applications. EFM represents the Cloud environment resources, e.g., web server, data base, execution environment. This framework helps developers selecting the best solution based on specific customer criteria. We extend these previous results to include SH environment to SALOON and adapt feature modeling for the deployment purpose. In [2], the authors analyze the deployment of health monitoring application variants in different Cloud platforms using SPL in order to select the possible deployment with the lower price. Our work focus on introducing deployment constraints to adapt feature modeling for deployment analysis.

6   Conclusion

Our approach proposes to include deployment constraint in EFM that is not proposed by other researches. We have used and extended the SALOON framework [10] to introduce a new process for mapping application components onto deployment nodes using feature modeling. This paper raises a preliminary validation of how to adapt feature modeling for the deployment purpose. However, it does not characterize the limits of this method. The given example is restricted to SHEA with only one SH node, e.g., HAB and other examples should be checked to get better insight in the approach added value.

References

1. Apt, K.: Principles of constraint programming. Cambridge University Press (2003)
2. Cavalcante, E., Almeida, A., Batista, T., Cacho, N., Lopes, F., Delicato, F.C., Sena, T., Pires, P.F.: Exploiting software product lines to develop cloud computing applications. In: Proceedings of the 16th International Software Product Line Conference, vol. 2, pp. 179–187. ACM (2012)
3. Czarnecki, K., Hwan, C., Kim, P., Kalleberg, K.: Feature models are views on ontologies. In: 2006 10th International Software Product Line Conference, pp. 41–51. IEEE (2006)
4. Druilhe, R., Anne, M., Pulou, J., Duchien, L., Seinturier, L.: Energy-driven consolidation in digital home. In: Proceedings of the 28th Annual ACM Symposium on Applied Computing, pp. 1157–1162. ACM (2013)
5. Jussien, N., Rochart, G., Lorca, X.: Choco: an open source java constraint programming library. In: CPAIOR'08 Workshop on Open-Source Software for Integer and Contraint Programming (OSSICP'08), pp. 1–10 (2008)
6. Kang, K.C., Cohen, S.G., Hess, J.A., Novak, W.E., Peterson, A.S.: Feature-oriented domain analysis (foda) feasibility study. Technical report, DTIC Document (1990)
7. Lee, K.C.A., Segarra, M.T., Guelec, S.: A deployment-oriented development process based on context variability modeling. In: 2014 2nd International Conference on Model-Driven Engineering and Software Development (MODELSWARD), pp. 454–459. IEEE (2014)

8. Mell, P., Grance, T.: The nist definition of cloud computing. National Institute of Standards and Technology **53**(6), 50 (2009)
9. Pohl, K., Böckle, G., Van Der Linden, F.: Software product line engineering, vol. 10. Springer (2005)
10. Quinton, C.: Cloud Environment Selection and Configuration: A Software Product Lines-Based Approach. PhD thesis, Université Lille 1 (2014)
11. Szyperski, C.: Component Software: Beyond Object-oriented Programming. ACM Press/Addison-Wesley Publishing Co., New York (2002)

SmartyCo: Managing Cyber-Physical Systems for Smart Environments

Daniel Romero[1]([✉]), Clément Quinton[2], Laurence Duchien[1], Lionel Seinturier[1], and Carolina Valdez[3]

[1] Université Lille 1 & Inria, CRIStAL (UMR CNRS 9189) Laboratory,
Villeneuve-d'Ascq, France
{daniel.romero,laurence.duchien,lionel.seinturier}@inria.fr
[2] Politecnico di Milano, DEIB, Piazza L. Da Vinci, 32, 20133 Milano, Italy
clement.quinton@polimi.it
[3] Media.lab, Instituto Pladema, UNCPBA, Tandil, Argentina
Cvaldezgandara@alumnos.exa.unicen.edu.ar

Abstract. *Cyber-Physical Systems* (CPS) are composed of heterogeneous devices, communicating with each other and interacting with the physical world. Fostered by the growing use of smart devices that are permanently connected to the Internet, these CPS can be found in *smart environments* such as smart buildings, pavilions or homes. CPS must cope with the complexity and heterogeneity of their connected devices while supporting end-users with limited technical background to configure and manage their system. To deal with these issues, in this paper we introduce SMARTYCO, our approach based on *Dynamic Software Product Line* (DSPL) principles to configure and manage CPS for smart environments. We describe its underlying architecture and illustrate in the context of smart homes how end-users can use it to define their own CPS in an automated way. We then explain how such an approach supports the reconfiguration of smart devices based on end-users rules, thus adapting the CPS *w.r.t.* environment changes. Finally, we show that our approach is well-suited to handle the addition and removal of CPS devices while the system is running, and we report on our experience in enabling home inhabitants to dynamically reconfigure their CPS.

1 Introduction

Nowadays, the definition of *Cyber-Physical Systems* (CPS), *i.e.*, systems controlling physical elements in the real world from software applications, is a reality. This is due to the emerging Internet of Everything paradigm, where smartphones, tablets, PCs and different devices are connected to the Internet. These CPS enable a 'smart everywhere society', where roads, cars, trains, offices, public spaces or homes interact smartly. CPS must thus be context-aware, *i.e.*, able to react to environment changes by considering the technological heterogeneity, concurrency and availability of connected devices.

For instance, homes have recently been considered as smart environments and several works [5,7,13] focus on the Do-It-Yourself Smart Home paradigm.

© Springer International Publishing Switzerland 2015
D. Weyns et al. (Eds.): ECSA 2015, LNCS 9278, pp. 294–302, 2015.
DOI: 10.1007/978-3-319-23727-5_25

However, these approaches do not provide enough flexibility in terms of services that can be used, produce technological lock-in, or introduce additional costs. Thus, allowing end-users to configure, control and update their own CPS is a challenging task, as it requires a solution managing the variability of such CPS at design and runtime, while enabling these users to easily cope with this variability.

In order to face this challenge, we present in this article SMARTYCO, our *Dynamic Software Product Line* (DSPL) [6] based approach to capture smart environment configurations via extended *feature models* [1] and define smart CPS. In particular, SMARTYCO provides three main contributions: *(1)* A software product line for deriving the system configuration according to user requirements and available devices, *(2)* a support for runtime adaptation via end-user rules and *(3)* a bidirectional mechanism for keeping the software product line and the cyber-physical system synchronized in presence of adaptations. The context-awareness and the reactivity of the system are reified by defining event-condition-action rules, which execute tasks required by users under given conditions while maintaining the consistency of the whole system. The rules together with the possibility to incorporate new services into the system represent the dynamic part of the product line.

The next section presents the technologies that makes possible the definition of our approach. Then, Section 3 provides an overview of SMARTYCO and explains the rule definition mechanism. Sections 4 describes a prototype, while related work is discussed in Section 5. Section 6 concludes the paper.

2   Background Information and Enabling Technologies

As already mentioned, smart environments are equipped with several devices:

Set-top boxes, that provide interactive services such as search and configuration services. In recent years, these boxes have gained computation power by increasing their storage and processing capabilities, and have become more user-friendly by relying on well-designed interfaces. For instance, the Minix Neo X-7, an Android-based box, can be used to install, configure and control new software to manage cyber-physical systems.

Smartphones, that are permanently connected to the Internet through the 3G, 4G and Wi-Fi spots. Thanks to dedicated applications, smartphones can also be used to interact with physical equipments, *e.g.*, switching channels on television or listening to music on external loudspeakers.

Appliances and *devices*, which can be controlled via PC, smartphones and tablets. For example, light switches, thermostats, and cameras from the Belkin WeMo and Z-Wave families can be controlled via Internet services such as *If-This-Then-That* (IFTTT) [8] which is based on event-condition-action rules.

This variability in terms of technologies requires an approach enabling their coordination to run as a unified system. Furthermore, an automation solution has to consider different environment designs, has to be flexible, extensible, intuitive, trustworthy and has to make end-users feel that they are gaining control [14]. In the next section we introduce our approach to deal with these issues.

3 Managing Cyber-Physical Systems With SmartyCo

3.1 Overview

SMARTYCO relies on *Dynamic Software Product Line* (DSPL) principles [2]. A software product line reduces the efforts for producing a family of software products, *e.g.*, CPS. Within this family, products share common functionalities (*i.e.*, commonalities) and differ according to variable ones (*i.e.*, variability) [10]. A domain expert identifies this variability, which is reflected into a variability model, *e.g.*, a *feature model* [9]. Features from this variability model are mapped to concrete reusable software artifacts, or *assets*, which are bound together to yield the software product. In SMARTYCO DSPL, each CPS is thus a product. A DSPL supports binding variability at runtime, thus enabling a system to reconfigure itself while running. Such principles allow SMARTYCO to deal with the static configuration of CPS for smart environments while supporting the adaptation of such systems when required. The SMARTYCO DSPL generates controllers that are deployed on Android-based set-top boxes. Such controllers allow the definition of rules to manage the CPS as well as rules to deal with the context-awareness of the devices in use. Those controllers share a generic common configuration, but differ in some variation points according to the rules defined by the end-user and the available devices. SMARTYCO copes with this technological variability by describing CPS using feature models. Figure 1 provides an overview of SMARTYCO.

End-users rely on the `Configurator` for defining a CPS configuration by selecting the required devices and their location ①. The `Generator`, deployed on the SMARTYCO `Server` running in a private Cloud to ensure data privacy, processes such a configuration to check its validity. To do that, it translates extended feature models into a constraint satisfaction problem and solves it relying on the Choco solver [3], as described in [11]. Then, the `Generator` combines assets related to selected devices to produce the CPS `Controller` ②, which is deployed on the set-top box ③. Assets in SMARTYCO are channels (*i.e.*, sensors and actuators) and rules. End-users define rules when needed via the `Controller`

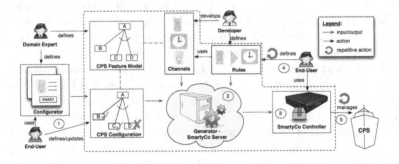

Fig. 1. Overview of the SmartyCo DSPL

④, which orchestrates the CPS ⑤. Channel developers also define rules to keep the system consistent. With such an approach, the SMARTYCO DSPL provides a customized CPS based on available devices.

3.2 Extended Feature Models to Manage CPS Variability

In SMARTYCO, we rely on model driven engineering principles [12] to define the feature models of smart environments. Figure 2 depicts our metamodels for such environments. These metamodels rely on and extend the *metamodel* we proposed in [11] to define feature models with cardinalities and attributes.

The `Channel Type` metamodel (*cf.* gray boxes) enables the definition of actuators and sensors providing actions and triggers (or events). Inspired by IFTTT [8], our approach allows smart objects to work for end-users through simple rules. Each rule has a trigger, an action and a priority to deal with conflicts. Rules with higher priority are executed and if two or more rules have the same priority, they will be executed in the order of their definition. Examples of channel types are smartphones and Belkin WeMo thermostats, while *if someone turns on the thermostat, send me a SMS* is a rule. The CPS metamodel (*cf.* blue boxes) is used to specify concrete channels. They can be fixed with a location (*e.g.*, a crock-pot is in the kitchen) or mobile (*e.g.*, smartphones). We also introduce `Fixed Controllers` that are installed on set-top boxes to control channels and rules. Finally, the `Smart Environment` metamodel (*cf.* degraded salmon boxes) enables the definition of the environment that hosts the CPS. The CPS metamodel uses the `Smart Environment` metamodel to specify the location of `Fixed Controllers`. Each smart environment can be configured independently by instantiating these metamodels. Below, we explain and illustrate their use.

Why extended feature models? The `Configurator` (*cf.* Figure 1) enables the user to deal with the variability of CPS and smart environments. This physical and software variability is reflected in the feature models, which are extended with cardinalities and attributes [1]. Feature models enhanced with such extensions allow the definition of *(1)* multiple instances for the same feature, and *(2)* complex constraints over these features. For example, several instances of the

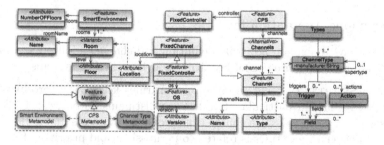

Fig. 2. Metamodels to manage variability in smart environments

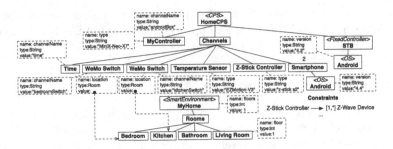

Fig. 3. CPS configuration in a smart home (Excerpt)

same feature (*e.g.*, a channel or a room) can be defined and configured, while attributes provide additional information about features such as location or type. Finally, these extended feature models support the definition of complex relationships involving cardinality and attribute values such as *the configuration of one or more Z-Wave Switches requires the configuration of at least one Z-Stick Controller* (to enable the definition of a Z-Wave device network).

Figure 3 depicts the use of these extensions with instances of the CPS and Smart Environment metamodels. The related Channel Type model (not shown here) contains types related to WeMo and Z-Wave devices. The lower part of the figure depicts the feature model of MyHome, an instance of a smart environment. This smart home is made up of a bedroom, a living room, a bathroom and a kitchen. The upper part depicts a CPS feature model (HomeCPS) that is composed by several devices. In particular, it describes two different cases involving the use of features whose cardinality upper bound is greater than one. On one hand, two different instances of the WeMo Switch feature are configured. Indeed, several devices of the same type may be present in the same home. On the other hand, two identical instances of Smartphone are also configured, meaning that two home inhabitants have the same smartphone model.

For the CPS to be consistent, some constraints must be defined. In this example, the configuration of an Aeotec Z-Stick Controller requires the presence of at least one Z-Wave device. This kind of constraints is properly handled by extended feature models and the related reasoning tools, *e.g.*, the Choco solver.

3.3   Dynamic Adaptation for CPS

In this section, we explain how rule definition and channel addition are used to modify running configurations of SMARTYCO cyber-physical systems.

Rules. In SMARTYCO, event-condition-action rules keep DSPL products consistent at runtime. In particular, SMARTYCO distinguishes between CPS rules and User rules. Both rules use channels as providers of events and actions. The difference between these rules is related to permissions and priorities. End-users cannot modify CPS rules, while User rules are defined and modified by end-users. Regarding priorities, CPS ones are specified by the channel developers while the

User rules are defined by the end-users. We provide below examples of CPS rules (CPS-R) and User Rules (User-R) for the scenario depicted in Figure 3.

```
CPS-R if(bedroomSwitch.state != available) then androidSetTopBox.disableRules(bedroomSwitch); priority = 10;
User-R1 if (bedroomTemperatureSensor.value >= 20) then bedroomSwitch.turnOff; priority = 10;
User-R2 if (time.value == 22:00) then bedroomSwitch.turnOn; priority = 5;
```

For instance, the rule User-R1 indicates that if the temperature in the bedroom is greater or equal to 20 degrees, then the bedroom switch is turned off. Some defined rules can conflict when dealing with the same actuator. For example, User-R1 and User-R2 can both be triggered at the same time. In such a case, the state of the switch would be on because of User-R2, the last executed rule. Such a state could be the one expected by the end-user or not. To avoid such an uncertainty, the end-user defines priorities on the rules as natural numbers. For instance, User-R1 has 10 as priority and User-R2 has 5. Thus, whenever both rules are triggered, the priority is given to User-R1. To process such priorities, we use a simplified version of the rule composition algorithm presented by Zave et al. [14]. We also consider the rule type to evaluate priorities. CPS rules have a higher priority than User rules, independently of the `priority`.

In order to avoid dysfunctions related to unreachable channels, when an end-user configures a cyber-physical system, three CPS rules are set for each channel: *(1)* a rule that disables the User rules related to the channel, so that they cannot be modified or executed. CPS-R is an example of this rule for `bedroomSwitch`; *(2)* a rule that notifies the end-users through their smartphone about the channel unavailability; *(3)* a rule that enables again the channel rules once the channel is available, *i.e.*, when an end-user solves the issue related to the channel.

As previously described, these default CPS rules avoid incorrect behaviors of the system at runtime. Additionally, each User rule checks the availability of channels before condition or trigger validation. To do this, SMARTYCO relies on a `state` trigger related to each channel. As most of rule triggers, the channel state is polled every 15 minutes by default, value that can be changed by the user.

Channel Addition. The SMARTYCO DSPL also enables end-users to change from one `Controller` configuration to another one through the removal and addition of channels at runtime. That is why SMARTYCO requires that end-users define the evolution of the cyber-physical system with these modifications. To integrate new channels into the system, end-users select from a list of channels the one related to the new device. If the channel functionality is already installed, the SMARTYCO `Controller` detects the new device and asks the end-user to configure the new channel by selecting the correct appliance and location. However, when a channel needs to be installed, an update is required through the SMARTYCO `Server`, which computes and executes the required changes on the current `Controller` configuration. After this, the end-user configures the new channel. Whether an update is required or not, a new channel cannot be available for rule definition if SMARTYCO cannot check its state. To remove a channel from the system, such a channel must not be required anymore. In such a case, all rules related to the removed channel are deleted.

4   Experience

We developed a prototype of SMARTYCO. The `Server`, implemented in Java, exposes the `Configurator` as a REST service deployed in a private Cloud based on OpenStack. Once generated by the DSPL, the Android-based Controller is installed manually in the set-top box. For our experiments, we used a smartphone based on the Android 4.2 version and a MiniX Neo X7 as set-top box. We also used an Aeotec Z-Stick Controller connected to this set-top box to interact with Z-Wave devices. This configuration was then deployed in a smart environment made of 4 rooms. In the current implementation, 5 Z-Wave devices and their channels are available, as well as a channel for Android phones. In the SMARTYCO DSPL, the extended feature model reflecting this configuration is translated into a constraint satisfaction problem with 14 constraints, leading to 20 different configurations. Even with a limited number of devices (*i.e.*, 6), end-users already have to deal with an important number of system configurations.

For the first experiment, we evaluate the time required to access devices when using channels. For this evaluation, we selected an On/Off switch and we performed 50 runs to turn it on and off using the dedicated channel deployed in the set-top box. We computed the average time for the two operations, which was measured at 824 ms for *turnOn* and 888 ms for *turnOff*. These low values show that our CPS rules can be executed in a reasonable time and that the state verification has a negligible impact on the execution time of user rules. The second experiment checks the correctness of the system's behavior when some devices become unreachable. A 3-in-1 motion-temperature-luminance sensor together with a switch are part of the system, and each one is configured with a User rule and the default CPS rules. These rules are desynchronized, which means that the system rules are executed first, and the end-user rule 2 minutes later (this last value was defined arbitrarily for testing purposes). Both devices are then turned off. The system rules successfully detect the problem and disable the user rule. Once the devices are turned back on, the `Controller` detects the presence of the devices and the system continues running properly.

5   Related Work

SPOK [4] is an End-User Development Environment for smart homes. The environment, based on OSGi, provides a middleware layer enabling interactions with different kind of devices and a pseudo natural language to define event-condition-action rules. The language proposed by SPOK could be integrated into SMARTYCO to provide a textual definition of event-condition-action rules including the loops usage. The Controller in SMARTYCO can play the middleware role by enabling access and control of the physical world via the channels.

Humle et al. [7] present a user-oriented approach based on JavaBean components that encapsulate sensors and actuators. Authors also propose a jigsaw-based editor, where each JavaBean component is represented as a jigsaw puzzle piece that can be composed with other pieces. On the other hand, CAMP [13] is a system enabling the definition of home applications without focusing on target devices. CAMP allows users to specify the application tasks and goals by means of a subset of natural language. We can exploit ideas related to GUIs proposed by these approaches in order to improve the SMARTYCO user interface.

Dey et al. [5] introduce iCAP, a system enabling end-users to build context-aware applications without writing any code. The users define if-then rules and spatial, temporal and personal relationship-based rules, together with the devices to be used. iCAP proposes an approach similar to SMARTYCO, where end-users can build and configure their system via rules. However, it is not clear how the system can be extended to include new devices, how they are configured or which actual devices available in the environment can be controlled. The dynamic part of SMARTYCO enables the inclusion of new devices when they become available.

6 Conclusions

In this paper we presented SMARTYCO, our solution for dealing with the variability of smart environment systems managed by end-users. SMARTYCO is based on DSPL principles to manage the variability of such systems at design and runtime. In particular, the runtime adaptations are twofold. First, they are defined via end-user rules requiring the activation or deactivation of certain devices under certain conditions, and validated by checking the related feature model configuration. Second, it is possible to easily add new devices when they become available. In such a case, the consistency of the DSPL is ensured by predefined rules avoiding the usage of unavailable devices.

Our experience in building a prototype confirms that we are close to enable an easy and partially automated configuration of *dynamic* CPS complying with any smart environments. Issues related to privacy and security as well as vulnerabilities related to devices must also be considered when modeling and generating the CPS. We also need to further consider conflicts between rules and their priorities by putting the accent in the behavior of the system regarding possible end-user behavior overriding action rules.

References

1. Benavides, D., Segura, S., Ruiz-Cortés, A.: Automated Analysis of Feature Models 20 Years Later: A Literature Review. Inf. Syst. **35**(6), 615–636 (2010)
2. Capilla, R., Bosch, J., Trinidad, P., Ruiz-Corts, A., Hinchey, M.: An overview of Dynamic Software Product Line architectures and techniques: Observations from research and industry. Journal of Systems and Software **91**, 3–23 (2014)
3. Choco Team: Choco: an Open Source Java Constraint Programming Library. Research report 10–02-INFO, École des Mines de Nantes (2010)
4. Coutaz, J., Demeure, A., Caffiau, S., Crowley, J.L.: Early lessons from the development of SPOK, an end-user development environment for smart homes. In: Proceedings of the 2014 ACM International Joint Conference on Pervasive and Ubiquitous Computing, UbiComp'14, pp. 895–902 (2014)

5. Dey, A.K., Sohn, T., Streng, S., Kodama, J.: iCAP: interactive prototyping of context-aware applications. In: Fishkin, K.P., Schiele, B., Nixon, P., Quigley, A. (eds.) PERVASIVE 2006. LNCS, vol. 3968, pp. 254–271. Springer, Heidelberg (2006)
6. Hallsteinsen, S., Hinchey, M., Park, S., Schmid, K.: Dynamic Software Product Lines. Computer **41**(4), 93–95 (2008)
7. Humble, J., Crabtree, A., Hemmings, T., Åkesson, K.-P., Koleva, B., Rodden, T., Hansson, P.: "Playing with the bits" user-configuration of ubiquitous domestic environments. In: Dey, A.K., Schmidt, A., McCarthy, J.F. (eds.) UbiComp 2003. LNCS, vol. 2864, pp. 256–263. Springer, Heidelberg (2003)
8. IFTTT: Put the internet to work for you (2015). https://ifttt.com/, (accessed April 16 2015)
9. Kang, K.C., Cohen, S.G., Hess, J.A., Novak, W.E., Peterson, A.S.: Feature-oriented domain analysis (foda) feasibility study. Tech. rep., Carnegie-Mellon University Software Engineering Institute, November1990
10. Pohl, K., Böckle, G., Linden, F.J.V.D.: Software Product Line Engineering: Foundations, Principles and Techniques (2005)
11. Quinton, C., Romero, D., Duchien, L.: SALOON: a platform for selecting and configuring cloud environments. In: Software - Practice and Experience P, January 2015. doi:10.1002/spe.2311
12. Schmidt, D.C.: Guest Editor's Introduction: Model-Driven Engineering. Computer **39**(2), 25–31 (2006)
13. Truong, K.N., Huang, E.M., Abowd, G.D.: CAMP: a magnetic poetry interface for end-user programming of capture applications for the home. In: Mynatt, E.D., Siio, I. (eds.) UbiComp 2004. LNCS, vol. 3205, pp. 143–160. Springer, Heidelberg (2004)
14. Zave, P., Cheung, E., Yarosh, S.: Toward User-Centric Feature Composition for the Internet of Things. Tech. rep., AT&T Laboratories Research (2014)

Analysis and Automation

Exploiting Traceability Uncertainty Between Software Architectural Models and Performance Analysis Results

Catia Trubiani[1]([✉]), Achraf Ghabi[2], and Alexander Egyed[2]

[1] Gran Sasso Science Institute, L'Aquila, Italy
catia.trubiani@gssi.infn.it
[2] Johannes Kepler University, Linz, Austria
a@ghabi.net, alexander.egyed@jku.at

Abstract. While software architecture performance analysis is a well-studied field, it is less understood how the analysis results (i.e., mean values, variances, and/or probability distributions) trace back to the architectural model elements (i.e., software components, interactions among components, deployment nodes). Yet, understanding this traceability is critical for understanding the analysis result in context of the architecture. The goal of this paper is to automate the traceability between software architectural models and performance analysis results by investigating the uncertainty while bridging these two domains. Our approach makes use of performance antipatterns to deduce the logical consequences between the architectural elements and analysis results and automatically build a graph of traces to identify the most critical causes of performance flaws. We developed a tool that jointly considers SOftware and PErformance concepts (SoPeTraceAnalyzer), and it automatically builds model-to-results traceability links. The benefit of the tool is illustrated by means of a case study in the e-health domain.

Keywords: Traceability · Uncertainty · Software modelling · Performance analysis

1 Introduction

In the software development domain there is a very high interest in the early validation of performance requirements because this ability avoids late and expensive repairs to consolidated software artifacts [1]. One of the proper ways to manage software performance is to systematically predict the performance of the software system throughout the development process. It is thus possible to make informed choices among architectural and design alternatives; and knowing in advance if the software will meet its performance objectives [2].

Advanced Model-Driven Engineering (MDE) techniques have successfully been used in the last few years to introduce automation in software performance modeling and analysis [3]. Nevertheless, the problem of interpreting the

© Springer International Publishing Switzerland 2015
D. Weyns et al. (Eds.): ECSA 2015, LNCS 9278, pp. 305–321, 2015.
DOI: 10.1007/978-3-319-23727-5_26

performance analysis results is still quite critical. A large gap exists between the representation of performance analysis results and the software architectural model provided by the engineers. In fact, the former usually contains numbers (e.g., mean response time, throughput variance, etc.), whereas the latter embeds architectural choices (e.g., software components, interaction among components, deployment nodes). Today, such activities are exclusively based on the analysts' experience and therefore their effectiveness often suffers from lack of automation.

In [4] we proposed a language capable of capturing model-to-code traceability while considering typical uncertainties in its domain. For example, the engineer knows that some given piece of code may implement an architectural element; however, not whether this piece of code also implements other architectural elements; or whether other pieces of code also implement this architectural element. This paper adapts this language to provide model-to-results traceability links while considering typical uncertainties from the performance analysis domain. We presume that engineers know when a given performance result is affected by an architectural element. However, they may not know whether this performance result is also affected by other architectural elements or whether other performance results are also affected by this architectural element.

The knowledge of the engineer is interwoven with software performance antipatterns [5] that represent bad practices in architectural models negatively affecting performance indices. A performance antipattern definition includes the description of a bad practice occurring in the architectural model (e.g., a software component sending an excessive number of messages), along with the solution that can be applied to avoid negative consequences (e.g., high network utilization). In previous work [6] we provided a more formal representation of performance antipatterns by introducing first-order logic rules that express a set of system properties under which an antipattern occurs. The benefit of this representation is that it already includes architectural elements (e.g., software components) and performance results (e.g., utilization) hence it can be used to make the knowledge of engineers less uncertain.

The contribution of this paper is to provide support in the process of identifying the architectural model elements that most likely contribute to the violation of performance requirements by jointly considering knowledge from engineers and performance antipatterns. To this end, we developed a tool, namely SoPe-TraceAnalyzer [7], that jointly considers SOftware and PErformance concepts: it takes as input a set of statements specifying the relationships between software elements and performance results, and provides as output model-to-results traceability links. The language defined in [4] is extended by adding a weighting methodology that quantifies the performance requirements' violation, thus to highlight the criticality of model elements despite performance results. The key feature of our tool is that the knowledge of performance antipatterns can be embedded in the specification of uncertainties to deduce the logical consequences between architectural elements and analysis results, thus to disambiguate the limited knowledge of engineers.

The paper is organized as follows: Section 2 presents related work; Section 3 describes our approach; Section 4 illustrates the case study; Section 5 discusses the threats to validity of the approach; Section 6 concludes the paper and outlines future research directions.

2 Related Work

The work presented in this paper relates to two main research areas and builds upon our previous results in these areas: (i) software performance engineering (SPE), and (ii) model-driven traceability.

Software performance engineering. SPE represents the entire collection of software engineering activities and related analyses used throughout the software development cycle, which are directed to meeting performance requirements [8]. Performance antipatterns [5] are very complex (as compared to other software patterns) because they are founded on different characteristics of software systems, spanning from static through behavioral to deployment. Antipatterns include features related to architectural model elements (e.g., *many* usage dependencies, *excessive* message traffic) as well as to performance results (e.g., *high, low* utilization). Our logic-based formalization [6] has been experimented to benefit across different modelling languages [9–11].

Model-driven traceability. In [4] we introduced a language for expressing uncertainties in traceability relationships between models and code, which is the main benefit of this technique compared with other traceability approaches. There are many other techniques exploiting the automatic recovery of different types of trace links [12] [13] [14]. Our work [4] out-passes these techniques by introducing a flexible methodology to express uncertainties. We proved in our recent work [15] that the same uncertainty expressions could be applied to trace arbitrary kinds of software artifacts.

In literature there are some approaches that work towards the specification of traceability links between model elements and performance results.

In [16] a mechanism to annotate performance analysis results back into the original performance models (provided by the domain experts) is presented. On the contrary, our approach includes the software models for traceability, and it supports the interpretation of analysis results by providing weights on the basis of requirements' violation. In [17] traceability links are maintained between performance requirements and Use Case Map (UCM) scenarios, however these links are used to build Layered Queueing Network (LQN) models only. In [18] traceability links are used to propagate the results of the performance model back to the original software model, however it applies to UML and LQN models only. Our approach instead aims to automatically build model-to-results traceability links to point out the architectural elements affecting the stated requirements.

The problem of dealing with uncertainty in early requirements and architectural decisions has been recognized by several works in literature. In [19] a language (i.e., RELAX) has been proposed to explicitly address uncertainty for specifying the behaviour of dynamically adaptive systems. In [20] a tool (i.e., GuideArch) has been presented to guide the exploration of the architectural solution space under uncertainty. In [21] a tool (i.e., Moda) has been introduced for multi-objective decision analysis by means of Monte-Carlo simulation and Pareto-based optimisation methods. However, all these works [19–21] do not explicitly consider performance analysis results and their traceability with software architectural elements.

3 Our Approach

Figure 1 illustrates the process we envisage to automate the traceability between architectural model elements and performance analysis results. Ovals in the figure represent operational steps whereas square boxes represent input/output data. Dashed vertical lines divide the process in four different phases.

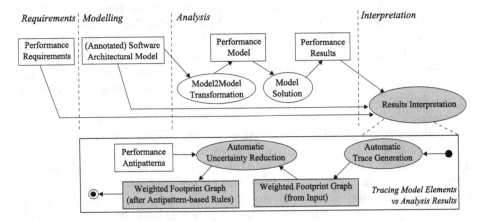

Fig. 1. Deriving automatically model-to-results traceability links by means of performance antipatterns.

We assume that a set of performance *requirements*, among others, is defined. Some examples of performance requirements are as follows: the response time of a service has to be less than 3 seconds, the throughput of a service has to be greater than 10 requests/second, the utilisation of a hardware device shall not be higher than 80%, etc. Performance requirements will be used to interpret the results from the model-based performance analysis. In the *modelling* phase, an annotated[1] software architectural model is built. In the *analysis* phase, a performance model is obtained through model transformation, and such model is solved to obtain the performance results of interest.

The focus of this paper is on the *interpretation* phase where the performance results must be interpreted in order to detect, if any, performance flaws[2] and

---

[1] Annotations are aimed at specifying information to execute performance analysis such as the incoming workload, service demands, hardware characteristics, etc.

[2] A performance flaw originates from a set of unfulfilled requirement(s), such as "the estimated average response time of a service is higher than the required one".

highlight the software architectural model elements responsible for that bad values. In fact, in case of unsatisfactory results a set of architectural refactoring actions can be introduced to generate new software architectural models[3] that undergo the same process shown in Figure 1.

The goal of our approach is to trace model elements vs analysis results, see shaded boxes of Figure 1. It starts with an automatic trace generation operational step that provides as output a weighted footprint graph (from input), i.e., a graph containing a node for every result element (called RE nodes) and a node for each model element (called ME nodes). The connections between these nodes describe the certainties of the input (trace or no-trace), and are refined with an automatic uncertainty reduction operational step aimed at generating a weighted foot print graph (after antipattern-based rules). This latter step is supported by performance antipatterns [5] that are suitable to deduce the logical consequences of the uncertainties, and contribute to automatically generate traces joining architectural elements and performance results.

3.1 Automatic Trace Generation

The automatic trace generation operational step (see Figure 1) takes as input: (i) performance requirements, (ii) annotated software architectural model, and (iii) performance results. It provides as output a weighted footprint graph.

Performance requirements are classified on the basis of the performance indices they address and the level of abstraction they apply. Here we consider the requirements that refer to the following performance indices [23]: *Response time* (RT) is defined as the time interval between a user request of a service and the response of the system; *Throughput* (TH) is defined as the rate at which requests can be handled by a system, and is measured in requests per unit of time; *Utilization* (U) is defined as the ratio of busy time of a resource and the total elapsed time of the measurement period; *Queue length* (QL) is defined as the number of users waiting for a resource; *Waiting time* (WT) is defined as the time interval required to access to a resource starting from when the resource is required up to when it is accessed.

Usually, *RT* requirements are upper bounds defined in "business" requirements by the end users of the system. *TH* requirements can be both "business" and "system" requirements, they can represent either an upper or a lower bound. *U*, *QL* and *WT* requirements are upper bounds defined in "system" requirements by system engineers on the basis of their experience, scalability issues, or constraints from other concurrent software systems.

Various levels of abstraction can be defined for a requirement: system, processor, etc. However, we do not consider all possible combinations of indices and levels of abstraction, we focus on the most common ones that are: RT and TH of services, U, QL, and WT of hardware devices.

---

[3] We do not detail the refactoring process here, as it is out of this paper focus. However, readers interested to this part can refer to [22].

Performance results represent the analysis values of the indices we consider for traceability. Note that such values are affected by a set of features such as system workload and operation profile that represent how the software system is used [23].

Annotated software architectural models may be constituted by elements belonging to different views [24]: *Static/Software View* (SW) includes the software elements, e.g., operations (SWop), components (SWcomp), services, and the static relationships among them; *Dynamic/Interaction View* (DY) includes the specification of the interaction, e.g., messages (DYmsg), that occurs between the software components to provide services; *Deployment/Hardware View* (HW) includes the hardware devices, e.g., processing nodes (HWnode), and communication networks (HWnet), and the mapping of software components and iterations onto hardware devices. Summarizing, SWop, SWcomp, DYmsg, HWnode, and HWnet represent the architectural elements we consider for traceability.

Language for Expressing Traceability. This paper adapts the language for model-to-code traceability introduced in [4] and extends it to express model-to-results traceability considering some of the unique aspects of this domain. The main benefit of our approach is that our language allows the engineer to express uncertainty constructs to the level of detail she or he is comfortable with.

Each construct is defined as $\{m^*\}$ relationship $\{r^*\}$ where $\{m^*\}$ is the set of model elements and $\{r^*\}$ is the set of results elements. The star symbol $(^*)$ expresses multiplicity in that m* stands for multiple model elements and r* for multiple results elements. The relationship term declares how the first set is related to the second one.

We distinguish between three major relationships: affectAtLeast, affectAtMost, affectExactly.

1) AffectAtLeast Construct: the input $\{m^*\}$ affectAtLeast $\{r^*\}$ defines that the model elements in $\{m^*\}$ affect all of the result elements in $\{r^*\}$ and possibly more. This input has a correctness constraint ensuring that every model element in $\{m^*\}$ individually must be affecting a subset of $\{r^*\}$. One example of this relationship is provided by the software components *SWcomp* and the subset of operations *SWop* involved in a service *S* that affect at least the response time (RT) and the throughput (TH) of the service *S*.
Input: $\{SWop^*, SWcomp^*\}$ affectAtLeast $\{RT, TH\}$

2) AffectAtMost Construct: the input $\{m^*\}$ affectAtMost $\{r^*\}$ defines that the model elements in $\{m^*\}$ affect some of the result elements in $\{r^*\}$ but certainly not more. This input expresses the certainty that every other model element not in $\{m^*\}$ must not affect any result element in $\{r^*\}$. One example of this relationship is provided by the software components *SWcomp* and the subset of operations *SWop* involved in a service *S* as well as the deployment nodes *HWnode* where the *SWcomp* components are deployed that affect at most the response time (RT) and the throughput (TH) of the service *S*.
Input: $\{SWop^*, SWcomp^*, HWnode^*\}$ affectAtMost $\{RT, TH\}$

3) AffectExactly Construct: the input $\{m^*\}$ affectExactly $\{r^*\}$ defines that every model element in $\{m^*\}$ affects one or more result elements in $\{r^*\}$ and that the results elements in {r*} are not affected in any other model element not in {m*}. This input defines no-trace between each result element in {r*} and each model element in the remaining M-{m*} (where M is the set of all input model elements), since each model element in {m*} affects only a subset of {r*}. However, this does not mean that these result elements could not be affected by other model elements in M-{m*}. One example of this relationship is provided by an hardware device *HWnode* and the performed operations *SWop* that affect exactly its utilization (U).

Input: {SWop*, HWnode} affectExactly {U}

Weighted Footprint Graph. The language we provided to express the uncertainty constructs between a set of architectural model elements and a set of analysis results elements is very flexible. Listing 1.1 reports one abstract example for the specification of the input. For example, the hardware devices HWnode and HWnet affect exactly the performance indices related to them, i.e., utilization (U), queue length (QL), and waiting time (WT). As another example, the software components *SWcomp* and the subset of operations *SWop* involved in a service *S* affect at least the response time (RT) and the throughput (TH) of the service *S*.

{HWnode, HWnet} **affectExactly** {U, QL, WT};
{SWop, SWcomp} **affectAtLeast** {RT, TH};
{SWop, DYmsg} **affectAtMost** {RT, TH, QL};
{SWcomp, DYmsg} **affectAtMost** {RT, TH, QL};

Listing 1.1. Input to trace generation.

The goal of our SoPeTraceAnalyzer tool [7] is to interpret these traceability expressions and automatically build (certainties and uncertainties) in a graph structure, which we call the weighted footprint graph (from input).

Figure 2 reports one abstract example of this graph and it refers to the input specified in Listing 1.1. The graph contains a node for every result element (called RE nodes) and a node for each model element (called ME nodes). RE nodes are: response time (RT), throughput (TH), utilization (U), queue length (QL), and waiting time (WT). ME nodes are: software operations (SWop), software components (SWcomp), dynamic interactions (DYmsg), hardware nodes (HWnode), and communication networks (HWnet).

The connections between RE nodes and ME nodes describe the certainties of the input (trace or no-trace) which are generated out of the logical consequences of the uncertainties. A trace (m, r) is depicted by a bold line between the ME node of m and the RE node of r. In Figure 2 no such lines are depicted because the logical interpretation of the input did not yield any traces. On the contrary, no-traces are depicted by dashed lines. Furthermore, the graph contains nodes to capture model element groups (MEG nodes) and results element groups (REG nodes). These two kinds of nodes describe the uncertainties of the input.

Note that each result element node RE has a weight (ω) that represents a value indicating how much the requirement is far from the analysed index, whereas each model element node ME has a weight that is a function ($\sum F(\omega)$)

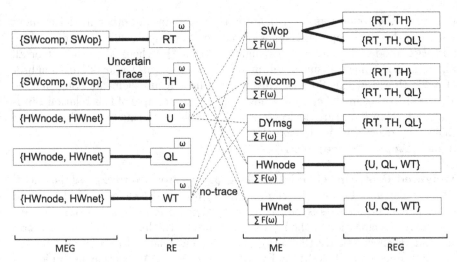

Fig. 2. Weighted Footprint Graph (from Input).

indicating how much the architectural element is critical for the violated requirements. Different heuristics (ω) and functions ($\sum F(\omega)$) can be used to weight RE and ME nodes in footprint graphs. Furthermore, the human intervention of engineers may help to add priorities to performance results and to specify legacy constraints for architectural elements. We provide preliminary heuristics in Section 4, and we intend to further investigate this aspect in the near future.

3.2   Automatic Uncertainty Reduction

The weighted footprint graph is the foundation for automatic trace generation, and several propagation rules can be introduced to reduce the initial uncertainty. Our approach makes use of performance antipatterns [5] to deduce the logical consequences between architectural elements and analysis results.

In our previous work [6] we provided a logic-based representation of performance antipatterns that supports the specification of further input to trace generation. Listing 1.2 reports the traceability rules while considering the specification of some performance antipatterns, i.e., Concurrent Processing Systems (CPS), Pipe & Filter (P&F), God Class/Component (BLOB), Extensive Processing (EP), Empty Semi Trucks (EST), One-Lane Bridge (OLB), and The Ramp (TR), respectively.

CPS: {HWnode} **affectExactly** {QL, U};
BLOB: {SWop, DYmsg} **affectAtLeast** {U};
P&F: {SWop, DYmsg} **affectAtLeast** {TH, U};
EP: {SWop, DYmsg} **affectAtLeast** {RT, U};
EST: {DYmsg} **affectAtLeast** {RT, U};
OLB: {SWcomp, SWop, DYmsg} **affectAtMost** {RT, WT};
TR: {SWop} **affectExactly** {RT, TH};

Listing 1.2. Antipattern-based rules to reduce model-to-results uncertainty.

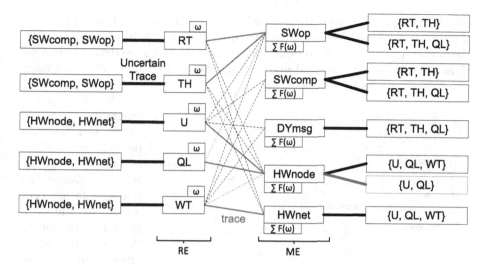

Fig. 3. Weighted Footprint Graph (after Antipattern-based Rules).

For example, detecting a CPS antipattern indicates that HWnode affects exactly QL and U. This rule comes from the logic-based formula of the CPS antipattern that has been defined in [6], and an excerpt is reported in Equation (1) where $\mathbb{P}$ represents the set of all the hardware devices. CPS is an antipattern that occurs when processes cannot make effective use of available hardware devices to a non-balanced assignment of tasks. The *over-utilized* hardware devices are detected by checking if the queue length and the utilization overcome pre-defined thresholds[4].

$$\exists P_x \in \mathbb{P} \mid F_{maxQL}(P_x) \geq Th_{maxQL} \wedge$$
$$F_{maxHwUtil}(P_x) \geq Th_{maxUtil} \tag{1}$$

Figure 3 reports the weighted footprint graph (after introducing antipattern-based rules) and, for figure readability, it is built considering CPS and TR rules only (see Listing 1.2). The inclusion of these two antipatterns generates five additional traces (bold lines) and two no-traces (dashed lines) between MEs and REs. Note that the specification of antipattern-based rules may also contribute to increase the overall uncertainty of the system since no logical consequences can be deduced while considering the addition of further constructs.

4 Illustrative Example

The proposed approach is illustrated on a case study in the e-health domain. Figure 4 depicts an excerpt of the E-Health System (EHS) software architectural

---

[4] A specific characteristic of performance antipatterns is that they contain numerical parameters representing thresholds (e.g., *high* utilization, *excessive* number of messages). For further details refer to [6].

model. The system supports the doctors' everyday activities, such as the retrieval of information of their patients. On the basis of such data doctors may send an alarm in case of warning conditions. Patients are allowed to retrieve information about the doctor expertise and update some vital parameters (e.g., heart rate) to monitor their health status.

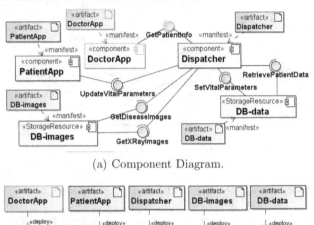

(a) Component Diagram.

(b) Deployment Diagram.

Fig. 4. EHS- Software Architectural Model.

The Component Diagram shown in Figure 4(a) describes the software components: *PatientApp* and *DoctorApp* components are connected to the *Dispatcher* component that forwards users' requests to the *DBdata* component and/ or retrieves images from the *DB-images* component. The Deployment Diagram depicted in Figure 4(b) shows that both the doctor's and the patient's applications have been deployed on a Personal Digital Assistant (PDA), i.e., a mobile device.

Hardware devices communicate through different networks, i.e., wide and local area networks.

The system workload has been defined as follows: (i) a closed workload is defined for the *getPatientInfo* service, with a population of 50 doctors and an average thinking time of 5 minutes; (ii) a closed workload is defined for the *updateVitalParameters* service, with a population of 2500 patients and an average thinking time of 1 hour.

The performance requirements that we consider, under the stated workload of 2550 users (i.e., 50 doctors and 2500 patients), are:

RT: The average response time of the UpdateVitalParameters service has to be less than 60 sec;

TH: The throughput of the UpdateVitalParameters service has to be greater than 4 requests/sec;

U: The utilization of the hardware devices has to be lower than 70%.

The performance analysis has been conducted by transforming the software architectural model into a Queueing Network (QN) performance model [25] and by solving the latter with two well-assessed techniques [23], i.e., mean value analysis (MVA) and simulation. Both solution techniques are supported by Java Modeling Tools (JMT) [26]. Table 1 shows the resulting performance results for the EHS software architectural model. In particular, the average response time (RT) and throughput (TH) for the *UpdateVitalParameters* service, and the utilization (U), queue length (QL), and waiting time (WT) for the hardware devices. Shaded entries of Table 1 highlight the violated performance requirements. For example, the RT of *UpdateVitalParameters* service is predicted to be 83.51 seconds, whereas it is required to be no more than 60 seconds.

Table 1. EHS- performance analysis results.

	UpdateVital Parameters	*dispatcher Host*	*DB-data Host*	*DB-imgs Host*
$RT[sec]$	83.51	-	-	-
$TH[reqs/sec]$	3	-	-	-
$U[\%]$	-	0.18	0.93	0.32
$QL[users]$	-	0.22	12.92	0.46
$WT[sec]$	-	0.69	43.72	4.99

4.1 EHS: Automatic Trace Generation

Listing 1.3 reports one example of the set of statements that can be specified by an engineer to express the relationships between software elements and performance results in EHS, and it is provided as input to our SoPeTraceAnalyzer tool [7]. Note that such statements represent one example of engineer understanding of the system, and other feasible specifications of traceability links can be provided as well. This unavoidable gap, that recurs in any specification task, requires a wider investigation to consolidate the definition of traceability links and is left for future work.

```
{HWdbDataHost, HWwan} affectExactly
    {UdbDataHost, QLdbDataHost, WTdbDataHost};
{SWuVP, SWdbData} affectAtLeast {RTuVP, THuVP};
{SWuVP, DYsetVP} affectAtMost
    {RTuVP, THuVP, QLdbDataHost};
{SWdbData, DYsetVP} affectAtMost
    {RTuVP, THuVP, QLdbDataHost};
```

Listing 1.3. EHS- Input to trace generation.

The weighted footprint graph (from input) for EHS has been automatically obtained with the SoPeTraceAnalyzer tool [7], according to the provided specification. In particular, RE nodes are all the performance results elements of interest: response time and throughput of the *UpdateVitalParameters* service (`RTuVP`, `THuVP`), utilization, queue length, and waiting time of the *DB-dataHost* device (`UdbDataHost`, `QLdbDataHost`, `WTdbDataHost`). ME nodes are all the architectural model elements involved in the *UpdateVitalParameters* service: software operations and components (`SWuVP`, `SWdbData`), dynamic interactions (`DYsetVP`), hardware nodes (`HWdbDataHost`), and communication networks (`HWwan`).

4.2 EHS: Automatic Uncertainty Reduction

Performance antipatterns have been detected by means of our rule-based engine [6], and we found the following two instances: (i) Concurrent Processing System (CPS) antipattern, i.e., *DB-dataHost* hardware device is over-utilized; (ii) The Ramp (TR) antipattern, i.e., the response time of the *UpdateVitalParameters* service is quite unstable along simulation time.

Listing 1.4 reports the set of statements specifying the relationships between software elements and performance results in EHS, as captured by performance antipatterns. Such statements contribute to the input provided to our SoPe-TraceAnalyzer tool [7].

CPS: {HWdbDataHost} **affectExactly**
    {QLdbDataHost, UdbDataHost};
TR: {SWuVP} **affectExactly** {RTuVP, THuVP};

Listing 1.4. EHS- Antipattern-based rules.

Figure 5 reports the weighted footprint graph (after antipattern-based rules) for EHS that has been automatically obtained with the SoPeTraceAnalyzer tool [7], after elaborating the rules provided by performance antipatterns.

The weight of RE nodes contribute to indicate the severity of the corresponding requirement's violation by quantifying the percentage gap between the requirement and the analysed index. Figure 5 shows that: RTuVP is 28% larger than the defined requirement of 60 seconds, THuVP is 25% lower than the defined requirement of 4 requests/sec, and UdbDataHost is 25% larger than the defined requirement of 70%. In fact, the *UpdateVitalParameters* service has an average response time of 83.51 sec, an average throughput of 3 requests/sec, and the utilization of the *DB-dataHost* device is 93% (see Table 1).

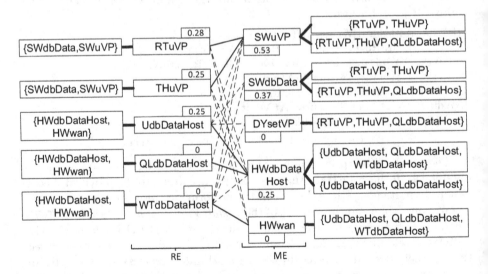

Fig. 5. EHS- Weighted Footprint Graph (after Antipattern-based Rules).

For sake of readability Figure 5 does not report the weights on the traceability links connecting RE and ME elements, however their values contribute to the weights of architectural model elements as follows. The SWuVP node is weighted with the value 0.53 (calculated as $0.28 * 1 + 0.25 * 1$) where the weight of 1 is assigned to the two links connecting the SWuVP node with RTuVP and THuVP nodes, respectively. Similarly, the HWdbDataHost node is weighted with the value 0.25 (calculated as $0.25 * 1$) where the weight of 1 is assigned to the link connecting HWdbDataHost with the UdbDataHost node. The SWdbData node is weighted with the value 0.37 (calculated as $0.28 * 0.44 + 0.25 * 1$) where the weights of 0.44 and 1 are assigned by using the guilt-based approach we defined in our previous work [11]. In particular, each model element is ranked on the basis of how much it contributes to the performance index under analysis: we calculate the index of the corresponding model element and we estimate how much it is participating. In EHS the RT of the *SWdbData* component is equal to 46.14 sec (i.e., 44% of RTuVP is provided by such component), whereas the TH is equal to 3 requests/sec, hence it is fully involved in the TH requirement. We recall that the *UpdateVitalParameters* service has an average response time of 83.51 sec and throughput of 3 requests/sec (see Table 1).

Table 2. EHS- performance analysis results while refactoring software model elements.

(a) *SWuVP* refactoring.

	Update Vital Parameters	dispatcher Host	DB-data Host	DB-imgs Host
$RT[sec]$	35.75	-	-	-
$TH[reqs/sec]$	6	-	-	-
$U[\%]$	-	0.35	0.51	0.17
$QL[users]$	-	0.56	1.05	0.2
$WT[sec]$	-	0.87	1.63	4.37

(b) *SWdbData* refactoring.

	Update Vital Parameters	dispatcher Host	DB-data Host	DB-imgs Host
$RT[sec]$	41.23	-	-	-
$TH[reqs/sec]$	5	-	-	-
$U[\%]$	-	0.18	0.77	0.04
$QL[users]$	-	0.22	3.52	0.03
$WT[sec]$	-	0.7	11.3	3.72

(c) *HWdbDataHost* refactoring.

	Update Vital Parameters	dispatcher Host	DB-data Host	DB-imgs Host
$RT[sec]$	82.9	-	-	-
$TH[reqs/sec]$	3	-	-	-
$U[\%]$	-	0.22	0.36	0.32
$QL[users]$	-	0.22	0.58	0.46
$WT[sec]$	-	0.71	1.82	48.3

RE and ME nodes related to undefined and/or inviolate requirements are weighted with a value equal to zero (e.g., QLdbDataHost, HWwan).

Several strategies can be devised to use the weighted footprint graph: (i) *RE-based traceability*, i.e., looking at RE nodes only it is possible to identify the ME that most likely contribute to each requirement violation by selecting the traceability link with the highest weight; (ii) *ME-based traceability*, i.e., looking at ME nodes only it is possible to identify the most critical causes of performance flaws by providing a link coverage for all the violated requirements.

We performed a preliminary validation of these traceability strategies while separately refactoring all the model elements with a consistent weight.

Table 2 shows the performance analysis results we obtained: Table 2(a) demonstrates that the SWuVP refactoring is actually beneficial to solve performance flaws, since all the stated requirements have been fulfilled; Table 2(b) shows that refactoring the SWdbData element is beneficial for the requirements to which it is strictly connected (see Figure 5) but there is still one requirement that is not satisfied and the SWuVP refactoring outperforms this refactoring; Table 2(c) finally reports that refactoring the HWdbDataHost element is beneficial only for the requirement to which it is strictly connected (see Figure 5).

We are aware that this is far from being a rigorous proof of the weighted footprint graph output soundness, but first validation results seem promising to track a direction for this goal.

5   Discussion

Besides inheriting all limitations of the underlying software performance engineering and model-driven traceability techniques [27,28], our approach exhibits the following threats to validity:

- *Correctness:* input is given by the engineer that defines uncertainty constructs to the level of detail she or he is comfortable with. This means that not every input combination is valid and it becomes increasingly unlikely that the input remains consistent, especially if the input is provided by different engineers.
- *Granularity:* it is difficult to establish at what level of granularity traces between model and results should be generated. Performance indices can be estimated at different levels of granularity, e.g. the response time index can be evaluated at the level of a cpu device, or at the level of a service that spans on different devices. Then, the engineer has the choice to establish traceability between the model elements and it is unrealistic to keep under control all performance results at all levels of abstraction.

An important aspect of future work is to provide correctness checks based on the consistency of the input, in fact consistency does not imply correctness. We can identify the input that is responsible for incorrectness and granularity problems, and provide support to engineers for resolving the detected issues.

Note that our approach makes use of performance antipatterns to deduce the logical consequences between the architectural elements and analysis results, however it does not a priori guarantee uncertainty reduction. As future work, we plan to integrate other approaches to derive model-to-results traceability links, e.g. bottleneck analysis [29] and model optimization methods [30] can be used to improve the uncertainty reduction.

6   Conclusion

This paper presents a new approach to automate the traceability between architectural model elements and performance analysis results, thus to support software architects in the identification of the causes that most likely contribute to the violation of performance requirements. To this end, we developed a tool (SoPeTraceAnalyzer) that is able to interpret a language capable of interpreting uncertainties while capturing model-to-results traceability links. The approach is illustrated by means of a case study in the e-health domain.

The benefit of the tool is that it allows to automatically visualize the dependencies between modelling elements in architectural models (e.g., software components) and performance analysis results (e.g., response time, throughput, and utilization). As input the tool takes on the one hand possible influences already known to the domain expert, and on the other hand performance antipatterns which express further such dependencies. The detection of performance antipatterns is used to make the domain expert dependencies more precise, e.g., by ruling out certain influences.

As future work we intend to apply our approach to other case studies, possibly coming from industrial experiences and different domains. This wider experimentation will allow us to deeply investigate the usefulness of performance antipatterns to reduce traceability uncertainty, thus studying the effectiveness and the scalability of our approach.

References

1. Smith, C.U., Woodside, M.: Performance validation at early stages of software development. In: System Performance Evaluation: Methodologies and Applications. CRC Press (1999)
2. Smith, C.U., Williams, L.G.: Performance Solutions: A Practical Guide to Creating Responsive, Scalable Software. Addison-Wesley (2002)
3. Cortellessa, V., Di Marco, A., Inverardi, P.: Model-Based Software Performance Analysis. Springer (2011)
4. Ghabi, A., Egyed, A.: Exploiting traceability uncertainty between architectural models and code. In: Joint Working IEEE/IFIP WICSA/ECSA. pp. 171–180 (2012)
5. Smith, C.U., Williams, L.G.: More new software antipatterns: even more ways to shoot yourself in the foot. In: International CMG Conference, pp. 717–725 (2003)
6. Cortellessa, V., Di Marco, A., Trubiani, C.: An approach for modeling and detecting software performance antipatterns based on first-order logics. Software and System Modeling 13, 391–432 (2014)

7. Trubiani, C., Ghabi, A., Egyed, A.: (SoPeTraceAnalyzer). http://www.sea. uni-linz.ac.at/tools/TraZer/SoPeTraceAnalyzer.zip
8. Woodside, C.M., Franks, G., Petriu, D.C.: The future of software performance engineering. In: Workshop on the Future of Software Engineering FOSE, pp. 171–187 (2007)
9. Cortellessa, V., Di Marco, A., Eramo, R., Pierantonio, A., Trubiani, C.: Digging into UML models to remove performance antipatterns. In: ICSE Workshop QUO-VADIS, pp. 9–16 (2010)
10. Cortellessa, V., De Sanctis, M., Di Marco, A., Trubiani, C.: Enabling performance antipatterns to arise from an adl-based software architecture. In: Joint Working IEEE/IFIP Conference WICSA/ECSA, pp. 310–314 (2012)
11. Trubiani, C., Koziolek, A., Cortellessa, V., Reussner, R.: Guilt-based handling of software performance antipatterns in palladio architectural models. Journal of Systems and Software **95**, 141–165 (2014)
12. Antoniol, G.: Design-code traceability recovery: selecting the basic linkage properties. Science of Computer Programming **40**, 213–234 (2001)
13. Egyed, A., Grunbacher, P.: Automating requirements traceability: beyond the record & replay paradigm. In: International Conference on Automated Software Engineering (ASE), pp. 163–171. IEEE (2002)
14. Cleland-Huang, J., Settimi, R., Romanova, E., Berenbach, B., Clark, S.: Best practices for automated traceability. Computer **40**, 27–35 (2007)
15. Ghabi, A., Egyed, A.: Exploiting traceability uncertainty among artifacts and code. accepted for Journal of Systems and Software (JSS) (to appear, 2014)
16. Fritzsche, M., Johannes, J., Zschaler, S., Zherebtsov, A., Terekhov, E.: Application of tracing techniques in model-driven performance engineering. In: European Conference on Model Driven Architecture - Foundations and Applications (ECMDA-FA) (2008)
17. Petriu, D.B., Amyot, D., Woodside, C.M., Jiang, B.: Traceability and evaluation in scenario analysis by use case maps. In: Leue, S., Systä, T.J. (eds.) Scenarios: Models, Transformations and Tools. LNCS, vol. 3466, pp. 134–151. Springer, Heidelberg (2005)
18. Alhaj, M., Petriu, D.C.: Traceability links in model transformations between software and performance models. In: Khendek, F., Toeroe, M., Gherbi, A., Reed, R. (eds.) SDL 2013. LNCS, vol. 7916, pp. 203–221. Springer, Heidelberg (2013)
19. Whittle, J., Sawyer, P., Bencomo, N., Cheng, B.H.C., Bruel, J.: Relax: Incorporating uncertainty into the specification of self-adaptive systems. In: IEEE International Conference on Requirements Engineering, pp. 79–88 (2009)
20. Esfahani, N., Malek, S., Razavi, K.: Guidearch: guiding the exploration of architectural solution space under uncertainty. In: International Conference on Software Engineering (ICSE), pp. 43–52 (2013)
21. Letier, E., Stefan, D., Barr, E.T.: Uncertainty, risk, and information value in software requirements and architecture. In: International Conference on Software Engineering (ICSE), pp. 883–894 (2014)
22. Arcelli, D., Cortellessa, V., Trubiani, C.: Antipattern-based model refactoring for software performance improvement. In: International Conference on Quality of Software Architectures (QoSA), pp. 33–42 (2012)
23. Jain, R.: The Art of Computer Systems Performance Analysis: Techniques for Experimental Design, Measurement, Simulation, and Modeling. SIGMETRICS Performance Evaluation Review **19**, 5–11 (1991)

24. Clements, P.C., Garlan, D., Little, R., Nord, R.L., Stafford, J.A.: Documenting software architectures: views and beyond. In: International Conference on Software Engineering (ICSE), pp. 740–741 (2003)
25. Cortellessa, V., Mirandola, R.: Prima-uml: a performance validation incremental methodology on early uml diagrams. Sci. Comput. Program. **44**, 101–129 (2002)
26. Casale, G., Serazzi, G.: Quantitative system evaluation with java modeling tools. In: International Conference on Performance Engineering (ICPE), pp. 449–454 (2011)
27. Smith, C.U.: Introduction to software performance engineering: origins and outstanding problems. In: Bernardo, M., Hillston, J. (eds.) SFM 2007. LNCS, vol. 4486, pp. 395–428. Springer, Heidelberg (2007)
28. Gotel, O., Cleland-Huang, J., Hayes, J.H., Zisman, A., Egyed, A., Grünbacher, P., Antoniol, G.: The quest for ubiquity: a roadmap for software and systems traceability research. In: IEEE International Requirements Engineering Conference (RE), pp. 71–80 (2012)
29. Franks, G., Petriu, D.C., Woodside, C.M., Xu, J., Tregunno, P.: Layered bottlenecks and their mitigation. In: International Conference on the Quantitative Evaluation of Systems (QEST), pp. 103–114 (2006)
30. Aleti, A., Buhnova, B., Grunske, L., Koziolek, A., Meedeniya, I.: Software architecture optimization methods: A systematic literature review. IEEE Trans. Software Eng. **39**, 658–683 (2013)

Automatic Translation of Architecture Constraint Specifications into Components

Sahar Kallel[1,2](✉), Bastien Tramoni[1], Chouki Tibermacine[1](✉), Christophe Dony[1], and Ahmed Hadj Kacem[2]

[1] Lirmm, Montpellier University, Montpellier, France
{sahar.kallel,bastien.tramoni,chouki.tibermacine,dony}@lirmm.fr
[2] ReDCAD, Sfax University, Sfax, Tunisie
sahar.kallel@redcad.org, ahmed.hadjkacem@fsegs.rnu.tn

Abstract. Architecture constraints are specifications defined by developers at design-time and checked on design artifacts (architecture descriptions, like UML models). They enable to check, after an evolution, whether an architecture description still conforms to the conditions imposed by an architecture pattern, style or any design principle. One possible language for specifying such constraints is the OMG's OCL. Most of these architecture constraints are formalized as "gross" specifications, without any structure or parameterization possibilities. This causes difficulties in their reuse. We propose in this work a process for translating architecture constraints into a special kind of components called constraint-components. This makes these specifications reusable (easily put and checked out in/from repositories), parametrizable (generic and applicable in different contexts) and composable with others. We implemented this process by considering the translation of OCL constraints into constraint-components described with an ADL called CLACS.

Keywords: Architecture constraint · UML metamodel · CLACS · Constraint-component · Reusability · OCL definition · Automatic translation

1   Introduction: Context and Problem Statement

Architecture constraints are specifications of invariants that are checked by analyzing architecture descriptions. This kind of constraints should not be confused with functional constraints, which are checked by analyzing the state of the running components constituting the architecture. For example, if we consider a UML model (an architecture description) containing a class Employee (a component in that architecture) which has an integer attribute age, a functional constraint presenting an invariant in this class could impose that the values of this attribute (slot of an object) must be included in the interval [16-70] for all instances of this class. This kind of constraints is inherently dynamic. They can be checked only at runtime.

© Springer International Publishing Switzerland 2015
D. Weyns et al. (Eds.): ECSA 2015, LNCS 9278, pp. 322–338, 2015.
DOI: 10.1007/978-3-319-23727-5_27

On the other side, architecture constraints are specifications where architecture descriptions, and not component states, are analyzed [28]. They define invariants imposed by the choice of a particular design principle, architectural style or pattern, like the layered architecture style [25], where "components in non-adjacent layers must not be directly connected together". This is an example of an architecture constraint. OCL(Object Constraint Language) [16] is an OMG standard which specify two types of constraints : functional (constraints navigate in UML models) and architectural (constraints navigate in MOF metamodels).

Functional constraints are used in Design by Contract for ensuring the definition of accurate and checkable interfaces for software components [21]. Architecture constraints are used during the evolution of a software architecture for guaranteeing that changes do not have bad side effects on the applied architecture patterns or styles, and thus on the quality [29].

Many architecture constraints have been formalized for the existing architecture patterns proposed in the literature and practice of software engineering [3,14,33]. But unfortunately, most of them are "gross" textual specifications. They do not offer any structure. Therefore, it is difficult to reuse them in other/different contexts. This is the reason why we propose in this paper a process to transform them into more structured assets in order to facilitate their reuse. In addition, our experience with architecture constraint specification leads us to say that most of the time, architecture constraints are composed of many "independent" parts that are assembled together via logical operators. Some of these parts are shared between several architecture constraints and have their own semantics. The idea of this paper is to propose a way to build OCL basic constraints as entities embedded in a special kind of software components, that can be reused, assembled, composed into higher-level ones and customized using standard component-based techniques.

In this paper, we propose to translate automatically architecture constraints specified in design stage into *"constraint-components"*. We propose a two-step process which takes as input a gross OCL architecture constraint specification expressed in the UML metamodel, and which provides as output constraints-components expressed with CLACS Architecture Description Language. We propose to generate architecture constraints as "constraint-components" [31] so that we can put them on "shelves" and thereafter make them reusable, customizable and composable with others to produce more complex constraints.

The remaining of this paper is organized as follows. In the following section, we give an illustrative example of the input and the output of the proposed process. These will serve as running examples throughout the paper. In Section 3, we describe in detail the steps of our process. In Section 4, we expose an evaluation of the approach. Before concluding and presenting the future work, we discuss the related work in Section 5.

2   Illustrative Example

To better understand the context of this work, we introduce an example of an architecture constraint (Listing 1.1) enabling the checking of the topological conditions imposed by the "Service Bus Architecture Pattern" [5]. This pattern introduces three kinds of components: the customers, the producers and the bus. The bus is defined as an adapter that establishes the communication between customers and producers as they may have mismatching interfaces. The architecture constraint which specifies the conditions imposed by this pattern is expressed in OCL using the UML metamodel [28] in the following listing.

```
 1  context Component inv :
 2  let bus:Component
 3  = self.realization.realizingClassifier
 4  ->select(c:Classifier | c.oclIsKindOf(Component)
 5    and c.oclAsType(Component).name='esbImpl')
 6  customers : Set(Component)
 7  = self.realization.realizingClassifier
 8  ->select(c:Classifier | c.oclIsKindOf(Component)
 9    and (c.oclAsType(Component).name='cust1'
10      or c.oclAsType(Component).name='cust2'
11      or c.oclAsType(Component).name='cust3'))
12  producers : Set(Component)
13  = self.realization.realizingClassifier
14  ->select(c:Classifier | c.oclIsKindOf(Component)
15    and (c.oclAsType(Component).name= 'prod1'
16  or c.oclAsType(Component).name='prod2'
17  or c.oclAsType(Component).name='prod3'))
18  in
19  -- The bus should have at least one input port
20  -- and one output port
21  bus.ownedPort->exists(p1,p2:Port|
22      p1.provided->notEmpty() and p2.required->notEmpty())
23  and
24  --Customers should have output ports only
25  customers->forAll(c:Component|
26      c.ownedPort->forAll(required->notEmpty()
27        and provided->isEmpty()))
28  and
29  --Customers should be connected to the bus only
30  customers->forAll(com:Component|
31      com.port->forAll(p:Port|p.end->notEmpty()
32        implies
33          self.ownedConnector ->exists(con:Connector |
34              bus.ownedPort->exists( pb:Port|
35                con.end.role->includes(pb)) and
36                  con.end->includes(p.end))))
37  and
38  --Producers should have input ports only
39  producers->forAll(c:Component|
40      c.ownedPort->forAll(provided->notEmpty()
41        and required->isEmpty()))
42  and
43  --Producers should be connected to the bus only
44  producers->forAll(com:Component|
45      com.port->forAll(p:Port|p.end->notEmpty()
46        implies
47          self.ownedConnector->exists(con:Connector|
48              bus.ownedPort->exists( pb:Port|
49                con.end.role->includes(pb)) and
50                  con.end->includes(p.end))))
```

Listing 1.1. Bus architecture pattern constraint in OCL/UML

When applying our proposed approach, we change the format of the constraint (Listing 1.1) from a textual "gross" specification into an architecture description made of "constraint-components" and "query-components". These components are described with an ADL named CLACS [31] (pronounced Klax). By "gross" specification, we mean a specification that does not offer enough structure, reusability and parameterization.

In the literature, there are many languages enabling the specification of architecture constraints (see [28] for a survey). Each one has its advantages and its particular application context. However, CLACS is the only language that provides a component model for software architecture constraint specification. The architecture constraints modeled with this language are constraint-components in which the checked invariants are still specified using OCL. But these OCL constraints navigate in CLACS metamodel and not in the UML's one. The choice of UML is simply motivated by the fact that it is an industrial standard[1], and that OCL is its original constraint language. We can consider here a repository of architecture constraints that can be fed by the software architecture community, by using these general modeling languages, which are UML and OCL. The result of our translation process is shown in Fig. 1. We notice the presence of two kinds of component descriptors (query and constraint). Query-components embed OCL **definition** constraints that return a value whose type is different from Boolean and constraint-components embed OCL **definition** constraints that return only Boolean values. Indeed, our architecture constraint specification will be decomposed in a set of OCL **definition** constraints and these constraints will be embedded in these two kinds of components to reuse them.

There are three let expressions in the architecture constraint (Listing 1.1). Each one (Lines 2–5, 6–11, 12–17) is supposed to be defined basically in a separate query-component descriptor. But let expressions 2 and 3 are similar according to a similarity measure which is defined in the following section. That is why they are represented by only one query-component (**ParticipantsIdentification**).

There are five constraint-components on the right of the figure. These components represent the OCL **definitions** that are extracted from our initial constraint and then parametrized. These **definitions** are called throughout the constraint and they will potentially serve other constraints.

There are in total five sub-constraints in the architecture constraint (Listing 1.1). Each one (Lines 21–22, 25–27, 30–36, 39–41 and 44–50) is supposed to be defined basically in a separate component descriptor. But in this example, sub-constraints 2 and 4 can be grouped in the same component descriptor (**PortConstraint**) because they check similar "aspects". They check if all the components in a given set of instances (**customers** in the first sub-constraint and **producers** in the second) have specific kinds of ports (input or output).

---

[1] Even if a recent empirical study [23] found out that UML is not fully (but selectively) used by developers in industry, and that it is used informally, there is a general agreement that UML is the *de facto* standard modeling language known by a large number of developers.

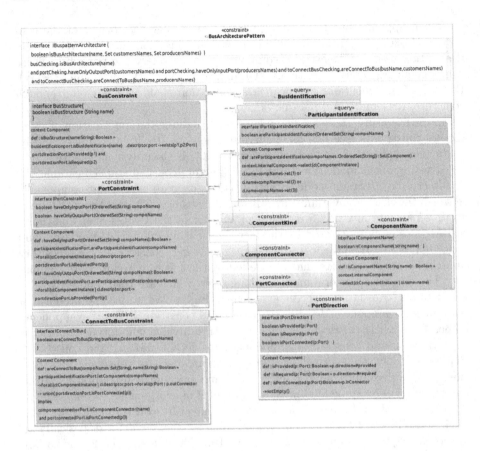

Fig. 1. Sample of approach results

`PortConstraint` descriptor provides two operations which enable the checking of these two sub-constraints. On the other side, sub-constraints 3 and 5 check exactly the same invariant (in contrast to sub-constraints 2 and 4), except that they apply on different sets of components (`customers` for sub-constraint 3 and `producers` for sub-constraint 5). Thus, there is a single component descriptor (`ConnectToBusConstraint`) which is generated for these two sub-constraints. This constraint-component provides a single operation which is parameterized with the set of components on which the constraint should be checked.

We can see (on the top of the figure) the constraint checked by the composite, in which there are five operation invocations to the three internal components (on the left of the figure). These internal components (that constitute our initial constraint) call the operations that are declared in the others components using the name of the provided port. These later descriptors will be registered in a repository and will be potentially useful for other constraints. In other words, for each new "gross" constraint specification to decompose, we will measure the similarity between the OCL `definitions` extracted from it i.e. after applying the decomposition and the paramterization (see Section 3, subsection 3.1), and the registered OCL `definitions` embedded in the components, According to the similarity result, we can reuse an existing OCL `definition` constraint and also modify it, if necessary.

For this example, we will obtain, in addition to the descriptor of the "main" component (`BusPatternArchitecture`), three constraint-component descriptors (instead of five) corresponding to our initial constraint. These three components are connected to the two query-components (`BusIdentification` and `ParticipantsIdentification`) and five other constraint-components. These query-components provide queries that are shared between the constraint- components.

Through this *"componentization"*, CLACS constraint-component and query-component descriptors can be reusable (instantiated many times in different contexts), composable (instances of them can be connected together or connected within a composite component to build complex constraint-components) and parameterizable (to check that **customers** or **producers** are connected only to the **bus**, we can pass the right arguments to the operation of `ConnectToBusConstraint` descriptor).

In the following section, we describe in detail the steps of the constraint translation process illustrated with examples.

3   Transformation of Constraints into Components

Our process is composed of two main steps. The first one consists in extracting sub-constraints from the constraint. These sub-constraints will be specified as parametrized OCL `definitions`. The second step consists in embedding these generated OCL `definitions` into components in order to make them reusable. We will detail these two steps in the following subsections.

Note that OCL constraints are predicates in the first order logic. They have a simple and intuitive concrete syntax. Even if the transformations presented in this paper apply on OCL, the proposed work can be generalized to any equivalent predicate logic language. This is not demonstrated experimentally in our work, but as the reader can notice, the syntactic tokens handled in our transformations are general to predicate logic.

3.1   Constraint Refactoring

We propose first to extract sub-constraints as OCL `definitions` and then we identify parameters for them and we will obtain at the end an invariant which uses these definitions. These **definitions** are parametrizable and will be registered in a repository to be used by other constraints. To obtain this new form of our invariant, we propose a multi-step transformation micro-process. All steps use as input the abstract syntax tree of the initial constraint.

Variable Declaration Extraction. Sometimes a sub-expression is used several times in an OCL constraint. The operator `let` allows to report and set the value (i.e initialize) a variable that can be used in the expression which follows the `inv`. `def` is a type of constraints which is used to declare and define the values of attributes or returned values of operations. The first step in our approach is to extract the let expressions from our textual constraint specification and define them as constraints stereotyped with `def`. These OCL `definition` constraints must return a value whose type is different from Boolean. At the same time, we modify our textual constraint i.e, the constraint undergoes changes and call these generated OCL `definitions` in their appropriate places. At this level, our initial constraint will be as follows:

```
 1  context Component
 2  ---let expressions extraction
 3  def: letBus(): Component = self.realization.
 4  realizingClassifier->select(c : Classifier | c.oclIsKindOf(
       Component)
 5    and c.oclAsType(Component).name = 'esbImpl')
 6  def: letCustomers(): Set(Component) = self.realization.
 7  realizingClassifier->select(c : Classifier | c.oclIsKindOf(
       Component)
 8  and (c.oclAsType(Component).name = 'cust1' or
 9   c.oclAsType(Component).name = 'cust2' or
10   c.oclAsType(Component).name = 'cust3'))
11  def: letProducers(): ...
12  inv:
13  letBus().ownedPort ->includes(p1, p2 : Port | p1.provided
14      ->notEmpty() and p2.required ->notEmpty())
15  and
16  letCustomers()->forAll(c:Component|c.ownedPort
17  ->forAll(required ->notEmpty()and provided->isEmpty()))
18    and ...
19    and ...
20    and ...
```

Listing 1.2. Constraint after extracting let expressions

Constraint Decomposition. Second, we decompose automatically the obtained constraint into a set of sub-constraints. This decomposition is primary based on logical operators used at the top level (Lines 15, 18, 19 and 20 in Listing 1.2). Operands of these operators are considered here as sub-constraints. This set of sub-constraints is refined recursively into a tree of sub-constraints if these sub-constraints can be decomposed again. The stopping condition of the recursion is that no logic operator is found in the sub-constraint. All these sub-constraints will be represented as OCL `definition` constraints. The refactoring of the constraint (i.e modification of the constraint invariant) is performed every time we generate a new `definition`. At this level we obtain a bag of OCL `definition` constraints that return a Boolean value. Listing 1.3 represents an excerpt of our constraint during the decomposition stage.

```
1  context Component
2  def: def1(c: Classifier): Boolean = c.oclIsKindOf(Component)
3  def: def2(c: Classifier): Boolean = c.oclAsType(Component).name
4  = 'esbImpl'
5  def: letBus(): Component = self.realization.realizingClassifier
6  ->select(c : Classifier | def1(c) and def2(c))
7  def: def3(c : Classifier): Boolean = c.oclIsKindOf(Component)
8  def: def4(c : Classifier): Boolean = c.oclAsType(Component).name
9   = 'cust1' or c.oclAsType(Component).name = 'cust2' or
10  c.oclAsType(Component).name = 'cust3'
11 def: letCustomers(): Set(Component) = self.realization.
12 realizingClassifier->select(c : Classifier | def3(c) and def4(c))
13 ...
14 def: part1(): Boolean = letBus().ownedPort
15 ->includes(p1, p2 : Port | def7(p1) and def8(p2))
16 def: part2(): ...
17 def: def11(p: Port): Boolean = p.end->notEmpty()
18 def: def12(p: Port): Boolean = self.ownedConnector
19 ->exists(con : Connector | letBus().ownedPort ->exists(pb:Port|
20 con.end.role ->includes(pb)) and con.end ->includes(p.end))
21 def: part3(): Boolean = letCustomers()
22 ->forAll(com : Component | com.port
23     ->forAll(p : Port |def11(p) implies def12(p)))
24 def: part4(): ...
25 def: part5(): ...
26 inv:
27 part1() and part2() and part3() and part4() and part5()
```

Listing 1.3. Bus architecture pattern Constraint during the decomposition stage

In Listing 1.3, the constraint is composed of five "main" OCL sub-constraints (part1(), part2(), part3(), part4() and part5()). These sub-constraints can be decomposed again into other sub-constraints due to the recursive process[2]. For instance def4() contains the operator or, so it will be decomposed again. All these sub-constraints are defined as OCL definitions (def:) presented before the inv:. We can observe that there are some OCL definitions that have parameters. The reason to make some parameters at this stage (the decomposition) is to have the possibility to define all the generated OCL definitions with the same context as that of the constraint (Line 1).

Redundancy Removal. After the constraints decomposition, we obtain a bag of OCL definitions. In this step, we remove all redundant definitions and then we update the constraint. For instance, in Listing 1.3 def1() and def3() are syntactically identical. Now we have a set of OCL definition constraints that constitute our textual constraint.

Constraint Parameterization. When creating the signature of the operation that wraps a constraint, we add a parameter in this signature everywhere we find a literal value of a given data type. The type of these parameters is obtained from the abstract syntax tree of the constraint. For instance def2() in Listing 1.3 will be defined as follows:

---

[2] In Listing 1.3, the decomposition is stopped in part4().

```
1  context Component
2  def: def2(c: Classifer , name: String ): Boolean = c.oclAsType(Component
        ).name = name
```

Listing 1.4. OCL definition constraint paramatrizable

In this stage, we need to measure the similarity between the OCL definitions. This measure allows to optimize our process, i,e. remove some redundant OCL definitions (obtained in the parametrization stage). For example def4() in Listing 1.3 will be defined at this stage as follows:

```
1  context Component
2  def: def17(c: Classifier , name1: String ): Boolean =
3  c.oclAsType(Component).name = name1
4  def: def18(c: Classifier , name2: String ): Boolean =
5  c.oclAsType(Component).name = name2
6  def: def19(c: Classifier , name3: String ): Boolean =
7  c.oclAsType(Component).name = name3
8  def: def4(c: Classifier , name1: String ,name2: String ,name3: String ):
9  Boolean = def17(c,name1)and def18(c,name2) and def19(c,name3).
```

Listing 1.5. Example of parametrization

We remark that def2() (see Listing 1.4), def17(), def18() and def19() are similar. They are different only by the name of the parameter (the same type of the parameter). Then, we remove def17(), def18() and def19() and replace them by def2() presented in Listing 1.4. We also optimize the def4() definition which will take as parameter c:Classifier and consumersNames: Set(String). This is performed when comparing the OCL expressions before the "=" (c.name) in each literal value. This comparison is done using the AST of the OCL constraint. Concerning how we measured the similarity between OCL definitions, we implemented an automated process by analyzing the abstract syntax trees of definitions body. Each pair of trees is compared. These should share a common root and a minimal sub-tree (obtained in a breadth-first traversal). This ensures, to some extent, that constraints define predicates on the same kind of architectural elements, which are obtained through navigations in the OCL definition (reflected by these sub-trees). For the remaining sub-tree, an edit distance [27] is measured between each pair of sub-trees. If this measure is less than a threshold[3], we consider that the two definitions are similar.

At the end of this step, our invariant is completely decomposed in OCL definition constraints. These constraints will be registered in a repository in order to reuse them to create others constraint specifications.

---

[3] The value of this threshold will be fixed empirically.

3.2   Constraint Transformation into CLACS Components

In this section, we describe the transformation of OCL definitions generated
in the first step into CLACS components. A CLACS component is an instance
of a component descriptor (like an object is an instance of a class). A component
has a name, a description and a kind (business or constraint). It declares ports,
which are characterized by a direction (required or provided) and a visibility
(internal or external). Each port has an interface which specifies a set of operation signatures. Ports are linked via connectors. A connector receives operation
invocations through its source port and transmits them through its target port.
For generating CLACS components, we proposed a multi-step transformation
micro-process:

Operation Grouping. Each CLACS query-component descriptor will embed
an OCL definition which returns a value whose type is different from Boolean
and each CLACS constraint-component will embed an OCL definition which
returns only boolean values. From the other side, among the generated OCL
definitions, each one that corresponds to a let in the constraint (Subsection 3.1, like letConsumers()) will be embedded in a query-component descriptor and each one among the others will be embedded in a constraint-component.
In this case, we can obtain a large number of components. Therefore, we propose to put together OCL definitions that check similar "aspects" in the
same component descriptors. By checking similar aspects, we mean checking
the connection, testing the kind, or some other property of a given architectural element (a port or a connector for example). For that we use the same
technique of similarity measurement described before (Subsection 3.1, step *Constraints Parametrization*). For example, the OCL definitions part2() and
part4() check the same aspect which is the kind of an architectural element
(a Port). The two trees of these two sub-constraints have a common root
which is a component and a common sub-tree generated from the expression
.ownedPort->includes(p1,p2:Port|). For the remaining sub-trees generated
from the remaining expressions of the two sub-constraints, we can observe that
there is a similarity between them (only two edit operations (node substitu-
tions): required and provided tokens are inverted). So these are grouped as
two operations in the same component descriptor.

Metamodel Migration. In this step, we transform constraint navigations written in OCL/UML into OCL/CLACS. This is performed using a simple set of
declarative mappings that we have specified between the two metamodels (UML
and CLACS). These have been defined using the same template as in [30]. For
reasons of space limitation, we do not show these mappings. But note that, the
self keyword [4] is replaced by context, which is resolved to an implicit required
port connected to a meta-descriptor of the business component on which the constraint is checked. This connection resolution is made (lazily) when the checking
is launched.

---

[4] *self* is located in the initial constraint written in UML metamodel.

CLACS Architecture Description Generation. Starting from the tree obtained in the first step, a component-based architecture description in CLACS is generated. This architecture description contains all the necessary constraint-components and query-components (instances) connected together. These components embed the refactored [5] architecture constraints that navigate henceforth in CLACS metamodel. These generated components will be instantiated and then connected to the business components in order to be verified.

4   Process Evaluation

We collected 25 architecture constraints that characterize patterns which concern only structural allure of the architecture. In order to measure the reusability obtained in the result of our transformation process, we choose the metric proposed by Gaffney and Durek in [13]. It allows to calculate the proportion and the number of the reuse constraints. This metric is defined as follows:

$$C = \left(b + \left(\frac{E}{n} \right) - 1 \right) R + 1$$

where:

- C: is the cost of software development (specification of an architecture constraint)
- b: is the cost of integrating the reused elements into the new artifact (integration of constraint-components in a composite)
- E: is the cost of developing a reusable element (a constraint-component)
- n: is the number of uses of reused elements
- R: is the proportion of reused elements

C is an important indicator of the effectiveness of the reuse obtained in the final result of our transformation process. If there is no reuse at all, C is equal to 1. The more effective the reuse is, the less C is. b and E relate to the estimated cost of incorporating and developing, respectively, the reused elements. b is supposed to be greater than 0 because it always takes effort to reuse an element. E is supposed to be greater than 1 because the creation of a reusable element requires an extra effort. E is the sum of the costs of developing a new element (without reuse support) and reusing elements. For our experiment, R represents the proportion of the patterns (constraint's) structure which is reused to construct other patterns (constraints). R is the number of the reused constraints divided by the total number of constraints in the same pattern.

Fig 2 shows the values of R for all patterns. As we can observe, the R value is in the range 20-100. We can also observe that there are 13 (out of 25) patterns having 100 % of their structure reused elsewhere. This reinforces our idea to transform architectural constraints into a reusable structure.

---

[5] A constraint is refactored when the different steps described above have been applied on it.

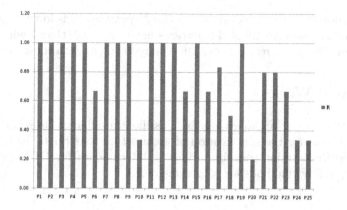

Fig. 2. R values for all patterns

Another value that we have measured is n, which represents how many times a structure is reused in the whole set of evaluated constraints. Fig. 3 depicts the frequency of reusable constraints in each pattern. This demonstrates the potential to promote the reusability of pattern structure in the construction of a pattern library. We can see in Fig. 3 that the pattern P8 is composed of constraint-components that are reused 55 times by other patterns. We have six patterns that have a reusable structure called more than 50 times.

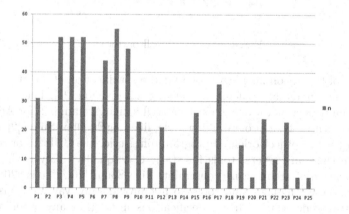

Fig. 3. n values for all patterns

b and E are difficult to measure because of various reasons as explained in [12]. We take the b and E values estimated by [10] since our evaluation falls into the polylithic category[6]. Thus, b and E are equal to 0.15 and 1.2 respectively in our experiment.

---

[6] This category concerns structures that can be divided into individual parts and each of them can be independently manipulated.

Fig. 4 shows the cost of constructing the 25 patterns. C is in the range of 18 to 89. As we can observe, all of the patterns have a cost less than 1 which means that the obtained reuse really has an effect in reducing pattern construction cost.

5   Related Works

Works related to our approach can be classified in different categories: i) languages and tools for the specification of architecture constraints, ii) techniques for predicate/constraint transformations, iii) techniques for OCL constraints refactoring and iv) methods for constraint reuse.

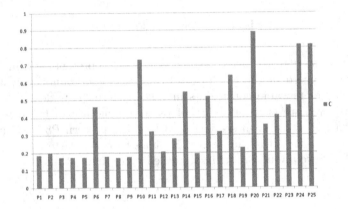

Fig. 4. C values for all patterns

A state of the art on languages used for the specification of architecture constraints at design and at implementation stages is given in [28]. These languages vary from embedded notations in existing ADLs, like Armani [22] for Acme [15], to notations with a logic programming style, like LogEn [9] or Spine [2], or notations with (or for) object-oriented programming style, like CDL [19]or SCL [18]. In practice there are several tools for static code quality analysis that enable the specification of architecture constraints, like Sonar [26], Lattix [20], among others. All these languages and tools do not provide any way for transforming or generating code starting from specifications in OCL or any other predicate language. In addition, they provide either no or a limited parameterization and reusability of architecture constraints.

Hassam et al. [17] proposed a method for transforming OCL constraints during UML model refactoring, using model transformations. Their approach uses first an annotation method for marking the initial UML model in order to obtain an annotated target model. Then, a mapping table is created from these two annotations in order to use it for transforming OCL constraints of the initial model into OCL constraints of the target one. Their solution of constraint transformation cannot be used straightforwardly because it needs some knowledge about model transformation languages and tools. In our work, constraint transformation is performed in a simple an ad-hoc way without using additional modeling and transformation languages. In [11], the authors propose an approach for generating (instantiate) models from metamodels taking into account OCL constraints. Their approach is based on CSP (Constraint Satisfaction Problem). They defined some formal rules to transform models and constraints associated to them. Cabot *et al.* [4] worked also on UML/OCL transformation into CSP in order to check quality properties of models. These approaches are similar to our transformation process since the transformed/handled artifacts are the same (OCL specifications and metamodels). They use the same OCL compiler as us (DresdenOCL [8]) to analyze constraints. In contrast to CSP, this does not require an external tool for the interpretation of constraints. In addition, in our approach, we transform only constraints. In the other approaches, everything should be transformed into a CSP to be solved (the constraints + the models/metamodels). Moreover, Bajwa and Lee presented in [1] a two-step process for transforming SBVR rules (Semantics of Business Vocabulary and Business Rules) into OCL constraints. The first step consists in realizing a mapping between SBVR rules elements and UML model elements. This step ensures that the OCL constraint that will be generated is semantically checkable in a UMl model. The second step consists in transforming an OCL model instance from SBVR model instance using a mapping between the two metamodels (OCL and SBVR). This paper uses model transformations techniques. Their process is troublesome when the constraints have a gross specification (very large models). The generated constraints are complex, not reusable and parametrizable.

OCL refactoring consists in simplifying the constraints and making them more expressive. In [7], Correa *et al.* have as goal to improve the readability and the comprehensibility of the constraint. Therefore, they prepared a catalog of smells. They proposed refactorings for removing a given smell in the constraint. It is true that this refactoring allows a greater comprehensibility of the constraints (validation in the paper) but these do not consider reuse. Besides, the authors consider in their approach only the functional constraints and not architectural ones. In [24], Reimann *et al.* complete the previous work of Correa *et al.*, they proposed new smells and new refactorings like a decomposition of OCL constraints in atomic sub-constraints. These new refactorings does not address the parameterization of the constraint which enables more reuse.

In [6], Chimak-Opoka proposed a library OCLLib which contains a group of valid OCL constraints. The main objective of this library is to offer a set of OCL constraints that are reliable, tested and can be reusable. But, no method explain how to make the constraints customizable is presented. In [32], Ton That *et al.* proposed a catalog of architecture pattern as constraint-components. They defined for each pattern its architectural constraints, they decomposed the constraints manually and embarked them in components. The component-constraints built are reusable and parametrizable. In our approach, we realized these transformations automatically and we use the result of this paper as an oracle for our experimentation.

6   Conclusion and Future Work

Architecture constraints are predicates that bring a valuable help for preserving architecture styles, patterns or general design principles in a given application after having evolved its architecture description. Such kind of specifications is subject to reuse. They are frequently assembled together to build more complex architecture constraints [31]. We have presented in this paper a process for translating architecture constraints into components. Our process is composed of two main steps. The first one consists in describing OCL constraints, extracted from "gross" textual constraint specifications, as OCL definitions. The second step consists in generating automatically constraint-components from these definitions. These components provide operations for checking the constraints. They are specified in an ADL named CLACS.

As a future work, we plan first to demonstrate the generality of our approach studying other predicate logic language than OCL and then we propose to make these generated constraint-components checkable in the implementation stage on component-based programs. We would like to automatically translate these constraint-components into checkable descriptors at runtime.

References

1. Bajwa, I.S., Lee, M.G.: Transformation rules for translating business rules to OCL constraints. In: France, R.B., Kuester, J.M., Bordbar, B., Paige, R.F. (eds.) ECMFA 2011. LNCS, vol. 6698, pp. 132–143. Springer, Heidelberg (2011)
2. Blewitt, A., Bundy, A., Stark, I.: Automatic verification of design patterns in java. In: Proceedings of the 20th IEEE/ACM International Conference on Automated Software Engineering (ASE 2005), pp. 224–232. ACM (2005)
3. Buschmann, F., Henney, K., Schmidt, D.C.: Pattern-Oriented Software Architecture. On Patterns and Pattern Languages, vol. 5. Wiley, April 2007
4. Cabot, J., Clarisó, R., Riera, D.: Umltocsp: a tool for the formal verification of uml/ocl models using constraint programming. In: Proceedings of the 22nd IEEE/ACM International Conference on Automated Software Engineering, pp. 547–548. ACM (2007)
5. Chappell, D.: Enterprise Service Bus: Theory in Practice. O'Reilly Media (2004)
6. Chimiak-Opoka, J.: OCLLib, OCLUnit, OCLDoc: pragmatic extensions for the object constraint language. In: Schürr, A., Selic, B. (eds.) MODELS 2009. LNCS, vol. 5795, pp. 665–669. Springer, Heidelberg (2009)
7. Correa, A., Werner, C., Barros, M.: Refactoring to improve the understandability of specifications written in object constraint language. IET Software 2, 69–90 (2009)
8. Demuth, B.: The dresden OCL toolkit and its role in information systems development. In: ISD 2004 (2004)
9. Eichberg, M., Kloppenburg, S., Klose, K., Mezini, M.: Defining and continuous checking of structural program dependencies. In: Proceedings of the 30th International Conference on Software Engineering (ICSE 2008). ACM (2008)
10. Favaro, J.: What price reusability?: a case study. In: ACM SIGAda Ada Letters, vol. 11. ACM (1991)

11. Ferdjoukh, A., Baert, A.-E., Chateau, A., Coletta, R., Nebut, C.: A CSP approach for metamodel instantiation. In: IEEE Internationnal Conference on Tools with Artificial Intelligence, ICTAI 2013, pp. 1044–1051 (2013)

12. Frakes, W., Terry, C.: Software reuse: metrics and models. ACM Computing Surveys (CSUR) **28** (1996)

13. Gaffney, J.E., Durek, T.A.: Software reuse key to enhanced productivity: some quantitative models. Information and Software Technology **31**(5) (1989)

14. Gamma, E., Helm, R., Johnson, R., Vlissides, J.: Design patterns: Elements of Reusable Object-Oriented Software. Addison Wesley, October 1994

15. Garlan, D., Monroe, R.T., Wile, D.: Acme: Architectural description of component-based systems. In: Leavens, G.T., Sitaraman, M. (eds.) Foundations of Component-Based Systems, pp. 47–68. Cambridge University Press (2000)

16. OMG: Object Management Group. Object constraint language (ocl), v2.4, specification: Omg document formal/2014-02-03, February 2014. http://www.omg.org/spec/OCL/2.4/

17. Hassam, K., Sadou, S., Fleurquin, R., et al.: Adapting OCL constraints after a refactoring of their model using an mde process. In: BElgian-NEtherlands software eVOLution seminar (BENEVOL 2010), pp. 16–27 (2010)

18. Hou, D., Hoover, H.J.: Using scl to specify and check design intent in source code. IEEE Transactions on Software Engineering **32**(6), 404–423 (2006)

19. Klarlund, N., Koistinen, J., Schwartzbach, M.I.: Formal design constraints. In: Proceedings of the 11th ACM SIGPLAN Conference on Object-Oriented Programming, Systems, Languages, and Applications, San Jose, CA, USA, pp. 370–383. ACM Press (1996)

20. Lattix. http://lattix.com/

21. Meyer, B.: Touch of Class. Springer, June 2013

22. Monroe, R.T.: Capturing software architecture design expertise with armani. Technical report, School of Computer Science, Carnegie Mellon University, Pittsburgh, Pennsylvania, USA (2001)

23. Petre, M.: Uml in practice. In: Proceedings of the 35th International Conference on Software Engineering (ICSE 2013), pp. 722–731. IEEE Press, May 2013

24. Reimann, J., Wilke, C., Demuth, B., Muck, M., Aßmann, U.: Tool supported OCL refactoring catalogue. In: Proceedings of the 12th Workshop on OCL and Textual Modelling, pp. 7–12. ACM (2012)

25. Shaw, M., Garlan, D.: Software Architecture: Perspectives on an Emerging Discipline. Prentice Hall (1996)

26. Sonar. http://www.sonarqube.org/

27. Tai, K.-C.: The tree-to-tree correction problem. Journal of the ACM **26**(3), 422–433 (1997)

28. Tibermacine, C.: Software Architecture 2, chapter Architecture Constraints. John Wiley and Sons, New York (2014)

29. Tibermacine, C., Fleurquin, R., Sadou, S.: On-demand quality-oriented assistance in component-based software evolution. In: Gorton, I., Heineman, G.T., Crnković, I., Schmidt, H.W., Stafford, J.A., Ren, X.-M., Wallnau, K. (eds.) CBSE 2006. LNCS, vol. 4063, pp. 294–309. Springer, Heidelberg (2006)

30. Tibermacine, C., Fleurquin, R., Sadou, S.: Simplifying transformations of architectural constraints. In: Proceedings of the ACM Symposium on Applied Computing (SAC 2006), Track on Model Transformation, Dijon, France. ACM Press. April 2006

31. Tibermacine, C., Sadou, S., Dony, C., Fabresse, L.: Component-based specification of software architecture constraints. In: Proceedings of the 14th ACM Sigsoft Symposium on Component Based Software Engineering (CBSE 2011). ACM (2011)
32. That, T.M.T., Tibermacine, C., Sadou, S.: Catalogue of architectural patterns characterized by constraint components, Version 1.0. Technical report, July 2013, 53p
33. Zdun, U., Avgeriou, P.: A catalog of architectural primitives for modeling architectural patterns. Information and Software Technology **50**(9) (2008)

The Layered Architecture Recovery as a Quadratic Assignment Problem

Alvine Boaye Belle[1], Ghizlane El Boussaidi[1(✉)], Christian Desrosiers[1],
Sègla Kpodjedo[1], and Hafedh Mili[2]

[1] Department of Software and IT Engineering, École de Technologie Supérieure,
Montreal, Canada
ghizlane.elboussaidi@etsmtl.ca
[2] Department of Computer Science, Université du Québec à Montréal, Montreal, Canada

Abstract. Software architecture recovery is a bottom-up process that aims at
building high-level views that support the understanding of existing software
applications. Many approaches have been proposed to support architecture recovery using various techniques. However, very few approaches are driven by
the architectural styles that were used to build the systems under analysis. In
this paper, we address the problem of recovering layered views of existing
software systems. We re-examine the layered style to extract a set of fundamental principles which encompass a set of constraints that a layered system must
conform to at design time and during its evolution. These constraints are used to
guide the recovery process of layered architectures. In particular, we translate
the problem of recovering the layered architecture into a quadratic assignment
problem (QAP) based on these constraints, and we solve the QAP using a heuristic search algorithm. In this paper, we introduce the QAP formulation of the
layering recovery and we present and discuss the results of the experimentation
with the approach on four open source software systems.

Keywords: Software architecture · Architecture recovery · Layered style ·
Architecture evolution · Quadratic assignment problem

1 Introduction

Software architects rely on a set of patterns, commonly named architectural styles [1],
to design systems. An architectural style embodies design knowledge [2] that applies
to a family of software systems [1]. Common architectural styles include layered,
pipes and filters, and service-oriented styles [1-3]. Each style has its own vocabulary
and constraints, and it promotes some specific quality attributes. However, researchers observed that the as-built architecture of a software system does not conform to
the initial style that guided its design. This is mainly due to: 1) the continuous
changes undergone by the system, which increase its complexity and lead to a deviation from its initial design; and 2) violations of the style constraints due to the conceptual gap between the elements defined by the style and the constructs provided by

© Springer International Publishing Switzerland 2015
D. Weyns et al. (Eds): ECSA 2015, LNCS 9278, pp. 339–354, 2015.
DOI: 10.1007/978-3-319-23727-5_28

programming languages [4]. Therefore, understanding and properly evolving a software system often require recovering its architecture as it is implemented.

Architecture recovery may be achieved using a bottom-up process that starts from source code to progressively construct a more abstract representation of the system [5]. In this context, various clustering-based approaches have been proposed and discussed [5 and 7]. However, these approaches generally rely on properties such as high-cohesion and low-coupling to reconstruct architectures (e.g., [6, 8]) and they do not consider the architectural style of the analyzed system. Our focus in this paper is the recovery of layered architectures as the layered style is a widely used pattern to structure large software systems. Some approaches were proposed to reconstruct layered architectures (e.g., [9-15]). However, most of these approaches propose greedy algorithms that partition elements of the analyzed system into layers using some heuristics or some particular criterion (e.g., the number of fan-in and fan-out dependencies of a module [12, 13]). This may result in partitions with very few layers (e.g., in case of a heuristic based on highly connected modules [10, 15]) or too many layers (e.g., in case of heuristics to resolve cyclic dependencies [11]) which may be too permissive with violations of the style's constraints.

In this paper, we propose an approach that aims at recovering the layered architecture of object oriented systems while relying on: 1) a set of constraints that convey the essence of the layered architectures and 2) the user's input which reveals how strictly he applied the layered principles when designing a given system. Thus, we analyze the layered style and extract a set of principles that we use to define cost factors corresponding to possible types of assignments of dependent packages to the layers of a given system. These cost factors were used to formulate the layering recovery problem as a quadratic assignment problem (QAP), a well-established combinatorial optimization formulation which has been used to model problems such as layout design or resource allocation. Experimentation with the approach on four open source projects yielded interesting results and observations.

The main contributions of this paper are: 1) the formalization of a layered architecture as a special case of a QAP; 2) an algorithm that solves the QAP to recover layered architectures; and 3) an evaluation on four open source projects. The paper is organized as follows. Section 2 discusses the layered style and the limitations of existing approaches to recover such architectures. Section 3 introduces the layering principles that we retained from our analysis of this style. In accordance with these principles, we define in section 4 a set of cost factors related to layers' assignments of dependent packages and we formulate the layering recovery problem as a special case of the QAP. Section 5 discusses the experimentation results. Related works are discussed in section 6 and we conclude and outline some future works in section 7.

2   Background and Limitations of Existing Approaches

2.1   Analysis of the Layered Style

To analyze the layered style, we studied many reference books and papers (e.g., [1-3, 10-18]). The layered style promotes a set of quality attributes which include reuse, portability and maintainability [1-3]. It is an organized hierarchy where each layer is providing services to the layer above it and serves as a client to the layer be-low [1]. Different strategies can be used to partition a software system into layers. The most common layering strategies are the responsibility-based and the reuse-based layering strategies [16]. The responsibility-based strategy aims at grouping compo-nents of the system according to their responsibility and assigning each responsibility group to a layer. The reuse-based layering strategy aims at grouping components of the system according to their level of reuse and assigning the most reusable compo-nents (through applications) to the bottom layers.

In an ideal layered architecture, a layer may only use services of the next lower layer. This is referred to as strict [3] or closed [17] layering and is often violated in practice. For example, the dependence of a layer to much lower layers is a violation (named a skip-call violation in [10] and layer bridging in [2]) that is considered as a regular feature in open [17] or relaxed [3] layering. On the other hand, intra-dependencies, which are dependencies between services of the same layer, are not recommended [2, 18] but can be implemented under considerations such as portability [2]. Exceptionally, a layer may need to rely on a service offered by an upper layer. These back-calls [10] are discussed in [2] as "upward usage" and should be rare as they threaten the quality attributes promoted by the layered style.

2.2   Limitations of Existing Approaches to Recover Layered Architectures

Based on the above analysis of the layered style, the structure of a layered architecture must be a directed acyclic graph or at least a directed graph with very few cycles con-necting different layers. The existence of cyclic dependencies between entities of the system (i.e., packages) makes it difficult to identify its layers [11]. Hence most of the approaches that were proposed to recover software layers focused their effort on pro-posing methods and heuristics to handle entities involved in cyclic dependencies (e.g., [10, 11, 15]). To illustrate the limitations of these approaches, we will use as an ex-ample the software system illustrated by Fig. 1(a). The latter displays a dependency graph where nodes are packages of the system and edges are dependencies between these packages. The weight of a dependency between two packages is derived from the number of dependencies between their respective classes.

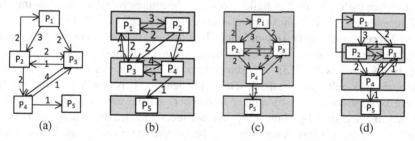

Fig. 1. An example of a system, its architecture and the layering obtained applying different existing approaches

Fig. 1(b) shows the expected layered architecture of our example system. Using a clustering algorithm that relies on modularity (e.g., [6, 8]), the recovered architecture of the system is depicted in Fig. 1(c). The clustering, in this case, puts all packages involved in a cyclic dependency in the same layer/cluster as they are tightly coupled. This is also the case for approaches relying on strongly connected components (e.g., [10, 15]). Other approaches use some heuristic to resolve cyclic dependencies and then assign packages to layers using a depth traversal of the resulting dependency graph. Using such approach as in [11], the recovered architecture of our example system is depicted in Fig. 1(d): it possesses too many layers and may be too permissive with violations such as skip-calls and back-calls.

In our example system, the architect defined three responsibilities embodied in the sets $\{P_1, P_2\}$, $\{P_3, P_4\}$ and $\{P_5\}$. He then assigned each set to a layer according to its abstraction level (Fig. 1(b)). In doing so, the architect applied the responsibility-based strategy while trying to best comply with the layered style constraints. Hence, to obtain the most accurate results (i.e., a layering as in Fig. 1(b)), the layering recovery approach proposed in this paper is based on the principles of the layering style and on how strictly the architect applied them when designing his system.

3   Principles for Layers Recovery

Applying the layered style means partitioning the system into a set of layers that must be ordered according to the abstraction criterion that rules the flow of communication between components of the system. This observation encompasses two fundamental principles that should guide both design and recovery of layered architectures. These two principles are discussed in details in [27]:

- **The Layer Abstraction Uniformity**: This principle states that components of the same layer must be at the same abstraction level so that the layer has a precise meaning. The level of abstraction of a component often refers to its conceptual distance from the "physical" components of the system [3], i.e. hardware, database, files and network. Components at the highest levels are application specific; they generally contain the visible functionalities provided by the system. This principle led to many algorithms that build layered architectures based on a depth-traversal of dependency graphs built from the studied system (e.g., [10-12, 19]).
- **The Incremental Layer Dependency**: This principle is related to the "ideal layering" property that states that a component in a layer (j) must only rely on services of the layer below ($j-1$) [3]. This principle is the one that is mostly violated, either through back-calls, skip-calls or intra-dependencies. It is worth pointing out that there is no clear consensus among researchers on the use of intra-dependencies which are accepted by some [20] and not recommended by others [2, 18]. Our analysis of the various descriptions of the layered style and several open source projects led us to conclude that the acceptance of the intra-dependencies depend on the granularity of the components (e.g., packages) of the layer: the higher the granularity, the lower the number of intra-dependencies. The incremental dependency property should thus be stated in a way that allows the intra-dependencies and the

skip-calls and—to some extent—back-call violations. Hence, we formulate this property as "components of layer *j-1* are mainly geared towards offering services to components of layer *j*". This means that, for a given layered system, the number of skip-call and back-call dependencies must be much lower than the number of downward dependencies between adjacent layers and intra-dependencies.

In the context of this paper, we focus on object oriented systems and we work at the package level; i.e., we rely on existing decomposition of object oriented systems into packages. To comply with the first principle, the packages of the same layer should be at the same distance from the "physical" components of the system. However, the existence of back-call and skip-call dependencies introduces a discrepancy between the packages' distances, even when they belong to the same layer. Hence, compliance with the first principle derives largely from compliance with the second principle (i.e., incremental layer dependency). The latter will be used to formulate the layered architecture recovery problem as a QAP in the following section.

4   Translating the Layering Recovery into a Quadratic Semi-Assignment Problem

To formalize the incremental layer dependency principle, we define a number of cost factors related to layers assignment of two dependent packages. These cost factors are used to formulate the problem of recovering layered architectures as a special case of the QAP known as the Quadratic Semi-Assignment Problem (QSAP) [21].

4.1   Cost Factors for Layers Assignment

Let packages i and j be two distinct packages of the system with a directed dependency from i to j. The dependency between two packages is derived from the dependencies between their respective classes and it includes class references, inheritance, method invocation and parameters. Let c_{kl} be the cost of assigning packages i and j to layers k and l, respectively. Following the incremental layer dependency principle, we distinguish four possible types of layers' assignments for packages i and j:

- Adjacent layers assignment: in this case $k = l+1$; this is the optimal and desirable assignment of two dependent packages and thus, has no cost attached to it ($c_{kl} = 0$).
- Same layer assignment: in this case $k = l$; this introduces an intra-dependency which is not recommended, unless there is a system portability concern, and has a non-zero cost $c_{kl} = \gamma$ attached to it.
- Skip layers assignment: in this case $k \geq l+2$; i.e., this introduces a skip-call dependency that can be tolerated (e.g., for performance reasons [4]) in small numbers and has a non-zero cost $c_{kl} = \alpha$ attached to it.
- Back layers assignment: in this case $k \leq l-1$; this introduces a back-call dependency that can hamper the quality attributes promoted by the layered style and is thus assigned a non-zero cost $c_{kl} = \beta$.

Consider the layered system illustrated in Fig. 2(a). The assignment of packages P_1 and P_2 to layers L_4 and L_3, respectively, has a cost value of β because of the back-call dependency relating P_2 to P_1. The assignment of packages P_1 and P_5 to layers L_4 and L_1, respectively, has a cost value of $2*\alpha$ because it introduces a skip-call dependency having a weight of 2. The assignment of packages P_2 and P_3 to the same layer L_3, has a cost value of γ because of the intra-dependency relating P_2 to P_1. The other assignments do not introduce any additional skip-calls, back-calls or intra-dependencies. Hence, the total cost of this layered system is: $(\gamma + 2*\alpha + \beta)$.

In accordance with the incremental layer dependency principle, we want to minimize the number of skip-calls and back-calls and the number of intra-dependencies. This means that, apart from the adjacent layers assignment as described above, we must minimize the number of the other assignment types. However, in practice, intra-dependencies and skip-calls are more accepted than back-calls which lead to a poorly structured system. Furthermore, according to the analysis of the open or relaxed layering ([3, 17]), skip-calls are more often used and tolerated in practice than intra-dependencies. Accordingly, we make the assumption that the values of the cost factors γ, α and β should be constrained as follows: $\alpha < \gamma < \beta$. This assumption should be validated through experimentation by analyzing a number of software systems purported to be all 1) of a layered style, and 2) of good quality.

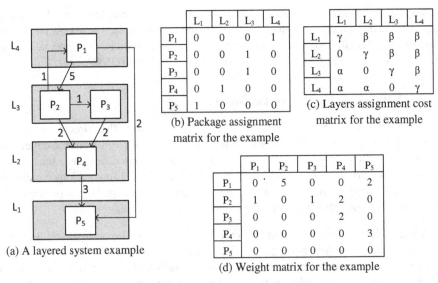

(b) Package assignment matrix for the example

	L_1	L_2	L_3	L_4
P_1	0	0	0	1
P_2	0	0	1	0
P_3	0	0	1	0
P_4	0	1	0	0
P_5	1	0	0	0

(c) Layers assignment cost matrix for the example

	L_1	L_2	L_3	L_4
L_1	γ	β	β	β
L_2	0	γ	β	β
L_3	α	0	γ	β
L_4	α	α	0	γ

(a) A layered system example

(d) Weight matrix for the example

	P_1	P_2	P_3	P_4	P_5
P_1	0	5	0	0	2
P_2	1	0	1	2	0
P_3	0	0	0	2	0
P_4	0	0	0	0	3
P_5	0	0	0	0	0

Fig. 2. An example of a layered system and its related matrices

4.2 Layers Recovery as a Quadratic Semi-Assignment Problem

Recovering the layered architecture of a given system consists in finding a mapping function that assigns each package to a given layer while minimizing the intra-, skip-call and back-call dependencies as discussed in the previous section. Let m be the number of packages and n the number of layers of the system under analysis. Let w_{ij}

be the weight of the directed dependency relating package i to package j. Recall that the dependency between two packages derives from the dependencies between their respective classes. Let W ($[W]_{ij} = w_{ij}$) be the $m \times m$ dependency weight matrix, and C ($[C]_{kl} = c_{kl}$) be the $n \times n$ matrix of layer assignment costs. Fig. 2(c) displays the layer assignment cost matrix and Fig. 2(d) displays the weight matrix corresponding to the system of Fig. 2(a). Let x_{ik} be the binary decision variable representing the assignment of package i to layer k (i.e., x_{ik} is set to 1 if package i is assigned to layer k, otherwise to 0), and let X ($[X]_{ik} = x_{ik}$) be the $m \times n$ package assignment matrix. Fig. 2(b) displays the package assignment matrix corresponding to the system of Fig. 2(a).

The layering recovery problem can be expressed as the following QSAP:

$$\min f(X) = \sum_{i,j=1}^{m} \sum_{k,l=1}^{n} w_{ij} \, c_{kl} \, x_{ik} \, x_{jl} \tag{1}$$

$$x_{ik} \in \{0, 1\} \quad i = 1, \ldots, m, \ k = 1, \ldots, n \tag{2}$$

$$\sum_{k=1}^{n} x_{ik} = 1 \quad i = 1, \ldots, m \tag{3}$$

The quadratic cost function of Eq. 1, called the layering cost in our context, defines a penalty for each possible set of assignments of packages to layers. Thus, the penalty of assigning package i to layer k, if a package j is assigned to layer l corresponds to $w_{ij} * c_{kl}$. Eq. 3 constrains the possible solutions to Eq. 1 by stating that a package may be assigned only to one layer.

4.3 Solving the Layers Recovery Problem

Because the NP-hard clustering problem is a particular case of the QSAP, finding a globally optimal solution for this problem is also a difficult task. However, since it plays a central role in many applications, much effort has been spent to solve this problem efficiently. Exact methods proposed for the QSAP, which guarantee the global optimum, include the cutting-plane and branch-and-bound algorithms. However, these methods are generally unable to solve large problems (i.e., $m \geq 20$). For large problem instances, heuristic algorithms like tabu search, local improvement methods, simulated annealing and genetic algorithms have been proposed [21]. Among these, the tabu search method [22] and the local improvement method are known to be the most accurate heuristic methods to solve the QAP. Hence, to solve the layering recovery problem, we adapted the tabu search method using our layering cost (Eq.1) as a fitness function. Briefly, the tabu search [23] starts with a feasible solution as the current solution. At each iteration, neighbors of the current solution are explored through some moves and the best neighbor is accepted as the current solution provided the related move does not belong to a tabu list. The latter records moves which are marked as tabu (i.e. forbidden) to prevent cycling and to escape from local optima. The search process stops when a termination criterion is met.

Fig. 3 gives a simplified view of our adaptation of the tabu search technique to the layering problem. The algorithm, takes as input: 1) an initial layered partition of the system under analysis; 2) a set of values for the cost factors; and 3) the maximum number of iterations (max_it) after which the algorithm terminates. The initial partition is a 3-layer solution where packages are randomly assigned to these layers. The initial partition is then considered as the current and the best solution of the algorithm (lines 1 to 2). In the following iterations (lines 5 to 18), all the neighboring solutions of the current solution are explored to find a better layering. A neighbor is computed by moving a single package from a layer A to a layer B, provided these two layers are different (line 7). This neighbor is considered as a candidate solution if it is produced using a package move that does not belong to the tabu list (lines 8 to 10). Note that a package move may introduce an additional layer (i.e., the final layering may have more than 3 layers). The candidate solution having the lowest layering cost value is the best candidate solution and it is accepted as the current solution (line 12) to be used for the next iteration. In this case, the tabu list is updated to include the package move that led to this solution (line 13). It is also accepted as the best solution if its cost is lower than the current best-known solution (lines 14 to 16).

```
Input: initialLayeredPartition, max_it,   γ, α, β
Output: LayeredSolution
1. currentSolution ← initialLayeredPartition
2. bestSolution ← currentSolution
3. tabuList ← null
4. K ← 0
5. while (K < max_it){
6.         candidates ← null
7.         for each neighborSolution of currentSolution {
8.                 if (neighborSolution is produced using a move not belonging to
tabuList){
9.                 candidates ← candidates + neighborSolution
10.         }
11.    } //end for
12.    currentSolution ← locateBestSolution(candidates)
13.    tabuList ← updateTabuList(currentSolution.move)
14.    if (LC(currentSolution) < LC(bestSolution)) {
15.       bestSolution ← currentSolution
16.    }
17.    K ← K +1
18. } //end while
19. return bestSolution
```

Fig. 3. A high level view of the layering algorithm

5   Experimentation with the Approach

To experiment our QSAP formulation of the layering recovery problem, we implemented a tool within the Eclipse™ IDE. This tool is made of two modules. The first module was built on top of the MoDisco open source tool [24] which enables to

analyze source code files of the system under study and to generate platform independent representations that are compliant with the Knowledge Discovery Metamodel
(KDM). The KDM was introduced by the OMG as a standard and platform-
independent meta-model for representing legacy systems [25]. In our context, the
KDM representation is used by our module to extract the system's facts, i.e. packages
and their dependencies. These facts are used to build the initial partition that is the
input to the second module. This module implements our layering algorithm for
which we set the maximum number of iterations to 1000 and the tabu list length to 10
(i.e., the tabu list records the last ten best packages' moves). Results were computed
on a 2.8 GHz Intel octo-core CPU with 16Gb of RAM and took less than a second for
any of the systems. For each system and setup, we ran 50 times the algorithm and
retained the best (lowest layering cost) result.

5.1   Research Questions and Experimental Setup

Experimentations with our approach aimed at answering the following questions:

*1) What are the (relative) values of the cost factors (γ, α, β) that best correspond to
the common understanding of the layered style?* For any given layered software sys-
tem, assuming we already know its layered architecture, we look for the values of the
cost factors that yield a set of layers that best match the known architecture of the
system. However, as the system may be an imperfect application of the layered style,
we need to look into a set of well-designed software systems that are known to be
layered systems. The answer to this question will help assessing the extent to which
the layering principles, as discussed in section 3, are applied by designers.

*2) How does the layering cost evolve across revisions of a software system and
what does it tell us about the architectural evolution of the system?* This question is
related to two aspects: 1) the stability of our layering recovery algorithm and 2) the
stability of the set of values of the cost factors that yield the layering that matches the
known architecture of the system across its revisions. The latter aspect can be reph-
rased into *"when a layered system evolves, does it maintain the same level of conformity to the layering principles?"*.

To answer these questions, we carried out an experiment on four different open
source projects and four different versions of one of these projects. Some characteristics of these projects are given in Table 1. All the projects (Apache Ant, JUnit, JFree-
Chart and JHotDraw) are purported layered systems that are actively maintained and
that were analyzed in related work (e.g., [11, 12]). We performed several executions
on each of these projects using different values for the layering cost factors γ, α, β.
For lack of space, we present the results for 5 setups. Recall that downward adjacent
dependencies are rewarded and, hence, no cost factor was associated to them. Briefly,
setups 1 and 2 penalize more skip-calls than intra-dependencies while setups 3, 4 and
5 penalize more intra-dependencies than skip-calls. Thus setups 1 and 2 are appropriate for systems that favor portability over reuse. Conversely, setups 3, 4 and 5 are
appropriate for systems that comply with a reuse-based layering strategy where the
most (re)used packages are assigned to bottom layers. Setups 3, 4 and 5 differ in the
value they assign to the back-call cost β and they are meant to analyze the extent to

which the back-calls are tolerated in the analyzed systems. It should be noted that we performed tests using other setups where the cost γ of intra-dependencies was set to zero. However, in this case, the algorithm behaves as a modularity-based clustering algorithm and it assigns all highly dependent packages to the same layer.

To find out which ones of the setups return layered solutions that best match the actual layered organizations of the analyzed systems, we compare the returned solution for each setup and system with an authoritative decomposition of the system. We rely on previous works (e.g. [15 and 26]) to specify the authoritative decomposition of the analyzed systems (e.g., Apache Ant and JUnit). For systems for which the authoritative decomposition was not available (e.g., JHotDraw and JFreeChart), we had 3 PhD students with intensive experience in software design and with a good knowledge of these systems to manually decompose them. We used the harmonic mean (F-measure) of precision and recall as introduced in [12] to evaluate each solution with respect to both correctness and completeness of its layers compared to the authoritative decomposition. Thus, we compute the precision as the number of packages correctly assigned by our tool over the total number of packages assigned by our tool. We compute the recall as the number of packages correctly assigned by our tool over the number of the packages assigned to layers in the authoritative decomposition.

Table 1. Statistics of the analyzed open source projects

Project	Number of files	LOC	Numb. of packages	Package dependencies
Apache Ant	681	171 491	67	229
JUnit 4.10	162	10 402	28	106
JFreeChart 1.0.14	596	209 711	37	207
JHotDraw 6.0.b1	498	68 509	17	72
JHotDraw 7.0.6	310	51 801	24	89
JHotDraw 7.4.1	585	111 239	62	365
JHotDraw 7.6	680	118 938	65	358

5.2   Results and Discussions

Table 2 summarizes the results of executing our layering algorithm on the analyzed projects using 5 setups. The first column indicates for each setup the values of the cost factors. For each solution returned by the algorithm, Table 2 displays: 1) the layering cost (LC); 2) the number of layers (NL); 3) the total weight of all dependencies relating adjacent layers (Adj); 4) the total weight of all intra-dependencies (Intra); 5) the total weight of all skip-calls (Skip); 6) the total weight of all back-calls (Back); and 7) the F-measure. Recall that the layering cost is the value of the quadratic function in Eq. 1. Cells that are greyed in Table 2 correspond to the solutions with the highest F-measures.

As shown by Table 2, for Apache Ant and JUnit, the layering solution that best matches the actual layering of the system is returned using setup 2. In general, the most accurate results are produced by our algorithm for these two systems when using setups where the intra-dependencies cost γ is less than the skip-calls cost α (e.g., setups 1 and 2). This means that the designers of these two systems have favored intra-dependencies over skip-calls and back-calls. This is consistent with the fact that both Apache Ant and JUnit are frameworks that target different platforms and, thus, portability is one of the concerns that drive their design. As for JFreeChart, we obtained the best match using setup 5. JFreeCHart contains several subsystems that are composed

Table 2. Results returned by the layering recovery algorithm

		Ant	JFreeC	JUnit	JHD.60b1	JHD.706	JHD.741	JHD.76
Setup 1 γ=1 α=2 β=4	LC	569	1069	152	383	385	1176	1089
	NL	3	3	3	3	3	3	3
	Adj	153	1018	234	864	623	1547	1522
	Intra	521	629	110	335	353	1036	909
	Skip	0	64	3	4	8	12	6
	Back	12	78	9	10	4	29	42
	F-measure	74	35.97	57	58	29	22	21
Setup 2 γ=1 α=2 β=15	LC	692	1411	247	493	429	1316	1245
	NL	3	3	3	3	3	3	3
	Adj	150	450	168	864	623	1362	1325
	Intra	557	1332	181	335	353	1247	1141
	Skip	0	2	3	4	8	12	7
	Back	9	5	4	10	4	3	6
	F-measure	76	59	67	58	29	12	12
Setup 3 γ=2 α=1 β=4	LC	102	1476	234	587	572	1910	1719
	NL	4	4	3	3	4	4	5
	Adj	156	998	248	887	665	1622	1580
	Intra	417	409	78	213	222	455	526
	Skip	48	290	14	97	92	396	275
	Back	36	92	16	16	9	151	98
	F-measure	59	13	53	82	87	51	60
Setup 4 γ=2 α=1 β=15	LC	120	2368	357	715	589	2263	2039
	NL	4	4	4	3	4	4	4
	Adj	152	870	234	891	647	1396	1398
	Intra	494	637	109	239	234	993	874
	Skip	36	224	4	72	106	232	201
	Back	12	58	9	11	1	3	6
	F-measure	65	18	53	76	91	75	70
Setup 5 γ=2 α=1 β=20	LC	137	2725	402	770	594	2278	2069
	NL	3	3	4	3	4	4	4
	Adj	149	474	234	891	647	1396	1398
	Intra	533	1277	109	239	234	993	874
	Skip	36	31	4	72	106	232	201
	Back	9	7	9	11	1	3	6
	F-measure	23	65	53	76	91	75	70

of subsets of highly dependent packages; i.e., it includes a high number of cyclic dependencies. In this case, the layering result that matches best the authoritative architecture is produced using a setup where the back-calls cost β is set to a very high value compared to the intra-dependencies cost γ (e.g., setup 5). Finally, in the case of JHotDraw, we hypothesized that the best matches for the 4 analyzed versions would be produced using the same setup. As displayed by Table 2, this is the case for JHotDraw 7.0.6, 7.4.1 and 7.6 for which the best results are generated using both setups 4 and 5. But, for JHotDraw 60b1, the best match is generated using setup 3. This is due to: 1) JHotDraw 60b1 containing more layering violations compared to the 3 other versions; and 2) each of the subsequent versions 7.0.6 and 7.4 introducing substantial changes to the framework. Yet, the setups producing the best matches for all JHotDraw versions are the setups that enforce more strictly the layering principles as discussed in this paper (i.e., $\alpha < \gamma < \beta$).

Based on these observations and on the fact that JHotDraw was designed as an example for a well-designed framework, we hypothesized that the setup that produces the best matches for most of the versions of JHotDraw is the one that corresponds to the common understanding of the layered style constraints. This is the case of Setup 4 (i.e., the results of setup 4 and 5 are the same but we consider the first setup that gives most of the best results). To verify our hypothesis, we analyzed the density of violations found in each project. To do this, for each solution that best matches the system's architecture (greyed cells in Table 2), we compared the number of each type of dependency (i.e., intra-dependencies, skip-calls and back-calls) to the total number of dependencies in the system. Fig. 4 displays the dependencies by type for the best matched solution of each project. JFreeChart have the highest percentage of intra-dependencies (71%) relative to the other dependencies. JHotDraw 6.0.b1 has the lowest percentage of intra-dependencies (17%) while JHotDraw 7.0.6 has the lowest percentage of back-calls (0.1%). For the four versions of JHotDraw, the density of violations relative to the project size is smaller than the density of violations in the two of the three projects (i.e., JUnit and JFreeChart). These findings confirm our hypothesis which is consistent with the fact that JHotDraw is known to be well-designed. They also strongly suggest that setup 4 is the one that most corresponds to the common understanding of the styles constraints with respect to our first research question. This will be investigated more in future works.

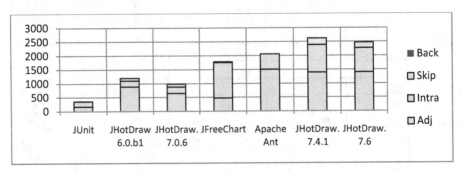

Fig. 4. Dependencies by type for the best matched solution of each project

Regarding our second question, the analysis of four versions of JHotDraw led us to some interesting observations. The best solutions for both versions 6.0.b1 and 7.0.6 have approximately the same layering cost (LC). Furthermore, the layering solutions are stable, i.e., an existing package in both versions is assigned to the same layer in the two best layering solutions. The same observations were made when we compared the results for versions 7.4.1 and 7.6. This confirms the stability of our layering recovery algorithm. Moreover, for the versions 7.0.6, 7.4.1 and 7.6., the best results are returned by the same setup. This suggests the stability of the set of cost values that yield the layering that matches best the architecture of the system across its revisions. It also suggests that JHotDraw maintains the same level of conformity to the layering principles through its evolution. To confirm this, we analyzed eight (8) versions of JHotDraw. Fig. 5 displays for each of these versions their layering cost (LC) using setup 4 and their total weight of package dependencies. Interestingly, Fig. 5 reveals that the evolution of the layering cost of JHotDraw through these 8 versions followed a linear trend line. This strongly suggests that JHotDraw maintains the same level of conformity to the layering principles through its evolution. Future work will investigate whether this trend line applies or not to other layered systems.

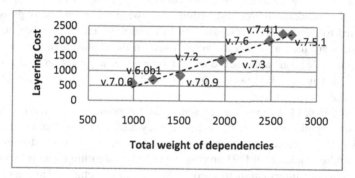

Fig. 5. Evolution of the layering cost of JHotDraw using setup 4

5.3   Threats to Validity

Conclusion Validity: To find out which setups return the most accurate layered solutions, we compared these solutions to authoritative architectures which come in part from the manual work of students. This issue is related to the lack of comparison baselines in the software architecture community. However, the students who participated to the experimentation were chosen based on their experience and knowledge of the analyzed systems.

Internal Validity: The parameters of the tabu search were set through preliminary tests and may not have the best possible values. In any case, as a meta-heuristic, tabu search cannot guarantee a global optimal solution. We were however able to confirm that for the smallest system (JHotDraw 60b1), the algorithm was returning the global optimum. Indeed, with 3 layers and 17 packages, it was possible to examine and evaluate (with a run time of about half an hour) each of the 3^{17} possible solutions.

External Validity: The experiment has been conducted on a sample of four open source Java projects. While all these projects are known to be layered systems, the observed results may not be generalizable to other projects. To minimize the threats, we have analyzed several versions of a layered system that is purported to be of good quality (i.e., JHotDraw). We plan as a future work to analyze other existing layered systems including commercial software systems.

6   Related Work

The work in this paper is related to the approaches proposed to recover layered architectures (e.g., [9-15]). Most of these approaches rely on some criterion or heuristics (e.g. [10-14]) in the process. Muller et al. [9] propose an approach aiming at supporting users in discovering, restructuring and analyzing subsystem structures using a reverse engineering tool. The proposed process involves the identification of the layered subsystem structures. The layered structure is obtained through the aggregation of system's entities into building blocks using composition operations based on principles such as low coupling and high cohesion. Schmidt et al. [28] introduced a framework that supports the reconstruction of software architectures. A greedy algorithm is used to generate clusters based on low coupling and high cohesion criteria. These clusters are then assigned to layers based on their ratio of fan-in and fan-out. Unlike [9] and [28], our approach does not include an aggregation phase since we work at the package level. However, our approach can be applied at a lower level of granularity (i.e., at class level).

Hassan and Holt [14] propose a semi-automatic approach to reconstruct the architecture of web applications. For this purpose, they analyze the source code to extract artifacts which are clustered according to some heuristics and refined using human expertise. Andreopoulos et al [13] propose a clustering algorithm which exploits both static and dynamic information to recover layered architectures. This approach assigns highly interdependent files to top layers and less interdependent files to bottom layers. Laval et al. [11] propose an approach which resolves cyclic dependencies and decomposes a system into layers. They rely on two heuristics to find undesired cyclic dependencies which are ignored when building layers of the system. In [10], the authors proposed 3 layering principles (skip-call, back-call and cyclic dependency) and a set of metrics that measure the violation of these principles. Although these principles are focused on detecting violations, they are related to the principles discussed in this paper. In [12], a semi-automatic approach is proposed to identify software layers. Classes that are used by many other classes are grouped in the lowest layer while classes that rely on many other classes are grouped in the highest layer. The remaining classes are assigned to a middle layer. The same technique is used in [29] where a lexical-based clustering is performed to further decompose each layer into modules. In [11, 12, 13 and 29], it is assumed that a module that does not have fan-out dependencies belongs to the lowest-level layer and conversely a module that does not have fan-in dependencies belongs to the highest-level layer. However, a module encapsulating a common subtask exclusive to components of a middle-level layer, will not have any fan-out dependency but still belongs to this middle-level layer. Likewise, a module that starts some specific service of a middle-layer may not have any fan-in dependency but still belongs to this middle-level layer. Unlike all these approaches, we do not rely on any heuristic or criteria. Our approach relies on the constraints of the layering style and a set of parameters that express how rigorously the designer applied these constraints.

7   Conclusion

Recovering architectural views from existing software systems remains a challenging problem and will remain a topical issue in software engineering. In this paper, we proposed an approach to recover the layered architecture of object oriented systems using the principles of the layering style and the designer's input which describes how strictly he applied these principles when designing the analyzed system. We revisited and analyzed the layered style and retained two important principles. These principles were translated into a set of layers assignment cost factors that help formulating the layering recovery problem as a specific case of QAP, namely a Quadratic Semi-Assignment Problem (QSAP). To experiment this formulation, we implemented a tool that extracts packages' dependencies from object oriented java systems, and an algorithm to solve the layering recovery QSAP. We tested the approach on four open source Java projects using several setups with different sets of values for the layering cost factors. This experimentation yielded interesting results.

While the results of the approach are promising, we plan to extend it in different ways. In the short-term, we want to handle issues related to library components also called omnipresent modules. Library components obscure the system's structure if considered during the decomposition of the system [9]. These components may be clustered into a vertical layer (called transversal layer in [2]) to ease the recovery of the layered architecture. In the mid- to long-term, we need to perform more experiments and analysis to properly tune the cost factors. We would also like to experiment on domain-specific systems and find out if particular setups (i.e., a set of cost factors) are related to specific domains or classes of systems. In this context, the availability of such systems and some architecture description of these systems is a challenging issue. As a future work, we plan to investigate how a given setup can be enforced so that an architect is notified when some changes made to the system introduce a "deviation" from that setup. Finally, we plan to strategy to experiment the approach on software systems implemented using other programming languages and paradigms.

References

1. Shaw, M., Garlan, D.: Software Architecture: Perspectives on an Emerging Discipline. Prentice Hall (1996)
2. Clements, P., Bachmann, F., Bass, L., Garlan, D., Ivers, J., Little, R., Nord, R., Stafford, J.: Documenting Software Architectures: Views and Beyond. Addison-Wesley (2003)

3. Buschmann, F., Meunier, R., Rohnert, H., Sommerlad P., Stal, M.: Pattern-Oriented Software Architecture: A System of Patterns. John Wiley & Sons (1996)

4. Harris, D.R., Reubenstein, H.B., Yeh, A.S.: Recognizers for Extracting Architectural Features from Source Code. The 2nd WCRE, pp. 252–261 (1995)

5. Ducasse, S., Pollet, D.: Software Architecture Reconstruction: A Process-Oriented Taxonomy. IEEE Trans. on Soft. Eng. 35(4), 573–591 (2009)

6. Mitchell, B.S., Mancoridis, S.: On the Evaluation of the Bunch Search-Based Software Modularization Algorithm. Soft Comput. 12(1), 77–93 (2007)

7. Maqbool, O., Babri, H.A.: Hierarchical Clustering for Software Architecture Recovery. IEEE Transactions on Software Engineering 33(11), 759–780 (2007)

8. Lung, C.H., Zaman, M., Nandi, A.: Applications of Clustering Techniques to Software Partitioning, Recovery and Restructuring. JSS Journal 73, 227–244 (2004)

9. Muller, H.A., Orgun, M.A., Tilley, S.R., Uhl, J.S.: A reverse engineering approach to subsystem structure identification. Journal of Software Maintenance 5(4), 181–204 (1993)

10. Sarkar, S., Maskeri, G., Ramachandran, S.: Discovery of architectural layers and measurement of layering violations in source code. JSS Journal 82(11), 1891–1905 (2009)

11. Laval, J., Anquetil, N., Bhatti, M.U., Ducasse, S.: OZONE: Layer Identification in the presence of Cyclic Dependencies. submitted to Science of Computer Programming (2012)

12. Scanniello, G., D'Amico, A., D'Amico, C., D'Amico, T.: Architectural layer recovery for software system understanding and evolution. SPE Journal 40(10), 897–916 (2010)

13. Andreopoulos, B., Aijun, A., Tzerpos, V., Wang, X.: Clustering large software systems at multiple layers. Information and Software Technology 49(3), 244–254 (2007)

14. Hassan, AE., Holt, RC.: Architecture recovery of web applications. In: The 24th International Conference on Software Engineering, pp. 349–359. ACM Press, New York (2002)

15. Sangal, N., Jordan, E., Sinha, V., Jackson, D.: Using dependency models to manage complex software architecture. In: Proceedings of OOPSLA 2005, pp. 167–176 (2005)

16. Eeles, P.: Layering Strategies. Rational Software White Paper, TP 199, 08/01 (2002)

17. Szyperski, C.A.: Component Software. Addison Wesley (1998)

18. Bourquin, F., Keller, R.K.: High-impact refactoring based on architecture violations. In: The 11th CSMR, pp. 149–158 (2007)

19. El-Boussaidi, G., Boaye-Belle, A., Vaucher, S., Mili, H.: Reconstructing architectural views from legacy systems. In: The 19th WCRE (2012)

20. Avgeriou, P., Zdun, U.: Architectural patterns revisited-a pattern language. In: EuroPlop (2005)

21. Pardalos, P.M., Rendl, F., Wolkowicz, H.: The quadratic assignment problem-a survey and recent developments. In: DIMACS. Americ. Mathemat. Society, vol. 16, pp. 1–42 (1994)

22. Skorin-Kapov, J.: Tabu search applied to the quadratic assignment problem. ORSA Journal on Computing 2(1), 33–45 (1990)

23. Glover, F., Laguna, M.: Tabu Search. Kluwer Academic Publishers, Boston (1997)

24. MoDisco site. http://www.eclipse.org/MoDisco/

25. OMG Specifications. http://www.omg.org/

26. Barros, MdO, Farzat, FdA, Travassos, G.H.: Learning from optimization: A case study with Apache Ant. Information and Software Technology 57, 684–704 (2015)

27. Boaye, B.A., El-Boussaidi, G., Desrosiers, C., Mili, H.: The layered architecture revisited is it an optimization problem. In: Proc. 25th Int. Conf. SEKE, pp. 344–349 (2013)

28. Schmidt, F., MacDonell, S.G., Connor, A.M.: An automatic architecture reconstruction and refactoring framework. In: SERA 2011, pp. 95–111 (2011)

29. Scanniello, G., D'Amico, A., D'Amico, C., D'Amico, T.: Using the Kleinberg algorithm and vector space model for software system clustering. In: ICPC, pp. 180–189 (2010)

Services and Ecosystems

Design of a Domain-Specific Language Based on a Technology-Independent Web Service Framework

Florian Rademacher$^{(\boxtimes)}$, Martin Peters, and Sabine Sachweh

Department of Computer Science, University of Applied Sciences
and Arts Dortmund, Dortmund, Germany
{florian.rademacher,martin.peters,sabine.sachweh}@fh-dortmund.de

Abstract. Nowadays web services gain more and more importance in allowing a standardized access to remote information without being tied to a specific form of presentation. The majority of such data interfaces is either based on the architectural REST style following World Wide Web specifications or the more protocol-oriented SOAP, which allows the definition of XML transfer structures.

In this paper we introduce an extensible framework for the abstraction of technological differences between service technologies like REST and SOAP. It provides the basis for the design of a domain-specific language (DSL), which allows the technology-independent declaration of web services. A code generator derived from the DSL grammar translates the service declarations into corresponding framework elements and creates stub methods for the implementation of the services' business logic.

Keywords: Domain-specific languages · Code generation · Service-oriented architectures · Web services

1 Introduction

The Internet becomes more and more heterogeneous in the way its information are retrieved and processed by users and applications. Web services constitute one established mechanism to provide interfaces to online resources. Clients can access the supplied data in a specified way, process it and propagate changes back to the web service host. REST [1] and SOAP [2] are the web service technologies most commonly applied [3].

REST stands for Representational State Transfer and denotes an architectural style for distributed hypermedia systems. It abstracts from the concrete architectural elements within such systems and introduces *resources* as time dependent mappings to a set of information entities. A resource may be referenced by a Uniform Resource Identifier (URI) like http://www.example.com/resource. Additionally, REST defines a generic interface to resources, consisting of methods like GET for requesting and POST for creating resource *representations*. Within the World Wide Web (WWW), client applications like browsers

© Springer International Publishing Switzerland 2015
D. Weyns et al. (Eds.): ECSA 2015, LNCS 9278, pp. 357–371, 2015.
DOI: 10.1007/978-3-319-23727-5_29

or mobile apps may invoke one of these methods, for example via the Hypertext Transfer Protocol (HTTP), and retrieve a representation from a server hosting a certain resource. XML or JavaScript Object Notation (JSON) [4] are widely used to encode the transmitted representation.

SOAP is another mechanism used to implement web services. Information is solely structured in XML and mostly sent to clients via HTTP. The content of a SOAP message is embraced by an `<Envelope>`-element, which itself consists of at least one `<Body>`-element.

When implementing a web service, the choice of a concrete service technology is crucial from the beginning. Regardless of the purpose a web service may serve, its implementation heavily depends on the applied service technology and thus on how data is transferred between a client and a server. Providing a web service for both, REST and SOAP clients, often results in redundant service implementations, although the semantic of the service is the same.

In this paper we address the problem of semantically equivalent web services, which need to be provided using different service technologies for different types of clients. To do so, an extensible framework that allows the implementation of REST, SOAP and any other kind of web service technology is presented in Section 3. Its utilization automatically leads to reusable code within all provided service interfaces. Starting from the framework, a DSL for the concise and efficient definition of service interfaces is designed in Section 4. Section 5 describes the implementation of a code generator that translates service declarations expressed with the DSL into Java code based on the framework. Service developers only need to implement the declared services' business logic within generated stub methods, which then are accessible for clients through the different service technologies supported by the framework. We show the framework's specification, the DSL design and its usage by means of a case study described in the next section.

2   Case Study

The case study involves a scenario taken from a research project, which focused, among others, on providing a Java EE based infrastructure for the remote maintenance of wastewater treatment systems (WTS). Each WTS communicates with a server platform using a custom communication protocol. WTS owners can monitor their systems' state and change the parameters of a WTS using a mobile app. The server platform acts as an intermediate between mobile clients and WTSs. Figure 1 shows the structure and the participants of the case study in a SoaML diagram [5].

The server platform offers web services for the retrieval and update of a WTS's parameters. These parameters control the behavior of the WTS, e.g. the pressure of its valves. A `ParameterType` is associated with a `ParameterValue` indicating the value's allowed range. The `MobileApp` participant may use the `Parameters` interface to retrieve and update the current parameters of a WTS.

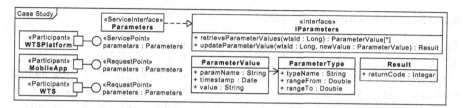

Fig. 1. Structure of the case study. A mobile app and a set of WTSs interact with a server platform for monitoring and maintenance of WTSs via web services.

It communicates with the server platform via REST because of its better integration with the mobile operating system. The control unit of the WTS participant will call updateParameterValue when it was forced to adjust a parameter value due to changing environmental conditions such as temperature variations. WTSs use SOAP for platform interaction due to its advanced QoS support concerning security and reliability of exchanged information [6]. The platform is accessible at http://www.example.com/wts. In case of RESTful communication, an HTTP GET request is issued to www.example.com/wts/{wtsId} to retrieve a WTS's current parameter values. A parameter update is performed by sending PUT to www.example.com/wts/{wtsId}/{paramName} together with the new value. The REST services use JSON as transfer format. In the case of SOAP-based communication, XML packets are transmitted to the server platform via HTTP. Listing 1 and 2 show the data transferred when performing REST- and SOAP-based parameter updates in contrast.

```
{"new_value": "{new_value}"}
```

Listing 1. REST request to update a WTS parameter's value. The new value is sent within a JSON packet.

```
<Envelope><Body><updateParameterValue>
  <wtsId>{wtsId}</wtsId>
  <paramName>{paramName}</paramName>
  <new_value>{new_value}</new_value>
</updateParameterValue></Body></Envelope>
```

Listing 2. Structure of a SOAP packet sent to update a parameter's value.

3   Specification of a Technology-Independent Web Service Framework

Following, an analysis of the WTS platform's architectural requirements and technology-specific aspects of the involved web services is undertaken. Based on the results abstractions are defined, which hide characteristics specific to a certain web service technology from a service developer. The main goal of this section is the specification of a framework that allows the reusable, technology-independent implementation of a web service's business logic, which then may be provided for client access by REST, SOAP or any other kind of technology-dependent service interface.

3.1   Reusable Business Logic

The service framework has to support the reusability of business logic in web services provided by different technologies. For example, the `updatePara-meterValue` service of the case study has to be available via REST (for the mobile app) and SOAP (for a WTS). However, its semantic and functionality is independent of a concrete service technology. To model reusable service implementations, a technology-independent interface for the invocation of a web service's business logic is introduced. It is based on the Command pattern described in [7].

Figure 2 shows the abstract Command-class `Operation` whose `logic` method has to be implemented by a subclass to realize a service's behavior. The technology-independent generalization of the information exchange between an `Operation` and its invokers is realized by two data transfer objects (DTOs). Depending on its communication direction, a DTO implements one of the *marker interfaces* `ItoI` (inbound transfer object for service requests) or `OtoI` (outbound transfer object for service responses). An `Operation` and its DTOs are always specific to a certain web service.

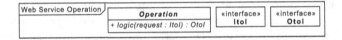

Fig. 2. Technology-independent abstraction of a web service's logic. The `Operation` class contains a service's business logic. The marker interfaces `ItoI` and `OtoI` subsume DTOs used for information exchange between service invoker and business logic.

3.2   Support for Arbitrary Web Service Technologies

The case study demands the provisioning of web services following the REST and SOAP paradigms. In Java EE based applications like the WTS platform this is achieved by JAX-RS [8] and JAX-WS [9] compliant implementations. Both specifications define rules on how to implement web services. JAX-RS utilizes class and method annotations like `@Path` and `@GET` for the specification of a REST service's URI and the HTTP method for business logic invocation. In contrast, JAX-WS relies on a Java interface annotated with `@WebService`, which defines the contract for calling a SOAP service's business logic in form of a method marked with `@WebMethod`. This Service Endpoint Interface (SEI) needs to be implemented by a Service Implementation Bean (SIB), i.e. a Java class annotated with `@WebService`. While the SEI specifies the name of the port type, the SIB defines further SOAP-characteristics such as port name, service name and endpoint interface.

However, the service framework has to allow the realization of web service technologies without relying on the existence of frameworks implementing specifications like JAX-RS or JAX-WS. For example, it is conceivable that the WTS

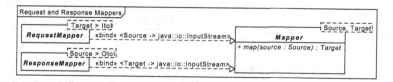

Fig. 3. The abstract `Mapper` class and its subclasses. Request mappers create inbound DTOs from input streams, whereas response mappers map outbound DTOs to technology-dependent client responses.

platform will offer a service interface based on the WebDAV[1] protocol allowing clients to browse connected WTSs and view their current parameters in the form of virtual files. This would require the `RetrieveParameterValues` service described in Section 2 being able to understand requests sent by WebDAV clients and produce corresponding responses.

To support arbitrary web service technologies, the framework applies the Mapper concept as suggested by [10]. Figure 3 shows all components the framework provides for the utilization of the Mapper concept.

An abstract `Mapper` is responsible for the transformation of a `Source` object into a `Target` instance. The depicted subclasses limit the types applicable for both generic parameters in the cases of inbound and outbound traffic conversion. Thus, an inbound request, in the form of a "raw" Java `InputStream`, has to be deserialized into a DTO implementing the `ItoI` interface so that the business logic of a service, located in the appropriate `Operation` subclass, is able to handle it. This conversion is done by a concrete mapper inheriting from `RequestMapper`. The outbound response, resulting from business logic execution, will be serialized from an `OtoI`-marked DTO instance into an `InputStream` and sent back to the requesting client. A technology-dependent subclass of `ResponseMapper` performs the serialization.

Concrete mappers are associated with a set of service `Operations` by an `@Mapper` annotation. It specifies the mapper's direction, i.e. inbound or outbound, the name of the service technology the mapper supports, e.g. "WebDAV", and the Multipurpose Internet Mail Extensions (MIME) type [11] being interpreted or produced. The annotation enables the framework to find and invoke the appropriate mappers when clients access the business logic via different service technologies.

3.3   Service Interfaces

Service interfaces are the key abstractions of the service framework. These classes act as façades between a service client, such as the mobile app or a WTS, and an `Operation` like `UpdateParameterValue`. Figure 4 shows the `ServiceInterface` class.

---

[1] http://www.webdav.org

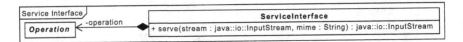

Fig. 4. A service interface launches a service's business logic. It further handles the traffic conversion between client and business logic by calling appropriate mappers.

Each class that receives data directly from a service client has to extend `ServiceInterface` and call the predefined `serve()` method. In case of JAX-RS, this would be all classes annotated with `@Path`. For services compliant with JAX-WS, the SIBs need to derive from `ServiceInterface` and call `serve()`. WebDAV service interfaces would have to be located on a lower level of the communication stack where it is possible to retain the raw network request in the form of a Java `InputStream`.

The `serve()` method takes an inbound stream and a MIME type as its arguments. Depending on this information, the framework invokes the `Mapper` appropriate for technology-dependent inbound and outbound traffic conversion. Every derived `ServiceInterface` class has to be annotated with `@ServiceInterface` to specify the name of the web service technology and the associated `Operation` to handle client requests.

3.4   Framework Overview

Figure 5 shows the interactions between the different framework elements. The interactions are consecutively numbered in their order of occurrence. Three clients issue requests to the WTS platform via REST, WebDAV and SOAP. The eponymous service interfaces forward the raw requests to the framework, which may utilize the appropriate `RequestMappers` to create instances of inbound DTOs. After the mapping process has finished, the `ServiceInterface` will execute the requested service's `Operation`. A resulting outbound DTO is then sent back to the client after it has been mapped to a stream by a technology-specific `ResponseMapper`.

4   Design of a Web Service DSL

To improve the efficiency of implementing web services with the framework and to let a service developer focus on the business logic, a DSL that can be used to declare web services and their technology-dependent interfaces, is introduced. Based on its definition and the framework, infrastructural code for the provisioning of semantically equivalent web services through interfaces of different service technologies can be generated.

In this section, a design model, which outlines the semantic concepts of the language and their relations, is presented first. It is expressed in the form of a "mixed" UML diagram shown in Figure 6. The model utilizes classes to present language concepts and inheritance to cluster sub-concepts, which may be used

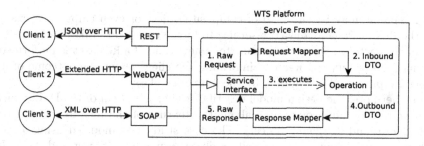

Fig. 5. Interactions between the different framework elements using the example of three clients issuing REST, WebDAV and SOAP requests. Solid arrowheads represent communication directions, whereas the semantics of all other kinds of arrowheads and lines follow UML notations for inheritance and dependencies.

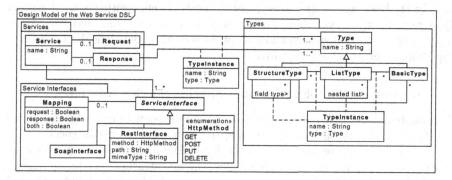

Fig. 6. Design model of the web service DSL. Different concepts of the language are expressed as classes and clustered in separate packages.

synonymously when declaring web services with the DSL. Associations connect different semantic concepts. Additionally, packages are used to group concepts for a better separation of concerns in the process of language implementation. The model was derived from the framework's specification and determines the basis for the DSL's grammar, syntactic rules and linkage between language expressions and generated code.

4.1   Service Generalization

Creating the DSL, the complexity of the service framework and its concrete utilization is hidden from the service developer keeping the language as expressive and concise as possible. For that purpose, in the design model a web service is viewed as a "black box" receiving a service request as stimulus and producing a suitable response. At this level, the service's business logic implementation is irrelevant. Instead, a `Service` is identified by a name and the information it receives and produces. Thus, the DSL allows the declaration of web services and their interfaces only, excluding concrete implementations. `Request` and `Response` may be any kind of composite object or even empty. For example, the `UpdateParameterValue` service from the case study takes an identifier unique for each WTS and the parameter's new value if a `Request` is performed. The method produces a `Result`, informing the client about the outcome of its request, represented in Figure 6 by the `Response` class.

Furthermore, the design model describes the type-system of the DSL, which for example contains constraints about the texture of the mentioned composite `Request` and `Response` objects. The case study was modeled using Java's built-in primitive types [12] as well as object types like `String` and `Date`. In the following, both kinds of types are subsumed under the term "basic types". More complex structures like the case study's `ParameterValue` are assembled of basic types. Additionally, the `RetrieveParameterValues` service returns a list of `ParameterValues`. Thus, the DSL needs to support a variety of types, namely (i) basic types, (ii) lists, possibly nested, representing sets of named `TypeInstances`, i.e. variables storing data of a certain type, and (iii) structured types, which themselves may contain structure typed fields, i.e. named `TypeInstances` of other structured types.

4.2   Representation of Technology-Specific Service Interfaces

As described in Section 3, the framework communicates with clients using service interfaces. These façades bridge the gap between characteristics specific to a concrete web service technology and the technology-independent business logic of a service's `Operation`. New technologies may be "attached" to the framework in the form of specialized mapper classes, which perform inbound and outbound traffic conversion. Both, service interfaces and mappers, need to be covered by the design model.

A service interface is modeled in the form of an abstract `ServiceInterface` extended by concrete REST- and SOAP-specific concepts. While the latter is characterized only by the name of its assigned `Service`, a `RestInterface` has to be specified in more detail by further properties, e.g. the `HttpMethod` for its invocation. Alternative service approaches, like the already mentioned WebDAV, may be integrated in the design model by inheriting from `ServiceInterface` and declaring the attributes needed for its specification.

A `Mapping` may be assigned to a `ServiceInterface`, given a mapping direction, which may be inbound only, outbound only or both, as the eponymous attributes of the `Mapping` concept imply.

4.3   Derivation of the DSL Grammar

The introduced design model already specifies some of the DSL's characteristics. The structure of each language concept is defined by the depicted classes, their attributes and the associations, which link two different concepts. Multiplicities mark optional or mandatory language elements. For example, a `Service` has to be specified by a name. A `Request` and a `Response` may be assigned, which themselves need to be assembled from a number of named type instances. Inheritance

```
Service: 'service' name = ID ':'
  otoName = 'receives' otoVariables = TypeInstances itoName = 'returns'
  itoVariables = TypeInstances interfaces += ServiceInterface
  (interfaces += ServiceInterface)* ';' ;
ServiceInterface: name = 'interface'
  type = (RestInterface | SoapInterface) (mapping = MappingSpec)? ;
RestInterface: name = 'rest'
  'method' method = HttpMethod 'path' path = STRING 'handles' mime = MimeSpec ;
HttpMethod: name = ('get' | 'post' | 'put' | 'delete') ;
SoapInterface: {SoapInterface} name = 'soap' ;
MappingSpec: name = 'maps' (request ?= 'request' | response ?= 'response' | both ?= 'both') ;
```

Listing 3. Excerpt from the Xtext-based grammar of the DSL. It shows those parts relevant for the definition of REST- and SOAP-based service interfaces.

is used to cluster semantic concepts: At least one concrete `ServiceInterface`, acting as an adapter for a certain service technology, is linked to a `Service` and thus enables technology-dependent clients to invoke a web service's business logic.

Listing 3 shows the substantial part of the grammar definition derived from the design model. The excerpt specifies how REST and SOAP services may be declared using the DSL. The grammar is expressed using Xtext[2], a Java-based framework we employed to implement the web service DSL. Definitions targeting the type-system and MIME types are omitted due to lack of space.

The `Service` concept of the design model is represented by the eponymous grammar rule and syntactically introduced by the `service` keyword, the service's name and a colon. The `Request` and `Response` concepts of the design model are linked with a service through the `receives` and `returns` keywords, followed by a number of `TypeInstances`.

Furthermore, in the design model the `Service` concept is associated with the `ServiceInterface` concept. This allows the service developer to provide web services leveraging different technologies. Within the grammar, the linkage between a service and its technology-dependent interfaces is realized by the `ServiceInterface` rule. Each interface declaration starts with the `interface` keyword and one of the identifiers `rest` or `soap`, representing the `RestInterface` and `SoapInterface` sub-concepts.

As shown in the design model, a `RestInterface` consists of attributes for the HTTP method it may be invoked by, its URI path and the handled MIME type. These attributes are grammatically expressed by the keywords `method`, `path` and `handles` of the `RestInterface` rule. The `SoapInterface` sub-concept doesn't have any attributes and thus the eponymous grammar rule hasn't either. In fact, a SOAP interface is solely assigned to a service through the `soap` identifier.

A mapping for inbound requests, outbound responses or both may be attached to a REST or SOAP service interface, allowing the service developer to implement custom mappers in environments where automatic traffic conversion, e.g. by specialized frameworks, may not be available.

Using the grammar the case study's `UpdateParameterValue` service offering REST and SOAP access might be declared as shown in Listing 4.

---

[2] http://www.eclipse.org/Xtext

```
1   service UpdateParameterValue:
2     receives long wtsId, String paramName, Date timestamp, String value
3     returns int returnCode
4     interface rest method put path "wts/{wtsId}/{paramName}" handles "application/json"
5     interface soap;
```

Listing 4. Declaration of `UpdateParameterValue` with the DSL. The service is accessible via REST and SOAP.

5   Implementation of a Code Generator for the DSL

Based on the design model of the web service DSL and the derived grammar, the implementation of a code generator becomes straightforward. It has to parse service declarations like the one in Listing 4 and create an Abstract Syntax Tree (AST). An AST consists of a number of subtrees, each representing a collection of instances of the design model elements. However, at the stage of code generation, the `Request` and `Response` concept instantiations contain no values. This is because in the DSL both concepts are used to describe composite type structures, whose AST "instances" are classes composed of the declared fields.

Figure 7 shows the subtree corresponding to the `UpdateParameterValue` service expressed in Listing 4 in the form of a UML object diagram.

5.1   Mapping Between AST Elements and Java Code

The code generator traverses the AST and translates each subtree into a piece of Java code leveraging the framework introduced in Section 3 to gain reusability of business logic across different service technologies. Thus, the code generator is used to bridge the gap between service modeling and implementation. As already stated, the DSL only allows the declaration of web services. For each declared service the code generator produces a stub method wherein the technology-independent business logic needs to be implemented. This lets a service developer focus on the correctness of a service's concrete realization instead of its provisioning by different service technologies for different clients. As the stub methods are generated only once to prevent existing business logic implementations from being overwritten, all other framework-related code is generated every time a new service interface is declared. This provides a better maintenance of the generated code as outdated versions of the framework may immediately be replaced by new ones.

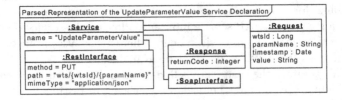

Fig. 7. AST subtree for the `UpdateParameterValue` service.

Table 1. Coherences between concepts of the DSL's design model and generated Java code based on the web service framework.

Language Concept	Generated Java Code
StructureType	Java class, consisting of the assigned TypeInstances in the form of attributes with getters and setters.
ListType	Java class, containing a generic java.util.List attribute whose type parameter is a class composed of the TypeInstances stored in the list.
BasicType	Attribute of the assigned type in either a ListType, StructureType, Request or Response.
Request	Java class, marked with ItoI containing getters and setters for the assigned TypeInstances.
Response	Like Request, but marked with OtoI.
Service	Class, extending Operation and providing a stub method for business logic implementation by a service developer.
RestInterface	JAX-RS class, extending ServiceInterface. The class contains a request handler method, which is annotated with @Path specifying the service URI and @Consumes/@Produces for MIME type handling. The method calls ServiceInterface.serve().
SoapInterface	JAX-WS compliant SEI and SIB. The latter extends ServiceInterface and invokes ServiceInterface.serve().
Mapping	Class, extending either RequestMapper or ResponseMapper and containing a stub method for the mapping logic yet to be implemented by a service developer.

Table 1 shows the coherences between the language concepts defined in the design model and the framework-based code produced by the generator. A mapping isn't defined for abstract concepts, which cluster concrete ones, depicted in the design model in the form of super classes.

5.2 Evaluation of the Generator's Efficiency

All boilerplate code demanded by the service framework is automatically generated as listed in Table 1 from a service declaration based on the DSL. This leads to an increased developer productivity being one of the advantages of a code generator [13].

For the case study's UpdateParameterValue service the corresponding declaration using the proposed DSL was already given in Listing 4. The five lines of DSL code (LODC) result in the following Java-based classes produced by the code generator (the arabic numerals in brackets determine the generated lines of boilerplate code): (i) a Request class (46), (ii) a Response class (21), (iii) a JAX-RS handler class (35), (iv) a JAX-WS SEI and SIB (44), (v) an Operation class (12) containing a stub method for subsequent business logic implementation. All generated classes comprise 158 lines of boilerplate code (LOBC) excluding empty lines. To measure the generator's efficiency, the quotient of the LOBC and LODC metrics, denoting the average number of LOBC each line of DSL code produces

(ALOBC), is calculated first. A second measure is the difference between LOBC and LODC, denoting the LOBC a service developer need not to implement and maintain (NLOBC). Both metrics are only used to assess changes made in the context of the framework and the DSL. Thus, their values are not comparable to those of other DSLs. When applying them to the `UpdateParameterValue` declaration expressed in the service DSL, the ALOBC is 31.6 and the NLOBC is 153.

To make an even more reliable statement on the efficiency of the code generator and to take a wider range of web services into account for a measurement, the DSL was used to implement 25 web services for a more complex case study. At first, 20 structured types were declared. These types contained 114 fields in total, which results in an average of 5.7 fields per declared type. Of these 114 fields the types of 17 fields corresponded to one of the 20 structured types, seven represented lists of the structured types and the remaining 90 were declared using basic types. Each of the defined 25 web services provided a REST and a SOAP interface. 15 services expected a `Request` object with an average of two fields per object each of a basic type. Ten out of 25 services didn't expect a `Request`, as these only returned a list of predefined, immutable master data. Overall, 21 out of 25 services returned a `Response` object. 13 `Responses` were lists comprising one of the 20 structured types. This resulted in each list containing an average of 7.85 basic typed fields. Seven `Responses` corresponded to one of the 20 structured types with an average field count of 6.43. One service returned a `Response` consisting of a single `String`. For the type and service declarations 252 LODC were needed. The generator produced the following Java-based classes (LOBC stated by bracketed arabic numerals): (i) 20 type classes (919), (ii) 15 `Request` classes (504), (iii) 21 `Response` classes (559), (iv) 25 JAX-RS handler classes (939), (v) 25 JAX-WS SEIs and SIBs (1104), (vi) 25 `Operation` classes (359). The generated code consisted of 4384 LOBC. Thus, the ALOBC measure amounted to 17.4, the NLOBC measure to 4132.

6 Related Work

In this section, we first present related work concerning web service DSLs. Following, we give an overview of papers targeting the simultaneous provisioning of REST- and SOAP-based web services. The section closes with a placement of the service DSL in the field of DSL-based web engineering.

In [3] a model-driven approach for the generation of REST interfaces is introduced. A presentation layer is applied to an application, condensing a number of existing web services from the latter, using "Use Case-specific interfaces". Service developers may declare these interfaces utilizing a DSL whose statements will be translated into JAX-RS-based code. However, SOAP isn't taken into account as the modeled services target clients with limited resources. In [14] Nguyen et al. describe a DSL called SWSM (Simple Web Service Modeling) for the modeling of SOAP services and propose a methodology for its usage. [15] presents a DSL for web service *mashups* based on different technologies. The paper involves an example of combining a SOAP-based service for web searching and a RESTful photo API, both hosted by different companies. [16] and [17] discuss the simultaneous integration of REST and SOAP by converting services based on one technology into services based on the other technology. With such an approach developers don't have to learn a new language to provide the same business logic via different technologies. However, for each new service technology transformation rules have to be defined for each possible direction of conversion, while with the introduced framework and DSL there are always only two mapping directions no matter how many service technologies have already been integrated: from service protocol to Java objects and vice versa. In [18] Shi introduces an approach for defining service semantics requester-oriented, i.e. independent from concrete technologies like REST and SOAP. The framework and DSL introduced above may serve as the technological basis behind a requester-oriented service interface that abstracts from different information exchange formats demanded by different web service technologies. The utilization of DSLs in the domain of web applications is described in [19] by means of a case study. The presented WebDSL allows the definition of data models and simple web pages. As web services aren't considered, combining WebDSL and the introduced service DSL would allow a web engineer to efficiently design web pages and provide data exchange with clients.

7   Conclusion and Future Work

In this paper, we first presented a framework for the provisioning of semantically equivalent business logic via different web service technologies. Furthermore, we introduced a DSL for the technology-independent declaration of web services and showed the implementation of a code generator, which creates all necessary boilerplate code for subsequent business logic implementation. We bridged the gap between framework model and language design by means of a design model, that was used to derive the DSL grammar regarding associations between different language concepts.

The DSL enables a service developer to concentrate on the correct implementation of business logic without keeping requirements of different web service technologies in mind. In addition, the code generator not only increases developer productivity, but guarantees a certain quality of the framework-based boilerplate code, which surrounds the business logic.

However, there are some limitations concerning the DSL. At first, the DSL implementation isn't as extensible as the underlying design model and the framework. Both allow the rapid integration of additional service interfaces, e.g. for the WebDAV protocol. The DSL's architecture may not be extended in a flexible manner, yet. In future work, we plan to enhance the design model in a way that enables the automatic inheritance of the DSL's grammar and architecture through model transformation. Another shortcoming is the DSL's limited expressiveness concerning SOAP. Currently there are no language constructs for

370 F. Rademacher et al.

standards defined in the WS-* stack of W3C's Web Services Activity[3]. They might act as case studies when applying model transformation to inherit parts of the DSL from its design model. In addition, in the future the code generator shall be extended to produce code, which clients like mobile apps may leverage to invoke the declared services' interfaces.

References

1. Fielding, R.T.: Architectural styles and the design of network-based software architectures. PhD thesis, University of California, Irvine (2000)
2. Gudgin, M., Hadley, M., Mendelsohn, N., Moreau, J.J., Nielsen, H.F., Karmarkar, A., Lafon, Y.: Soap version 1.2. W3C Recommendation 24 (2003)
3. Gulden, M., Kugele, S.: A concept for generating simplified restful interfaces. In: Proceedings of the 22nd International Conference on World Wide Web, pp. 1391–1398. ACM (2013)
4. Crockford, D.: The application/json media type for javascript object notation (json). The Internet Society, Request for Comments 4627 (2006)
5. Object Management Group: Service oriented architecture modeling language (soaml). OMG Formal Versions Of SoaML (ptc/2009-04-01) (2009)
6. Pautasso, C., Zimmermann, O., Leymann, F.: Restful web services vs. "big" web services: making the right architectural decision. In: Proceedings of the 17th International Conference on World Wide Web, pp. 805–814. ACM (2008)
7. Gamma, E., Helm, R., Johnson, R., Vlissides, J.: Design patterns: Elements of Reusable Object-Oriented Software, 40th edn. Addison-Wesley, Boston (2012)
8. Hadley, M., Sandoz, P.: Jax-rs: Java api for restful web services. Java Specification Request 311 (2009)
9. Kotamraju, J.: The java api for xml-based web services (jax-ws) 2.2. Java Specification Request 224 (2011)
10. Daigneau, R.: Service Design Patterns: Fundamental Design Solutions for SOAP/WSDL and RESTful Web Services. Addison-Wesley, Boston (2011)
11. Freed, N., Borenstein, N.: Multipurpose internet mail extensions (mime) part two: Media types. Network Working Group, Request for Comments 2046 (1996)
12. Gosling, J., Joy, B., Steele, G., Bracha, G.: The Java Language Specification, 2nd edn. Addison-Wesley, Reading (2000)
13. Kieburtz, R.B., McKinney, L., Bell, J.M., Hook, J., Kotov, A., Lewis, J., Oliva, D.P., Sheard, T., Smith, I., Walton, L.: A software engineering experiment in software component generation. In: Proceedings of the 18th International Conference on Software Engineering, pp. 542–552. ACM (1996)
14. Nguyen, V.C., Qafmolla, X., Richta, K.: Domain specific language approach on model-driven development of web services. Acta Polytechnica Hungarica 11(8), 121–138 (2014)
15. Maximilien, E.M., Wilkinson, H., Desai, N., Tai, S.: A domain-specific language for web APIs and services mashups. In: Krämer, B.J., Lin, K.-J., Narasimhan, P. (eds.) ICSOC 2007. LNCS, vol. 4749, pp. 13–26. Springer, Heidelberg (2007)
16. Peng, Y.Y., Ma, S.P., Lee, J.: Rest2soap: a framework to integrate soap services and restful services. In: IEEE International Conference on Service-Oriented Computing and Applications, pp. 106–109. IEEE (2009)

---

[3] http://www.w3.org/2002/ws

17. Upadhyaya, B., Zou, Y., Xiao, H., Ng, J., Lau, A.: Migration of soap-based services to restful services. In: 13th IEEE International Symposium on Web Systems Evolution, pp. 105–114. IEEE (2011)
18. Shi, X.: Sharing service semantics using soap-based and rest web services. IT Professional **8**(2), 18–24 (2006)
19. Visser, E.: WebDSL: a case study in domain-specific language engineering. In: Lämmel, R., Visser, J., Saraiva, J. (eds.) GTTSE 2007. LNCS, vol. 5235, pp. 291–373. Springer, Heidelberg (2008)

Tailoring the ATAM for Software Ecosystems

Simone da Silva Amorim[1,4](✉), John D. McGregor[2],
Eduardo Santana de Almeida[3,4], and Christina von Flach G. Chavez[4]

[1] Federal Institute of Education, Science and Technology of Bahia,
Salvador, Bahia, Brazil
simone.amorim@ifba.edu.br
[2] Clemson University, Clemson, SC, USA
johnmc@cs.clemson.edu, esa@dcc.ufba.br
[3] Fraunhofer Project Center for Software & Systems Engineering,
Federal University of Bahia, Salvador, Bahia, Brazil
[4] Federal University of Bahia, Salvador, Bahia, Brazil
flach@dcc.ufba.br

Abstract. Software ecosystems often form around a platform which is
defined by a reference architecture. None of the existing architecture
evaluation methods evaluate the unique aspects of the architectures that
drive a software ecosystem. These architectures emphasize properties,
such as Extensibility, Flexibility, and Scalability, that should be considered during an architecture evaluation. An evaluation method must also
allow stakeholders, who are spread around the world, to participate in the
evaluation. To address these issues, this paper proposes a method, Architectural Analysis Method for Evolving Ecosystems (AAMEE), to evaluate the architecture that is the basis for a software ecosystem. AAMEE,
a variant of ATAM, analyzes architectural scenarios covering both the
platform and product architectures in the ecosystem. The method has
been piloted through its application to the architecture of the Noosfero
ecosystem. We report some lessons learned.

Keywords: Software ecosystems · Software architecture · Architectural
evaluation

1 Introduction

The ecosystem strategy is based on an organization developing a partial product
and exposing its interfaces to the outside world. This partial product, referred
to as a platform, is defined by a reference architecture that describes a complete
product. For the ecosystem to be successful a product architecture should be able
to be derived from the reference architecture quickly and easily [8]. If the product
architecture can be quickly and easily derived from the reference architecture
future product builders will be encouraged to use the platform and the ecosystem
thrives.

Previous research and experience have shown that having an effective and
efficient architecture evaluation method is critical to success. The Architecture

D. Weyns et al. (Eds.): ECSA 2015, LNCS 9278, pp. 372–380, 2015.
DOI: 10.1007/978-3-319-23727-5_30

Tradeoff Analysis Method (ATAM) evaluates architecture-level designs that consider multiple quality attributes [9]. ATAM has been tailored in several ways to meet specific evaluation objectives and differing architecture patterns [12]. In this paper we present the Architectural Analysis Method for Evolving Ecosystems (AAMEE), a specialization of ATAM that is effective in the context of the ecosystem strategy.

In our previous research on ecosystem architectures [1–3] we identified several issues that an architecture evaluation method should be able to address to be effective in an ecosystem. The evaluation method must accommodate this multi-purpose environment with a community making decisions about the platform architecture and multiple business strategies defined by the different organizational contributors to the ecosystem. AAMEE is designed to address the issues described above. It works with ecosystems of different granularity levels, analyzes the point view of different roles in the community, and operates through asynchronous communication channels. To make the evaluation efficient, as well as effective, we will narrow the evaluation technique to only consider the high priority attributes of Extensibility, Flexibility, and Scalability, identified in our previous work [1–3].

The remainder of this paper is organized as follows: Section 2 presents related work; Section 3 describes characteristics of ecosystem architectures, their viewpoints and the quality attributes used in this evaluation; Section 4 presents the AAMEE approach and explains some differences from the ATAM approach; Section 5 shows a pilot experience of an application of to a real-world ecosystem; and Section 6 presents conclusions and perspectives for future directions.

2   Related Work

Kazman *et al.* developed the Architecture Tradeoff Analysis Method (ATAM), which evaluates quality attribute requirements by examining the consequences of architectural decisions [9]. It also identifies risks, sensitive points and tradeoffs, besides evaluating multiple quality attributes and can be used in different environments. However, ATAM does not address directly some ecosystem characteristics such as having numerous external developer organizations with conflicting requirements and strategies; a community that influences directly the platform architecture; and a varied, perhaps conflicting, set of business strategies resulting from the diversity of organizations participating in the ecosystem.

Several variations on ATAM have been defined. Bengtsson *et al.* [4] introduced the Architecture Level Modifiability Analysis (ALMA). This is a scenario-based software architecture analysis method that focuses only on the modifiability quality attribute. It can be used to achieve one of three goals: comparing software architectures, predicting maintenance effort or doing risk assessment.

Knodel *et al.* [10] proposed Rapid ArchiTecture Evaluation (RATE). RATE also works with architectural scenarios that are used to identify risks, sensitivity points, tradeoffs, strengths, and weaknesses. Besides, it verifies the suitability of the documentation to development process and how it is readable and updated, and validates the conformity of implementation with the designed architecture. RATE can evaluate different quality attributes, however, it does not define strategies to support ecosystem architectures and their community environment with multiple concrete architectures and applications and developers spread around world.

Graff *et al.* [6] reported on a modification of ATAM to address reference architectures similar to that for an ecosystem. They used a scenario approach similar to that reported here but only from a single abstract perspective. We will analyse the reference architecture as it is defined for the ecosystem of products and as it is used for individual products.

3   Quality Attributes

The software architecture for an ecosystem is a reference architecture for a set of products. That architecture is the basis for both the platform and for apps built on the platform. These architectures are developed in a shared market to meet community needs [7]. Regarding the characteristics of these architectures, AAMEE analyzes three quality attributes:

- Extensibility reflects how easily the architecture will accommodate the future growth, e.g. adding new requirements, of the system [5].
- Scalability is the effort required to adapt the system to new requirement that modify the size and scope of the computation[13].
- Flexibility expresses how easy, cheap, and fast necessary changes to software systems, i.e. existing requirements, can be accomplished [11].

Our previous work [1–3] indicate the significant impact of these quality attributes on evolving ecosystems architectures, so we chose them as the primary considerations when evaluating an evolving ecosystem architecture.

4   AAMEE Approach

AAMEE is an adaptation of the ATAM for ecosystem architectures. The main ATAM steps are retained but the way in which they are applied supports both the ecosystem platform and the applications built on the platform. The specific goal of AAMEE is to promote a rational evaluation and analysis of ecosystem architectures covering three quality attributes. The evaluation identifies risks and problems with respect to these attributes and gathers suggestions from application developers for architectural improvement. AAMEE can be applied during any stage of software development; however, it is most effective when the software architecture is already implemented and applications have been created using the platform. AAMEE can be applied to small, medium and large ecosystems; to ecosystems with different sizes of modules from micro-services to subsystems used in systems-of-systems, and different governance models from proprietary to open source.

Benefits of the AAMEE are: classification of quality attributes state, detection of risks and problems, and analysis of two-sided view (applications and platform developers) of the platform. AAMEE has different roles: evaluators, application developers, and platform developers. Evaluators are responsible for conducting all steps of the method. Application developers participate evaluating interactions between platform and applications. Lastly, evaluators and platform developers evaluate the platform, analyze all scenarios and generate a list of risks and problems of the architecture. Moreover, they analyze feedback collected from application developers about relevant architectural points regarding the three quality attributes. Templates of AAMEE artifacts can be found at http://homes.dcc.ufba.br/~ssamorim/aamee/.

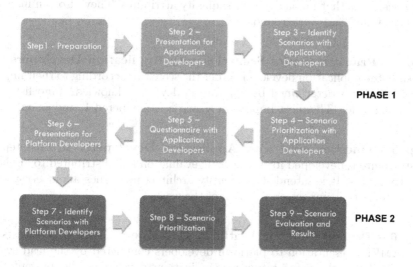

Fig. 1. AAMEE Steps

The AAMEE activities are divided into two phases and 9 steps. The first phase, encompassing the first 6 steps, involves the evaluation conducted with application developers and the second phase, consisting of 3 steps, presents the evaluation conducted with platform developers. Figure 1 shows the complete flow of the AAMEE.

4.1 Phase 1

Step 1 - Preparation. In this first step, some stakeholders prepare all the material to be used during the application of the method. The evaluative team prepares a presentation of the AAMEE, a questionnaire for application developers, and forms, which we describe later. Concurrently, the lead architects of the platform prepare an architecture presentation.

Step 2 - Presentation to Application Developers. The second step is the lead evaluators' AAMEE presentation to application developers. This presentation explains the goals of AAMEE, roles and responsibilities of participants, and the steps in the method. Moreover, the evaluators explain the outputs for the evaluation and define outlines according to available time of the application developers.

Step 3 - Identification of Scenarios with Application Developers. The third step includes processes for the identification of evolution scenarios. These scenarios are created based on interactions between the platform's architecture and application's architecture. Application developers define present day and future scenarios that impact the three quality attributes. They also can indicate problems found and workarounds.

Step 4 - Prioritization of Scenarios with Application Developers. In this step, the application developers order the scenarios according to their importance. Priority is determined by application developer knowledge and listed in descending order. The most important scenario is numbered 1, and so on.

Step 5 - Questionnaire with Application Developers. In this step, a questionnaire is developed for the specific evaluation and distributed to application developers. It is intended to identify architectural issues about ecosystem architectures that impact on progress of the work.

Step 6 - Presentation for Platform Developers. This step consists of the AAMEE presentation to platform developers conducted by the lead evaluators. Similar to the presentation for applications developers, this presentation explains the goals of AAMEE, roles and responsibilities of participants, and the steps in the method. The focus of the presentation is on the platform core and the platform team is presented questions that help to identify scenarios related specifically to quality attributes of the platform.

4.2   Phase 2

Step 7 - Identification of Scenarios with Platform Developers. In this step, platform developers identify scenarios that impact the three quality attributes. These scenarios encompass different situations which influence design decisions and can increase or decrease the level of the quality attributes focusing on the platform core.

Step 8 - Prioritization of Scenarios with Platform Developers. This step consist of prioritizing the scenarios according to the level of impact on the quality attributes. Platform developers determine the ordering by considering all the scenarios created by both groups. Application developers prioritized their scenarios previously, but platform developers analyze that classification and judge if these prioritizations should be kept or modified in accordance with the view of the platform core. At the end, all scenarios are prioritized regarding descending order starting by the most important scenario is assigned with number 1.

Step 9 - Scenario Evaluation and Results. This final step consists of recognizing and analyzing limitations imposed by the current platform architecture on the scenarios and identifying risks to successful implementation of the prioritized scenarios. These scenarios populate an result matrix and are classified in accordance with its influence degree for each quality attribute. The influence degree can be ranked as negative, positive or neutral. Besides, the negative and positive scale can be categorized as low, medium and high depending on its impact. These values are gathered through scenario forms for application and platform developers. Evaluation team analyzes limitations and risks found by both groups, summarizes results eliminating duplicative information, and makes recommendations for future versions of the platform. These results are available for all participants of AAMEE process.

4.3 Tailoring ATAM

ATAM is a well-established method and have been used to evaluate software architectures over time. We designed AAMEE to take advantage of the ATAM's strengths and changed some aspects to address weaknesses. AAMEE's heavier reliance on scenarios allows sessions to be held remotely and even asynchronously. Presentations, discussions, voting, etc. are conducted online in response to ecosystem characteristics such as having people around the world collaborating. Meetings can be scheduled and conducted using social media tools and collaborative meeting tools, as well as making videos of the presentations of the approach and architecture available online for all members of the community. Discussions occur via forums or mailing lists and scenario voting is available in specific forms accessible on the Internet. Regarding the quantity of participants and distance among them, AAMEE can be conducted in a period from 1 to 3 months in order for all interested parties to have time to share their vision and experience.

5 Experience

We illustrate how to use AAMEE for architectural evaluation with a pilot experience performed in the Noosfero ecosystem (http://Noosfero.org). Noosfero is an open source web platform for social and solidarity economy networks. It was created and has been maintain by Colivre (http://colivre.coop.br/). Noosfero is a young and small ecosystem that has a community of around 219 developers and 475,000 lines of code (https://www.openhub.net/p/noosfero).

5.1   Applying AAMEE

The Noosfero architecture was presented by the lead architect in an online meeting. He introduced all the main components of the system, business drivers, and technologies used such as database management systems and middleware servers. Due to the large number of components and lines of code, the evaluator and architect, decided to reduce the scope of the evaluation. A small component of Noosfero core called *Conteudo* was chosen as the target of the case study. This component was chosen because of the important tasks it performs and its interaction with several external applications.

Scenario elicitation occurs in two phases of the AAMEE. In step 3, our case study had the participation of two application developers belonging to different organizations outside of Colivre. Developers identified 15 scenarios of interactions with their application and answered the questionnaire. In step 7, we had participation of one platform developer, who is also the leader architect of Noosfero. He identified 4 scenarios.

5.2   Noosfero Results

The questionnaire answered by applications developers offered data about their level of work experience, their activities, and their opinions about Noosfero architecture. These answers were used to complement the list of problems and risks gathered by scenario elicitation. Furthermore, the evaluator conducted the process of voting for all scenarios elicited to establish the priority for each scenario. Only platform developers voted and prioritized scenarios. In the Noosfero case, the leader architect considered all scenarios important and agreed with the priority defined previously by application developers. Using the scenario priorities and information collected from the questionnaire, the evaluator built a result matrix for all scenarios and created lists composed by risks and problems that influence the three quality attributes. Analyzing all scenarios, it was concluded that the majority of the scenarios were viewed positively for the Extensibility and Scalability attributes. However, the Flexibility attribute was viewed negatively, requiring actions and changes by Noosfero team to improve the architecture with respect to this quality attribute.

6   Conclusion and Future Work

In this paper, we propose AAMEE, a method for evaluation of software ecosystem architectures focusing on Extensibility, Scalability and Flexibility quality attributes. This method is an adaptation of ATAM and addresses the two distinct audiences in an ecosystem: platform developers and application developers. The approach is based on scenarios analysis, but it is adapted to support development processes of the large distributed communities present in ecosystems. We applied this approach in a component of a real-world ecosystem, the Noosfero ecosystem, for validation.

The next step is to extend the application of the AAMEE to the whole Noosfero ecosystem. Furthermore, apply the AAMEE in medium and large ecosystems to validate this approach for ecosystems with different size, scope, and granularity. Going forward, we will adapt and apply an evaluation considering other quality attributes.

Acknowledgments. The authors would like to thank to Victor Costa, Arthur Del Esposte and Antonio Terceiro, application and platform developers of the Noosfero ecosystem. Their contribution in the evaluation process was essential for the accomplishment of this work. This work was partially supported by the National Institute of Science and Technology for Software Engineering (INES - http://www.ines.org.br), funded by CNPq and FACEPE, grants 573964/2008-4 and APQ-1037-1.03/08 and CNPq grants 305968/2010-6, 559997/2010-8, 474766/2010-1 and FAPESB. McGregors work was partially funded by the National Science Foundation grant #ACI-1343033.

References

1. Amorim, S.d.S., de Almeida, E.S., McGregor, J.D.: Extensibility in ecosystem architectures: an initial study. In: Proceedings of the 2013 International Workshop on Ecosystem Architectures, WEA 2013, pp. 11–15, August 2013
2. Amorim, S.d.S., de Almeida, E.S., McGregor, J.D.: Scalability of ecosystem architectures. In: Proceedings of the 11th Working IEEE/IFIP Conference on Software Architecture, WICSA 2014, pp. 49–52, April 2014
3. Amorim, S.d.S., de Almeida, E.S., McGregor, J.D., Chavez, C.v.F.G.: Flexibility in ecosystem architectures. In: Proceedings of the 2014 European Conference on Software Architecture Workshops, ECSAW 2014, pp. 14:1–14:6 (2014)
4. Bengtsson, P., Lassing, N., Bosch, J., van Vliet, H.: Architecture-level modifiability analysis (ALMA). Journal of Systems and Software **69**, 129–141 (2004)
5. Buschmann, F., Meunier, R., Rohnert, H., Stal, M.: vol. 1. Wiley (1996)
6. Graaf, B., Van Dijk, H., Van Deursen, A.: Evaluating an embedded software reference architecture. In: Proceedings of the Ninth European Conference on Software Maintenance and Reengineering, CSMMR 2005, pp. 354–363, March 2005
7. Jansen, S., Finkelstein, A., Brinkkemper, S.: A sense of community: a research agenda for software ecosystems. In: Proceedings of the 31st International Conference on Software Engineering: Companion Volume, ICSE 2009, pp. 187–190, May 2009
8. Jansen, S.: How quality attributes of software platform architectures influence software ecosystems. In: Proceedings of the 2013 International Workshop on Ecosystem Architectures, WEA 2013, pp. 6–10 (2013)
9. Kazman, R., Klein, M., Barbacci, M., Longstaff, T., Lipson, H., Carriere, J.: The architecture tradeoff analysis method. In: Proceedings of the Fourth IEEE International Conference on Engineering of Complex Computer Systems, ICECCS 1998, pp. 68–78, August 1998
10. Knodel, J., Naab, M.: Software architecture evaluation in practice - retrospective on more than 50 architecture evaluations in industry. In: Proceedings of the 2014 IEEE/IFIP Conference on Software Architecture, WICSA 2014, pp. 115–124, April 2014

11. Naab, N., Stammel, J.: Architectural flexibility in a software-systems life-cycle: systematic construction and exploitation of flexibility. In: Proceedings of the 8th international ACM SIGSOFT conference on Quality of Software Architectures, QoSA 2012, pp. 13–22, June 2012
12. Ram, N.S., Rodrigues, P.: Enhanced quantitative trade-off analysis in quality attributes of a software architecture using bayesian network model. JDCA **3**(4)
13. Taylor, R.N., Medvidovic, N., Dashofy, E.M.: Wiley, January 2009

Author Index